Nanak C. Kakwani

Income Inequality and Poverty
Methods of Estimation and Policy Applications

Published for the World Bank
Oxford University Press

Oxford University Press

NEW YORK OXFORD LONDON GLASGOW
TORONTO MELBOURNE WELLINGTON HONG KONG
TOKYO KUALA LUMPUR SINGAPORE JAKARTA
DELHI BOMBAY CALCUTTA MADRAS KARACHI
NAIROBI DAR ES SALAAM CAPE TOWN

Library of Congress Cataloging in Publication Data

Kakwani, Nanak.
  Income inequality and poverty.

  Bibliography: p. 399
  Includes index.
  1. Income distribution—Mathematical models.
2. Poverty—Mathematical models.   I.   Title.
HC79.I5K34   339.2'01'51   80-14229
ISBN 0-19-520126-4
ISBN 0-19-520227-9 pbk.

Contents

Kuznets' Hypothesis and the Skewness
of the Lorenz Curve   *382*
Intercountry Comparison of Income Inequality   *384*
An International Comparison of Poverty   *390*

Tables

Figures

Preface

THE METHODOLOGY of the size distribution of income deals with the distribution of income among individuals. Ideally, its analysis should employ both theoretical economics and statistical inference, although empirical data have been the main analytic tool in the last hundred years. Thus Professor Tinbergen's study, *Income Distribution: Analysis and Policy* (1975), which provided the first thorough and systematic treatment of alternative theories of the size distribution of income, was most welcome. The present study could be considered a complement to his book. It deals with income distribution methods and their economic applications; appropriate techniques developed to analyze the problems of size distribution of income using actual data; and the use of these techniques in the evaluation of alternative fiscal policies affecting income distribution.

This study represents the past six years of my research on income distribution and draws heavily upon a number of my articles both published and forthcoming. My interest in the field was first aroused in 1971 through discussions with Nripesh Podder in connection with his Ph.D. thesis. I later collaborated with him on several studies on income distribution financed by the Reserve Bank of Australia, the Australian Taxation Review Committee, and the Poverty Inquiry Commission. But the major research for this book was done at the Development Research Center of the World Bank, where I spent my sabbatical leave from July 1974 to February 1976.

I wish to express my gratitude to the following people. Nripesh Podder read the entire first version of the manuscript and offered many criticisms that reoriented my thinking on a number of issues. Useful insights were contributed at various stages of this study by colleagues at the World Bank and the University of New South Wales. Particular thanks go to Graham Pyatt, Montek Ahluwalia, Roger Norton, Jack Duloy, Bela Belassa, Suresh Tendulkar, Clive

Bell, Constantine Lluch, Eric Sowey, and Murray Kemp. In addition, I am grateful to Amartya Sen and an unknown referee, who made valuable comments on the draft manuscript, and to Malathy Parthasarathy, who provided computational assistance. Sue Zerby typed successive versions of the manuscript with great accuracy and patience. Kathleen McCaffrey edited the final manuscript for publication. Proofs of the text and tables were corrected by Marie Hergt through the Word Guild, the charts were prepared by Pensri Kimpitak of the World Bank's Art and Design Section, and the text was indexed by Ralph Ward.

Finally, because this study has been completed at the cost of neglecting my family for a number of years, acknowledgment is due to my wife, Kamal Kakwani, and to my daughter, Anu, for their forbearance during the period.

NANAK C. KAKWANI

CHAPTER 1

Introduction

IN A CLOSED ECONOMY, income is created in production with the aid of factors such as land, labor, capital, and entrepreneurship. Production takes place within different firms and government organizations, and, at the same time, income is created and distributed to income units. From this process, a pattern of distribution emerges that has been found to be stable over time and space. This feature of income distribution has provoked a number of alternative theories explaining the generation of income.

Three Topics in the Theory of Income Distribution

There is a vast literature on distribution theory that seeks to account for: (a) the functional distribution of income, or factor prices, (b) factor shares, or the share of the total national income that each factor of production receives, and (c) the size distribution of income, or personal distribution.

The first two topics relate to the determination of the distribution of income among factors of production. Most of the economic literature on distribution has focused on these two topics.[1] The present volume, however, concerns the distribution of income among individuals, households, and other units. A brief review of alternative theories of the size distribution of income is presented in this chap-

---

1. The most comprehensive and up-to-date discussion of these topics is available in Bronfenbrenner (1971).

1

ter. In addition, the scope and limitations of the study are described and its major contributions summarized.

Theories of Size Distribution of Income: A Brief Review

The various theories that have been proposed to explain the distribution of income among individuals have emerged from two main schools of thought. The first may be called the theoretic statistical school and is represented by such authors as Gibrat (1931), Roy (1950), Champernowne (1953), Aitchison and Brown (1954), and Rutherford (1955). These authors explain the generation of income with the help of certain stochastic processes.[2] The most serious criticism of stochastic models is that they provide only a partial explanation of the income generation process and, as Mincer (1958) pointed out, shed no light on the economics of the distribution process.

The second school of thought, which may be called the socio-economic school, seeks the explanation of income distribution by means of economic and institutional factors, such as sex, age, occupation, education, geographical differences, and the distribution of wealth. Three groups of authors belong to this school. The first follows the human capital approach, based on the hypothesis of lifetime income maximization. This approach was initiated by Mincer (1958) and subsequently developed by Becker (1962, 1967), Chiswick (1968, 1971, 1974), Husen (1968), and De Wolff and Van Slijpe (1972). A number of criticisms have been leveled against the human capital approach, the most serious being that it deals mainly with the supply side of the market, which provides labor of various levels of education.[3]

The second group of authors, which concentrates on the demand side of the market, has been referred to as the education planning school by Tinbergen and is represented by such authors as Bowles (1969), Dougherty (1971, 1972), and Psacharopoulos and Hinchliffe

2. A brief survey of stochastic models is provided by Bjerke (1961).

3. See Tinbergen (1975), p. 4. In addition, see Blinder (1974) for a consideration of other criticisms.

(1972). This group holds that the demand for various kinds of labor is derived from production functions.

The third group of authors is called the supply and demand school. The major contribution of this approach is represented by Tinbergen (1975), who considers income distribution a result of the supply and demand for different kinds of labor. His analysis applies not only to labor income, but also to incomes from other factors of production.[4]

Scope and Limitations of the Present Study

The present study focuses on the following issues: (a) income distribution functions, (b) measurement of degree of income inequality, (c) government policies affecting personal distribution of income, and (d) measurement of poverty.

The regularities displayed by observed income distributions over time and space provide sufficient justification to describe them with the help of some statistical distribution functions. These provide not only a useful summary of the phenomenon of income distribution, but also a technique to study the effects of alternative redistributive policies.

The phenomenon of income inequality has been a source of worldwide social upheaval. It has become a weapon in the hands of social reformers and a point of intellectual debate among academics. The two main aspects of this debate, ethical evaluation and statistical measurement, are not always clearly distinguishable. For this reason, the present study considers some welfare aspects of income inequality, although its major concern is the statistical measurement of inequality and analysis of income distribution.

Since the introduction of progressive income tax, the fiscal policies of many governments have included the redistribution of income as a major goal. And, with the recent emergence of welfare states, redistributive policies have even been accepted as a social norm. It has become important, therefore, to develop techniques of evaluating alternative fiscal policies affecting income distribution. The ideal means of achieving this is to develop a general equilibrium model that explicitly incorporates the income distribution function

4. For further details of this analysis, see Tinbergen (1975).

as an indispensable component. This task is, in its entirety, too formidable to be undertaken in the present study, although some techniques developed to study the effect of alternative fiscal policies on income distribution in isolation from other economic variables are presented below.

Finally, an awareness of the existence of poverty in western societies has increased during the past fifteen years. Social attitudes toward poverty have changed, and the fact that many of the western economies have achieved a level of affluence where poverty can be eliminated without causing any significant hardship to the nonpoor sections of the community is increasingly recognized. It is highly probable that the developing countries will continue to need outside assistance to eliminate poverty, or at least to reduce its intensity.[5] The prior problem, however, is to identify the poor and measure the intensity of their poverty so that methods can be devised to wage a war against it. In this study, alternative measures of intensity of poverty are discussed rather than the conceptual problems of poverty.

Outline and Major Contributions

This study is divided into six parts. The first three concern income distribution methods, and the remaining three, beginning with chapter 9, provide economic applications.

The problem of the shape of observed income distributions has attracted the attention of several scholars during the past eighty years. Pareto, one of the first to find a certain regularity in the distribution of incomes in various countries, arrived at a formulation of his famous law of distribution in 1897 using inductive reasoning. This law provided a fixed relationship between income x and the number of people with income x or more. Pareto believed that this law was universally true and applicable to the distribution of income in all countries, at all times. Subsequent empirical studies indicated, however, that the Pareto law applies only to higher incomes. These observations have led a number of authors to propose alternative probability laws that purport to describe observed

5. For a number of years, the World Bank has been particularly interested in financing projects in the developing countries leading to a reduction in poverty.

distributions over the whole range of income. A critical review of these laws is provided in chapter 2.

As mentioned above, the second issue considered in this study is the measurement of income inequality. To this end, the Lorenz curve, which provides a readily interpretable picture of inequalities in distribution, is used. Lorenz proposed this curve in 1905 in order to compare and analyze inequality of wealth of different countries, and, since then, the curve has been widely used as a convenient graphical device to represent size distributions of income and wealth.

In this study, the concept of the Lorenz curve is extended and generalized to introduce distributional considerations into various fields of economic analysis; chapters 3 and 4, therefore, are devoted to a detailed discussion of the Lorenz curve and its properties. The statistical and mathematical properties of the curve are discussed in chapter 3, and chapter 4 deals with its normative properties related to social welfare.

It is argued in chapter 4 that the Lorenz curve can be used as a criterion for ranking income distributions, although this function is fulfilled only partially by the curve. For example, if two Lorenz curves intersect, neither distribution can be said to be more equal than the other. A number of inequality measures have been proposed to provide complete orderings of income distributions. A critical review of these measures is provided in chapter 5, where they are examined according to their social welfare implications.

Chapter 6 concerns the problem of the estimation of various inequality measures from grouped observations. A general interpolation device is provided, which facilitates the derivation of explicit formulae for most of the inequality measures in common use. A numerical illustration based on Australian data indicates that this approach provides fairly accurate estimates of various inequality measures.

Part 3, consisting of chapters 7 and 8, deals with some further properties of the Lorenz curve, which have many interesting economic applications.

A new coordinate system for the Lorenz curve is introduced in chapter 7, where particular attention is paid to a special case that has wide empirical applications. The density function underlying this equation of the curve provides a good fit to a wide range of observed income distributions from different countries.

Chapter 8 concerns ways in which the Lorenz curve technique

can be used to analyze relationships among the distributions of different economic variables. A number of theorems are provided that have many applications in economics, particularly in the field of public finance, where the effect of taxation and public spending on income distribution is investigated. The other areas in which these theorems can be applied are inflation as it affects income distribution, estimation of Engel curve elasticities, disaggregation of total inequality by factor components, as well as economic growth and income distribution. Some of these applications are discussed in this chapter, and many other important applications are given in the remaining three parts of the book.

The relationships between the consumption of different commodities and disposable income (or total expenditure) play a central role in the models of income distribution and growth. This kind of relationship is called an Engel curve, and Engel curves of all the commodities taken together are called expenditure systems. Chapter 9 deals with several income distribution models based on the linear expenditure system. The major contribution of this chapter is an evaluation of the effect of relative price changes on the inequality of real income.

Chapter 10 concerns the estimation of Engel curve elasticities from the Lorenz curve by means of the new coordinate system of the Lorenz curve discussed in chapter 7. The concept of a concentration index is used to derive a new index of elasticity (inelasticity) of a commodity. The empirical results given in this chapter are based on Indonesian data obtained from the *National Social and Economic Survey*, 1969.

Part 5, consisting of chapters 11, 12, 13, and 14, is devoted to a discussion of government policies affecting income distribution. Chapter 11 provides a number of models used to investigate the effect of taxation on income distribution. These models, although simple, have interesting policy implications, which are also discussed in this chapter.

Chapter 12 focuses on two problems. The first concerns the measurement of tax progressivity and its effect on income distribution. The second deals with the measurement of the degree of built-in flexibility. A new measure of tax progressivity, derived from the notion of concentration curves discussed in chapter 8, is given. Empirical analysis for four countries (Australia, Canada, the United States, and the United Kingdom) is also provided.

Because negative income tax is a commonly suggested fiscal measure used to transfer income from rich to poor in order to reduce poverty, a number of negative income tax plans have been proposed in the professional literature. Chapter 13 concerns the redistributive effects of alternative plans; in chapter 14 a theoretical model is developed in order to evaluate the effect of negative income tax on income inequality through its effects on the individual's choice between income and leisure. An empirical analysis is provided, using data from the United States.

Part 6 is devoted to the measurement of poverty, to an empirical analysis of poverty, and to income inequality.

Problems concerning the measurement of poverty are closely considered in chapter 15. Most of the existing literature on poverty deals with the estimation of the number of people below the poverty line. Because this measure, as such, does not reflect the intensity of poverty suffered by the poor, chapter 15 deals with the problem of deriving a suitable measure of poverty. A general class of poverty measures that makes use of three poverty indicators — the percentage of poor, the aggregate poverty gap, and the distribution of income among the poor — is proposed. Two numerical illustrations are provided by means of Malaysian and Indian data.

Because the economic welfare of households depends, in addition to income, on household size and composition, the latter is an essential consideration in any accurate measurement of income inequality or poverty. In chapter 16 a new model is provided that helps to estimate both the effect of family composition on income inequality and the extent of poverty. The model is applied to Australian data.

The last chapter provides an international comparison of income inequality and poverty. The investigation is based on income distribution data from fifty countries. An alternative method is provided to test Kuznets' hypothesis concerning the relationship between economic growth and distribution of income by size. This method is based on the skewness of the Lorenz curve. The poverty indexes discussed in chapter 14 are used to determine the effect of different countries or regions on world poverty.

PART ONE

Distribution Patterns and
Descriptive Analysis

CHAPTER 2

Income Distribution Functions

THE BASIC CONCEPTS of income distribution functions are taken up in this first section. Suppose x represents the income of a unit and there are n units that have been grouped into $(T + 1)$ income classes: $(0$ to $x_1)$, $(x_1$ to $x_2)$, $\ldots$, $(x_T$ to $x_{T+1})$. This can be conceptualized as a probability experiment. Assume that a unit belongs to the $(t + 1)^{\text{th}}$ income class if it gets t heads in the tossing of T coins. It can be seen that the probability of a unit selected at random having income in the interval x_t and x_{t+1} is $^T C_t$ divided by 2^T where $^T C_t$ is the number of combinations of T objects taken t at a time. This probability has been computed on the assumption that all the outcomes of this experiment are equally likely. Each coin yields either head or tail; therefore, with T coins there will be 2^T possible outcomes. An event in this experiment is the number of heads obtained. It is not difficult to see that exactly t heads will be obtained by tossing T coins in $^T C_t$ number of ways.

Suppose 1,000 income units are placed in four income classes: (0 to 1,000), (1,000 to 2,000), (2,000 to 3,000), and (3,000 and over), with the income limits for each class marked by an appropriate unit of money. For each income unit three coins will be tossed, and, depending on the number of heads obtained, the unit will be placed in one of the four income classes. Thus if no head is obtained, the unit will be placed in the first class; with one head it will be placed in the second class, and so on. This process is expected to generate the following income distribution:

	Expected
Income classes	*frequency*
0–1,000	125
1,000–2,000	375
2,000–3,000	375
3,000–over	125
Total	1,000

Each conceivable outcome of a probability experiment is defined as a sample point. The sample space denoted by Ω is the totality of conceivable outcomes or sample points. An event is defined as a subset of the sample space. The set of all events is defined as the event space, which may be denoted by A. In the experiment considered above, the sample space Ω consists of eight sample points, whereas the event space A has four elementary events.

A function, say $f(x)$, is a rule which transforms each point in one set of points into one and only one point in another set of points. The first collection of points is called the domain, and the second collection, the counterdomain of the function. A function $X(a)$ whose domain is the event space A and whose counterdomain is a set of real numbers is called a random variable. An event that belongs to the event space A is denoted by a. Although the random variable $X(a)$ is a function, it is in practice denoted by X.

Assuming that income X of a unit is a random variable whose counterdomain is a set of real numbers in the range zero to infinity, the function $F(x)$ defined by

$$(2.1) \qquad\qquad F(x) = Pr[X \leq x]$$

is called the probability distribution function, with Pr standing for probability. The function $F(x)$ is interpreted as the probability that a unit selected at random will have an income less than or equal to x. The important properties of this function are as follows:

(a) $\lim\limits_{x \to +\infty} F(x) = F(\infty) = 1;$

(b) $\lim\limits_{x \to 0} F(x) = F(0) = 0;$

(c) $F(x)$ is a monotone, nondecreasing function of x.

It is obvious that the function $F(x)$ has the domain $(0, \infty)$ and the counterdomain $(0, 1)$. Furthermore, if it is assumed that the function $F(x)$ is continuous and has a continuous derivative at all values of x, then it follows that

(2.2) $$\frac{d}{dX} F(X) = f(X)$$

where $f(X) \geq 0$. The fundamental theorem of integral calculus yields

$$F(x) - F(0) = \int_0^x f(X) dX,$$

which, by means of property (b), yields

$$F(x) = \int_0^x f(X) dX.$$

The probability density function is denoted by $f(x)$.

The main problem in the statistical description of an income distribution is the specification of the density function $f(x)$. A number of density functions have been proposed to approximate observed income distributions. These functions are reviewed in the following sections.

The Normal Distribution

The normal distribution, most widely used to describe the probability behavior of a large number of random phenomena, was found in 1733 by De Moivre and later rediscovered by Gauss in 1809 and Laplace in 1812. Both arrived at this function in connection with their work on the theory of errors of observations. The distribution is also referred to as the Gaussian law.

A large number of distributions observed in reality are at least approximately normal. A theoretical explanation of this empirical phenomenon is provided by the well-known Central Limit Theorem, which states that the sum of a large number of random variables is normally distributed under fairly general assumptions.

The shape of observed income distributions is invariant with respect to time and space. Many authors have, therefore, attempted to explain the generation of income by some stochastic process. If income can be conceived of as the result of the sum of a large number of random variables, the variable income should, according to the Central Limit Theorem, approximately follow the normal distribution. This conclusion may also follow from a different phenomenon. If the level of income depends on the intelligence of the individual, which can be assumed to be normally distributed, one should expect that income is at least approximately normally distributed. This, however, is not true in reality. The normal distribution is symmetric with a finite mean and variance. It is bell shaped, which means that much of the probability mass is concentrated around the mean. But observed income distributions are always positively skewed with a single mode and a long tail. Thus, the normal distribution cannot describe either the frequency distribution or the generation of income. In the following sections, the distribution functions that exhibit positive skewness in accordance with observed income data are examined.

The Pareto Law

The Pareto law of income distribution states: *In all places and at all times the distribution of income is given by the empirical formula*

(2.3)
$$R(x) = \left(\frac{x}{x_0}\right)^{-\alpha} \quad \text{when} \quad x > x_0$$
$$= 1 \quad \text{when} \quad x < x_0$$

where $R(x) = 1 - F(x)$ *is the proportion of income units having income x or greater, and* α *is found to be approximately 1.5.*[1]

The density function of the Pareto distribution is obtained by differentiating (2.3) with respect to x:

(2.4)
$$f(x) = \alpha x_0^{\alpha} x^{-1-\alpha} \quad \text{when} \quad x > x_0$$
$$= 0 \quad \text{when} \quad x < x_0$$

where x_0 is the scale factor, and α the Pareto parameter. The curve (2.3) can be transformed to the logarithmic form

$$\log R(x) = \alpha \log x_0 - \alpha \log x,$$

and, therefore, the graph of this curve on the double logarithmic scale will be a straight line with the slope $-\alpha$.

1. See Pareto (1897).

Equation (2.3) implies that the elasticity of $R(x)$ with respect to x is $-\alpha$. In other words, if income x increases by 1 percent, the proportion of units having income greater than or equal to x declines by α percent. The parameter α can, therefore, be interpreted as the elasticity of decrease in the number of units when passing to a higher income class.

The mean of the Pareto distribution is given by

$$E(x) = \alpha x_0^\alpha \int_{x_0}^\infty x^{-\alpha}\, dx,$$

which will be finite only if $\alpha > 1$. If this condition is met, it follows that

$$E(x) = \frac{x_0 \alpha}{(\alpha - 1)}.$$

This equation implies that the mean of the Pareto distribution is proportional to the initial income x_0.

The variance of the Pareto distribution is derived as equal to

$$V(x) = \frac{x_0^2 \alpha}{(\alpha - 2)(\alpha - 1)^2},$$

which exists only if $\alpha > 2$. Pareto observed that the value of α is approximately 1.5, which means that the variance of the estimated Pareto distribution will not be finite.

That the Pareto law applies only to higher incomes can be theoretically shown by finding the first derivative of the density function

$$f'(x) = -\alpha(1 + \alpha) x_0^\alpha x^{-2-\alpha},$$

which is negative for all positive values of α. The density function of the Pareto distribution, therefore, decreases monotonically for all values of x greater than x_0. From this it can be concluded that the Pareto law can be valid only for that range of income for which the density function is decreasing. It is demonstrated below that the Pareto law is valid only for an even shorter range of income.

If the elasticity of $R(x) = 1 - F(x)$ with respect to x is denoted by $-r(x)$, where $F(x)$ is a general distribution function, (2.2) yields

(2.5)
$$r(x) = \frac{x f(x)}{[1 - F(x)]}$$

where $r(x) \geq 0$. Note that for the Pareto distribution, $r(x)$ is equal to α for all values of x. The first derivative of $r(x)$ with respect to x is obtained as

$$(2.6) \qquad r'(x) = \frac{r(x)}{x} \left[1 + \epsilon(x) + r(x) \right]$$

where $\epsilon(x) = xf'(x)/f(x)$ is the elasticity of the probability density function $f(x)$ with respect to x.

Because the observed income distributions are unimodal, the elasticity $\epsilon(x)$ will be positive up to the mode; then it becomes negative.[2] Equation (2.6) implies that $r'(x) > 0$ for $x \leq x^*$ where x^* satisfies

$$(2.7) \qquad \epsilon(x^*) = -1 - r(x^*).$$

This proves that $r(x)$ is a monotonically increasing function of x up to the point x^*. Consequently, the Pareto distribution, for which $r(x)$ is always constant, cannot apply to income levels less than x^*. It is clear from (2.7) that $\epsilon(x^*)$ is strictly negative. Because $\epsilon(x)$ is positive for incomes below the mode and equals zero at the modal value, the point x^* must be strictly greater than the mode. This demonstrates that the Pareto distribution will be valid only for incomes strictly greater than the mode. It is difficult to say, theoretically, how far beyond the mode the income level x^* will extend. Because income distribution is positively skewed with a long tail, the proportion of units having income less than or equal to x^* is almost invariably greater than 50 percent. This means that the Pareto distribution is suitable to describe income distributions of, at most, 50 percent of the population, a fact that has now been universally recognized, although Pareto asserted that the law was true over the whole range of income. Shirras, after a detailed examination of income tax and supertax statistics, arrived at the following conclusion: "There is indeed no Pareto law. It is time that it should be entirely discarded in studies on distribution."[3]

2. Mode is the level of income that gives the maximum value of the density function.

3. See Shirras (1935), p. 681.

Generation of Income Distribution:
Champernowne's Model

It has been pointed out that the shape of income distributions is stable over time and space. This feature has inclined a number of authors to think that income generation might be explained by a stochastic process. Gibrat (1931) was the first to advance this line of thought. He proposed the "law of proportionate effect," which generates a positively skewed distribution, and which will be discussed briefly later in this chapter. In this section a short account is given of a simple stochastic process suggested by Champernowne in 1953. His model demonstrates that, under suitable conditions, any initial distribution of income will, in the course of time, approach the Pareto distribution. Because the generalizations considered by Champernowne do not alter his main conclusions, only the simplest version of the model will be considered.

Champernowne divides the income scale above a certain minimum income x_0 into an enumerably infinite number of income classes. The ith income class given by (x_{i-1} to x_i) satisfies the condition that $x_i = kx_{i-1}$ for $i = 1, 2, \ldots, \infty$ where k is a constant. This condition assumes that the end points of income classes are equidistant on a logarithmic scale. Obviously, the width of income classes on such a scale is log k. The income units move across these income classes from one discrete time period to the next.

If $P_t(r, u)$ is denoted as the transitional probability that a unit belonging to class r at time t will move to class $r + u$ by time $t + 1$, then

$$\sum_{u=-(r-1)}^{\infty} P_t(r, u) = 1,$$

which implies that a unit in class r at time t will be in one of the income classes $1, 2, 3, \ldots, \infty$ with probability 1. If $P_t(r)$ is denoted as the probability that at time t a unit is in income class r, the income distribution $P_{t+1}(s)$ at time $(t + 1)$ will be generated according to

$$(2.8) \qquad P_{t+1}(s) = \sum_{u=-\infty}^{s-1} P_t(s - u)P_t(s - u, u).$$

This equation is called the transition equation because it links the income distribution at time $(t + 1)$ with the income distribution at time t through transition probabilities $P_t(r, u)$.

The assumptions underlying Champernowne's model are:

ASSUMPTION 2.1. *For every dying income receiver there is an heir to his income in the following year.*

This assumption implies that the number of incomes is constant over time.

ASSUMPTION 2.2. *For every value of t and r, and for some fixed integer n,*

$$(2.9) \qquad\qquad P_t(r, u) = 0$$

if $u > 1$ or $u < -n$, and

$$(2.10) \qquad\qquad P_t(r, u) = p_u > 0$$

if $-n \leq u \leq 1$ and $u > -r$.

Equation (2.9) implies that no income unit moves up by more than one or down by more than n income classes in a year. At the same time, equation (2.10) has two implications. First, that the transitional probabilities $P_t(r, u)$ are constant with respect to time; second, that they are independent of income level r and determined fully by u alone. Note that u is the number of income classes a unit moves in a single period. In other words, a transitional probability depends only on the number of income classes a unit jumps at a single time period. Because the income classes are equidistant on a logarithmic scale, any given proportionate income change is equiprobable at all levels of income.

ASSUMPTION 2.3.

$$\sum_{u=-n}^{1} u p_u < 0.$$

This assumption means that in all units, initially in any one of the income classes $n + 1, n + 2, \ldots$, the expected number of income classes shifted during the following time period is negative. This assumption is needed to prevent income from increasing indefinitely without stabilizing to an equilibrium distribution.

If $P^*(s)$ is used to denote the equilibrium distribution, the transition equation (2.8) becomes under assumption 2.2

(2.11) $$P^*(s) = \sum_{u=-n}^{1} P^*(s - u)p_u$$

for all $s > 1$. And

$$P^*(1) = \sum_{u=-n}^{0} P^*(1 - u)q_u$$

for $s = 1$ where $q_u = \sum_{v=-n}^{u} p_v$. In order to determine $P^*(s)$, it is necessary to find a nontrivial solution of (2.11). For this purpose, $P^*(s) = cZ^s$ is substituted into (2.11), yielding

(2.12) $$g(Z) = \sum_{u=-n}^{1} p_u Z^{1-u} - Z = 0$$

where $g(Z)$ is a polynomial of degree $(n + 1)$.

Descartes' rule of signs establishes the fact that (2.12) has no more than two real positive roots. One root is obviously unity. To determine the second root, calculate $g'(Z)$ from (2.12) at $Z = 1$:

$$g'(1) = - \sum_{u=-n}^{1} up_u,$$

which under assumption 2.3 is always positive. Because $g(0) = p_1 > 0$, $g(1) = 0$, and $g'(1) > 0$, it is implied that the second real positive root must lie between zero and unity. If this root is denoted by b, the equilibrium distribution will be given by

(2.13) $$P^*(s) = c_1 b^s$$

where $0 < b < 1$. The constant c_1 is determined so as to make the probability sum to unity.

In order to establish the link between the equilibrium distribution (2.13) and the Pareto law, calculate the probability

$$R(x_s) = Pr(X \geq x_s) = \sum_{r=s}^{\infty} P^*(r) = c \sum_{r=s}^{\infty} b^r,$$

which is the sum of a geometric series and is given by

(2.14) $$R(x_s) = \frac{cb^s}{(1 - b)}.$$

Note that this geometric series is convergent because b is positive and less than unity. Because the income classes satisfy the condition that $x_i = kx_{i-1}$, it follows that

$$(2.15) \qquad x_s = k^s x_0$$

where x_0 is the minimum income. Transforming equations (2.14) and (2.15) into logarithms and eliminating s yields

$$(2.16) \qquad \log R(x_s) = \gamma - \alpha \log x_s$$

where

$$\alpha = -\frac{\log b}{\log k} \quad \text{and} \quad \gamma = \log \frac{cx_0^\alpha}{(1 - b)},$$

α being identified as the Pareto parameter. Because $0 < b < 1$, α will always be positive. Equation (2.16) shows that the logarithm of the probability of income exceeding x_s is a linear function of the logarithm of x_s, which is the Pareto law in its exact form.

The model considered here is extremely simple and can be generalized in several directions. Although Champernowne has relaxed some of the assumptions to allow for the influence of age and occupation, his general conclusions do not change with these generalizations. In addition, he introduces two further generalizations: (a) allowing income units to shift upward by more than one income class in a year, and (b) limiting assumption 2.2 (that the prospects of various amounts of proportionate change of income are independent of initial income) to apply to higher incomes only.

With these two generalizations, the Pareto law ceases to be obeyed exactly. The law continues to apply asymptotically, however, to the occupants of high income groups. This aspect of the Pareto law is discussed in greater detail in the following section.

The Pareto-Levy Law

In the section "The Pareto Law," it was concluded that the Pareto distribution is unsuitable for graduating observed income distributions over the entire income range. The vast amount of empirical work done so far confirms this observation and shows that the Pareto distribution fits rather well toward the upper tail covering about 40 percent of income recipients. This empirical evidence led Mandelbrot (1960) to introduce the weak Pareto law:

$$R(x) \text{ behaves like } \left(\frac{x}{x_0}\right)^{-a}, \text{ as } x \rightarrow \infty,$$

which implies that

(2.17) $$\lim_{x \rightarrow \infty} \frac{R(x)}{\left(\dfrac{x}{x_0}\right)^{-\alpha}} = 1.$$

For an unspecified value of the parameter α, the Pareto law defined in (2.3) has been referred to as the strong Pareto law by Mandelbrot. When α assumes value 1.5, the Pareto law in (2.3) is referred to as the strongest Pareto law. On the basis of empirical evidence, the strong Pareto law is not strictly applicable; in contrast, there will be little disagreement over the validity of the weak Pareto law.

Before introducing the Pareto-Levy law, it is necessary to define stable probability law. Suppose the observed income X is equal to the sum of n independent random variables $X_1, X_2, \ldots, X_n$, such that all X_i follow the same probability distribution up to a linear transformation. This would assume the existence of coefficients $a_i > 0$ and b_i, so that all $a_i X_i + b_i$ have the same distribution. If X has the same distribution as individual X_i, again, up to the linear transformation, such a probability law is said to be stable. Mathematically this can be written as

(2.18) $$(a_1 X_1 + b_1) \oplus (a_2 X_2 + b_2) \oplus \ldots, (a_n X_n + b_n) = aX + b$$

where a and b are two constants that always exist for whatever values a_i and b_i take, so that $a_i > 0$. The sign $\oplus$ denotes the addition of random variables. Equation (2.18) implies that the probability distribution of $(aX + b)$ is the same as that of individual random variables $(a_1 X_1 + b_1)$, $(a_2 X_2 + b_2), \ldots, (a_n X_n + b_n)$. If this idea is applied to incomes, it is implied that the distribution of income continues to be the same, regardless of the number of components that constitute income. In this context, it is worth mentioning that, although, in general, the set of components constituting income differs from country to country, the shape of the observed income distribution in each country is the same.

The Gaussian law, which is the well-known normal distribution, is a stable probability law. Levy (1925) constructed the family of stable laws that are non Gaussian and satisfy the weak Pareto law with the parameter α restricted to the range $0 < \alpha < 2$. Mandelbrot (1960) defined the Pareto-Levy (P-L) law as the class of stable probability laws that satisfy the weak Pareto law with α lying in the range $1 < \alpha < 2$.

The density function of the P-L law cannot, unfortunately, be expressed in a closed analytic form but is determined indirectly with a Laplace transform. The probability distribution function can, however, be expressed for large x as

$$F(x) \sim 1 - x^{-\alpha}[u^*\Gamma(1-\alpha)]^\alpha$$

where $\Gamma(1-\alpha)$ is the gamma function,[4] α is the Pareto parameter lying in the range $1 < \alpha < 2$, and u^* is a positive scalar parameter.

The P-L distribution has a finite mean and infinite variance. As long as α is not close to 2, the distribution very rapidly becomes indistinguishable from a strong Pareto curve of the same α. If α approaches 2, the P-L density will tend toward a Gaussian density. From this observation, Mandelbrot concluded that the P-L density should be worth considering only if α is not too close to 2. The distribution has never been empirically tested, perhaps because of its complexity.

A Family of Distribution Functions

In this section a family of distribution functions that satisfy the weak Pareto law is considered. The strong Pareto law asserts that the elasticity $r(x)$ defined in (2.5) is constant and equal to α; the weak Pareto law implies that

$$\lim_{x \to \infty} r(x) = \alpha,$$

which means that $r(x)$ approaches α as x approaches infinity. Consider the following general form of $r(x)$:

$$(2.19) \qquad r(x) = \frac{\alpha x^\beta}{(c^\beta + x^\beta)}$$

---

4. $\Gamma(1-\alpha) = \displaystyle\int_0^\infty e^{-x} x^{-\alpha}\, dx$ where e is the base of Napierian logarithms, so that $\log e = 1$.

where α represents the Pareto parameter and c and β are additional parameters. It can be seen that if $\beta > 0$ as x approaches infinity, $r(x)$ approaches α, which means that the weak Pareto law is satisfied by this specification of $r(x)$. Differentiating (2.19) with respect to x yields

$$r'(x) = \frac{\alpha\beta c^\beta x^{\beta-1}}{(c^\beta + x^\beta)^2},$$

which is always positive if the parameters α, β, and c are strictly positive. Therefore, $r(x)$ is a monotonically increasing function of x.

Substituting (2.2) and (2.5) into (2.19), the following first-order differential equation is obtained:

$$\frac{dF(x)}{dx} = \frac{\alpha[1 - F(x)]x^{\beta-1}}{(c^\beta + x^\beta)},$$

which on integration gives

(2.20) $$[1 - F(x)] = k[c^\beta + x^\beta]^{-(\alpha/\beta)}$$

where k is the constant of the integration. So that $F(x)$ can satisfy the conditions (a), (b), and (c) as stated at the beginning of this chapter, it should follow that $\beta > 0$ and $k = c^\alpha$. With these restrictions, notice that $F(x) = 0$ for $x = 0$, and $F(x)$ approaches 1 as x approaches infinity. The density function corresponding to this function is obtained by differentiating (2.20) with respect to x as

$$f(x) = \alpha c^\alpha x^{\beta-1}(c^\beta + x^\beta)^{-(\alpha/\beta)-1},$$

from which the jth moment of x yields

(2.21) $$E(x^j) = \alpha c^\alpha \int_0^\infty x^{j+\beta-1}(c^\beta + x^\beta)^{-(\alpha/\beta)-1}\, dx$$

where E denotes the expectation operator.

Transforming x into y using the relation $y = \left(\dfrac{x}{c}\right)^\beta$, the integral in the right-hand side of (2.21) reduces to the Beta distribution of second kind. In this case, the jth moment of x obtained is

(2.22) $$E(x^j) = \frac{\alpha}{\beta} c^j B\left(\frac{j}{\beta} + 1, \frac{\alpha - j}{\beta}\right)$$

where $B(m, n)$ is the Beta function with parameters m and n.[5] So that this integral will converge, it should follow that $m > 0$ and $n > 0$, which from (2.22) implies that the jth moment of this distribution exists only if $j < \alpha$. It is empirically observed that the Pareto parameter α tends to have values in the range $1 < \alpha < 3$; thus, at the most, the first two moments of x can be deduced from the parameters of this distribution. If α is restricted to the range $1 < \alpha < 2$, which may be called the Pareto-Levy range, the distribution will have a finite mean and infinite variance.

The distribution function (2.20) was first proposed by Burr (1942). Later, in an unpublished paper presented at the 1958 meeting of the Econometric Society, Sargan applied it to income data.[6]

Three special cases of the family of distribution functions (2.20) are of considerable interest. If $c = 0$, the function (2.20) reduces to the Pareto distribution function as given in (2.3). If $\beta = 1$, however, the function (2.20) becomes

$$(2.23) \qquad 1 - F(x) = k(c + x)^{-\alpha},$$

which is called the Pareto distribution of second kind. This function was suggested by Pareto himself but has rarely been applied to empirical data.

The third case is obtained by introducing $\beta = \alpha$ into the density function (2.20). Thus

$$f(x) = \alpha c^{\alpha} x^{\alpha-1}(c^{\alpha} + x^{\alpha})^{-2},$$

which can be transformed into

$$(2.24) \qquad dF(x) = \frac{e^{\phi}d\phi}{(1 + e^{\phi})^2}$$

by means of the transformation $\left(\dfrac{x}{c}\right)^{\alpha} = e^{\phi}$.

The distribution function (2.24) is the well-known sech square distribution that is widely used in bioassay problems. Fisk (1961b)

---

5. $B(m, n) = \displaystyle\int_0^1 x^{m-1}(1 - x)^{n-1}dx$, which is also equal to $\Gamma(m)\Gamma(n)/\Gamma(m + n)$.

6. Singh and Maddala (1976) derived this distribution function using an alternative approach of hazard rate or failure rate.

proposed using this distribution for graduating income distributions. His investigation suggests that the sech square distribution may prove useful in examining distributions of income in populations that are homogeneous in at least one characteristic, such as occupation. He arrived at this distribution as the limiting case of the distribution function proposed by Champernowne (1952).

Champernowne's Distribution

In 1937 Champernowne proposed a family of functions for the purpose of graduating pretax income distributions.[7] Later, in 1952, he provided further explanations of the properties of these functions. Of the three forms of the distribution function he considered, only one gave good fit to the majority of the income distributions he studied.

The general form of Champernowne's distribution is written as

$$\phi(z) = \frac{n}{\cosh\{\alpha\,\gamma(z - z_0)\} + \lambda}$$

where $z = \log x$ is the income power, and $\phi(z)$ is the density function of z. The parameters are n, α, z_0 and λ; z_0 is the median income power.

The majority of the income distributions Champernowne studied gave a value of λ less than 1. In this case, the distribution function is given by

$$1 - F(x) = \frac{1}{\theta}\tan^{-1}\frac{\sin\theta}{\cos\theta + (x/x_0)^\alpha}$$

where $\cos\theta = \lambda$ and $z_0 = \log x_0$. The parameters α and θ are restricted to the ranges $\alpha > 0$ and $0 \le \theta < \pi$, these restrictions being required for $F(x)$ to be a single, valued, and monotonically increasing function of x. Fisk (1961b) has noted that moments of x exist up to order j where $j < \alpha$. Further, it can be seen that for this distribution, $r(x)$ approaches α as x approaches infinity. The distri-

7. Champernowne's Ph.D. dissertation, submitted in 1937 to Cambridge University, was published in 1973 by Cambridge University Press as *Distribution of Income Between Persons.*

bution satisfies the weak Pareto law, therefore, and α is the Pareto parameter. The parameter θ, however, has no simple interpretation. Fisk investigated the effect of θ on the shape of the distribution of x, concluding that the shape of the curve is relatively insensitive to changes in value of θ over the range $0°$ to $45°$, where it will, therefore, be reasonable to put $\theta = 0$. He argued that for sections of the population that are homogeneous in one character (for example, occupation), it is possible that θ may be zero. It can be seen that, as θ approaches zero, the Champernowne distribution approaches the sech square distribution. Thus Fisk derived the sech square distribution as a limiting case of Champernowne's distribution.

Laws of Income Distribution That Do Not Satisfy the Weak Pareto Law

The distribution functions so far considered have the common property that, for large values of income, they can be approximated by Pareto's formula given in (2.3). More technically speaking, they satisfy the weak Pareto law. This section concerns the distribution functions that do not obey the weak Pareto law. In this class, the lognormal distribution is most widely used. An elaborate history of this distribution has been given by Aitchison and Brown (1957), who indicate that several authors, among whom Gibrat is the best known, have contributed to the development of the lognormal distribution. In 1931, Gibrat published an extensive study of this distribution and presented his theory of the law of proportionate effect, which generates a positively skewed distribution. A brief outline of this law follows.

Suppose an individual's income begins with X_0 and subsequently undergoes a series of random, independent, proportional changes $m_1, m_2, \ldots, m_t$ where m_i can be either negative or positive. After t periods during which these changes have taken place, his income becomes

$$X_t = X_0(1 + m_1)(1 + m_2) \ldots (1 + m_t),$$

the logarithm of which will be

(2.25) $$\log X_t = \log X_0 + \sum_{i=1}^{t} u_i$$

where $u_i = \log (1 + m_i)$.

If the u_i are mutually independent, the distribution of log X_t will, according to the Central Limit Theorem, tend toward normality as t becomes large, and the random variable X_t will then follow the lognormal distribution. The lognormal distribution is, therefore, defined as the distribution of a random variable whose logarithm follows the normal probability law.

This simple stochastic process has been criticized by Kalecki (1945) on the grounds that the standard deviation of the logarithm of income increases continuously with the passage of time. This can be demonstrated by the fact that the variance of a sum of mutually independent random variables is the sum of the variances. Thus (2.25) yields

$$\text{var} (\log X_t) = \sum_{i=1}^{t} \text{var} (u_i),$$

which shows that, with the passage of time, the variance of log X_t grows steadily. Because the tendency for such an increase has not been observed in the real world, Kalecki suggested a modification of this process by introducing a negative correlation between X_t and m_t, which is just sufficient to prevent the variance of log X_t from growing steadily. Although a simple economic interpretation of this negative correlation is that the percentage increase in income is likely to be lower for the rich than for the poor, it is difficult to justify or refute this assumption without evidence.

The distribution function of the lognormal distribution is derived by assuming that $Y = \log X$ is normally distributed with mean μ and variance σ^2. The distribution function $F(x)$ of the random variable X is, therefore, given by

$$F(x) = \int_0^x \frac{1}{X\sigma\sqrt{2\pi}} \exp \{ - \frac{1}{2\sigma^2} (\log X - \mu)^2\} dX, \qquad X > 0$$

(2.26) $= 0, \qquad X \leq 0,$

which is usually denoted by $\Lambda(x|\mu, \sigma^2)$.

It can now be seen that $r(x)$ (defined in (2.5)) for the lognormal distribution approaches infinity as x approaches infinity, which violates the weak Pareto law.

The lognormal distribution has several attractive properties.[8]

---

8. See Aitchison and Brown (1954).

First, it is closely related to the normal distribution, which provides ready access to efficient estimation procedure and statistical inference. Second, the distribution gives reasonable fit in the middle ranges of income, covering about 60 percent of the population. Third, it produces a positively skewed distribution in accordance with observed income data.

Although the lognormal distribution is widely used in empirical work, it has a number of limitations: it fits poorly toward the tails; it tends to overcorrect for the positive skewness of the income distribution (this is demonstrated by the fact that the logarithmic transform of observed income distribution exhibits negative skewness, whereas the lognormal distribution assumes symmetry); the distribution is defined only over positive income levels. This limitation is of little consequence because the observations on negative or zero incomes are relatively few compared to the total number of observations.

Rutherford (1955) suggested an interesting extension of Gibrat's law of proportional effect by introducing "birth" and "death" considerations into the model. He based his model on the following assumptions: (a) Newcomers enter the labor force at a constant rate. (b) The income distribution of the newcomers is lognormal. (c) Mortality is unrelated to income power. (d) The number of survivors declines exponentially with age.

From these assumptions he deduced that the resulting income distribution will eventually approach the Gram-Charlier Type A distribution.[9] He also provided a tentative method of fitting this distribution, but it does not give as close an approximation to observed distributions as the distributions considered by Champernowne and Fisk.

Still two other distributions do not satisfy the weak Pareto law. One, suggested by Pareto himself (1919), has the probability distribution function

$$(2.27) \qquad F(x) = 1 - \frac{c^{\alpha} e^{-\beta x}}{(x + c)^{\alpha}}$$

where α and β are two parameters. As defined in (2.5) for this dis-

---

9. The Gram-Charlier series of type A represents the expansion in orthogonal polynomials. For more details, see Cramer (1946), p. 222.

tribution, $r(x)$ is given by

$$r(x) = \frac{x(\beta x + \beta c + \alpha)}{(x + c)},$$

which obviously approaches infinity as x approaches infinity. The weak Pareto law is, therefore, violated unless, of course, $\beta = 0$, in which case the function (2.27) reduces to the Pareto distribution of second kind as given in (2.23). Pareto estimated β from empirical statistics and found its value so small that he neglected it.[10]

The other distribution that does not satisfy the weak Pareto law is the Gamma density, fitted to income data by Amoroso (1925) and later proposed by Salem and Mount (1974). The Gamma density function is given by

$$f(x) = \frac{\lambda^{\alpha}}{\Gamma(\alpha)} x^{\alpha-1} e^{-\lambda x}$$

where $0 < x < \infty$ and α and λ are positive parameters. The Gamma function is $\Gamma(\alpha)$; the parameter α is directly related to the standard inequality measures; and the second parameter λ is a scale parameter.

Salem and Mount fitted the Gamma distribution to personal income data in the United States for the years 1960 to 1969. Their empirical results show that the Gamma distribution fits the data better than the lognormal but still is not entirely satisfactory; it exaggerates the skewness, although this tendency is even more marked in the fit of the lognormal.

10. See Hayakawa (1951).

CHAPTER 3

The Lorenz Curve

THE LORENZ CURVE, widely used to represent and analyze the size distribution of income and wealth, is defined as the relationship between the cumulative proportion of income units and the cumulative proportion of income received when units are arranged in ascending order of their income. Lorenz proposed this curve in 1905 in order to compare and analyze inequalities of wealth in a country during different epochs, or in different countries during the same epoch. The curve has been used principally as a convenient graphical device to represent size distribution of income and wealth.

In this chapter, the Lorenz curve is introduced in formal and rigorous terms. Its derivation from certain well-known income distribution functions is outlined and a direct approach, suggested by Kakwani and Podder (1973), of specifying a functional form for the Lorenz curve is considered. In addition, an alternative definition of the Lorenz curve suggested by Gastwirth (1971) is discussed, with the aid of illustrations. Finally, a number of important mathematical and statistical properties of the Lorenz curve are presented in a number of lemmas.

A Formal Definition of the Lorenz Curve

Suppose income X of a unit is a random variable with the probability density function $f(X)$.[1] This function, as defined in (2.1), would then be given by

---

1. The income X can be negative for some units but is assumed to be non-negative here for notational convenience.

$$(3.1) \qquad\qquad F(x) = \int_0^x f(X)\,dX$$

where $F(x)$ can be interpreted as the proportion of units having an income less than or equal to x; $F(x)$ obviously varies from 0 to 1. Further, if it is assumed that the mean μ of the distribution exists, the first-moment distribution function of X is defined as

$$(3.2) \qquad\qquad F_1(x) = \frac{1}{\mu}\int_0^x Xf(X)\,dX$$

where $F_1(x)$ also varies from 0 to 1. It follows that $F_1(x)$ is interpreted as the proportional share of total income of the units having an income less than or equal to x. If $f(X)$ is continuous, the derivate of $F_1(x)$ exists and is given by

$$(3.3) \qquad\qquad \frac{dF_1(x)}{dx} = \frac{x\,f(x)}{\mu}\,,$$

which implies that $F_1(x)$ is a monotonically nondecreasing function of x.

The Lorenz curve is the relationship between the variables $F(x)$ and $F_1(x)$ and is obtained by inverting functions (3.1) and (3.2), and eliminating x if the functions are conveniently invertible. Alternatively, the curve can be plotted by generating the values of $F(x)$ and $F_1(x)$ from (3.1) and (3.2) by considering the arbitrary values of x. The curve is represented in a unit square (figure 1). The ordinate and abscissa of the curve are $F_1(x)$ and $F(x)$, respectively.

By means of (3.3) and (2.2), the slope of the Lorenz curve is obtained as

$$(3.4) \qquad\qquad \frac{dF_1}{dF} = \frac{x}{\mu}\,,$$

which is always positive for positive income. Similarly, the second derivative of the curve is

$$(3.5) \qquad\qquad \frac{d^2F_1}{dF^2} = \frac{d}{dF}\left(\frac{dF_1}{dF}\right) = \frac{1}{\mu f(x)} > 0,$$

which is also positive. These two derivatives imply that the slope of the Lorenz curve is positive and increases monotonically; in other words, the curve is convex to the F-axis. From this it follows that $F_1 \leq F$. The straight line $F_1 = F$ is called the egalitarian line.

Figure 1. *The Lorenz Curve*

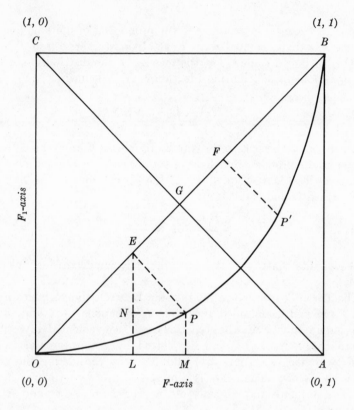

In figure 1 the egalitarian line is the diagonal *OB* through the origin of the unit square. The Lorenz curve falls below this line. If the curve coincides with the egalitarian line, it is implied that each unit receives the same income; this is the case of perfect equality of incomes. In the case of perfect inequality of incomes, the Lorenz curve coincides with *OA* and *AB*, which implies that all the income is received by only one unit in the population.

Lorenz Curve for Several Well-Known Income Distribution Functions

Before deriving the equation of the Lorenz curve for several well-known distribution functions, it would be useful to express the relationship as

(3.6) $$L(p) = F_1(x)$$

where

(3.7) $$p = F(x),$$

and $0 \le p \le 1$. The functional form $L(p)$, obtained by eliminating x from (3.6) and (3.7), is interpreted as the fraction of total income received by the lowest p^{th} fraction of the families. It satisfies the following conditions (Kakwani and Podder, 1973):

(a) if $p = 0$, $L(p) = 0$;

(b) if $p = 1$, $L(p) = 1$;

(c) $L'(p) = \dfrac{x}{\mu} \ge 0$ and $L''(p) = \dfrac{1}{\mu f(x)} > 0$;

(3.8)   (d) $L(p) \le p$.

Conditions (a) and (b) follow immediately from (3.1) and (3.2). Condition (c) is obvious from (3.4) and (3.5). And condition (d) follows from condition (c), which implies that the Lorenz curve lies below the egalitarian line.

The equation of the Lorenz curve implied by the Pareto distribution whose probability distribution function is given by

(3.9) $$F(x) = 1 - \left(\frac{x}{x_0}\right)^{-\alpha} \quad \text{when} \quad x \ge x_0$$

(see equation [2.3]) can be derived as follows.

If the mean of the Pareto distribution exists and is given by μ, the first-moment distribution function can be expressed as

(3.10) $$F_1(x) = \frac{1}{\mu} \int_{x_0}^{x} \alpha x_0^{\alpha} u^{-\alpha} du$$

where use has been made of the Pareto density function $f(x)$ as given in equation (2.4). Equation (3.10) is equal to

(3.11) $$F_1(x) = \frac{1}{\mu} \frac{\alpha x_0}{(\alpha - 1)} \left[1 - \left(\frac{x_0}{x}\right)^{\alpha - 1}\right].$$

In equation (3.10), $F_1(x)$ should approach unity as x approaches infinity. It can be seen that this limit exists only if $\alpha > 1$, which, if satisfied, gives

$$\mu = \frac{\alpha x_0}{(\alpha - 1)}.$$

Substituting (3.6) and (3.7) into (3.9) and (3.11) gives the equation of the Lorenz curve as

(3.12) $$L(p) = 1 - (1 - p)^\delta$$

where $\delta = [(\alpha - 1)/\alpha]$. The restriction $\alpha > 1$ implies that $0 < \delta < 1$. When $\delta = 1$, the Lorenz curve coincides with the egalitarian line.

Next, the equation of the Lorenz curve for the family of distribution functions discussed in chapter 2 can be derived. The distribution function derived in (2.20) yields

(3.13) $$\left(\frac{x}{c}\right)^\beta = [(1 - p)^{-(\beta/\alpha)} - 1].$$

The first-moment distribution function for this distribution is given by

(3.14) $$F_1(x) = \frac{1}{\mu} \int_0^x \alpha c^\alpha u^\beta (c^\beta + u^\beta)^{-(\alpha/\beta)-1} \, du$$

where the mean μ is

$$\mu = \frac{\alpha}{\beta} cB\left(\frac{1}{\beta} + 1, \frac{\alpha - 1}{\beta}\right),$$

$B(m, n)$ being the Beta function with parameters m and n. The integral (3.14) is evaluated by substituting $y = [(u/c)]^\beta$, which gives

(3.15) $$F_1(x) = B_z\left(\frac{1}{\beta} + 1, \frac{\alpha - 1}{\beta}\right)$$

where $z = [(x/c)]^\beta$, and $B_z(m, n)$ is the incomplete Beta distribution of second kind and is defined by

$$B_z(m, n) = \frac{1}{B(m, n)} \int_0^z \frac{y^{m-1} dy}{(1 + y)^{m+n}}.$$

From (3.13) and (3.15), the equation of the Lorenz curve becomes

(3.16) $$L(p) = B_z\left(\frac{1}{\beta} + 1, \frac{\alpha - 1}{\beta}\right)$$

where

(3.17) $$z = [(1 - p)^{-(\beta/\alpha)} - 1].$$

The particular cases can now be considered. Substituting $\beta = 1$ into (3.16) gives

$$L(p) = 1 - \alpha(1 - p)^{\delta} + (\alpha - 1)(1 - p),$$

which is the equation of the Lorenz curve for the Pareto distribution of second kind. Similarly, the Lorenz curve for the sech square distribution considered by Fisk (1961b) is obtained by substituting $\beta = \alpha$ into (3.16) and (3.17).

Next, the equation of the Lorenz curve implied by the lognormal distribution can be derived. The probability distribution function is denoted by

$$F(x) = \Lambda(x|\mu, \sigma^2)$$

where

(3.18) $$\Lambda(x|\mu, \sigma^2) = \int_0^x \frac{1}{X\sigma\sqrt{2\pi}} \exp\{-\frac{1}{2\sigma^2}(\log X - \mu)^2\}dX.$$

The first-moment distribution function can then be written as

$$F_1(x) = \int_0^x Xd\Lambda(X|\mu, \sigma^2)/\int_0^1 Xd\Lambda(X|\mu, \sigma^2)$$

$$= \int_0^x \frac{1}{X\sqrt{2\pi}\sigma} \exp\{-\frac{1}{2\sigma^2}(\log X - \mu)^2\}dX/e^{\mu+(\sigma^2/2)}$$

$$= \int_0^x \frac{1}{X\sqrt{2\pi}\sigma} \exp\{-\frac{1}{2\sigma^2}(\log X - \mu - \sigma^2)^2\}dX$$

(3.19) $$= \Lambda(x|\mu + \sigma^2, \sigma^2).$$

Note that $e^{\mu+(\sigma^2/2)}$ is the mean of the lognormal distribution with parameters μ and σ^2. Define the relation

(3.20) $$x = \phi(t)$$

so that

$$t = \frac{1}{\sqrt{2\pi}}\int_0^x e^{-1/2X^2}dX.$$

Then, if $p = \Lambda(x|\mu, \sigma^2)$, it follows that

(3.21)
$$\frac{\log x - \mu}{\sigma} = \phi(p).$$

Similarly, if $L(p) = F_1(x)$, equation (3.19) becomes

(3.22)
$$\frac{\log x - \mu - \sigma^2}{\sigma} = \phi[L(p)].$$

Eliminating $\log x$ from (3.21) and (3.22) gives the equation of the Lorenz curve as

(3.23)
$$\phi[L(p)] = \phi(p) - \sigma,$$

which depends only on the parameter σ.

An alternative approach to the equation of the Lorenz curve was suggested by Kakwani and Podder (1973). They proposed that, instead of the Lorenz curve being derived from a well-known income density function, the functional form for the Lorenz curve be specified directly. They suggested the following form of the Lorenz curve:

(3.24)
$$L(p) = pe^{-\gamma(1-p)}$$

where $\gamma > 0$ is the parameter. If $\gamma > 0$, the curve lies below the egalitarian line; if $\gamma = 0$, the curve coincides with the egalitarian line. The first two conditions given in (3.8) are obviously satisfied by the curve. Differentiating (3.24) twice yields

(3.25)
$$L'(p) = e^{-\gamma(1-p)}(1 + p\gamma)$$

(3.26)
$$L''(p) = 2\gamma e^{-\gamma(1-p)}(2 + p\gamma).$$

Following (3.25) and (3.26) note that if $\gamma > 0$, both derivatives are positive for all values of p in the interval 0 to 1. This implies that the curve (3.24) is sloping upward and increasing monotonically, thereby satisfying the third condition given in (3.8).

Kakwani and Podder (1973) fitted the curve (3.24) to Australian data using ordinary least squares on the transformed equation

$$\log L(p) = \log p - \gamma \log (1 - p),$$

but their empirical fit was unsatisfactory. Following a similar approach, the same authors proposed (1976) a new coordinate system for the Lorenz curve, paying particular attention to a special case

with wide empirical validity. This approach will be discussed in
detail in chapter 7.

An Alternative Definition of the Lorenz Curve

Gastwirth (1971) provided an alternative definition of the Lorenz
curve, which applies to discrete as well as to continuous variables,
and which is expressed in terms of the inverse of the distribution
function $F(x)$ defined as

$$(3.27) \qquad F^{-1}(t) = \text{Min}[x: F(x) \geq t].$$

This equation requires some explanation. If $F(x)$ has a continuous
derivative—that is, the density function $f(x)$ is continuous—, it
follows that for a given value of $F(x)$, one can always find a value
of x. But in the case of a discrete distribution corresponding to some
values of $F(x)$, x will not exist. The definition of inverse in (3.27)
ensures the existence of x for all values of $F(x)$. This definition
implies that the minimum value of x is chosen so that $F(x) \geq t$. If
the density function is continuous, this new definition of inverse is
identical to the usual definition of an inverse function. Because
$x = F^{-1}(t)$ and $f(x)dx = dt$ where t varies from zero to unity when
x varies from zero to infinity, the mean μ is given by

$$\mu = \int_0^\infty xf(x)\,dx = \int_0^1 F^{-1}(t)\,dt.$$

The Lorenz curve corresponding to the distribution function $F(x)$
is defined as

$$(3.28) \qquad L(p) = \frac{1}{\mu} \int_0^p F^{-1}(t)\,dt$$

where $0 \leq p \leq 1$.

As an illustration of the process of deriving the Lorenz curve by
means of this definition, consider the exponential distribution function

$$F(x) = 1 - e^{-\lambda x}, \qquad x > 0,$$

which gives the inverse function

$$F^{-1}(t) = -\frac{1}{\lambda} \log (1 - t).$$

The Lorenz curve for this function is, therefore, given by

$$L(p) = -\frac{1}{\mu} \int_0^p \frac{1}{\lambda} \log(1 - t)\, dt,$$

which, after integrating by parts, simplifies to

$$L(p) = \frac{1}{\mu\lambda} [p + (1 - p) \log (1 - p)]$$

where μ is the mean of the distribution and is equal to $1/\lambda$.

Another illustration is provided by Gastwirth who considers a distribution in which a fraction f of the population receives income A and the remaining fraction $(1 - f)$ of the population receives income according to the Pareto law with origin A and parameter α. According to this example,

$$F(x) = f \qquad\qquad , \qquad x = A$$

$$= 1 - (1 - f) \left(\frac{A}{x}\right)^\alpha, \qquad A < x < \infty,$$

which has the mean income

$$\mu = \frac{A(\alpha - f)}{(\alpha - 1)}.$$

The inverse is

$$F^{-1}(t) = A \qquad\qquad , \qquad 0 < t \leq f$$

$$= A \left\{\frac{(1 - f)}{(1 - t)}\right\}^{1/\alpha}, \qquad f < t < 1.$$

Then, applying formula (3.28) yields the following equation of the Lorenz curve:

$$L(p) = \frac{(\alpha - 1)p}{\alpha - f}, \qquad 0 < p \leq f$$

$$= 1 - \frac{\alpha(1 - f)^{1/\alpha}}{(\alpha - f)} (1 - p)^\delta, \qquad f < p < 1$$

where $\delta = [(\alpha - 1)/\alpha]$. Note that when $f = 0$, $L(p)$ reduces to the equation of the Lorenz curve for the Pareto law as derived in equation (3.12).

Some Useful Lemmas

The perpendicular distance between the Lorenz curve and the egalitarian line is $\phi(p) = p - L(p)$. It can be seen from (3.8) that $\phi(p)$ vanishes at $p = 0$ and $p = 1$. The first and second derivatives of $\phi(p)$ are given by

$$\phi'(p) = 1 - L'(p)$$

$$\phi''(p) = -L''(p),$$

which show that $\phi'(p)$ vanishes at the point where the Lorenz curve has slope unity and that the second derivative of $\phi(p)$ is always negative. If p_μ is the point at which the Lorenz curve has slope unity, $\phi(p)$ is maximum at $p = p_\mu$. Equation (3.4) clearly indicates that p equals p_μ at income level $x = \mu$. Thus the following lemma is proved.

LEMMA 3.1. *The distance between the Lorenz curve and the egalitarian line is maximum at income level $x = \mu$.*

Next, divide the population into two groups, all units having an income less than the population mean income belonging to the first group, and the rest belonging to the second group. If μ_1 and μ_2 denote the mean incomes of the first and the second group, respectively, it follows that

$$L(p_\mu) = \frac{p_\mu \mu_1}{\mu}$$

(3.29) $$1 - L(p_\mu) = \frac{(1 - p_\mu)\mu_2}{\mu}$$

where $\mu = p_\mu \mu_1 + (1 - p_\mu)\mu_2$.

If some income is transferred from the second group to the first group so that both have the same mean income, the gain in income of the first group as a percentage of the total income of the population is $[p_\mu(\mu - \mu_1)/\mu]$, which by means of (3.29) simplifies to $p_\mu - L(p_\mu)$. This, obviously, is the maximum distance between the egalitarian line and the Lorenz curve and leads to the following lemma.

LEMMA 3.2.   *If the population is divided into two groups so that in the first (second) group all the income units have income less (greater) than the population mean, the proportion of income that should be transferred from the second group to the first so that both have the same mean income is given by the maximum distance between the Lorenz curve and the egalitarian line.*

The symmetry of the Lorenz curve is defined with respect to the diagonal drawn perpendicular to the egalitarian line. Suppose that in figure 1, PE and $P'F$ are the perpendiculars drawn on the egalitarian line from any two points P and P', respectively, on the Lorenz curve. If $EG = GF$, it follows that for a symmetric Lorenz curve, $PE = P'F$. If the Lorenz curve is not symmetric, it is skewed either toward $(0, 0)$ or toward $(1, 1)$. The curve is defined as skewed toward $(0, 0)$ if $P'F$ is greater than PE. Similarly, the curve is skewed toward $(1, 1)$ if $P'F$ is less than PE. A formal condition of symmetry is derived in the following lemma.

LEMMA 3.3.   *The Lorenz curve $q = L(p)$ is symmetric if, and only if,*

$$(3.30) \qquad 1 - p = L(1 - q).$$

Proof.   If P is any point on the curve with coordinates (p, q), it can be seen from figure 1 that $OM = OL + LM$ and $EL = EN + NL$. Further, $OL = LE = (1/\sqrt{2})OE$ and $EN = NP = (1/\sqrt{2})PE$. Because $OM = p$ and $NL = PM = q$, it follows that

$$p = \frac{1}{\sqrt{2}}(OE + PE) \quad \text{and} \quad q = \frac{1}{\sqrt{2}}(OE - PE),$$

which, on solving for OE and PE, gives

$$(3.31) \qquad OE = \frac{1}{\sqrt{2}}(p + q) \quad \text{and} \quad PE = \frac{1}{\sqrt{2}}(p - q).$$

Similarly, if p' is any other point on the curve with coordinates (p', q'),

$$(3.32) \qquad OF = \frac{1}{\sqrt{2}}(p' + q') \quad \text{and} \quad P'F = \frac{1}{\sqrt{2}}(p' - q').$$

If the point P' is such that $EG = GF$, it is obvious that $OF = \sqrt{2} - OE$, which from (3.31) and (3.32) gives

$$(3.33) \qquad p' + q' = 2 - p - q.$$

If the Lorenz curve is symmetric, it should follow that $PE = P'F$, which gives

(3.34) $$p' - q' = p - q$$

where use has been made of (3.31) and (3.32).

Solving equations (3.33) and (3.34) for p' and q' yields

(3.35) $$p' = (1 - q) \quad \text{and} \quad q' = (1 - p).$$

Because (p', q') is a point on the Lorenz curve $q = L(p)$, the result given in (3.30) follows immediately from (3.35). This proves the necessity part of the condition. To prove sufficiency, it must be shown that if P' is a point on the Lorenz curve with coordinates $(1 - q)$, $(1 - p)$, $EG = GF$ and $P'F = PE$. This follows immediately from equations (3.31) and (3.32) and completes the proof of lemma 3.3.

Lemma 3.3 implies that if (p, q) is any point on a Lorenz curve, the point $(1 - q, 1 - p)$ also lies on the curve. This can be interpreted as follows: If the bottom p percent of the population earns q percent of the total income, the top q percent of the population earns p percent of the total income.

Differentiating equation (3.30) with respect to p gives

(3.36) $$L'(1 - q)L'(p) = 1.$$

According to lemma 3.1, $L'(p)$ equals unity at $p = p_\mu$ where p_μ is the value of p at which $x = \mu$. Thus equation (3.36) at point $p = p_\mu$ gives

$$L'(p_\mu) = 1 \quad \text{and} \quad L'[1 - q_\mu] = 1$$

where $q_\mu = L(p_\mu)$. Because $L''(p) > 0$ for all p in the range $0 \le p \le 1$, it is implied that $L'(p)$ is a monotonically increasing function of p. There cannot, then, be two different values of p at which $L'(p) = 1$. Thus these equations imply that

$$p_\mu + L(p_\mu) = 1,$$

which leads to the following lemma.

LEMMA 3.4. *If the Lorenz curve $q = L(p)$ is symmetric, the point $[p_\mu, L(p_\mu)]$ corresponding to the mean income μ lies on the diagonal perpendicular to the egalitarian line.*

An alternative condition of symmetry of the Lorenz curve in terms of density function is provided in the following lemma.

LEMMA 3.5. *The necessary and sufficient condition for the Lorenz curve $q = L(p)$ to be symmetric is*

$$(3.37) \qquad \frac{f(\mu^2/x)}{f(x)} = \left(\frac{x}{\mu}\right)^3$$

for all x where $f(x)$ is the density function.[2]

Proof. The necessary and sufficient condition for the Lorenz curve $q = L(p)$ to be symmetric is provided in (3.30). Differentiating this equation with respect to p yields equation (3.36), which on differentiating again yields

$$(3.38) \qquad [L'(p)]^3 = \frac{L''(p)}{L''(1-q)}$$

where use has been made of (3.36). If p corresponds to income level x and $p = 1 - q$ to income level x', condition (c) of equation (3.8) yields

$$(3.39) \qquad L'(p) = \frac{x}{\mu} \quad \text{and} \quad L''(p) = \frac{1}{\mu f(x)}$$

$$(3.40) \qquad L'(1-q) = \frac{x'}{\mu} \quad \text{and} \quad L''(1-q) = \frac{1}{\mu f(x')}\,.$$

Substituting these results into (3.36) gives

$$(3.41) \qquad x' = \frac{\mu^2}{x}\,,$$

which demonstrates that, if p corresponds to income level x, $p = 1 - q$ corresponds to income level μ^2/x. Combining (3.39), (3.40), and (3.41) with (3.38) yields (3.37). This proves the necessity aspect of the condition in lemma 3.5.

In order to prove the sufficiency aspect of lemma 3.5, it must be shown that equation (3.37) implies equation (3.30). If the point

---

2. This lemma was suggested by Champernowne (1956), but he did not provide its proof.

$[p', L(p')]$ corresponds to the income level μ^2/x, then

(3.42) $\qquad L'(p') = \dfrac{\mu}{x}$ and $L''(p') = \dfrac{1}{\mu f(\mu^2/x)}$.

Equations (3.39), (3.42), and (3.37) yield

(3.43) $\qquad\qquad\qquad L'(p)L'(p') = 1$

(3.44) $\qquad\qquad\qquad L''(p') = L''(p)[L'(p')]^3.$

Differentiating (3.43) with respect to p and using (3.44) yields

(3.45) $\qquad\qquad\qquad L'(p')\dfrac{dp'}{dp} = -1,$

which on integration gives

(3.46) $\qquad\qquad\qquad L(p') = c - p$

where c is the constant of integration. Substituting (3.43) into (3.45) yields

$$\frac{dp'}{dp} = -L'(p),$$

which on integration becomes

(3.47) $\qquad\qquad\qquad p' = c_1 - L(p),$

c_1 being the constant of integration.

Equations (3.46) and (3.47) yield

$$L(c_1 - q) = c - p$$

$$L(c - q') = c_1 - p'$$

where $q' = L(p')$. Fulfilling the conditions that $q = 0$ when $p = 0$ and $q' = 0$ when $p' = 0$, these two equations become

$$L(c_1) = c$$

$$L(c) = c_1,$$

which can be true if either $c = c_1 = 0$ or $c = c_1 = 1$. It is clear from (3.46) and (3.47) that c and c_1 cannot be equal to zero; if they were, p' and $L(p')$ would be negative. Consequently, $c = c_1 = 1$, and, therefore, it follows that

$$p' = 1 - q \quad \text{and} \quad L(p') = 1 - p.$$

These two equations together lead to (3.30). This completes the proof of lemma 3.5.

LEMMA 3.6.   *The Lorenz curve for the lognormal distribution is symmetric.*

The proof of this lemma follows immediately from lemma 3.5 if the density function of the lognormal distribution in equation (3.37) is used. Now, lemma 3.5 can be used to construct a family of distribution functions that give a symmetric Lorenz curve. Condition (3.37) will be satisfied if[3]

$$f(x) = \left(\frac{\mu}{x}\right)^{3/2} g\left(\log\frac{x}{\mu}\right)$$

where $g(y)$ is an even function of y.[4] If $\log(x/\mu) = u$, the density function of u becomes

$$h(u) = g(u)e^{-u/2},$$

and in the specific case of $g(u) = 1/\sqrt{2\pi}\, e^{-u^2/2}$, it becomes

$$h(u) = \frac{1}{\sqrt{2\pi}} e^{-1/2(u+1/2)^2},$$

which shows that u is normally distributed with a mean $-\frac{1}{2}$ and variance unity. Because $u = \log(x/\mu)$, it is implied that x is lognormally distributed with parameter $\log \mu - \frac{1}{2}$ and unity. The lognormal distribution is derived, therefore, as a particular case of the family of distribution functions that give a symmetric Lorenz curve.

In figure 2, if P_μ is the point on the Lorenz curve corresponding to the mean income μ, it follows from lemma 3.1 that the perpendicular $P_\mu E_\mu$ is of maximum length. In a symmetric Lorenz curve the point P_μ lies on the diagonal perpendicular to the egalitarian line. This diagonal will now be referred to as the alternative diagonal. If the Lorenz curve is skewed toward $(0, 0)$, it is clear from figure 2 that P_μ will lie above the alternative diagonal. This implies that the distance OE_μ will be greater than the distance OG. Because $OE_\mu = 1/\sqrt{2}\,[p_\mu + L(p_\mu)]$ and $OG = 1/\sqrt{2}$, the Lorenz curve

---

3. See Kendall (1956).
4. $g(y)$ is said to be an even function if $g(y) = g(-y)$.

Figure 2. *Skewed Lorenz Curve*

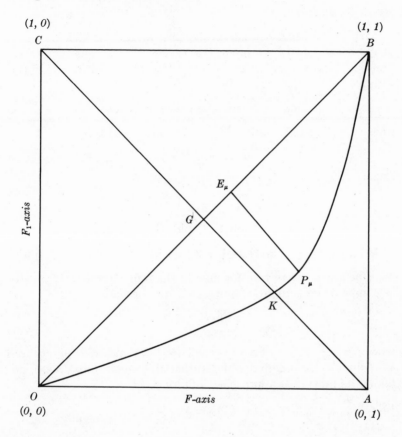

that is skewed toward $(0, 0)$ implies that $P_\mu + L(p_\mu)$ will always be greater than unity. Further, it is clear from figure 2 that, if $p_\mu + L(p_\mu) > 1$, OE_μ will be greater than OG, in which case the Lorenz curve must be skewed toward $(0, 0)$. Thus the following lemma has been proved.

LEMMA 3.7. *The Lorenz curve $q = L(p)$ is skewed toward $(0, 0)$ if, and only if,*

$$(3.48) \qquad\qquad p_\mu + L(p_\mu) > 1.$$

From this the following lemma concerning the skewness of the Paretian Lorenz curve can be proved.

LEMMA 3.8.   *The Lorenz curve for the Pareto distribution is skewed toward (0, 0).*[5]

Proof. The proof consists in demonstrating that the inequality (3.48) holds for the Paretian Lorenz curve. The equation of the Paretian Lorenz curve is given by (3.12), which, on differentiating with respect to p, gives

$$L'(p) = \delta(1 - p)^{\delta-1}$$

where $0 \leq \delta \leq 1$. Equating $L'(p)$ with unity yields

$$p_\mu = 1 - \delta^{1/(1-\delta)},$$

which, on substituting into (3.12), gives

$$p_\mu + L(p_\mu) = 2 - \delta^{1/1-\delta} - \delta^{\delta/1-\delta}.$$

So that the inequality (3.48) can hold, the function

(3.49) $$q(\delta) = 1 - \delta^{1/1-\delta} - \delta^{\delta/1-\delta}$$

must be greater than zero for all δ in the range $0 < \delta < 1$. Clearly, as δ approaches zero, $q(\delta)$ approaches zero because

$$\lim_{\delta \to 0} \delta^\delta = 1.$$

Since $\delta = (1 - 1/\alpha)$ where α is the Pareto parameter, δ approaches 1 as α approaches infinity. Substituting this result into (3.49) and taking its limit as α approaches infinity yields

(3.50) $$\lim_{\delta \to 1} q(\delta) = 1 - 2e^{-1}$$

because

$$\lim_{\alpha \to \infty} \left(1 - \frac{1}{\alpha}\right)^\alpha = e^{-1}.$$

Obviously, the expression in the right-hand side of (3.50) is always positive. Differentiating $q(\delta)$ with respect to δ gives

(3.51) $$\frac{dq(\delta)}{d\delta} = -\delta^{\delta/1-\delta}[1 + (1 + \delta)(1 - \delta)^{-2}(\log \delta + 1 - \delta)],$$

---

5. This result has already been proved by Quandt (1966). A simpler proof is provided here.

which, by means of logarithmic expansion, simplifies to

$$\frac{dq(\delta)}{d\delta} = (1-\delta)\delta^{\delta/1-\delta}\left[\frac{1+\delta}{12} + \frac{\delta(1-\delta)}{4}\right.$$

$$\left. + (1+\delta)\left\{\frac{(1-\delta)^2}{5} + \frac{(1-\delta)^3}{6} + \ldots \infty\right\}\right].$$

The expression in the right-hand side of (3.51) is, therefore, positive for $0 < \delta < 1$. This implies that $q(\delta)$ increases monotonically from zero to $(1 - 2e^{-1})$ for all δ in the range $0 < \delta < 1$. Thus $q(\delta)$ can never become negative. This proves lemma 3.6.

CHAPTER 4

The Lorenz Curve and Social Welfare

BECAUSE THE LORENZ CURVE displays the deviation of each individual income from perfect equality, it captures, in a sense, the essence of inequality. Consequently, the Lorenz curve could be used as a criterion for ranking income distributions. However, the ranking provided by the curve is only partial. When the Lorenz curve of one distribution is strictly inside that of another, it can safely be concluded that the first distribution is more equal than the second. But when two Lorenz curves intersect, neither distribution can be said to be more equal than the other. This partial ranking need not, however, be considered a weakness of Lorenz curves. In fact, Sen (1973) criticized complete ranking of distributions on the grounds that the concept of inequality has different facets and is, therefore, essentially a question of partial ranking.

Atkinson (1970) provided a justification of the Lorenz curve ranking in terms of social welfare by showing that the ranking of income distributions according to the Lorenz curve criterion is identical to the ranking implied by social welfare, regardless of the form of the utility function of the individuals (except that it is increasing and concave), and provided the Lorenz curves do not intersect. If the Lorenz curves do intersect, however, two functions that will rank them differently can always be found.

Atkinson's result relies on the assumptions that the social welfare function is equal to the sum of the individual utilities, and that every individual has the same utility function. These assumptions have been criticized by Das Gupta, Sen and Starrett (1973) as well as by

Rothschild and Stiglitz (1973), who have demonstrated that the result is, in fact, more general and would hold for any symmetric welfare function that is quasi-concave. In this chapter these results will be discussed and some new corollaries given.

Some Useful Definitions and Lemmas

DEFINITION 4.1.   *The distribution X is said to be Lorenz superior (inferior) to the distribution Y if the Lorenz curve for X lies above (below) the Lorenz curve for Y at all points.*

The above definition implies that the distribution X is Lorenz superior to the distribution Y if, and only if,

(4.1) $$L_x(p) \geq L_y(p)$$

for all p in the interval $0 \leq p \leq 1$ where $L_x(p)$ is the Lorenz curve for the distribution X. If (4.1) holds, $X \underset{L}{\geq} Y$. Note that both $X \underset{L}{\geq} Y$ and $Y \underset{L}{\geq} X$ will be true if, and only if, $L_x(p) = L_y(p)$ for all p; that is, if both distributions have an identical Lorenz curve.

The definition of the Lorenz curve for a finite collection of individuals, the distribution of which must be discrete, follows. If there are n income units arranged in ascending order of their incomes, $x_1 \leq x_2 \leq \ldots, \leq x_n$, the ordinate of the Lorenz curve at $p = i/n$ for $i = 0, 1, 2, \ldots, n$ will be

$$L(0) = 0$$

(4.2) $$L\left(\frac{i}{n}\right) = \sum_{k=1}^{i} x_k / \sum_{k=1}^{n} x_k$$

where $i \leq n$.

If X and Y are two ordered distributions,

$$x_1 \leq x_2 \leq \ldots, \leq x_n \quad \text{and} \quad y_1 \leq y_2 \leq \ldots, \leq y_n,$$

the condition $X \underset{L}{\geq} Y$ is equivalent to

$$\sum_{k=1}^{i} x_k / \sum_{k=1}^{n} x_k \geq \sum_{k=1}^{i} y_k / \sum_{k=1}^{n} y_k$$

for all i. If the two distributions have the same mean income, the above condition simplifies to

$$(4.3) \qquad \sum_{k=1}^{i} x_k \geq \sum_{k=1}^{i} y_k$$

for all i.

The following definition of regressive transfers (RT) was proposed by Rothschild and Stiglitz (1973).

DEFINITION 4.2. *Suppose X is an ordered income distribution and $\hat{X}$ is another distribution obtained from X by transferring income d from individual j to the richer k so that*

$$\text{(a)} \ \ \hat{x}_j = x_j - d,$$

$$\text{(b)} \ \ \hat{x}_k = x_k + d,$$

$$\text{(c)} \ \ \hat{x}_i = x_i$$

for $i \neq j, k$.

where $x_j \leq x_k$. Such a transfer is called a regressive transfer, and $\hat{X}$ is said to differ from X by a single regressive transfer.

If the distribution Y can be obtained from the distribution X by a sequence of regressive transfers, it is expressed symbolically as

$$X \underset{T}{\geq} Y.$$

The following definitions relate to the concavity and quasiconcavity of a function.

DEFINITION 4.3. *The function $u(\mathbf{x})$ is concave if, and only if,*

$$\lambda u(\mathbf{x}) + (1 - \lambda)u(\mathbf{y}) \leq u[\lambda\mathbf{x} + (1 - \lambda)\mathbf{y}]$$

for any λ with $0 < \lambda < 1$, and for any two vectors $\mathbf{x}$ and $\mathbf{y}$ in the domain of the function u.

DEFINITION 4.4. *The function $u(\mathbf{x})$ is strictly concave if, and only if,*

$$(4.4) \qquad \lambda u(\mathbf{x}) + (1 - \lambda)u(\mathbf{y}) < u[\lambda\mathbf{x} + (1 - \lambda)\mathbf{y}]$$

for any λ with $0 < \lambda < 1$, and for any two vectors $\mathbf{x}$ and $\mathbf{y}$ in the domain of the function u.

The above definitions indicate that a strictly concave function is necessarily concave, but that the converse may not be true. For example, a linear function is concave but not strictly concave.

LEMMA 4.1. *Suppose a function $u(x)$ possesses a second derivative $u''(x)$ in some open interval. Then a necessary and sufficient condition for $u(x)$ to be concave in the interval is*

$$u''(x) \leq 0.$$

The proof of this lemma follows from theorem 94 of Hardy, Littlewood, and Polya (1934).

LEMMA 4.2. *If $u''(x) < 0$, $u(x)$ is strictly concave.*

The proof of this lemma follows from theorem 95 of Hardy, Littlewood, and Polya (1934).

The following lemma will be useful in proving Atkinson's theorem.

LEMMA 4.3. *Suppose g and h are two increasing functions. Then the necessary and sufficient condition for*

$$\int_a^b u(g(x))\,dx \geq \int_a^b u(h(x))\,dx$$

to be true for every concave and continuous u is

$$\int_a^l g(x)\,dx \geq \int_a^l h(x)\,dx$$

for $a \leq l \leq b$, with equality for the extreme values of l.

The proof follows from theorem 10 of Hardy, Littlewood, and Polya (1929).

DEFINITION 4.5. *A function $u(\mathbf{x})$ is quasi-concave if, and only if,*

$$(4.5) \qquad \text{Min}\,[u(\mathbf{x}), u(\mathbf{y})] \leq u[\lambda\mathbf{x} + (1 - \lambda)\mathbf{y}]$$

for any λ with $0 < \lambda < 1$, and for any two vectors $\mathbf{x}$ and $\mathbf{y}$ in the domain of u.

DEFINITION 4.6. *A function $u(\mathbf{x})$ is strictly quasi-concave if, and only if,*

$$\text{Min}\,[u(\mathbf{x}), u(\mathbf{y})] < u[\lambda\mathbf{x} + (1 - \lambda)\mathbf{y}]$$

for any λ with $0 < \lambda < 1$, and for any two vectors $\mathbf{x}$ and $\mathbf{y}$ in the domain of u.

Note that quasiconcavity is a weaker condition than concavity.

Utilitarianism and Income Inequality

Suppose a society comprises n individuals who have incomes $x_1, x_2, \ldots, x_n$. Let $u_i(x)$ represent the utility of income x for individual i. The utilitarian social welfare function is then equal to the sum of individual utilities

$$(4.6) \qquad W = \sum_{i=1}^{n} u_i(x_i).$$

This social welfare function is clearly an additive separable, which is not necessarily utilitarian. This can be seen by considering the additive separable welfare function

$$W = \frac{1}{\alpha} \sum_{i=1}^{n} [u_i(x_i)]^{\alpha},$$

which will be a utilitarian welfare function only if α is unity. If it is assumed that every individual has the same utility function, the social welfare function (4.6) becomes

$$(4.7) \qquad E[u(X)] = \sum_{i=1}^{n} u(x_i)$$

where X denotes the distribution $(x_1, x_2, \ldots, x_n)$ and E stands for expected value defined over the probability distribution X.

Assume that distribution X is characterized by the continuous random variable x that has the density function $f(x)$. The social welfare function (4.7) will then be written as

$$(4.8) \qquad E[u(X)] = \int_{0}^{\infty} u(x)f(x)\,dx$$

where the income is assumed to vary from zero to infinity.

It can be demonstrated that the maximization of utilitarian social welfare from a given total income leads to an egalitarian distribution only if every individual has the same utility function; if each individual has a different utility function, the maximization of social welfare may lead to a highly unequal distribution of income.[1]

1. See Sen (1972).

An inequality measure is usually defined in terms of the deviation of a given distribution of income from the "ideal distribution." As will be discussed in chapter 5, all the existing measures of inequality represent deviation from perfect equality. Obviously, perfect equality is too extreme to be accepted as a social norm, although the justification provided by utilitarianism for perfect equality is based on the assumption that every individual has an identical utility function with diminishing marginal utility. Sen (1973) demonstrated that any resort to welfare economics in search of an ideal distribution invariably fails.

Atkinson's Theorem

THEOREM 4.1. *If X and Y are two distributions having the same mean income, the following statements are equivalent:*

(a) $X \geq Y$,
    _{L}

(b) $E[u(X)] \geq E[u(Y)]$

where $u(x)$ is an increasing function of x and is concave.

Atkinson proved this theorem by making use of a well-known theorem in the theory of choice under uncertainty.[2] An alternative proof will be presented here by means of lemma 4.3.

Assume that distributions X and Y are characterized by random variables x and y, respectively, which have the same mean μ. If $q = L_x(p)$ and $q = L_y(p)$ denote the Lorenz curves for the two distributions, equation (3.8) yields

(4.9) $x = \mu L_x'(p)$ and $y = \mu L_y'(p)$

where p varies from zero to unity when incomes x and y vary from zero to infinity. Because $dp = f(x)dx$, substituting (4.9) into (4.8) yields

$$E[u(X)] = \int_0^1 u[\mu L_x'(p)]dp$$

2. For proof of this theorem, see Hadar and Russell (1969), Hanoch and Levy (1969), and Rothschild and Stiglitz (1970).

and

$$E[u(Y)] = \int_0^1 u[\mu L_y'(p)]dp.$$

Applying lemma 4.3 provides the necessary and sufficient condition for

$$E[u(X)] \geq E[u(Y)]$$

to be true for every concave and continuous u as

(4.10) $$\int_0^l \mu L_x'(p)dp \geq \int_0^l \mu L_y'(p)dp$$

for $0 \leq l \leq 1$, with equality for extreme values of l. When the integrals have been evaluated, equation (4.10) becomes

$$L_x(l) \geq L_y(l)$$

for all l in the interval $0 \leq l \leq 1$, which is clearly equivalent to condition (a) of theorem 4.1. This completes the proof of that theorem.

The above theorem implies that if social welfare is the sum of the individual utilities and every individual has an identical utility function, the ranking of distributions according to the Lorenz curve criterion is identical to the ranking implied by the social welfare function, provided the Lorenz curves do not intersect; indeed, condition (a) requires that the Lorenz curves do not intersect. One can judge between the distributions without knowing the form of the utility function $u(x)$, except that it is increasing and concave.

Consider the hypothesis that proportional additions to income, in excess of that required for bare subsistence, make equal additions to individual utility. This is Bernoulli's hypothesis considered by Dalton (1920); it leads to the utility function

(4.11) $$u(x) = \log x + c,$$

which is an increasing function x and concave. Applying Atkinson's theorem, it follows that

(4.12) $$E[\log x] \geq E[\log y]$$

if, and only if, the distribution corresponding to variable x is Lorenz superior to the distribution corresponding to variable y, and the two distributions have the same mean income. Let X^* and Y^* be any two distributions corresponding to random variables x^* and y^*, respectively, so that

$$x^* = \frac{\mu_x^*}{\mu} x$$

$$y^* = \frac{\mu_y^*}{\mu} y$$

where $\mu_x^* = E(x^*)$ and $\mu_y^* = E(y^*)$. These equations then imply that the distributions corresponding to variables x and y have the same mean income μ. Substituting x and y from these equations into (4.12) yields

$$E[\log x^*] - \log \mu_x^* \geq E[\log y^*] - \log \mu_y^*,$$

which leads to the following corollary.

COROLLARY 4.1. *If X^* and Y^* are two distributions with mean incomes μ_x^* and μ_y^*, respectively, the distribution X^* is Lorenz superior to the distribution Y^* if, and only if,*

$$\frac{G_{x^*}}{\mu_x^*} \geq \frac{G_{y^*}}{\mu_y^*}$$

where G_{x^*} and G_{y^*} are the geometric means of the two distributions.

It is obvious from this corollary that if X^* is Lorenz superior to Y^* and both distributions have the same geometric mean, Y^* must have a higher mean than X^*.

Now consider the utility function

(4.13) $$u(x) = c - \frac{1}{x}$$

where c is constant. This utility function satisfies the following conditions:[3]

(a) An increase in utility when income has reached a certain level, should correspond to a more than proportionate increase in income.
(b) Utility should tend to a finite limit as income increases indefinitely.

3. See Dalton (1920), p. 350.

(c) Utility should be zero for a certain amount of income and negative for smaller amounts.

These conditions are satisfied if the utility is of the form

$$du = \frac{dx}{x^2} \, ,$$

which leads to the functional form (4.13). The utility is an increasing function of income and is concave. Again, applying Atkinson's theorem leads to the following corollary.

COROLLARY 4.2. *If X^* and Y^* are two distributions with mean incomes μ_x^* and μ_y^*, respectively, the distribution X^* is Lorenz superior to the distribution Y^* if, and only if,*

$$\frac{H_{x^*}}{\mu_x^*} \geq \frac{H_{y^*}}{\mu_y^*}$$

where H_{x^*} and H_{y^*} are the harmonic means of the two distributions.

Stronger Versions of Atkinson's Theorem

To arrive at stronger versions of Atkinson's theorem, a class of social welfare functions, which are not necessarily utilitarian, must be considered. The concept of a general social welfare function was introduced by Bergson in 1938 and subsequently developed by Samuelson in 1947. In its most general form, the Bergson-Samuelson social welfare function is defined as

(4.14) $W = W(X) = W(x_1, x_2, \ldots, x_n)$

where $X = (x_1, x_2, \ldots, x_n)$ is a social state belonging to the set S, S being a set of all possible social states. Arrow's (1951) concept of social welfare is, however, defined as a collective choice rule that specifies orderings for the society.[4] The distinction between the two concepts has been adequately discussed by Sen (1969). This section shall concern only the Bergson-Samuelson kinds of social welfare functions.

---

4. Using this definition, Arrow proved his famous impossibility theorem, which rules out the existence of all possible social welfare functions under mild-looking conditions.

DEFINITION 4.7.   *The welfare function $W(X)$ is said to be symmetric if*

$$W(X) = W(\pi(X))$$

where π is any permutation of X.

The symmetry of the social welfare function requires that if two individuals interchange their incomes, the social welfare function remain unchanged. Note that the utilitarian social welfare function is symmetric only if every individual has the same utility function.

The generalized version of Atkinson's theorem as provided by Rothschild and Stiglitz follows.

THEOREM 4.2.   *If X and Y are two distributions having the same mean income, the following statements are equivalent:*

(a) $X \underset{L}{\geq} Y$;

(b) $X \underset{T}{\geq} Y$;

(c) $W(X) \geq W(Y)$

where $W(X)$ is symmetric and quasi-concave in individual incomes.

Proof.   The proof consists in demonstrating the chain of implications: (a) $\Rightarrow$ (b) $\Rightarrow$ (c) $\Rightarrow$ (a).

1. (a) $\Rightarrow$ (b). If condition (a) is true, it must be shown that distribution Y can be obtained from distribution X by a sequence of regressive transfers. If X and Y are two ordered distributions, condition (a) is equivalent to (4.3). Let k be the first integer so that $x_k > y_k$; this yields a new distribution $X(k)$ as follows. Transfer an amount $(x_k - y_k)$ from individual k to $(k + 1)$, which lowers the income of the kth individual to y_k and raises the income of $(k + 1)^{\text{th}}$ by the same amount. The distribution $X(k)$ is given by

$$x_i(k) = y_i, \qquad i \leq k$$

$$x_{k+1}(k) = x_{k+1} + (x_k - y_k)$$

$$x_i(k) = x_i, \qquad i > k + 1.$$

It is evident that distribution $X(k)$ is Lorenz superior to Y and that $X(k)$ agrees with Y in k places (one more than X). Applying the same procedure to $X(k)$ yields a new distribution $X(k + j)$, which is again Lorenz superior to Y and agrees with Y in $(k + j)$ places. When $j = (n - k)$, Y is obtained. Thus Y can be obtained from X by a sequence of less than n regressive transfers.

2. (b) $\Rightarrow$ (c). It will suffice to show that a single regressive transfer does not increase the value of $W(X)$ where $W(X)$ is quasi-concave and symmetric. Suppose, without loss of generality, that Y is obtained from X by a single regressive transfer affecting the income of the first two persons. Thus

$$y_1 = x_1 - d$$
$$y_2 = x_2 + d$$
$$y_i = x_i, \qquad i \geq 3.$$

By considering function

$$Q(t) = W(x_1 - t, x_2 + t, \ldots, x_n),$$

it can be seen that if W is quasi-concave, so is $Q(t)$, which by means of (4.5) gives

$$(4.15) \qquad \text{Min}[Q(t), Q(t^*)] \leq Q\left[\frac{t + t^*}{2}\right]$$

where λ is assumed to be equal to $\frac{1}{2}$. Because $W(X)$ is symmetric, $Q(t) = Q(t^*)$ where $t^* = x_1 - x_2 - t$; therefore, (4.15) becomes

$$Q(t) \leq Q\left(\frac{x_1 - x_2}{2}\right),$$

which implies that $Q(t)$ attains the maximum when $t = (x_1 - x_2)/2 < 0$. For $t > (x_1 - x_2)/2$, $Q(t)$ decreases. Because $d \geq 0$, $Q(0) \geq Q(d)$; this proves that $W(X) \geq W(Y)$.

3. (c) $\Rightarrow$ (a). Consider the welfare function

$$W^k(X) = \sum_{i=1}^{k} x_i,$$

which is symmetric and quasi-concave. Thus

$$W^k(X) \geq W^k(Y)$$

implies that

$$\sum_{i=1}^{k} x_i \geq \sum_{i=1}^{k} y_i,$$

which is equivalent to condition (a). This completes the proof of the theorem.

Das Gupta, Sen, and Starrett (1973) considered the following social welfare function, which is a function of individual utilities:

$$S(X) = S[u(x_1), u(x_2), \ldots, u(x_n)]$$

where S is increasing, symmetric, and quasi-concave in individual utilities, and u is concave. Because the function is necessarily symmetric and quasi-concave, $S(X)$ is a special case of $W(X)$ as given in (4.14). Thus $W(X) \geq W(Y)$ implies that $S(X) \geq S(Y)$. Furthermore, $E(u(X))$ in (4.7) is a special case of $S(X)$; therefore, $S(X) \geq S(Y)$ implies that $E[u(X)] \geq E[u(Y)]$. According to Atkinson's theorem, $E[u(X)] \geq E[u(Y)]$ implies that $X \underset{L}{\geq} Y$, which, according to theorem 4.2, implies that $W(X) \geq W(Y)$. This proves the following theorem, proposed by Das Gupta, Sen, and Starrett.

THEOREM 4.3.   *The following statements are equivalent:*

(a) $X \underset{L}{\geq} Y$,

(b) $S(X) \geq S(Y)$.

PART TWO

===

Measurement of Income Inequality

CHAPTER 5

Measures of Income Inequality

WHEREAS THE LORENZ PREFERENCE provides only a partial ordering of distributions, measures of income inequality have been devised to provide complete orderings; of all these measures, the Gini index is the most widely used. In addition, the coefficient of variation, the relative mean deviation, and the standard deviation of logarithms of income are frequently utilized in the empirical literature. And in 1967 Theil proposed two new inequality measures, which are derived from the notion of entropy in information theory.

It is now widely recognized that alternative inequality measures do not provide the same ranking of distributions. Yntema (1933) was the first to demonstrate such conflicts in ranking. Conducting an empirical study by means of ten wealth and seven income distributions, he arrived at the conclusion that, although some consistency may be found in the ranking of distributions by certain subgroups of measures, there is little overall uniformity in the ranking of these distributions. In his study of Puerto Rico, Argentina, and Mexico, Weisskoff (1970) observed that, on the basis of the Gini index and the standard deviation of logarithms of income, Puerto Rico displayed a more equal distribution of income than did Mexico. When the coefficient of variation was used as a measure of inequality, however, Mexico's income distribution appeared more equal. Atkinson (1970), in summarizing Ranadive's conclusions (1965), argued that the differences in ranking are so contradictory that no clear picture emerges of the relative degree of inequality in advanced and developing countries.

Because the conflicting results displayed by conventional inequality measures have continued to be a major source of dissatisfaction, much of the literature has concerned the problem of choice among alternative measures. In 1974, Champernowne conducted a detailed simulation study to judge the relative merits of various inequality measures. He concluded that there can be no single "best" measure; that the choice of a measure should depend on the particular aspect of inequality in which one is interested; and that some measures are more suited to reflect particular aspects of distribution than others.

In his classic 1920 article, Dalton pioneered an attack on conventional inequality measures from a welfare standpoint, and, about fifty years later, Aigner and Heins (1967), Bentzel (1970), Atkinson (1970), and others pursued the attack. Their criticisms focus on the fact that these measures are statistical devices that measure the relative dispersion of a frequency distribution without reference to the normative notion of social welfare. Arguing that any inequality measure must incorporate society's preferences, Dalton proposed a measure based on the idea of proportional welfare loss resulting from income inequality. Atkinson criticized Dalton's measure on the grounds that it is variant with respect to linear transformations of the utility function, and proposed an alternative inequality measure by introducing "the equally distributed equivalent level of income." In addition, Sen (1973), Allingham (1972), and Muellbauer (1975b) proposed alternative measures based on more general assumptions about social welfare than the measures considered by Dalton and Atkinson.

Because the inequality measures proposed by Dalton, Atkinson, and others rely heavily on the value judgments represented by the social welfare functions chosen, they are normative measures. The conventional measures, in contrast, are called positive measures because they do not make explicit use of any concept of social welfare. Sen (1973) argued that the distinction between the two kinds of measures is not a firm one, and that every positive measure embodies some form of social welfare function. The various assumptions about the form of the social welfare function that are implied by different conventional inequality measures have been discussed in a series of articles by Atkinson (1970), Das Gupta, Sen, and Starrett (1973), Newbery (1970), Sheshinski (1972b), and Rothschild and Stiglitz (1973). This chapter deals with these issues in detail and presents a number of new interpretations.

Axioms for Inequality Comparisons

If $x_1 \leq x_2 \leq \ldots, \leq x_n$ is an ordered income distribution among n individuals denoted by a nonnegative vector

$$\mathbf{x} = (x_1, x_2, \ldots, x_n),$$

the inequality measure $\theta(\mathbf{x})$ is defined as a unique function of x_1, $x_2, \ldots, x_n$, satisfying certain desirable properties. These properties are presented below in the form of a number of axioms. Note that these axioms may not all be considered desirable at the same time. The purpose here is not so much to justify them as to provide a framework for comparing various inequality measures.

AXIOM 5.1.   *If* $\mathbf{y} = \alpha\mathbf{x}(\alpha > 0)$*, then* $\theta(\mathbf{x}) = \theta(\mathbf{y})$.

This axiom implies that the inequality measure should remain unaffected if each income is altered by the same proportion and requires, therefore, that the inequality measure be independent of the scale of measurement. Because the Lorenz curve is scale-independent, the inequality measures associated with it will always satisfy this axiom.

Dalton's suggestion that equal proportionate additions to all incomes should diminish inequality and that equal proportionate subtractions should increase it is called the principle of proportionate additions to incomes; it clearly contradicts axiom 5.1. An argument against Dalton's principle is that the inequality of income can be diminished simply by calculating all incomes in cents instead of in dollars. But as Dalton himself pointed out, this is obviously unacceptable. If units of money income in any two cases are to be compared, he argued, they must have approximately equal purchasing power.

AXIOM 5.2.   *If the new distribution* $\mathbf{y}$ *is obtained from* $\mathbf{x}$ *by adding to incomes of all individuals a constant amount d, it follows that*

(a) *if* $d > 0$, $\theta(\mathbf{y}) < \theta(\mathbf{x})$;

(b) *if* $d < 0$, $\theta(\mathbf{y}) > \theta(\mathbf{x})$.

This axiom corresponds to Dalton's principle of equal additions to incomes, which implies that equal additions to all incomes diminish inequality, and equal subtractions increase it. The following lemma is related to this axiom.

LEMMA 5.1.   *If the new distribution* **y** *is obtained from* **x** *by adding to incomes of all individuals a constant amount* d, *the distribution* **y** *is Lorenz superior (inferior) to the distribution* **x**, *if* d *is greater (less) than zero.*

Proof.   The distribution **y** is given by

$$(5.1) \qquad\qquad y_i = x_i + d$$

for $i = 1, 2, \ldots, n$. If μ is the mean income of the distribution **x**, the new distribution **y** will have the mean income $(\mu + d)$. If $L(k/n)$ is denoted as a point on the Lorenz curve for the distribution **x** at $p = k/n$, equation (4.2) yields

$$(5.2) \qquad\qquad L\left(\frac{k}{n}\right) = \sum_{i=1}^{k} x_i/n\mu.$$

Similarly, if $L^*(k/n)$ is denoted as the Lorenz curve for the distribution **y**, equation (4.2) yields

$$L^*\left(\frac{k}{n}\right) = \sum_{i=1}^{k} y_i/n(\mu + d),$$

which, by means of (5.1), simplifies to

$$(5.3) \qquad\qquad L^*\left(\frac{k}{n}\right) = (\sum_{i=1}^{k} x_i + kd)/n(\mu + d).$$

Equations (5.2) and (5.3) give

$$(5.4) \qquad\qquad L^*\left(\frac{k}{n}\right) - L\left(\frac{k}{n}\right) = \frac{kd(\mu - \mu_k)}{n\mu(\mu + d)}$$

where μ_k is the mean income of the first k individuals, μ being the mean income of the whole distribution, which is clearly greater than the mean income of the first k individuals. The sign of the expression on the right-hand side of (5.4), therefore, depends on the sign of d. It follows then that $L^*(k/n)$ is greater (less) than $L(k/n)$ if d is greater (less) than zero. This completes the proof of lemma 5.1.

AXIOM 5.3.   *Inequality remains unaffected if a proportionate number of persons are added at all income levels.*

This axiom corresponds to Dalton's principle of proportionate additions of persons; the Lorenz curve clearly remains unchanged if proportionate additions are made to the number of persons receiving incomes at all levels. The inequality measures associated with the Lorenz curve will, therefore, always satisfy this axiom.

AXIOM 5.4. *If a transfer of income $d < h/2$ takes place from a person with income x to a person with lower income $(x - h)$, the inequality is strictly diminished.*

This axiom corresponds to Dalton's principle of transfers, which is equivalent to the concept of regressive transfers introduced by Rothschild and Stiglitz (1973). It follows from theorem 4.2, therefore, that if a transfer of income takes place from rich to poor, subject to the restriction $d < h/2$, the new distribution is Lorenz superior. Because the restriction $d < h/2$ ensures that the transfer not be so large as to reverse the relative positions of two individuals, any number of such transfers taking place between any two consecutive income units subject to this restriction will not alter the ranking of income units. This process of transfers is called the rank-preserving equalization.[1] In addition, there will be a maximum reduction in inequality if the transfer is equal to half the difference between the two incomes, that is, when $d = h/2$.

Axiom 5.4 requires that the inequality measures be sensitive to transfers at all levels of income. The following lemma gives the condition under which axiom 5.4 is always satisfied.

LEMMA 5.2. *Any inequality measure that is the arithmetic mean of a strictly convex function of income satisfies Dalton's principle of transfers.*

Proof. Let $\theta(\mathbf{x}) = \theta(x_1, x_2, \ldots, x_n)$ be the inequality measure. If the partial derivative $\partial\theta/\partial x_i$ exists for all x_i, the change in inequality due to an infinitesimal transfer of income from individual i to individual j is expressed by

$$(5.5) \qquad d\theta = \frac{\partial\theta}{\partial x_i}(-dx_i) + \frac{\partial\theta}{\partial x_j}(dx_i),$$

which, according to axiom 5.4, should be negative for all $dx_i > 0$

1. See Fields and Fei (1974).

and $x_i > x_j$. Axiom 5.4 will, therefore, be satisfied if

$$(5.6) \qquad \frac{\partial \theta}{\partial x_i} - \frac{\partial \theta}{\partial x_j} > 0$$

for all $x_i > x_j$. If the inequality measure is expressed as

$$(5.7) \qquad \theta(\mathbf{x}) = \sum_{i=1}^{n} V(x_i),$$

condition (5.6) becomes

$$V'(x_i) - V'(x_j) > 0$$

for all $x_i > x_j$ where $V'(x_i)$ stands for the first derivative of $V(x_i)$ with respect to x_i. Clearly, this condition will always be satisfied if the function $V(x_i)$ is strictly convex for all i. This proves lemma 5.2.

LEMMA 5.3.   *If the income inequality is expressed as*

$$(5.8) \qquad \theta = \int_0^\infty V(x)f(x)\,dx,$$

the relative sensitivity of inequality to an infinitesimal transfer of income from a person with income x to a person with income $(x - h)$ depends on the magnitude of $T(x)$ where[2]

$$(5.9) \qquad T(x) = V'(x) - V'(x - h).$$

Proof.   Note that equation (5.8) in the discrete case is equivalent to (5.7). Substituting $x_i = x$ and $x_j = x - h$ into equation (5.5) yields

$$d\theta = -dx[V'(x) - V'(x - h)],$$

which shows that the magnitude of change in inequality depends on $T(x)$ where $T(x)$ is already defined. This proves lemma 5.3.

Lemma 5.3 facilitates an examination of the relative sensitivity of the inequality measure at different income levels. For example, if the function $T(x)$ is constant, it is implied that the effect of transfer would be independent of the income level at which it is made.

---

2. Atkinson (1970) also used expression (5.9) to examine the relative sensitivity of the measure, but he did not provide a proof.

Further, if $T(x)$ is a monotonically decreasing function of x, the inequality measure gives higher weight to transfers at the lower end of the distribution, and the weight decreases monotonically as income increases. Similarly, if $T(x)$ is a monotonically increasing function of x, weights attached to transfers increase with income. It can also occur that $T(x)$ increases first and then decreases. This would imply that the inequality measure attaches more weight to transfers in the middle of the distribution than at the tails.

AXIOM 5.5. $\theta(\mathbf{x}) = \theta(\pi(\mathbf{x}))$ *where π is any permutation of* $\mathbf{x}$.

This axiom implies a symmetric inequality measure, which means that if two individuals interchange their income positions, inequality remains unchanged. Moreover, the axiom ensures impartiality between individuals; the inequality depends only on the frequency distribution of incomes and not on the order in which individuals are ranked within the distribution.

AXIOM 5.6.   *The inequality measure lies in the range of zero to one.*

This axiom will be satisfied if the inequality measure takes the value zero when every individual has equal income, and takes the value unity in the limit as the number of individuals increases, with one individual getting all the income.

The Gini Index and the Relative Mean Difference

Of all the inequality measures, whether positive or normative, the Gini index is the one most widely used to analyze the size distributions of income and wealth. The measure as proposed by Gini in 1912 is defined as

(5.10) $$G = \frac{\Delta}{2\mu}$$

where

$$\Delta = \frac{1}{n(n-1)} \sum_{i=1}^{n} \sum_{j=1}^{n} |x_i - x_j|,$$

x_i being the income of the ith unit, and n the total number of units.

In the continuous case, Δ is written as

$$\Delta = \int_0^\infty \int_0^\infty |x - y| f(x) f(y) \, dx \, dy.$$

Note that Δ is the arithmetic average of the $n(n - 1)$ differences taken as absolute values, and that 2μ is the maximum possible value of Δ, which would be obtained when one unit receives all the income. The minimum value of Δ is obviously zero and would be obtained when every individual receives the same income. Thus, the Gini index lies in the range of zero to unity (satisfying axiom 5.6).

A number of intuitive interpretations of the Gini index are possible; that the Gini index arises from differences in incomes between individuals is itself appealing. For example, Pyatt (1976) provided an interpretation of the Gini index based on the expected gain of having the option of being someone better off. Suppose for each individual an income is selected at random from the population. He is then given the option to choose between his present income and that of the random selection. It is reasonable to assume that the individual will choose the randomly selected income only if it is larger than his own. There will always be, therefore, a positive expected gain for each individual from this process. If x is the actual income of an individual, his expected gain from the option of being someone else will be

$$E[\text{gain}/x] = \int_x^\infty (y - x) f(y) \, dy,$$

considering that the probability of selecting any income y from the population is $f(y) \, dy$. Averaging these expected gains over all individuals yields the following average expected gain for the whole population:

$$E[\text{gain}] = \int_0^\infty \int_x^\infty (y - x) f(x) f(y) \, dx \, dy$$

$$= \tfrac{1}{2} \int_0^\infty \left[\int_0^x (x - y) f(y) \, dy + \int_x^\infty (y - x) f(y) \, dy \right] f(x) \, dx,$$

which is equal to $\Delta/2$. Thus, the Gini index is interpreted as equal to the average gain expected by an individual from the option of being someone else in a population divided by average income.

Sen (1973) suggested another interesting interpretation. In any pairwise comparison, the individual with the lower income may suffer from depression upon discovering that his income is the lower. If it is assumed that this depression is proportional to the difference in incomes, the average of all such depressions in all possible pairwise comparisons leads to the Gini index.

The Gini Index and the Lorenz Curve

Subsequently, in 1914, Gini proposed an inequality measure that is equal to one minus twice the area under the Lorenz curve. He demonstrated that this new measure corresponds to his earlier measure, defined in terms of relative mean difference. The following lemma expresses this correspondence.

LEMMA 5.4.   *The Gini index as defined in (5.10) is equal to one minus twice the area under the Lorenz curve.*

Proof.

$$G = \frac{1}{2\mu} \int_0^\infty \int_0^\infty |x - y| f(x) f(y) \, dx \, dy$$

$$= \frac{1}{2\mu} \int_0^\infty \left[\int_0^x (x - y) f(y) \, dy + \int_x^\infty (y - x) f(y) \, dy \right] f(x) \, dx$$

$$(5.11) \quad = \frac{1}{\mu} \int_0^\infty \left[x F(x) - \mu F_1(x) \right] f(x) \, dx$$

where (3.1) and (3.2) are used. Note that $F(x)$ is the probability distribution function, and that $F_1(x)$ is the first-moment distribution function. Integrating the first term into (5.11) by parts yields

$$(5.12) \quad \frac{1}{\mu} \int_0^\infty x F(x) f(x) \, dx = 1 - \int_0^\infty F_1(x) f(x) \, dx,$$

which, on substituting into (5.11), yields

$$(5.13) \quad G = 1 - 2 \int_0^\infty F_1(x) f(x) \, dx.$$

The right-hand side in (5.13) is clearly equal to one minus twice the area under the Lorenz curve. This completes the proof of lemma 5.4.

LEMMA 5.5. *If the distribution* **y** *is Lorenz superior (inferior) to the distribution* **x**, $G(\mathbf{y})$ *is less (greater) than* $G(\mathbf{x})$ *where* $G(\mathbf{x})$ *stands for the Gini index of the distribution* **x**.

The proof of this lemma follows immediately from lemma 5.4. Note that the converse of this lemma may not be true: if the two Lorenz curves cross, $G(\mathbf{y}) > G(\mathbf{x})$ does not imply that $\mathbf{x} \geq \mathbf{y}$.
$$L$$

From lemmas 5.1 and 5.5 it immediately follows that the Gini index always satisfies Dalton's principle of equal additions to incomes. This principle is stated as axiom 5.2. Axiom 5.3, concerning Dalton's principle of proportionate additions of persons, will obviously be satisfied by the Gini index because of its relation to the Lorenz curve.

It was observed in "Axioms for Inequality Comparisons" that if a transfer of income takes place from rich to poor, subject to the restriction $d < h/2$, the new distribution will be Lorenz superior. This result, with lemma 5.5, implies that axiom 5.4, corresponding to Dalton's principle of transfers, is always satisfied by the Gini index.

LEMMA 5.6. *The Gini index attaches more weight to transfers of income near the mode of the distribution than at the tails.*

Proof. Substituting equation (5.12) into (5.13), the Gini index can be expressed as

$$G = \frac{2}{\mu} \int_0^\infty x[F(x) - \tfrac{1}{2}]f(x)\,dx,$$

which yields

$$V(x) = \frac{2}{\mu} x[F(x) - \tfrac{1}{2}].$$

If the income x of an individual changes to $x + dx$ because of rank-preserving transfers from rich to poor, $F(x)$ will not be affected. The derivative of $V(x)$ with respect to x is, therefore, equal to

$$V'(x) = \frac{2}{\mu}[F(x) - \tfrac{1}{2}],$$

which yields

(5.14) $$T(x) = \frac{2}{\mu} \left[F(x) - F(x-h) \right].$$

The sensitivity of the Gini index to transfers depends on $T(x)$. Equation (5.14) shows that for a typical unimodal distribution, $T(x)$ first increases with x and then decreases. This means that $T(x)$ will have a maximum at the mode of the distribution. Thus, the Gini index will give more weight to transfers near the mode of the distribution than at the tails. This proves the lemma.

Welfare Implications of the Gini Index

The welfare implications of the Gini index have been debated by Atkinson (1970), Newbery (1970), Kats (1972), Sheshinski (1972b), Das Gupta, Sen, and Starrett (1973), Rothschild and Stiglitz (1973), Chipman (1974), and Sen (1973, 1974a). A brief review of this debate follows.

Consider a number of distributions with the same mean income. Lemma 5.5, with theorem 4.2, shows that the Gini index will rank these distributions in the same order as any quasi-concave and symmetric social welfare function, provided the Lorenz curves of these distributions do not intersect. Using this result, Atkinson criticized the Gini index by arguing that if the Lorenz curves do intersect, one can always find a social welfare function that will rank the distributions in a reverse order to the one given by the Gini index. Newbery strengthened Atkinson's criticism of the Gini index by proving that there exists no additive social welfare function that ranks income distributions in the same order as the Gini index. Thus a strong case is made for rejecting the Gini index as a measure of inequality.

The supporters of the Gini index argue that additive separability is too strong a condition to impose on a social welfare function. Sheshinski maintained, moreover, that an additive welfare function has no particular significance, and he provided an example of a nonadditive welfare function that ranks the distributions in the same order as the Gini index. Das Gupta, Sen, and Starrett, as well as Rothschild and Stiglitz, in contrast, demonstrated that there exists no strictly quasi-concave welfare function that would give the same ranking of the distributions as the Gini index would give.[3] Sen does not, however, consider this criticism particularly serious: "The implied group welfare function may not be strictly concave, but it is concave all right, and furthermore any transfer from the poor to the rich or vice versa is strictly recorded in the Gini measure in the appropriate direction."[4]

So far, only the restrictions on the welfare functions implied by the Gini index have been considered. Chipman pursued an alternative approach by restricting the kinds of income distributions that are likely to be observed. He asked if any plausible form of income distribution would give the ranking of distributions provided by the Gini index in the same order as any social welfare function would give them. This question has been answered by Atkinson, Das Gupta, Sen, and Starrett, and Rothschild and Stiglitz: Any class of income distribution that gives nonintersecting Lorenz curves would permit the ranking of distributions by the Gini index.

It was demonstrated in chapter 3 that the Lorenz curves for the Pareto and lognormal distributions are functions of one parameter: α and σ, respectively. These distributions would, therefore, belong to the family of nonintersecting Lorenz curves. Thus theorem 4.2 and lemma 5.5 lead to the following lemma.

LEMMA 5.8.   *For both the Pareto and lognormal distributions,*

$$(5.15) \qquad\qquad \frac{\partial W}{\partial G} < 0$$

where W is the social welfare function, which is nondecreasing, symmetric, and quasi-concave.

Chipman proved inequality (5.15) for only the Pareto distribution. His proof is based on the assumption that the social welfare function is equal to the sum of individual utilities, and that every individual has the same utility function. Lemma 5.8 is clearly more general and follows immediately from theorem 4.2. In fact, the inequality in lemma 5.8 is valid for any income distribution that leads to a single-parameter Lorenz curve.

---

3. Note that the nonadditive welfare function considered by Sheshinski is quasi-concave, but not strictly quasi-concave.
4. See Sen (1973), p. 34.

An Axiomatic Approach

The criticisms of the Gini index so far discussed are, for the most part, based on the fact that the welfare function implied by the Gini index does not have desirable properties, such as additivity and strict quasiconcavity. Sen (1974a) derived a welfare function satisfying a set of axioms that gives the ranking of distributions in the same way as the Gini-index. He began with the following general form of the welfare function:

$$(5.16) \qquad W(\mathbf{x}) = \sum_{i=1}^{n} x_i v_i(\mathbf{x})$$

where x_i is the income of the ith person and $v_i(\mathbf{x})$ is a weight attached to x_i. Denote $(\mathbf{x}, i)$ as the position of being individual i with distribution $\mathbf{x}$, that is, having income x_i while the distribution is $\mathbf{x} = (x_1, x_2, \ldots, x_n)$. Now consider the following axioms proposed by Sen.

AXIOM 5.6 (weighting equity): If everyone prefers $(\mathbf{x}, i)$ to $(\mathbf{x}, j)$, then $v_j(\mathbf{x}) > v_i(\mathbf{x})$.

AXIOM 5.7 (limit equity): Each distribution $\mathbf{x}$ of a constant mean income μ over a constant population must have the same maximal $v_i(\mathbf{x})$ and the same minimal $v_i(\mathbf{x})$ for variation in i.

AXIOM 5.8 (independent monotonicity): For all $\mathbf{x}$, all individuals believe $(\mathbf{x}, i)$ to be at least as good as $(\mathbf{x}, j)$ if, and only if, $x_i \geq x_j$.

AXIOM 5.9 (ordinal information): If everyone prefers $(\mathbf{x}, i)$ to $(\mathbf{x}, j)$ and also $(\mathbf{x}, m)$ to $(\mathbf{x}, n)$, and there is no $(\mathbf{x}, k)$ such that anyone prefers $(\mathbf{x}, i)$ to $(\mathbf{x}, k)$ and $(\mathbf{x}, k)$ to $(\mathbf{x}, j)$, and there is no $(\mathbf{x}, p)$ such that anyone prefers $(\mathbf{x}, m)$ to $(\mathbf{x}, p)$ and $(\mathbf{x}, p)$ to $(\mathbf{x}, n)$, then

$$v_j(\mathbf{x}) - v_i(\mathbf{x}) = v_n(\mathbf{x}) - v_m(\mathbf{x}).$$

In any pairwise comparison, axiom 5.6 gives higher weight to the income of the person who is regarded by all as the worse off. Axiom 5.8 has each person decide his preference over pairs, such as $(\mathbf{x}, i)$ and $(\mathbf{x}, j)$, on the basis of income alone (higher income being preferred to lower income). These two axioms together imply that an individual with higher income receives the lower weight.

Axiom 5.7 requires that all income distributions have weights lying within the same range. If $v(\mathbf{x}, x)$ denotes the weight attached to an individual with income x when the distribution is $\mathbf{x}$, without loss of generality it can be assumed that minimal $v(\mathbf{x}, x)$ is zero and maximal $v(\mathbf{x}, x)$ is k for all income distributions $\mathbf{x}$. If income varies from zero to infinity, axioms 5.6 and 5.8 together imply that

$$v(\mathbf{x}, x) = 0 \quad \text{for} \quad x = \infty$$

(5.17) $$v(\mathbf{x}, x) = k \quad \text{for} \quad x = 0.$$

Axiom 5.9 seems to be the most controversial because it requires that the difference in weight given to two incomes depends solely on the difference in the number of persons between the two incomes (not on the difference of incomes). This axiom rules out, therefore, all cardinality about individual welfares, except that which is revealed by the number of intermediate income positions between any two incomes. Sen does not provide a justification for this axiom, but only shows its relevance to the Gini index. This axiom can also be expressed as

(5.18) $$v(\mathbf{x}, x) - v(\mathbf{x}, y) = k[F(y) - F(x)]$$

where $y > x$, implying that the difference in weights given to two incomes x and y is proportional to the percentage of individuals between the two incomes. As y approaches infinity, the probability distribution function $F(y)$ approaches unity, and $v(\mathbf{x}, y)$ from (5.17) approaches zero. Equation (5.18) then reduces to

(5.19) $$v(\mathbf{x}, x) = k[1 - F(x)]$$

where k is obviously the upper limit of $v(\mathbf{x}, x)$. Without loss of generality, it is assumed that k is equal to 2. If x is a continuous random variable, the social welfare function (5.16) becomes, by means of (5.19),

(5.20) $$W(\mathbf{x}) = 2 \int_0^\infty x[1 - F(x)] f(x) \, dx,$$

which simplifies to $\mu(1 - G)$. Thus, the following theorem proposed by Sen has been proved.

THEOREM 5.1. *A social welfare function $W(\mathbf{x})$ satisfying axioms 5.6, 5.7, 5.8, and 5.9 leads to*

(5.21) $$W(\mathbf{x}) = \mu(1 - G).$$

This theorem demonstrates that the social welfare function (5.16), satisfying Sen's four axioms, must rank the distributions with the same mean income in precisely the same order as the negative of the Gini index. An interesting corollary of this theorem follows.

If η_μ and η_G are denoted as the elasticities of the social welfare function $W(\mathbf{x})$ with respect to μ and G, respectively, (5.21) yields

$$\eta_\mu = 1$$

$$\eta_G = -\frac{G}{(1 - G)} \,,$$

which implies that

$$|\eta_G| < |\eta_\mu|$$

for $G < \frac{1}{2}$. This leads to the following corollary.

COROLLARY 5.1.   *The social welfare function derived in (5.21) is more (less) sensitive to the mean income than to the income inequality if the Gini index is less (greater) than one half.*

The following additional axioms will lead to an alternative welfare function related to the Gini index.

AXIOM 5.10.   *Each distribution* $\mathbf{x}$ *with a constant mean income* μ *over a constant population must have the same minimal* $v_i(\mathbf{x})$.

AXIOM 5.11.   *The sum of weights given to all incomes must be unity.*

AXIOM 5.12.   *If everyone prefers* $(\mathbf{x}, i)$ *to* $(\mathbf{x}, j)$, *and also* $(\mathbf{x}, m)$ *to* $(\mathbf{x}, n)$, *and there is no* $(\mathbf{x}, k)$ *so that someone prefers* $(\mathbf{x}, i)$ *to* $(\mathbf{x}, k)$ *and* $(\mathbf{x}, k)$ *to* $(\mathbf{x}, j)$, *and there is no* $(\mathbf{x}, p)$ *so that someone prefers* $(\mathbf{x}, m)$ *to* $(\mathbf{x}, p)$ *and* $(\mathbf{x}, p)$ *to* $(\mathbf{x}, n)$, *then*

$$\frac{v_j(\mathbf{x}) - v_i(\mathbf{x})}{x_i} = \frac{v_n(\mathbf{x}) - v_m(\mathbf{x})}{x_m} \,.$$

If the persons in $\mathbf{x}$ are ranked according to their income levels so that

$$x_1 < x_2 < x_3 \ldots, < x_n,$$

according to axiom 5.8 all individuals prefer $(\mathbf{x}, i + 1)$ to $(\mathbf{x}, i)$ for all $i \leq n - 1$. Axiom 5.12 yields

$$v_i(\mathbf{x}) - v_{i+1}(\mathbf{x}) = \alpha x_{i+1}$$

where α is the constant of proportionality. This equation is equivalent to

$$(5.22) \qquad v_i(\mathbf{x}) - v_{i+1}(\mathbf{x}) = \beta[F_1(x_{i+1}) - F_1(x_i)]$$

where $F_1(x_i)$ is the proportion of incomes of people having an income less than or equal to x_i, and β is another constant equal to $\alpha/n\mu$. For any $x_i > x_j$, equation (5.22) yields

$$v_j(\mathbf{x}) - v_i(\mathbf{x}) = \beta[F_1(x_i) - F_1(x_j)],$$

which shows that the difference in weight given to two incomes x_j and x_i depends on the proportion of total income between x_i and x_j. Because Sen's axiom 5.9 requires that this difference be proportional to the number of people between x_i and x_j rather than to their incomes, there is a fundamental difference between axiom 5.12 and Sen's axiom 5.9. The choice between the two alternative axioms depends on one's personal values. The following theorem indicates the relevance of axiom 5.12 to the Gini index.

THEOREM 5.2.   *A social welfare function* $W(\mathbf{x})$ *satisfying axioms 5.6, 5.8, 5.10, 5.11, and 5.12 can be written as*

$$(5.23) \qquad W(\mathbf{x}) = \frac{\mu}{(1 + G)}.$$

Proof.   Axiom 5.12 requires that

$$(5.24) \qquad v(\mathbf{x}, x) - v(\mathbf{x}, y) = \beta[F_1(y) - F_1(x)]$$

where $y > x$. Axiom 5.10 recommends that only the lower limit of the weights be the same for all income distributions. Without loss of generality, it can again be assumed that this lower limit is zero. If y then approaches infinity, $F_1(y)$ approaches unity, and $v(\mathbf{x}, y)$ approaches zero. Thus equation (5.24) becomes

$$(5.25) \qquad v(\mathbf{x}, x) = \beta[1 - F_1(x)]$$

where α is the upper limit of $v(\mathbf{x}, x)$. So that axiom 5.11 is satisfied, β is expressed by

$$\beta \int_0^\infty [1 - F_1(x)]f(x)dx = 1,$$

which, by means of (5.13) yields

$$(5.26) \qquad \beta = \frac{2}{(1 + G)}.$$

Then, by means of (5.25) and (5.26), the social welfare function (5.16) becomes

$$W(\mathbf{x}) = \frac{2}{(1 + G)} \int_0^\infty x[1 - F_1(x)] f(x) \, dx,$$

which, when integrated by parts, simplifies to $\mu/(1 + G)$. This completes the proof of theorem 5.2.

Theorem 5.2 provides an alternative normative justification of the Gini index as a measure of inequality and shows that the social welfare function, derived from a different set of axioms, ranks the distributions in precisely the same way as the negative of the Gini index.

The elasticities η_μ and η_G obtained for this new social welfare function are

$$\eta_\mu = 1$$

$$\eta_G = -\frac{G}{(1 + G)},$$

which implies that

$$|\eta_G| < |\eta_\mu|$$

for all values of G. This leads to the following corollary.

COROLLARY 5.2. *The social welfare function derived in (5.23) is always more sensitive to the mean income than to the income inequality.*

Relative Mean Deviation and Related Measures

The mean deviation as a measure of inequality was proposed by Von Bortkiewicz in 1898 (his results were published in 1930), and the relative mean deviation introduced later by Bresciani-Turroni (1910). The statistical properties of the measure were investigated by Pietra (1948).

The relative mean deviation is defined as

$$(5.27) \qquad R = \frac{1}{2\mu} \frac{1}{n} \sum_{i=1}^n |x_i - \mu|$$

where x_i is the income of the ith unit and i varies from 1 to n. If every unit receives the same income, $R = 0$. When one individual receives all the income, R becomes $(n - 1)/n$, which approaches unity as n approaches infinity. Thus axiom 5.6 is satisfied by this measure.

LEMMA 5.9. *The relative mean deviation is equal to the maximum discrepancy between the egalitarian line and the Lorenz curve.*

Proof. In the case of a continuous random variable, the relative mean deviation is written as

$$R = \frac{1}{2\mu} \int_0^\infty |x - \mu| f(x) \, dx$$

$$(5.28) \qquad = \frac{1}{2\mu} \int_0^\mu (\mu - x) f(x) \, dx + \frac{1}{2\mu} \int_\mu^\infty (x - \mu) f(x) \, dx,$$

which, by means of (3.1) and (3.2), simplifies to

$$(5.29) \qquad\qquad R = F(\mu) - F_1(\mu).$$

This equation shows that R is equal to the discrepancy between the egalitarian line and the Lorenz curve at the income level $x = \mu$. According to lemma 3.1, this discrepancy is indeed maximum. This completes the proof of lemma 5.9.

Lemma 3.2, in turn, leads to the following lemma.[5]

LEMMA 5.10. *If the population is divided into two groups, (a) those who receive less than or equal to mean income and (b) those who receive more than mean income, the relative mean deviation represents the percentage of total income that should be transferred from the second group to the first so that both groups have exactly the same mean income.*

This lemma provides an alternative definition of the relative mean deviation. Although this definition is intuitively more appealing, it reveals that the measure is completely insensitive to transfers of income among individuals on one side of the mean. Thus axiom 5.4, relating to Dalton's principle of transfers, is clearly violated, casting the relative mean deviation in an unattractive light.[6]

Schutz (1951) proposed a new inequality measure, which is based

---

5. See Kondor (1971).

6. See Atkinson (1970). Sen (1973) makes a stronger criticism, which is that the relative mean deviation fails to catch the commonly accepted ideas on inequality.

on a comparison of the slope of the Lorenz curve at various points. His measure is expressed by

$$(5.30) \qquad S = \int_0^{p_\mu} [1 - L'(p)]dp$$

where p_μ equals $F(\mu)$.[7] Note that S is the area between the curve $L'(p)$ and the straight line $p = 1$ in the region $0 \leq p \leq p_\mu$. The integration of (5.30) reduces S to $p_\mu - L(p_\mu)$, which is obviously equal to the relative mean deviation as given in (5.29). Schutz's new inequality measure is, therefore, identical to the relative mean deviation.[8]

Another measure that is related to the relative mean deviation was proposed by Kuznets (1957), who suggested it in connection with measuring the concentration of output of different sectors of the economy by the sum of the absolute differences between the percentage shares in the labor force and those in the output of various other sectors. In terms of the size distribution of income, his measure is the average of absolute differences between Δp and Δq where $q = L(p)$ is the proportional income of the bottom p percent of the population. As Δp approaches zero, Kuznets' measure can be expressed as

$$K = \tfrac{1}{2} \int_0^1 |1 - L'(p)|dp$$

$$= \tfrac{1}{2}\Big[\int_0^{p_\mu} [1 - L'(p)]dp + \int_{p_\mu}^1 [L'(p) - 1]dp \Big],$$

which simplifies to $p_\mu - L(p_\mu)$. Thus the Kuznets measure is also identical to the relative mean deviation.

Elteto and Frigyes' Inequality Measures

Elteto and Frigyes (1968) proposed a set of three inequality measures, which are defined as

$$u = \frac{\mu}{\mu_1}, \quad v = \frac{\mu_2}{\mu_1}, \quad \text{and} \quad w = \frac{\mu_2}{\mu}$$

7. See "Some Useful Lemmas," chapter 3.
8. See Rosenbluth (1951), who pointed out the similarity of Schutz's measure to the relative mean deviation.

where $\mu = E(x)$, $\mu_1 = E(x|x < \mu)$, and $\mu_2 = E(x|x \geq \mu)$. Note that $\mu_1(\mu_2)$ is the mean income of those with an income smaller (greater) than μ. These measures can also be expressed in terms of the Lorenz curve as

$$(5.31) \quad u = \frac{p_\mu}{L(p_\mu)}, \, v = \frac{1 - L(p_\mu)}{1 - p_\mu} \cdot \frac{p_\mu}{L(p_\mu)}, \text{ and } w = \frac{1 - L(p_\mu)}{1 - p_\mu}.$$

Although the range of the above measures is from one to infinity, it is possible to transform them so that they are confined within the finite range of zero to unity:

$$u' = 1 - \frac{1}{u}$$

$$v' = 1 - \frac{1}{v}$$

$$(5.32) \qquad w' = 1 - \frac{1}{w}.$$

Clearly, $v = uw$, and $v' = u' + w' - u'w'$, so that only two of the three measures are independent.

Equation (5.31) demonstrates that

$$\frac{(u - 1)(w - 1)}{(v - 1)} = p_\mu - L(p_\mu) = T$$

where T is only the relative mean deviation. Obviously, these three inequality measures convey no more information about inequality than the relative mean deviation conveys.[9] Further, they are completely insensitive, as is the relative mean deviation, to transfers of incomes within groups on either side of the mean. These measures are, therefore, subject to the same criticisms made of the relative mean deviation.

---

9. Kondor (1971) established the relationship between these inequality measures and the relative mean deviation. For the efficient estimation of the measures, see Kakwani (1974).

A New Inequality Measure

A new inequality measure, which is closely related to the Lorenz curve and sensitive to transfers at all levels of income, may now be considered. The derivation of this measure follows.

Let l be the length of the Lorenz curve. If every individual receives equal income, l is obviously equal to $\sqrt{2}$, which is the length of the egalitarian line. Further, if one individual receives all the income, l is equal to 2 in the limit as the number of units approach infinity. Thus l lies in the range $\sqrt{2} \leq l \leq 2$. The new inequality measure may, therefore, be defined as

$$(5.33) \qquad L = \frac{l - \sqrt{2}}{2 - \sqrt{2}},$$

Figure 3. *Length of the Lorenz Curve*

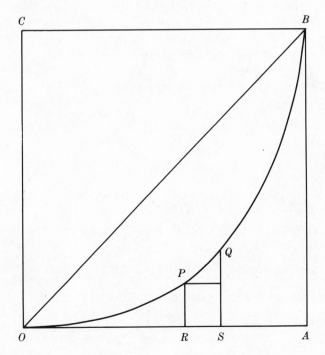

which obviously lies between zero and unity, thus satisfying axiom 5.6.

Consider two points P and Q on the Lorenz curve that have coordinates (p, q) and $(p + \Delta p, q + \Delta q)$, respectively. The distance PQ will then be expressed by

$$PQ = \sqrt{(\Delta p)^2 + (\Delta q)^2}.$$

Adding these lengths over the range $0 \leq p \leq 1$ gives l as Δp approaches zero. Thus, the proposed inequality measure can be written as

$$(5.34) \qquad L = \frac{1}{(2 - \sqrt{2})} \left[\int_0^1 \sqrt{1 + \left(\frac{dq}{dp}\right)^2} \cdot dp - \sqrt{2} \right]$$

where $dq/dp = L'(p)$ is the slope of the Lorenz curve at any value of p. If x is the income corresponding to the point (p, q) on the Lorenz curve, equation (5.34) becomes

$$(5.35) \qquad L = \frac{1}{(2 - \sqrt{2})} \left[\frac{1}{\mu} \int_0^\infty \sqrt{\mu^2 + x^2} f(x) dx - \sqrt{2} \right]$$

where the facts that $dp = f(x) dx$ and $L'(p) = x/\mu$ have been used.

Equation (5.35) shows that L is the arithmetic mean of a strictly convex function of income, which, according to lemma 5.2, implies that the measure is sensitive to transfers at all levels of income. The following lemma will aid in investigating the sensitivity of the measure to transfers at different levels of income.

LEMMA 5.11.   *The new measure of income inequality attaches higher weight to transfers at the lower end than at the middle and upper ends of the distribution.*

Proof. $V(x)$ as defined in (5.8) is

$$V(x) = \frac{1}{(2 - \sqrt{2})\mu} \left[\sqrt{\mu^2 + x^2} - \sqrt{2}\,\mu \right],$$

which, on differentiating with respect to x, becomes

$$V'(x) = \frac{1}{(2 - \sqrt{2})\mu} \cdot \frac{x}{\sqrt{\mu^2 + x^2}}.$$

$T(x)$, as defined in (5.9), is then expressed as

$$T(x) = \frac{1}{(2 - \sqrt{2})\mu} \left[\frac{x}{\sqrt{\mu^2 + x^2}} - \frac{x - h}{\sqrt{\mu^2 + (x - h)^2}} \right].$$

Lemma 5.3 shows that the sensitivity of the inequality to an infinitesimal transfer from a person with income x to a person with income $(x - h)$ depends on the magnitude of $T(x)$. The first derivative of $T(x)$ with respect to x is

$$T'(x) = \frac{\mu}{(2 - \sqrt{2})} \left[\frac{1}{[\mu^2 + x^2]^{3/2}} - \frac{1}{[\mu^2 + (x - h)^2]^{3/2}} \right],$$

which is obviously negative for all values of x. This demonstrates that $T(x)$ is a monotonically decreasing function of x. The conclusion is that weights given to transfers decrease monotonically as income increases. This proves the lemma.

An attractive quality of both the Gini index and the new measure of inequality is that they are closely related to the Lorenz curve. In addition, both are sensitive to transfers at all levels of income, although, unlike the Gini index, the new measure is more sensitive to transfers at the lower levels of income, making it particularly applicable to problems such as measuring the intensity of poverty.

Measures Not Directly Related to the Lorenz Curve

The coefficient of variation and the standard deviation of logarithms of income are also widely used, single measures of inequality. Because they are not directly related to the Lorenz curve, they do not offer a visual picture relating to the Lorenz diagram. (This might not be considered a serious criticism.)

The coefficient of variation as a measure of dispersion, suggested by Pearson, is defined as

$$(5.36) \qquad\qquad CV = \frac{\sigma}{\mu}$$

where σ is the standard deviation of the distribution. In the case of continuous distribution, σ is given by

$$(5.37) \qquad\qquad \sigma^2 = \int_0^\infty (x - \mu)^2 f(x)\,dx.$$

The lower limit of CV is obviously zero. The upper limit of the measure is $\sqrt{n - 1}$, which is obtained when one individual receives all the income. In addition, the upper limit approaches infinity as the number of persons increases. Thus the measure violates axiom 5.6.

Like the Gini index, the coefficient of variation can be interpreted in terms of the expected depression suffered by a person who discovers that his income is lower. In this connection the following lemma is presented.

LEMMA 5.12. *If, in any pairwise comparison, a person with lower income suffers some depression proportional to the square of the difference in incomes, the average of all such depressions in all possible pairwise comparisons leads to the coefficient of variation.*

Proof. A person with income x will, on the average, suffer depression equal to

$$E[\text{depression}|x] = \int_x^\infty (y - x)^2 f(y)\, dy$$

where the degree of depression is assumed to be proportional to the square of the difference in incomes. Accordingly, the average depression for the whole population may be expressed as

$$E[\text{depression}] = \int_0^\infty \left[\int_x^\infty (y - x)^2 f(y)\, dy \right] f(x)\, dx,$$

which can also be expressed as

$$E[\text{depression}] = 2[E(x^2) - \mu^2] - E(x^2) \int_0^\infty F_1(x^2) f(x)\, dx$$

$$(5.38) \qquad\qquad - \int_0^\infty x^2 F(x) f(x)\, dx + 2\mu \int_0^\infty x F_1(x) f(x)\, dx$$

where

$$(5.39) \qquad F_1(x^2) = \frac{1}{E(x^2)} \int_0^x u^2 f(u)\, du.$$

Integrating by parts yields

$$(5.40) \qquad \int_0^\infty x F_1(x) f(x)\, dx = \frac{\mu}{2}$$

$$(5.41) \quad E(x^2) \int_0^\infty F_1(x^2) f(x)\, dx = E(x^2) - \int_0^\infty x^2 F(x) f(x)\, dx.$$

And substituting (5.40) and (5.41) into (5.38) yields

$$E[\text{depression}] = E(x^2) - \mu^2,$$

which shows that the average depression for the whole population is equal to the variance of the distribution, and that μ^2 is the maximum possible depression, which occurs when one individual receives all the income. The average depression divided by the maximum possible depression, therefore, leads to the square of the coefficient variation. This proves the lemma.

It is clear from (5.37) that the square of the coefficient of variation can be expressed as the mean of a strictly convex function $V(x)$ given by

(5.42)
$$V(x) = \frac{x^2 - \mu^2}{\mu^2},$$

which shows that the measure is sensitive to transfers at all levels of income. The relative sensitivity, however, depends on $T(x)$, which is defined in (5.9). Equation (5.42) yields

$$T(x) = \frac{2h}{\mu^2},$$

which is independent of the level of income. Thus, the coefficient of variation is equally sensitive to transfers at all levels of income. Sen (1973) criticized the coefficient of variation because of this property. Although he agreed that our intuitive ideas of inequality are relatively vague, he expressed preference for the measures that attach greater importance to income transfers at the lower end of distribution. One such measure is the standard deviation of the income power, or the logarithms of income,[10] which is expressed by

$$\sigma_{\log} = \left[\int_0^\infty (\log x - \log G)^2 f(x)\, dx \right]^{1/2}$$

where G is the geometric mean. Note that some authors have taken the deviation from the logarithm of arithmetic mean rather than from that of geometric mean.[11]

The lower limit of $\sigma_{\log}$ is obviously zero, which implies complete

10. The new inequality measure proposed earlier also has this property.
11. See Atkinson (1970) and Stark (1972).

equality. The upper limit of the measure is difficult to obtain because the logarithm of zero income is not finite. According to Yntema (1933), complete inequality requires that all individuals have one dollar of income and that the richest individual receive the rest. This gives the upper limit as $\sqrt{n-1}$ log G, which approaches infinity as n becomes larger. Thus axiom 5.6 is violated by this measure. The square of the measure is of the form (5.8), which gives

$$(5.43) \quad T(x) = 2 \left[\frac{\log x - \log G}{x} - \frac{\log (x - h) - \log G}{x - h} \right].$$

Now consider the function

$$\phi(x) = \frac{\log x - \log G}{x},$$

the first derivative of which is

$$\phi'(x) = \frac{\log Ge - \log x}{x^2}$$

where e is the base of Napierian logarithms, so that log $e = 1$. This equation implies that $\phi(x)$ is not a monotonically increasing function of x for the whole range, but that it increases with x until $x = Ge$, and then decreases. Substituting this into (5.43) yields

$$T(x) > 0 \quad \text{for} \quad x < Ge$$
$$< 0 \quad \text{for} \quad x > Ge,$$

which implies that the function $V(x)$ becomes concave when the income level exceeds Ge. From lemma 5.2, then, it follows that the standard deviation of logarithms does not satisfy Dalton's principle of transfers when the income level exceeds Ge. This implies that any transfer of income from rich to poor at an income level greater than Ge would increase the inequality rather than decrease it, a factor that may constitute a strong objection to this inequality measure.

Information Measures of Inequality

Theil (1967) proposed two inequality measures that are based on the notion of entropy in information theory. Entropy is a measure of disorder in thermodynamics.

Let y_i be the fraction of total income earned by the ith individual where i varies from 1 to n. The entropy of income shares is then defined as

$$H(y) = \sum_{i=1}^{n} y_i \log \frac{1}{y_i},$$

which is the weighted average of the logarithms of the reciprocal of each income share, weights being the respective income shares. The upper limit of $H(y)$ is $\log n$, which is reached when all individuals earn equal income, and the minimum of $H(y)$ is zero, which represents one individual receiving all the income. It follows that $H(y)$ may be regarded as a measure of income equality. Thus the inequality measure proposed by Theil in 1967 is

$$\log n - H(y) = \sum_{i=1}^{n} y_i \log ny_i,$$

which varies from zero to $\log n$. The upper limit of this measure approaches infinity as n approaches infinity. Axiom 5.6 remains, therefore, unsatisfied.

It may be convenient to express this measure as

$$I(y:p) = \sum_{i=1}^{n} y_i \log \frac{y_i}{p_i}$$

where p_i is the population share that, in this case, is equal to $1/n$. One can interpret $I(y:p)$ as the expected information of the indirect message that transforms prior probabilities $p_1, p_2, \ldots, p_n$ into posterior probabilities $y_1, y_2, \ldots, y_n$.

The alternative measure proposed by Theil is

$$I(p:y) = \sum_{i=1}^{n} p_i \log \frac{p_i}{y_i},$$

which is interpreted as the expected information of the indirect message that transforms prior probabilities $y_1, y_2, \ldots, y_n$ into posterior probabilities $p_1, p_2, \ldots, p_n$.

When x is a continuous random variable, these measures are expressed as

$$I(y:p) = \frac{1}{\mu} \int_0^{\infty} x \log xf(x)\,dx - \log \mu$$

$$I(p:y) = \log \mu - \int_0^{\infty} \log xf(x)\,dx,$$

which shows that both are the arithmetic means of strictly convex functions of incomes. From lemma 5.2 it follows, then, that these measures satisfy Dalton's principle of transfers, that is, that any transfer from a rich to a poor person reduces inequality.

The sensitivity of the measures to transfers depends on the magnitude of $T(x)$. In both measures, for example, $T(x)$ is a monotonically decreasing function of x, which implies that the measures are sensitive to transfers at the lower incomes; this property is quite useful. Another attractive feature is that they can be decomposed between and within set inequalities. Thus, if a population is divided into a number of groups according to certain socioeconomic characteristics of individuals, this property can be useful in analyzing the contribution, so to speak, of inequality of each group to the aggregate inequality.[12]

Normative Measures of Income Inequality

In the preceding sections of this chapter, only the positive measures of income inequality were discussed, and their welfare implications examined. Dalton (1920), who was the first to argue that an inequality measure must be derived directly from a social welfare function, proposed a measure that is defined as the proportional welfare loss resulting from income inequality. The derivation of his measure follows.

It is assumed that social welfare is the sum of individual utilities that are functions of their respective incomes, and that each individual has the same utility function. The social welfare function will, therefore, be additive, separable, and symmetric. If the utility function is strictly concave, it immediately follows from equation (4.4) that[13]

$$\frac{1}{n} \sum_{i=1}^{n} u(x_i) < u(\mu).$$

This equation is true for any income distribution $\mathbf{x} = (x_1, x_2, \ldots, x_n)$ with a mean income μ. It is, then, evident that the aggregate

12. See Fishlow (1972) for application of this decomposition of inequality to U.S. data.

13. Dalton assumed that the marginal utility of income diminishes as income increases, that is, that the utility function is strictly concave.

welfare will be maximum when all incomes are equal, and that the proportional welfare loss resulting from income inequality will be

$$D = 1 - \sum_{i=1}^{n} u(x_i)/nu(\mu),$$

which is essentially the inequality measure proposed by Dalton. Clearly, this measure will assume zero value when all incomes are equal. In the case of complete inequality, when one individual receives all the income, D becomes

$$1 - \frac{(n-1)u(0) + u(n\mu)}{nu(\mu)},$$

which will be unity if, and only if,

$$(n-1)u(0) + u(n\mu) = 0.$$

Because there is no reason why this equation should always be true, the upper limit of Dalton's measure may not necessarily be equal to unity. A possible modification of Dalton's measure is

$$D^* = \frac{nu(\mu) - \sum_{i=1}^{n} u(x_i)}{nu(\mu) - (n-1)u(0) - u(n\mu)},$$

which clearly becomes unity when one individual receives all the income. Thus axiom 5.6 is satisfied by D^*.

Note that Dalton's measure is not independent of the unit of measurement. Dalton himself demonstrated that if the utility function $u(x)$ is of the form (4.11) or (4.13), proportional additions (subtractions) to all incomes will decrease (increase) the value of his measure.

Aigner and Heins (1967) computed Dalton's measure for the 1960 family income distributions in the fifty states and in the District of Columbia of the United States, using the following three functional forms of $u(x)$:

$$\text{(a)} \quad \alpha(1 - e^{-x/\alpha}),$$

$$\text{(b)} \quad \phi \log\left(\frac{x}{\phi} + 1\right),$$

$$\text{(c)} \quad \frac{\theta x}{\theta + x}.$$

Their results indicated that the inequality measures, based on the three selected forms of the utility function, gave almost similar ranking of the distributions. Atkinson criticized the numerical results of these authors, however, on the grounds that Dalton's measure is not invariant with respect to any positive linear transformations of the utility function. For example, if $u(x) = \log x$, Dalton's measure will be

$$D = 1 - \frac{b \int_0^\infty \log x f(x)\, dx + c}{b \log \mu + c}$$

where $b > 0$. The values of D clearly depend on b and c. Thus, the measure will take arbitrary values depending on which particular linear transformation is chosen. (Sen (1973), unlike Atkinson, argued that the ordering of Dalton's measure is not affected by positive linear transformations, and that the ordering property is a significant factor.)

Atkinson proposed a measure that is invariant with respect to any positive linear transformation of individual utilities. It is derived from the concept of the equally distributed equivalent level of income (x^*), the level, which, if received by every individual, would result in the same level of social welfare as the present distribution, that is,

$$u(x^*) = \frac{1}{n} \sum_{i=1}^n u(x_i).$$

The inequality measure proposed by Atkinson is

$$A = 1 - \frac{x^*}{\mu},$$

which is equal to one minus the ratio of the equally distributed equivalent level of income to the mean income of the actual distribution. In the derivation of this measure, Atkinson implicitly assumed that social welfare can be expressed as a function of two variables: total income (or average income) and a measure of inequality. He proposed the following form of the social welfare function:

(5.44) $$W = nu[\mu(1 - A)]$$

where A is the inequality measure and n is the number of persons in the population. This equation implies that social welfare is an increasing function of μ and a decreasing function of A. The definition of the equally distributed equivalent level of income (x^*) implies that the social welfare W is equal to $nu(x^*)$, which, when equated to (5.44), gives the measure proposed by Atkinson.

This measure has considerable intuitive appeal. For example, if $A = 0.3$, it is implied that, incomes being equally distributed, only 70 percent of the present total income is required to achieve the same level of welfare. Atkinson states that the measure A has the convenient property of lying between zero (complete equality) and unity (complete inequality). This may not necessarily be true. In fact, the lower limit of the measure is obviously zero if all incomes are equal. For complete inequality, one individual receives all the income. In this case A becomes

$$1 - \frac{x_m^*}{\mu}$$

where x_m^* is expressed as

$$nu(x_m^*) = (n - 1)u(0) + u(n\mu).$$

Clearly, x_m^* is not zero unless, of course, the utility function $u(x)$ is further restricted. For example, consider the utility function

$$u(x) = A + B \frac{x^{1-\epsilon}}{(1 - \epsilon)}, \qquad \epsilon \neq 1$$

(5.45) $$= \log_e (x) \qquad , \qquad \epsilon = 1.$$

For $\epsilon = 0$, $x_m^* = \mu$. If ϵ lies in the range $0 < \epsilon < 1$,

$$x_m = \mu \left(\frac{1}{n}\right)^{\epsilon/1-\epsilon},$$

which becomes zero only if n approaches infinity. A modified measure given by

$$A^* = \frac{\mu - x^*}{\mu - x_m^*}$$

would obviously lie between zero (complete equality) and unity (complete inequality).

Atkinson's measure does not necessarily satisfy axiom 5.1. If the measure is to be scale-independent, further restrictions on the form of the utility function must be considered. Applying the results of Pratt (1964) and Arrow (1965) in the theory of choice under uncertainty, it can be shown that the measure will be scale-independent if the utility function displays constant relative risk aversion. The measure of relative risk aversion for function $u(x)$ is defined as

$$R = - \frac{u''(x)x}{u'(x)} ,$$

which can be interpreted as equal to minus times the elasticity of the marginal utility $u'(x)$ with respect to x. If the relative risk aversion is constant for all values of x, there is one, and only one, admissible utility function, namely, the constant elasticity utility function as defined in (5.45), which is called homothetic.

Because of certain implications, this function may be unacceptable. Muellbauer (1975b) pointed out that the homotheticity assumption precludes the notion that some subsistence level of income is necessary for survival. He attempted to solve this problem by introducing an alternative inequality measure, whose definition is based on the distribution of utilities rather than incomes. But if his measure is to be scale-independent, the social welfare function must still be homothetic in utilities. This assumption, although less restrictive than the one required by Atkinson's measure, may also be unacceptable.

In addition, Atkinson's measure is derived from the assumption that the social welfare function is of the form $nu[\mu(1 - A)]$, a form that implies that the aggregate welfare is more (less) sensitive to the mean income than to the income inequality if A is less (greater) than one-half.[14] Alternatively, the social welfare function can take the form

$$W = nu\left[\frac{\mu}{1 + A}\right],$$

which also implies that social welfare is an increasing function of μ and a decreasing function of A. This specification leads to the fol-

---

14. This result can easily be proved by comparing the elasticities of the aggregate welfare with respect to μ and A.

lowing alternative inequality measure:

$$\hat{A} = \frac{\mu - x^*}{x^*} .$$

One may argue that since both measures A and $\hat{A}$ give the identical ranking of distributions, $\hat{A}$ will not provide any more information about inequality than A. Although this argument may be valid, the two measures still differ with respect to the relative sensitivity of the aggregate welfare. It can be shown that the aggregate welfare implied by $\hat{A}$ is always more sensitive to the mean income than to the income inequality.

Atkinson used the data collected by Kuznets (1963) covering the distribution of income in seven advanced and five developing countries, and computed his measure by means of the homothetic utility function (5.45) for $\epsilon = 1.0$, 1.5, and 2.0. His results indicate that measure A is sensitive to the choice of ϵ, that the range of variation is considerable, and that the ranking of the countries changes considerably with changes in the value of ϵ. These empirical observations raise the problem of selecting the appropriate value of ϵ, even if the social welfare function is additive, separable, and homothetic.

CHAPTER 6

Estimation of Income Inequality Measures from Grouped Observations

DATA ON THE DISTRIBUTION OF PERSONAL INCOMES (or household incomes) are often provided in grouped form, giving (a) the number of persons falling in different income ranges and (b) the total income in each range. Two methods are used to estimate various measures of income inequality from such data. The most common is the linear interpolation method, which assumes that inequality of income within each income range is zero. Obviously, this method may lead to substantial underestimation of the total inequality, especially when the income ranges are wide. The second method is that of fitting a function to the entire income range by ordinary least-squares and obtaining the inequality measures from the parameters of the fitted function.[1] The difficulty of this approach is that there is rarely a function that fits well to the entire income range.

Budd (1970) suggested fitting a single polynomial function to represent the Lorenz curve from the bottom to about the 85th percentile, and the Pareto function to the rest of the distribution. This method involves estimation of the polynomial function and the Pareto function by means of the ordinary least-squares method and the determination of the cutoff point. But there are difficulties with

---

1. See Fisk (1961a; 1961b), Champernowne (1952), Aitchison and Brown (1954), Kakwani and Podder (1973).

this approach as well. First, it is computationally cumbersome. Second, it does not permit utilization of available information on income ranges in estimating income inequalities.

In view of the inadequacies of these approaches, a general interpolation device was recently provided.[2] This method utilizes, within each income range, a separate, continuous differentiable function, which exactly fits the data points. The inequality measures are then computed by linking these functions. For the first and last income ranges, which are generally openended, a Pareto curve is used as a further refinement. The advantage of this approach is that it provides explicit formulas for each inequality measure in terms of observations on the distribution in a grouped form.

The general interpolation device is the main focus of this chapter. Four alternative functional forms are considered, in addition to the Pareto curves, which are fitted to the first and the last income classes. The estimation of different inequality measures by means of alternative functional forms is discussed, as well as the degree of accuracy of these estimates, tested against estimates made from individual observations. A method of deriving lower and upper bounds on the Gini index and the new inequality measure proposed in chapter 5 are also considered. (The bounds on the Gini index were derived by Gastwirth (1972) by means of certain inequality results given in Hardy, Littlewood, and Polya (1934). In this chapter the bounds on both these inequality measures are obtained by means of a geometric approach that seems intuitively appealing.) A numerical illustration using Australian data is provided.

Bounds on the Inequality Measures

The upper and lower bounds on the Gini index were derived by Gastwirth (1972) for an observed income distribution that is partitioned into several income classes. The lower bound on the index was readily obtained by assuming that inequality of income within each income range is zero. Gastwirth obtained the upper bound by distributing income receipts in such a way as to maximize the spread within each income group.

It is significant that the estimation of bounds on the Gini index

2. See Kakwani (1976).

requires no knowledge of the form of the distribution that generated the data. This implies that regardless of what form the distribution function takes, the unknown value of the Gini index must lie between the computed bounds. Clearly, if the Gini index, computed on the basis of a density function, lies outside the lower and upper bounds, the density function will be unsuitable for graduating the observed distribution. Gastwirth and Smith (1972) proposed, moreover, using these bounds on the Gini index to test the goodness of fit of a distribution to grouped data. This test will be used below to assess the suitability of the general interpolation approach.

The bounds on the Gini index are derived here by using a geometric approach that is further extended to provide bounds on the new inequality measure (L) proposed in chapter 5. The derivation is outlined as follows.

Suppose there are N income units that are grouped into $(T + 1)$ income classes, $(x_0 \text{ to } x_1)$, $(x_1 \text{ to } x_2)$, ..., $(x_T \text{ to } x_{T+1})$. If n_t is the number of income units in the tth income class, $f_t = n_t/N$ will be the relative frequency of the tth income class. Let μ_t be the mean income in the tth class. The proportion of units earning income less than or equal to x_t will then be $p_t = \sum_{r=1}^{t} f_r$, and the cumulative proportion of income received by these income units will be $q_t = 1/\mu \sum_{r=1}^{t} \mu_r f_r$ where $\mu = \sum_{r=1}^{T+1} \mu_r f_r$ is the overall mean income. The basic data are the x's, n's, and μ's; the derived data are the p's and q's. The Lorenz curve is the relationship between p and q. The slope of the Lorenz curve is given by

$$(6.1) \qquad \frac{dq}{dp} = \frac{x}{\mu}$$

where x is the income at a particular point on the curve.

Assume that points P and Q in figure 4 correspond to the lower and upper ends of the tth income class. The coordinates of P and Q will then be (p_{t-1}, q_{t-1}) and (p_t, q_t), respectively. The tangents at points P and Q are PR and RQ, which have the slopes x_{t-1}/μ and x_t/μ, respectively. From figure 4, then, the following areas are immediately obtained:

$$(6.2) \qquad \text{Area of triangle } PLQ = \tfrac{1}{2} \frac{f_t^2 \mu_t}{\mu}$$

Figure 4. *Calculation of Bounds on Inequality Measures*

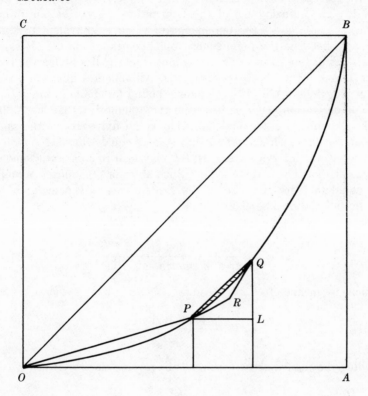

$$(6.3) \qquad \text{Area of triangle } PRQ = \tfrac{1}{2}\frac{f_t^2(\Delta x_t)\delta_t(1-\delta_t)}{\mu}$$

where $\delta_t = (\mu_t - x_{t-1})/(\Delta x_t)$, $\Delta x_t = x_t - x_{t-1}$, and use has been made of the facts that $p_t - p_{t-1} = f_t$ and $q_t - q_{t-1} = \mu_t f_t/\mu$. These results will now be used to derive the bounds on the Gini index.

First consider an approximate formula denoted by GL that is widely used to estimate the Gini index from grouped observations:[3]

$$GL = 1 - \sum_{t=1}^{T+1} f_t(q_t + q_{t-1})$$

3. See Yntema (1933) and Morgan (1962).

where $q_0 = 0$ and $q_{T+1} = 1$. Clearly, GL is equal to twice the area of the polygon with vertexes $(0, 0)$, (p_1, q_1), . . . , (p_T, q_T), and $(1, 1)$. The actual value of the Gini index is given as one minus twice the area under the Lorenz curve, which is equivalent to twice the area between the Lorenz curve and the egalitarian line. Because the straight line connecting the points P and Q lies above the convex Lorenz curve between them, GL will underestimate the true Gini index. Thus GL yields the lower bound for the Gini index G.

The derivation of GL is based on the assumption that inequality is zero within each income class; that is, all units receive the same income within each class, and that income equals the class average. If the income intervals are wide, GL may lead to substantial underestimation of the total inequality. Such an error of estimation would be equal to twice the sum of the shaded area (given in figure 4) within all the income classes.

Let G_t be the Gini index for the tth income class:

$$G_t = \frac{\text{shaded area}}{\text{area of the triangle } PLQ},$$

which, by means of (6.2), becomes

(6.4)
$$G_t = \frac{2\mu \times \text{shaded area}}{f_t^2 \mu_t}.$$

Adding the shaded areas within all the income classes yields

(6.5)
$$G = GL + \frac{1}{\mu} \sum_{t=1}^{T+1} f_t^2 \mu_t G_t,$$

which shows that the total inequality can be regarded as the sum of the two terms. The first term, GL, is the inequality between the income classes, and the second term is the inequality within the income classes. Thus $G = GL$ when $G_t = 0$ for all t, that is, when the inequality within each income class is zero.

Figure 4 indicates that the maximum value the shaded area between P and Q can assume is equal to the area PRQ. This, combined with (6.3), yields the following upper bound for G_t:

(6.6)
$$G_t \leq \frac{(\Delta x_t)\delta_t(1 - \delta_t)}{\mu_t}.$$

For the first and the last openended income classes, the upper bound for the Gini index can again be obtained from the Lorenz diagram. Following the same approach as above, the Lorenz diagram gives

$$(6.7) \qquad\qquad G_1 \leq 1 - \frac{\mu_1}{x_1}$$

$$(6.8) \qquad\qquad G_{T+1} \leq 1 - \frac{x_T}{\mu_{T+1}} .$$

Equations (6.6), (6.7), and (6.8) give the upper bounds on G_t regardless of the form of the underlying distribution. The Gini index will, therefore, always be between GL and $GL + \bar{D}$ where

$$(6.9) \qquad\qquad \bar{D} = \frac{1}{\mu} \sum_{t=1}^{T+1} f_t^2 (\Delta x_t) \delta_t (1 - \delta_t),$$

provided the first and the last income classes are not openended. If they are,

$$\bar{D} = f_1^2 \mu_1 \left(1 - \frac{\mu_1}{x_1} \right) + \sum_{t=2}^{T} f_t^2 (\Delta x_t) \delta_t (1 - \delta_t) + f_{T+1}^2 (\mu_{T+1} - x_T)$$

where use has been made of (6.7) and (6.8).

The result (6.9) is exactly the same as the one derived by Gastwirth. Here, however, a geometric approach, which is intuitively more appealing, has been used.

Consider now the derivation of the bounds on the new inequality measure L. Let L_t be the inequality measure for the tth income class. This yields

$$(6.10) \qquad\qquad L_t = \frac{l_t - PQ}{PL + LQ - PQ}$$

where l_t denotes the length of the Lorenz curve between P and Q. Clearly, l_t will be equal to PQ when all incomes in the tth income class are equal. The maximum value of l_t is equal to $(PL + LQ)$, which will be obtained when all the individuals in the tth income class receive the income x_{t-1}, and only one person receives the income x_t. Thus L_t will lie between zero (perfect equality) and one (perfect inequality). If $PL = f_t$ and $QL = \mu_t f_t / \mu$ are substituted into (6.10), L_t becomes

(6.11)
$$L_t = \frac{\mu l_t - f_t \sqrt{\mu^2 + \mu_t^2}}{f_t(\mu + \mu_t - \sqrt{\mu^2 + \mu_t^2})}$$

where use has been made of the fact that $PQ^2 = PL^2 + QL^2$. Obviously, $l = \sum_{t=1}^{T+1} l_t$, which in conjunction with (6.11) and (5.33) yields

$$L = \frac{1}{(2 - \sqrt{2})} \left[\frac{1}{\mu} \sum_{t=1}^{T+1} f_t \sqrt{\mu^2 + \mu_t^2} - \sqrt{2} \right]$$

$$+ \frac{1}{(2 - \sqrt{2})} \frac{1}{\mu} \sum_{t=1}^{T+1} L_t f_t (\mu + \mu_t - \sqrt{\mu^2 + \mu_t^2}).$$

(6.12)

This equation implies that total inequality can be decomposed into two components, the first being the inequality between the income classes, and the second the weighted sum of inequalities within the income classes.

Suppose that

$$\bar{L} = \frac{1}{(2 - \sqrt{2})} \left[\frac{1}{\mu} \sum_{t=1}^{T+1} f_t \sqrt{\mu^2 + \mu_t^2} - \sqrt{2} \right].$$

Then $L = \bar{L}$ when $L_t = 0$ for all t; that is, the inequality within each income class is zero. Clearly, $\bar{L}$ is the lower bound for L.

It is clear from figure 4 that the maximum value of l_t is equal to $(PR + RQ)$ where PR and RQ are expressed as

$$PR = \frac{f_t(1 - \delta_t)}{\mu} \sqrt{\mu^2 + x_{t-1}^2}$$

and

$$RQ = \frac{f_t \delta_t}{\mu} \sqrt{\mu^2 + x_t^2},$$

which yields

$$L_t \leq \frac{(1 - \delta_t) \sqrt{\mu^2 + x_{t-1}^2} + \delta_t \sqrt{\mu^2 + x_t^2} - \sqrt{\mu^2 + \mu_t^2}}{\mu + \mu_t - \sqrt{\mu^2 + \mu_t^2}}.$$

This equation gives the upper bound on L_t regardless of the form of the underlying distribution. The new inequality measure L, therefore, always lies between $\bar{L}$ and $\bar{L} + \bar{E}$ where

$$\bar{E} = \frac{1}{(2 - \sqrt{2})} \frac{1}{\mu} \sum_{t=1}^{T+1} f_t \left[(1 - \delta_t) \sqrt{\mu^2 + x_{t-1}^2} \right.$$

$$\left. + \delta_t \sqrt{\mu^2 + x_t^2} - \sqrt{\mu^2 + \mu_t^2} \right],$$

provided the first and the last income classes are not openended. If they are, the following results are required:

$$L_1 \leq \frac{\mu(x_1 - \mu_1) + \mu_1 \sqrt{\mu^2 + x_1^2} - x_1 \sqrt{\mu^2 + \mu_1^2}}{x_1(\mu + \mu_1 - \sqrt{\mu^2 + \mu_1^2})}$$

$$L_{T+1} \leq \frac{\sqrt{\mu^2 + x_T^2} - \sqrt{\mu^2 + \mu_{T+1}^2} + (\mu_{T+1} - x_T)}{(\mu + \mu_{T+1} - \sqrt{\mu^2 + \mu_{T+1}^2})},$$

which have been derived by means of figure 4.

The General Interpolation Device

The general interpolation device involves fitting a continuous differentiable function within each income class. Kakwani (1976) proposed several alternative functional forms for this purpose, a detailed discussion of which follows.

The third-degree polynomial function

Consider a polynomial of the third degree to represent the Lorenz curve within each income class, except the first and the last open-ended classes. Let this function for the tth income class be

$$(6.13) \quad q = \alpha_{0t} + \alpha_{1t}(p - p_{t-1}) + \alpha_{2t}(p - p_{t-1})^2 + \alpha_{3t}(p - p_{t-1})^3$$

where α_{0t}, α_{1t}, α_{2t}, and α_{3t} are the parameters. Because the end points (p_{t-1}, q_{t-1}) and (p_t, q_t) lie on the Lorenz curve, they should satisfy equation (6.13). Substituting (p_{t-1}, q_{t-1}) and (p_t, q_t) into (6.13) yields the following two equations:

$$(6.14) \qquad\qquad \alpha_{0t} = q_{t-1}$$

$$(6.15) \qquad \Delta q_t = \alpha_{1t}\Delta p_t + \alpha_{2t}(\Delta p_t)^2 + \alpha_{3t}(\Delta p_t)^3$$

where $\Delta q_t = q_t - q_{t-1}$ and $\Delta p_t = p_t - p_{t-1}$.

The relative frequency of the tth income class is $\Delta p_t = f_t$, and $\Delta q_t = \mu_t f_t / \mu$ is the relative share of income of the same income class. Equation (6.15) can, therefore, be written as

$$(6.16) \qquad \frac{\mu_t}{\mu} = \alpha_{1t} + \alpha_{2t} f_t + \alpha_{3t} f_t^2.$$

Differentiating (6.13) with respect to p yields

$$\frac{dq}{dp} = \alpha_{1t} + 2\alpha_{2t}(p - p_{t-1}) + 3\alpha_{3t}(p - p_{t-1})^2,$$

which, when combined with (6.1), yields

$$(6.17) \qquad \frac{x}{\mu} = \alpha_{1t} + 2\alpha_{2t}(p - p_{t-1}) + 3\alpha_{3t}(p - p_{t-1})^2.$$

When $p = p_{t-1}$, $x = x_{t-1}$, and when $p = p_t$, $x = x_t$. Substituting these into (6.17) yields

$$(6.18) \qquad \frac{x_{t-1}}{\mu} = \alpha_{1t}$$

$$(6.19) \qquad \frac{\Delta x_t}{\mu} = 2\alpha_{2t} f_t + 3\alpha_{3t} f_t^2.$$

Solving equations (6.14), (6.16), (6.18), and (6.19) for the α's yields

$$\alpha_{0t} = q_{t-1}$$

$$\alpha_{1t} = \frac{x_{t-1}}{\mu}$$

$$(6.20) \qquad \alpha_{2t} = \frac{(3\delta_t - 1)(\Delta x_t)}{\mu f_t}$$

$$\alpha_{3t} = \frac{(1 - 2\delta_t)(\Delta x_t)}{\mu f_t^2}$$

where $\delta_t = (\mu_t - x_{t-1})/(\Delta x_t)$ and $\Delta x_t = x_t - x_{t-1}$, which have already been defined.

The third-degree polynomial (6.13) will represent the Lorenz curve in the tth interval if, and only if, it is convex for all values of

p in the range $p_{t-1} \leq p \leq p_t$. To obtain the condition under which it is always convex, the sign of its second derivative must be examined. Differentiating (6.13) twice and substituting the α's from (6.20) yields

$$\frac{d^2q}{dp^2} = \frac{2(3\delta_t - 1)(\Delta x_t)}{\mu f_t} + \frac{6(1 - 2\delta_t)(\Delta x_t)(p - p_{t-1})}{\mu f_t^2},$$

which is obviously a monotonic function of p. It can be seen that the derivative d^2q/dp^2 will be strictly positive at $p = p_{t-1}$ if $\delta_t > 1/3$. Similarly, when $p = p_t$, $d^2q/dp^2 = 2\Delta x_t(2 - 3\delta_t)/\mu f_t$, which will be strictly positive when $\delta_t < 2/3$. It follows that the function d^2q/dp^2 will be strictly positive at the endpoints of the tth interval if δ_t lies in the range $1/3 < \delta_t < 2/3$. Because d^2q/dp^2 is a monotonic function of p, the condition that δ_t lie within the range $1/3 < \delta_t < 2/3$ is sufficient for the polynomial (6.13) to be always convex in the tth income class.

Derivation of the density function from the polynomial

The income density function can also be derived from the Lorenz curve (6.13) for the tth income range as follows. Equation (6.17) may be written as

$$3\alpha_{3t}(p - p_{t-1})^2 + 2\alpha_{2t}(p - p_{t-1}) + \left(\alpha_{1t} - \frac{x}{\mu}\right) = 0,$$

which is a quadratic equation in p. Its solution is

$$(6.21) \qquad p = p_{t-1} + \frac{-\alpha_{2t} \pm \sqrt{\alpha_{2t}^2 - 3\alpha_{3t}\alpha_{1t} + 3\alpha_{3t}\, x/\mu}}{3\alpha_{3t}}.$$

Equation (6.21) is the distribution function for the variable x, which, on differentiating with respect to x, yields the density function $f_t(x)$ for the tth income range. Thus

$$f_t(x) = \frac{1}{2\mu}\left[\alpha_{2t}^2 - 3\alpha_{1t}\alpha_{3t} + \frac{3\alpha_{3t}}{\mu}x\right]^{-1/2} = \frac{1}{\sqrt{a_t + b_t x}}$$

where

$$(6.22) \qquad\qquad a_t = 4\mu^2(\alpha_{2t}^2 - 3\alpha_{1t}\alpha_{3t})$$

$$(6.23) \qquad\qquad b_t = 12\mu\alpha_{3t},$$

and x varies from x_{t-1} to x_t.[4] Note that $(a_t + b_t x)$ will always be positive for all x in $x_{t-1} \leq x \leq x_t$ if $1/3 < \delta_t < 2/3$.

The Pareto curves

The first and the last income classes are generally openended, and, therefore, only two-parameter Lorenz curves can be fitted to them. The Pareto curves can be fitted to the first and last income classes, the equations of which are

(6.24) $$p = A_1 q^{\alpha_1}$$

and

(6.25) $$(1 - p) = A_{T+1}(1 - q)^{\alpha_{T+1}},$$

respectively. To estimate the parameters, two data points are needed for each curve; (p_1, q_1) and (p_T, q_T) lie on the first and second curves, respectively. From this, the following two equations are yielded:

(6.26) $$p_1 = A_1 q_1^{\alpha_1}$$

(6.27) $$(1 - p_T) = A_{T+1}(1 - q_T)^{\alpha_{T+1}}.$$

The remaining two data points are obtained by differentiating (6.24) and (6.25) with respect to p and using (6.1). This yields the following two equations:

(6.28) $$\frac{\mu}{x_1} = A_1 \alpha_1 q_1^{\alpha_1 - 1}$$

and

(6.29) $$\frac{\mu}{x_T} = A_{T+1} \alpha_{T+1}(1 - q_T)^{\alpha_{T+1} - 1}.$$

Solving the four equations (6.26), (6.27), (6.28), and (6.29) yields

(6.30) $$A_1 = f_1 \left[\frac{\mu}{\mu_1 f_1} \right]^{\alpha_1} \quad \text{and} \quad \alpha_1 = \frac{\mu_1}{x_1}$$

---

4. Note that differentiating (6.21) with respect to x yields $f_t(x) = \pm \dfrac{1}{\sqrt{a_t + b_t x}}$.

Because $f_t(x)$ is a density function, it obviously cannot be negative.

$$(6.31) \qquad A_{T+1} = f_{T+1} \left[\frac{\mu}{\mu_{T+1} f_{T+1}} \right]^{\alpha_{T+1}} \quad \text{and} \quad \alpha_{T+1} = \frac{\mu_{T+1}}{x_T}$$

where $p_1 = f_1$, $q_1 = \mu_1 f_1 / \mu$, $1 - p_T = f_{T+1}$, and $1 - q_T = \mu_{T+1} f_{T+1} / \mu$ have been used.

To investigate the conditions under which (6.24) and (6.25) represent the Lorenz curves in the first and last openended income classes, it is necessary to differentiate (6.24) and (6.25) twice to obtain

$$(6.32) \qquad \frac{d^2 q}{dp^2} = \frac{(1 - \alpha_1)}{A_1^2 \alpha_1^2} \left[\frac{p}{A_1} \right]^{(1 - 2\alpha_1)/\alpha_1}$$

and

$$(6.33) \qquad \frac{d^2 q}{dp^2} = \frac{(\alpha_{T+1} - 1)}{A_{T+1}^2 \alpha_{T+1}^2} \left[\frac{(1 - p)}{A_{T+1}} \right]^{(1 - 2\alpha_{T+1})/\alpha_{T+1}},$$

respectively. The second derivative will be positive for each curve if $\alpha_1 < 1$ and $\alpha_{T+1} > 1$. These conditions from (6.30) and (6.31) are equivalent to $x_1 > \mu_1$ and $\mu_{T+1} > x_T$, which are always true. Thus the Pareto curves (6.24) and (6.25) are always convex in the first and last income classes, respectively.

The density functions corresponding to the Pareto curves (6.24) and (6.25) can now be derived from (6.32) and (6.33) by means of

$$(6.34) \qquad \frac{d^2 q}{dp^2} = \frac{1}{\mu f(x)}$$

where $f(x)$ is the density function. Thus

$$(6.35) \qquad f_1(x) = \frac{\mu_1 f_1}{x_1 (x_1 - \mu_1)} \left[\frac{x}{x_1} \right]^{(2\mu_1 - x_1)/(x_1 - \mu_1)}$$

$$(6.36) \qquad f_{T+1}(x) = \frac{\mu_{T+1} f_{T+1}}{x_T (\mu_{T+1} - x_T)} \left[\frac{x_T}{x} \right]^{(2\mu_{T+1} - x_T)/(\mu_{T+1} - x_T)}$$

A reasonable requirement is that the density function $f_1(x)$ in the first income class increase with x. The sufficient condition for this to happen is that $\mu_1 > x_1/2$, which is generally satisfied by the observed data. Similarly, the density function $f_{T+1}(x)$ in the last openended interval should decrease with x. The sufficient condition for this to happen is that $\mu_{T+1} > x_T/2$. If these sufficient conditions are satisfied, equation (6.35) implies that $f_1(x)$ is zero at $x = 0$; similarly, equation (6.36) implies that the density function is zero at infinity.

The fourth-degree polynomial Lorenz function

It was proposed that a third-degree polynomial function be fitted within each income range and the Pareto curves in the first and last openended income classes. All these curves linked together give the Lorenz curve, which is continuous and smooth throughout the income range. The density functions derived from these curves for each income range, however, have only two parameters and will, therefore, involve discontinuity at each boundary point. In order to achieve a continuous density function throughout the whole range, an equation of the Lorenz curve with at least five parameters must be considered. One such equation is the fourth-degree polynomial function, which is expressed by

$$(6.37) \quad q = \alpha_{0t} + \alpha_{1t}(p - p_{t-1}) + \alpha_{2t}(p - p_{t-1})^2$$
$$+ \alpha_{3t}(p - p_{t-1})^3 + \alpha_{4t}(p - p_{t-1})^4.$$

The estimation of the third-degree polynomial required that the Lorenz curve and its slope be continuous at the endpoints of income classes. This procedure gave a smooth Lorenz curve throughout the entire range. It follows from (6.34) that in order to obtain a continuous density function, the second derivative of the Lorenz curve must also be continuous at the endpoints, a requirement used to estimate the additional parameter in (6.37). Thus, the parameters of function (6.37) are:

$$\alpha_{0t} = q_{t-1}$$

$$\alpha_{1t} = \frac{x_{t-1}}{\mu}$$

$$\alpha_{2t} = \frac{1}{\mu f_t(x_{t-1})}$$

$$\alpha_{3t} = \frac{(4\delta_t - 1)(\Delta x_t)}{f_T^2 \mu} - \frac{1}{\mu f_t f_t(x_{t-1})}$$

$$\alpha_{4t} = \frac{-(3\delta_t - 1)(\Delta x_t)}{f_t^3 \mu} + \frac{1}{2\mu f_t^2 f_t(x_{t-1})}$$

where $f_t(x_{t-1})$ is the density function at $x = x_{t-1}$. The relation between $f_t(x_{t-1})$ and $f_t(x_t)$ is expressed by

$$(6.38) \qquad \frac{1}{f_t(x_t)} - \frac{1}{f_t(x_{t-1})} = \frac{6(\Delta x_t)}{f_t}(-2\delta_t + 1).$$

After $f_1(x_1)$ has been computed from (6.35), equation (6.38) can be utilized to calculate the density function at each boundary point.

The linear and quadratic density functions

The advantage of directly fitting a Lorenz curve lies in the ease with which most inequality measures can then be derived; any percentile can be conveniently computed if the Lorenz curve is known, although this may not be the case if a density function is directly fitted, unless, of course, it is linear. This argument is not, however, powerful enough to ignore the alternative. Thus consider two alternative specifications of the density function, linear and quadratic. If the linear density function for the tth income class is expressed as

$$(6.39) \qquad f_t(x) = a_t + b_t(x - x_{t-1}),$$

its parameters are given by

$$(6.40) \qquad a_t = \frac{2f_t}{(\Delta x_t)}(2 - 3\delta_t)$$

$$b_t = \frac{6f_t}{(\Delta x_t)^2}(2\delta_t - 1).$$

Similarly, if the density function is quadratic, for example,

$$(6.41) \qquad f_t(x) = f_t(x_{t-1}) + b_t(x - x_{t-1}) + c_t(x - x_{t-1})^2,$$

then

$$b_t = \frac{-6f(x_{t-1})}{(\Delta x_t)} + \frac{6f_t}{(\Delta x_t)^2}(3 - 4\delta_t)$$

$$c_t = \frac{6f(x_{t-1})}{(\Delta x_t)^2} + \frac{12f_t}{(\Delta x_t)^3}(3\delta_t - 2).$$

And $f_t(x_{t-1})$ and $f_t(x_t)$ are related as

$$f_t(x_t) = f_t(x_{t-1}) + \frac{6f_t}{(\Delta x_t)}(2\delta_t - 1).$$

The linear density function given in (6.39) is again a two-parameter family and involves, therefore, discontinuities of $f(x)$ at each boundary point. The quadratic density function (6.41), consisting of three parameters, $f_t(x_{t-1})$, b_t, and c_t, is continuous at boundary points. Furthermore, if it is required that the density function have no corners at the bounds between ranges, the function would have to be specified with four parameters. This further refinement complicates the formulas so much that it has not been considered worthwhile to pursue here.

Estimation of Inequality Measures

The density functions proposed in the preceding section can be used to estimate a number of inequality measures. First, consider the estimation of the Gini index by using (6.5), which expresses the Gini index for the entire population as the sum of two components. Estimation of the first component, GL, which is the inequality between the income classes, requires no specific knowledge of the density function. The second component, the inequality within income classes, is equal to the weighted sum of the Gini indexes (G_t) within each income class. It is necessary to estimate G_t for all t in order to compute the second component.

Using (6.4) and figure 4, it can be seen that G_t is expressed by

$$G_t = 1 + \frac{2\mu q_{t-1}}{\mu_t f_t} - \frac{2\mu A_t}{\mu_t f_t^2}$$

where A_t is the area under the Lorenz curve for the tth income class. This area will be

$$(6.42) \qquad A_t = \int_{p_{t-1}}^{p_t} q \, dp,$$

which can be estimated directly from the equation of the Lorenz curve. If only the density function is known for each income class, however, q must be derived by means of the formula

$$q = q_{t-1} + \frac{1}{\mu} \int_{x_{t-1}}^{x} x f_t(x) \, dx,$$

which expresses q as a function of x. If this function is written as

$q_t(x)$, equation (6.42) becomes

$$A_t = \int_{x_{t-1}}^{x_t} q_t(x) f_t(x)\, dx$$

where the fact that dp in the range $p_{t-1} \leq p \leq p_t$ is equivalent to $f_t(x)\, dx$ in the range $x_{t-1} \leq x \leq x_t$ has been used.

Rather than give a detailed derivation of G_t under the alternative density functions proposed in the preceding section, only the results, which may be useful for empirical applications, are here supplied:

(a) third-degree polynomial Lorenz curve

$$G_t = \frac{1}{6} \frac{(\Delta x_t)}{\mu_t} \; ;$$

(b) fourth-degree polynomial Lorenz curve

$$G_t = \frac{1}{\mu_t} \left[\frac{-f_t}{30 f_t(x_{t-1})} + \frac{(\Delta x_t)}{10} (1 + 2\delta_t) \right] ;$$

(c) linear density function

$$G_t = \frac{2}{15} \frac{(\Delta x_t)}{\mu_t} \left[9\delta_t - 1 - 9\delta_t^2 \right] ;$$

(d) quadratic density function

$$G_t = \frac{(\Delta x_t)}{\mu_t f_t^2} \left[\delta_t^2 f_t^2 - \frac{1}{3} f_t^2(x_{t-1}) (\Delta x_t)^2 \right.$$

$$- \frac{5}{12} f_t(x_{t-1}) b_t (\Delta x_t)^3 - \frac{3}{10} c_t f_t(x_{t-1}) (\Delta x_t)^4 - \frac{2}{15} b_t^2 (\Delta x_t)^4$$

$$\left. - \frac{1}{14} c_t^2 (\Delta x_t)^6 - \frac{7}{36} b_t c_t (\Delta x_t)^5 \right]$$

where b_t and c_t are defined in (6.41).

For the first and last openended income ranges, where the Pareto density function was fitted, the Gini index is derived as

$$G_1 = \frac{x_1 - \mu_1}{x_1 + \mu_1}$$

and

$$G_{T+1} = \frac{\mu_{T+1} - x_T}{\mu_{T+1} + x_T}.$$

Next consider the estimation of the relative mean deviation denoted by R in (5.27). In lemma 5.9, R was shown to be equal to the maximum discrepancy between p and q, which occurs at the mean income.[5] It is necessary, therefore, to compute p and q at $x = \mu$ in order to determine R.

Suppose the mean income of the distribution falls in the tth income range where the equation of the Lorenz curve is given by either (6.13) or (6.37). One can calculate p at $x = \mu$ by equating the slope of the Lorenz curve with unity. Substituting this value of p into the equation of the Lorenz curve gives the value of q at $x = \mu$. Clearly, R is given by the difference between p and q at $x = \mu$.

For the linear and quadratic density functions, R can be directly derived from (5.28). Thus for the linear function,

$$R = (p_{t-1} - q_{t-1}) + \frac{(\Delta x_t) r_t^2 f_t}{\mu} \left[(2 - r_t) + \delta_t (2r_t - 3) \right],$$

and for the quadratic density function,

$$R = (p_{t-1} - q_{t-1}) + \frac{1}{2\mu} f(x_{t-1}) r_t^2 (\Delta x_t)^2 (1 - r_t)^2$$

$$+ \frac{r_t^3 (\Delta x_t) f_t}{\mu} \left[(3r_t - 4)\delta_t + (3 - 2r_t) \right]$$

where

$$r_t = \frac{(\mu - x_{t-1})}{(\Delta x_t)}.$$

The equations of the Lorenz curve given in (6.13), (6.24), (6.25), and (6.37) can be used to compute any percentile of the distribution. For a given value of p, the value of q can be obtained from the equations of the Lorenz curve, which provides the income share of the percentile.

5. See lemma 3.1.

Budd (1970) proposed comparing two distributions by the mean income of their quintiles relative to the mean income of the distributions. These measures can be regarded as the relative mean income for each quintile; they are equal to the slope of the chord connecting the lower and upper points on the Lorenz curve for the quintile.

Bowley's (1937) index of inequality is based on the quartiles and is defined as

$$(6.43) \qquad\qquad B = \frac{Q_3 - Q_1}{Q_3 + Q_1}$$

where Q_1 and Q_3 are the first and third quartiles.

The estimation of the other inequality measures discussed in chapter 5 require the evaluation of integrals of the type

$$(6.44) \qquad\qquad \int_0^\infty v(x) f(x)\,dx$$

where $f(x)$ is the density function, and $v(x)$ is any function of x, depending on the inequality measure. If the density function $f(x)$ is directly specified, it is possible to evaluate the integral within each income range and then aggregate the results. If the equation of the Lorenz curve is known for each income range, however, one can use (6.1) to evaluate the integral. Thus, the integral (6.44) for the tth income is expressed as

$$\int_{x_{t-1}}^{x_t} v(x) f_t(x)\,dx = \int_{p_{t-1}}^{p_t} v\left[\mu\, \frac{dq}{dp} \right] dp$$

where $\mu\, dq/dp$ can be derived from the equation of the Lorenz curve specified for the tth income range.

The following inequality measures were selected for the numerical illustration of the estimation technique given here:[6]

(a) L, the new inequality measure proposed in Chapter 5;

(b) CV, the coefficient of variation of income x;

(c) $\sigma_{\log}$, the standard deviation of income power, $z = \log x$;

---

6. The formulas for computing these inequality measures are given in the appendix to this chapter.

(d) A_1, the proportion by which the geometric mean falls below the arithmetic mean income;

(e) A_2, the proportion by which the harmonic mean income falls below the arithmetic mean income;

(f) $I(y{:}p) = \dfrac{1}{\mu} \displaystyle\int_0^\infty x \log xf(x)\,dx - \log \mu;$

(g) $I(p{:}y) = \log \mu - \displaystyle\int_0^\infty \log xf(x)\,dx.$

A_1 and A_2 are the special cases of Atkinson's (1970) inequality measure based on a given welfare function. When the marginal utility of income is inversely proportional to income, A_1 arises;[7] for A_2, the marginal utility of income is inversely proportional to the square of the income.[8] The information measures proposed by Theil (1967) are $I(y{:}p)$ and $I(p{:}y)$.

Empirical Illustrations

In this section the empirical results of using the methods discussed above of estimating various inequality measures from grouped observations are presented. The data used for this purpose are from *The Australian Survey of Consumer Expenditures and Finances,* 1966–68, stage two, by Drane, Edwards, and Gates. The first stage was an enquiry into the expenditures on different commodities made by the households; the second stage, a gathering of detailed information about income, taxes, assets, and liabilities of the 2,757 sample families. The variable considered is gross family income for the year 1966–67, Gross income being defined as total family income from all sources, including government cash benefits before income tax deductions. The data were originally based on individual families and then grouped into thirteen income classes; the grouped data are presented in table 6.1.

In addition to the frequency and mean income in each income class, table 6.1 provides the computed values of the cumulative

7. See equation (4.11).
8. See equation (4.13).

Table 6.1. *Distribution of Family Income, Australia, 1966–67*

Income range (Australian dollars)	Frequency (f_t)	Mean income (μ_t) (Australian dollars)	Cumulative frequency (p_t)	Cumulative income (q_t)
Under 1,000	0.059	664.5	0.059	0.009
1,000– 1,999	0.109	1,428.9	0.168	0.047
2,000– 2,999	0.161	2,562.9	0.329	0.146
3,000– 3,999	0.227	3,462.4	0.556	0.335
4,000– 4,999	0.166	4,451.5	0.722	0.512
5,000– 5,999	0.113	5,433.0	0.836	0.660
6,000– 6,999	0.061	6,465.7	0.897	0.756
7,000– 7,999	0.035	7,430.0	0.932	0.818
8,000– 8,999	0.026	8,438.6	0.958	0.871
9,000– 9,999	0.009	9,438.3	0.968	0.893
10,000–10,999	0.012	10,400.2	0.980	0.924
11,000–11,999	0.005	11,401.6	0.985	0.937
Over 12,000	0.015	17,498.1	1.000	1.000
Total	1.000	4,164.2	1.000	1.000

proportion of families p_t and the cumulative proportion of income q_t.

The first step was to estimate various inequality measures, discussed in the previous section, by means of the individual observations that provided the basis for assessing the accuracy of the interpolation method developed in this chapter. For the purpose of comparison, the commonly used approximate methods based on linear interpolation were also applied to compute the inequality measures.[9]

Table 6.2 presents the estimates of the Gini index for each income range. The last column in the table is the estimated upper bound for the Gini index as given in (6.6), (6.7), and (6.8). The table indicates that the estimates of G_t, computed from the four functions considered here, lie below the upper bound, thus qualifying the Gastwirth and Smith (1972) test for goodness of fit. Comparing them with the Gini indexes computed from the individual observations, however, the quadratic density function and the fourth-

9. Note that the linear interpolation assumes that the inequality of income within each income range is zero. This method provides only the lower bound to the inequality measures.

Table 6.2. *Estimates of Gini Indexes for Various Functions*

Income range (Australian dollars)	Estimated from individual observations	Linear density function	Quadratic density function	Third-degree polynomial	Fourth-degree polynomial	Upper limit
0– 1,000	0.153	0.202	0.202	0.202	0.202	0.335
1,000– 1,999	0.109	0.112	0.145	0.116	0.108	0.171
2,000– 2,999	0.061	0.063	0.075	0.065	0.048	0.095
3,000– 3,999	0.048	0.048	0.052	0.048	0.029	0.072
4,000– 4,999	0.039	0.037	0.040	0.037	0.025	0.056
5,000– 5,999	0.030	0.030	0.031	0.031	0.022	0.045
6,000– 6,999	0.026	0.025	0.028	0.026	0.022	0.038
7,000– 7,999	0.021	0.022	0.025	0.022	0.020	0.033
8,000– 8,999	0.018	0.019	0.021	0.020	0.016	0.029
9,000– 9,999	0.015	0.017	0.022	0.018	0.016	0.026
10,000–10,999	0.015	0.015	0.016	0.016	0.009	0.023
11,000–11,999	0.012	0.014	0.015	0.015	0.011	0.021
Over 12,000	0.221	0.186	0.186	0.186	0.186	0.314
Total	0.321	0.321	0.322	0.321	0.320	0.324

Note. The Pareto density function is fitted to the first and last group.

degree polynomial Lorenz function yield poor estimates in relation to the other two functions. Further, the estimates of G_t for the end-classes are less accurate than for the intervening classes because the openended classes are generally wider and use less information in the estimation of the density function than the other classes. Although the quadratic density function and the fourth-degree polynomial Lorenz function eliminate discontinuities of the density function at each boundary point, they perform poorly because the error of estimation of the density function at the endclasses is carried over to the estimation of the inequality measure in all classes. It is, therefore, safer not to impose the continuity requirement of the density function at each boundary point.

Table 6.3 presents the estimates of the new inequality measure L_t for each income range, along with its lower and upper bounds. The Pareto curve was used to estimate the measure in the first and last openended income classes; in the remaining classes, only the linear density function was used. The other three functional forms were not employed because explicit formulae for this measure could not be derived. The table indicates that the estimates of L_t computed from the linear density function lie below its upper bound in each income class. Furthermore, a comparison of these estimates

Table 6.3. *Estimates of the New Inequality Measure*

Income range (Australian dollars)	Estimated from individual observations	Linear approx- imations	Linear density function	Upper limit
0– 1,000	0.023	0.0	0.020	0.042
1,000– 1,999	0.018	0.0	0.018	0.021
2,000– 2,999	0.015	0.0	0.013	0.021
3,000– 3,999	0.013	0.0	0.013	0.020
4,000– 4,999	0.012	0.0	0.014	0.019
5,000– 5,999	0.013	0.0	0.012	0.020
6,000– 6,999	0.011	0.0	0.013	0.019
7,000– 7,999	0.011	0.0	0.011	0.019
8,000– 8,999	0.016	0.0	0.012	0.020
9,000– 9,999	0.018	0.0	0.014	0.025
10,000–10,999	0.023	0.0	0.024	0.031
11,000–11,999	0.024	0.0	0.024	0.038
Over 12,000	0.030	0.0	0.029	0.058
Total	0.018	0.005	0.019	0.026

Table 6.4. *Estimated Inequality Measures Associated with the Lorenz Curve*

Inequality measures	*Estimated from individual observations*	*Linear approx- imations*	*Linear density function*	*Third- degree polynomial*
Relative mean deviation	0.222	0.210	0.222	0.222
Bowley's index B	0.478	0.456	0.465	0.470
Budd's Measures				
1st quintile	0.315	0.333	0.317	0.316
2nd quintile	0.680	0.692	0.680	0.681
3rd quintile	0.894	0.883	0.893	0.893
4th quintile	1.164	1.161	1.165	1.164
Next 15 percent	1.622	1.605	1.620	1.622
Top 5 percent	2.922	2.904	2.916	2.916

with the estimates based on individual observations clearly shows that the linear density function provides sufficiently accurate estimates of the new inequality measure.

Table 6.4 presents the other estimates of the inequality measures that are directly associated with the Lorenz curve. This table clearly shows that the inequality estimates obtained from linear approximation are consistently lower than the actual values. The results, computed from the linear density function and the third-degree polynomial Lorenz function, are correct to at least two decimal places, which can be regarded as sufficient accuracy for practical purposes.

Table 6.5 presents estimates of the inequality measures that are not directly associated with the Lorenz curve.

The estimated coefficient of variation based on linear interpolation is significantly lower than its true value; the degree of accuracy is vastly improved, however, by using the linear density function or the third-degree polynomial Lorenz function.

The standard deviation of log income based on linear interpolation was obtained by means of the following formula:

$$\sigma_{\log} = \sum_{t=1}^{T+1} f_t (\log \mu_t - \log \mu)^2 .$$

The computed value is 0.665, which is much lower than that computed from individual observations (0.760). Although the standard

Table 6.5. *Estimated Inequality Measures Not Associated with the Lorenz Curve*

Inequality measure	Estimated from individual observations	Third-degree Lorenz function	Linear density function	Approximation based on linear interpolation
Coefficient of variation	0.740	0.696	0.695	0.640
Standard deviation of income power	0.759	0.725	0.721	0.665
Atkinson's Measures				
A_1	0.192	0.184	0.179	0.174
A_2	0.435	0.411	0.412	0.355
Theil's Information Measures				
$I(y:p)$	0.189	0.185	0.191	0.176
$I(p:y)$	0.213	0.204	0.197	0.192

deviation of log income computed by the general interpolation device is not highly accurate, it is definitely a significant improvement over the linear interpolation method. Kravis (1962) suggested the following approximation to the standard deviation of logarithms:

$$\sigma_{\log} = \frac{\log p_{80} - \log p_{20}}{1.6836}$$

where p_{80} is the income at the 80th percentile and p_{20} is the income at the 20th percentile.[10] This formula computes the standard deviation of log income to base 10, which can be easily converted to natural logarithms by multiplying the result by a constant. The value of $\sigma_{\log}$ by this approximation was calculated as 0.568, which is even less accurate than the approximation based on the linear interpolation.

The third-degree polynomial Lorenz function yields accurate estimates of Atkinson's inequality measures and Theil's measures up to two decimal places. Although the error in each of these cases does not exceed 5 percent, the linear density function leads to estimates with slightly larger errors.

10. There is an error in this formula given by Kravis.

In this chapter only four forms of the density function were tried, two of which yielded estimates of inequality measures close to their true values. In addition, these functions were used to derive explicit formulas for most of the inequality measures in common use. The computations involved are fairly straightforward and can be done with the use of a simple desk calculator.

Appendix

In this appendix the formulas for computing various inequality measures listed on page 63 are provided.

The new inequality measure

In equation (6.12) the new inequality measure L was expressed as the sum of two components. The first component $\bar{L}$, which is the inequality between income classes, can be estimated without fitting any form of the density function. The second component, the weighted sum of inequalities within the income classes, requires the estimation of L_t, the inequality measure in the tth income class. L_t is defined as

$$L_t = \frac{\mu l_t - f_t \sqrt{\mu^2 + \mu_t^2}}{f_t(\mu + \mu_t - \sqrt{\mu^2 + \mu_t^2})}$$

where l_t is the length of the Lorenz curve in the tth income class. If $f_t(x)$ is the density function in the tth income class, l_t will be given by

$$(6.45) \qquad l_t = \frac{1}{\mu} \int_{x_{t-1}}^{x_t} \sqrt{\mu^2 + x^2} f_t(x)\, dx$$

where (5.35) has been used. For a linear density function as given in (6.39), (6.45) simplifies to

$$l_t = \frac{2f_t(2\delta_t - 1)}{\mu(\Delta x_t)^2} \left[(\mu^2 + x_t^2)^{3/2} - (\mu^2 + x_{t-1}^2)^{3/2} \right]$$

$$+ \frac{(a_t - b_t x_{t-1})}{2\mu} \left[x_t \sqrt{\mu^2 + x_t^2} - x_{t-1} \sqrt{\mu^2 + x_{t-1}^2} \right]$$

$$+ \frac{(a_t - b_t x_{t-1})\mu}{2} \log \frac{x_t + \sqrt{\mu^2 + x_t^2}}{x_{t-1} + \sqrt{\mu^2 + x_{t-1}^2}}$$

where a_t and b_t are defined in (6.40). The explicit expressions for l_t could not be derived for the first and last openended income classes where the Pareto type function was fitted. Numerical integration was used, therefore, to compute the integral given in (6.45) for these intervals.

Coefficient of variation

The coefficient of variation was defined in (5.36) as σ/μ where σ is the standard deviation of the distribution. If σ_t is the standard deviation of the tth income class, it follows that

$$\sigma^2 = \sum_{t=1}^{T+1} f_t\mu_t^2 - \mu^2 + \sum_{t=1}^{T+1} f_t\sigma_t^2$$

where the values of σ_t^2 using the third-degree polynomial Lorenz curve (6.13) and the linear density function (6.39) are

$$(6.46) \quad \sigma_t^2 = \frac{6}{5}\mu_t f_t - \frac{\mu_t f_t}{5}(x_{t-1} + x_t) + \frac{1}{15}f_t(2x_{t-1}^2 + 2x_t^2 - x_{t-1}x_t)$$

and

$$\sigma_t^2 = (\Delta x_t)^2\left[\delta_t - \delta_t^2 - \frac{1}{6}\right],$$

respectively. For the first and last openended income ranges, where the Pareto function was fitted, σ_t^2 is derived as equal to

$$\sigma_1^2 = \frac{(x_1 - \mu_1)^2\mu_1}{(2x_1 - \mu_1)}$$

and

$$\sigma_{T+1}^2 = \frac{(\mu_{T+1} - x_T)^2\mu_{T+1}}{(2x_T - \mu_{T+1})}.$$

Atkinson's measures

Atkinson's measures A_1 and A_2, given above in "Estimation of the Inequality Measures," require the estimation of the geometric and harmonic means of the distribution. If G_t and H_t are denoted as the geometric and harmonic means for the tth income range, the geometric and harmonic means for the whole distribution are given by

$$\log G = \sum_{t=1}^{T+1} f_t \log G_t$$

and

$$\frac{1}{H} = \sum_{t=1}^{T+1} \frac{f_t}{H_t}.$$

For the linear and the third-degree polynomial density functions, G_t and H_t are derived to equal:

(a) linear density function

$$\log G_t = \frac{1}{f_t}\left(\frac{f_t}{\Delta x_t} - \frac{b_t}{2} x_t\right)\left(x_{t-1}\log\frac{x_t}{x_{t-1}} - \Delta x_t\right)$$

$$+ \log x_t - \frac{1}{4}\frac{b_t(\Delta x_t)^2}{f_t}$$

$$\frac{1}{H_t} = \frac{(x_{t-1} + x_t)}{x_{t-1}^2 + x_t^2} - \frac{b_t(\Delta x_t)}{2x_{t-1}^2 x_t^2 f_t}\left[(x_{t-1} + x_t)^2 - 2x_{t-1}^2 x_t^2\right]$$

where b_t is defined in (6.40);

(b) third-degree polynomial Lorenz curve

$$\log G_t = \frac{2}{b_t f_t}\left[2\mu\alpha_{2t}\log\frac{x_t}{x_{t-1}} + 6\mu\alpha_{3t}f_t(\log x_t - 2) - \frac{a_t f_t}{H_t}\right]$$

where

$$(6.47)\qquad \frac{1}{H_t} = \frac{2}{\sqrt{a_t}f_t}\log\frac{\sqrt{x_{t-1}}\,(\sqrt{a_t + b_t x_t} - \sqrt{a_t})}{\sqrt{x_t}\,(\sqrt{a_t + b_t x_{t-1}} - \sqrt{a_t})}$$

if $a_t > 0$. If $a_t < 0$, it follows that

$$\frac{1}{H_t} = \frac{2}{f_t\sqrt{-a_t}}\left[\tan^{-1}\sqrt{\frac{a_t + b_t x_t}{-a_t}} - \tan^{-1}\sqrt{\frac{a_t + b_t x_{t-1}}{-a_t}}\right]$$

where α_{3t} is given in (6.20) and a_t and b_t are defined in (6.22) and (6.23), respectively.

For the first and last openended income ranges, G_t and H_t are obtained as

$$\log G_1 = \log x_1 - (x_1 - \mu_1)/\mu_1$$

$$\log G_{T+1} = \log x_T + \frac{\mu_{T+1} - x_T}{\mu_{T+1}}$$

$$H_1 = \frac{x_1(2\mu_1 - x_1)}{\mu_1}$$

$$H_{T+1} = \frac{x_T(2\mu_{T+1} - x_T)}{\mu_{T+1}}.$$

The standard deviation of the income power

Let $\sigma_{\log t}$ be the standard deviation of the income power (or logarithm of income) for the tth income range; then for the whole distribution,

$$\sigma_{\log}^2 = \sum_{t=1}^{T+1} f_t \sigma_{\log t}^2 + \sum_{t=1}^{T+1} f_t (\log G_t)^2 - (\log G)^2.$$

For the linear density function $\sigma_{\log t}^2$ is derived as equal to

$$\sigma_{\log t}^2 = \frac{(a_t - b_t x_{t-1})}{f_t} \big[x_t \log x_t (\log x_t - 2)$$

$$- x_{t-1} \log x_{t-1} (\log x_{t-1} - 2)$$

$$+ 2(\Delta x_t) \big] + \frac{b_t}{4f_t} \big[2x_t^2 (\log x_t)(\log x_t - 1)$$

$$- 2x_{t-1}^2 \log x_{t-1} (\log x_{t-1} - 1)$$

$$+ (\Delta x_t)(x_{t-1} + x_t) \big] - (\log G_t)^2$$

where a_t and b_t are defined in (6.40).

For the first and last income ranges, the equality measure is computed to be equal to

$$\sigma_{log\ 1}^2 = (\log x_1)^2 - \frac{2(x_1 - \mu_1)}{\mu_1} \log G_1 - (\log G_1)^2$$

$$\sigma_{\log(T+1)}^2 = (\log x_T)^2 + \frac{2(\mu_{T+1} - x_T)}{\mu_{T+1}} \log G_{T+1} - [\log G_{(T+1)}]^2.$$

For the third-degree polynomial function, it is difficult to obtain an explicit expression. Equation (6.46) was used to estimate $\sigma^2_{\log t}$ after applying the logarithmic transformation to the original income distribution. Thus

$$\sigma^2_{\log t} = \frac{6}{5} (\log G_t)^2 f_t - \frac{(\log G_t) f_t}{5} \log x_{t-1} x_t$$

$$+ \frac{1}{15} f_t [2 (\log x_{t-1})^2 + 2 (\log x_t)^2 - (\log x_{t-1}) (\log x_t)].$$

Theil's information measures

Let $I_t(y{:}p)$ and $I_t(p{:}y)$ be Theil's inequality measures for the tth income range; then for the entire distribution these measures are equal to

$$I(y{:}p) = \frac{1}{\mu} \sum_{t=1}^{T+1} \mu_t f_t \log \mu_t - \log \mu + \frac{1}{\mu} \sum_{t=1}^{T+1} \mu_t f_t I_t(y{:}p)$$

$$I(p{:}y) = \log \mu - \sum_{t=1}^{T+1} f_t \log \mu_t + \sum_{t=1}^{T+1} f_t I_t(p{:}y).$$

Because $I_t(p{:}y) = \log \mu_t - \log G_t$, only the geometric mean is needed to obtain this measure. The formulae for computing the geometric mean are given in "Atkinson's measures" above.

By means of the linear density function, $I_t(y{:}p)$ is derived as equal to

$$I_t(y{:}p) = \frac{(a_t - b_t x_{t-1})}{2\mu_t f_t} \left[x_t^2 \log x_t - x_{t-1}^2 + \log x_{t-1} \right]$$

$$= \frac{b_t}{3\mu_t f_t} \left[x_t^3 \log x_t - x_{t-1}^3 \log x_{t-1} \right]$$

$$- \frac{1}{9} \frac{b_t}{\mu_t f_t} (x_t^3 - x_{t-1}^3) - \log \mu_t$$

where a_t and b_t are defined in (6.40).

Similarly, for the third-degree polynomial Lorenz function, $I_t(y{:}p)$

is obtained as equal to

$$I_t(y:p) = \frac{2}{3b_t^2} \frac{\sqrt{a_t + b_t x_t}}{\mu_t f_t} \left[-(2a_t - b_t x_t) \log x_t \right.$$

$$\left. + \frac{2}{3} (5a_t - b_t x_t) \right] - \frac{2}{3b_t^2} \frac{\sqrt{a_t + b_t x_{t-1}}}{\mu_t f_t}$$

$$\times \left[-(2a_t - b_t x_{t-1}) \log x_{t-1} \right.$$

$$\left. + \frac{2}{3} (5a_t - b_t x_{t-1}) \right] + \frac{4a_t^2}{3b_t^2 \mu_t H_t}$$

where a_t and b_t are defined in (6.22) and (6.23), and H_t is the harmonic mean of the tth income range. The formula for computing H_t by means of the third-degree polynomial density function is given in (6.47).

For the first and last openended income ranges, $I_t(y:p)$ is derived as equal to

$$I_1(y:p) = \log \frac{x_1}{\mu_1} - \frac{(x_1 - \mu_1)}{x_1}$$

$$I_{T+1}(y:p) = \log \frac{x_T}{\mu_{T+1}} + \frac{\mu_{T+1} - x_T}{x_T}.$$

PART THREE

Applications of Lorenz Curves in Economic Analysis

CHAPTER 7

A New Coordinate System for the Lorenz Curve

THE DERIVATION OF THE EQUATION of the Lorenz curve from a density function of income distribution was discussed in chapter 3. The density function is rarely known, however, and the usual approach has been to fit a well-known density function and derive the equation of the Lorenz curve from the specified function.[1] Furthermore, because the usual density functions rarely give good fit to a wide range of observed income distributions, an alternative approach has been suggested by Kakwani and Podder (1973).

Their approach is to directly specify a functional form of the Lorenz curve, which has a number of properties that can be effectively utilized to specify such an equation. Once the equation is specified and estimated from actual data, the inequality measures can be derived as functions of the parameters of the equation. Moreover, the standard errors of the inequality measures can also be computed from the standard errors of the estimated parameters of the Lorenz curve equation. (Needless to say, testing of the hypothesis on the inequality measures is possible only if their standard errors are known.) In addition, the density function can also be derived from the equation of the Lorenz curve and may serve a number of important purposes.

This chapter concerns a new coordinate system for the Lorenz

---

1. A discussion of several well-known density functions is given in chapter 2.

curve, introduced by Kakwani and Podder (1976),[2] and focuses on the estimation of different inequality measures by means of a special case of the new system.

Four alternative methods are employed to estimate the proposed Lorenz curve from grouped observations, and certain properties of the Lorenz curve that could be effectively utilized to improve the efficiency of the estimates are demonstrated. An empirical illustration is presented by means of *The Australian Survey of Consumer Expenditures and Finances*, 1966–68, by Drane and others.[3]

The empirical results indicate that the density function underlying the Lorenz curve considered here provides an extremely good fit to the entire range of the observed income distribution. Jain (1975) fitted the same equation of the Lorenz curve to about five hundred income distributions obtained from about seventy countries. Using this function to estimate the income share accruing to each decile of the population, her study clearly indicates that the density function underlying this equation of the Lorenz curve provides good fit to a wide range of observed income distributions from different countries. It must be added, however, that this function is not developed on the basis of some income-generating stochastic process, nor may it be interpreted in terms of income generation. The seriousness of this drawback is unclear because of the complexity of the process of income generation. The density function derived by means of the simple stochastic process may not, for example, be satisfactory from the economist's point of view. Mincer (1958) pointed out, in fact, that the stochastic models of personal income distribution shed no light on the economics of the distribution process.

A New Specification of the Lorenz Curve

Let P be any point on the Lorenz curve with coordinates (F, F_1) where $F(x)$ and $F_1(x)$ are defined in (3.1) and (3.2). PQ is the perpendicular drawn on the egalitarian line. Figure 5 shows that $OM = OL + LM$ and $QL = QN + NL$. Furthermore, $OL = LQ =$

---

2. This system was suggested by Professor A. Zellner in a letter to the authors that commented on an earlier paper by them (1973).

3. For a detailed discussion of the definitions and limitations of the survey, see Podder and Kakwani (1975a).

Figure 5. *New Coordinates for the Lorenz Curve*

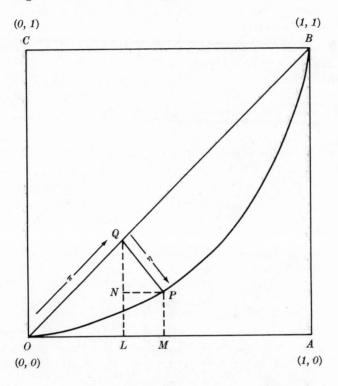

$1/\sqrt{2}\ \pi$ and $NQ = NP = 1/\sqrt{2}\ \eta$ where η is the length PQ, and π is the distance OQ. Combining these results yields

(7.1) $$\pi = \frac{1}{\sqrt{2}}\ (F + F_1) \quad \text{and} \quad \eta = \frac{1}{\sqrt{2}}\ (F - F_1).$$

Because the Lorenz curves lie below the egalitarian line, $F_1 \leq F$, which implies that $\eta \geq 0$. Further, if income is always positive, (7.1) will imply that η is always less than or equal to π.

The equation of the Lorenz curve in terms of π and η can now be written as

(7.2) $$\eta = g(\pi)$$

where π varies from zero to $\sqrt{2}$. The function $g(\pi)$ should satisfy the restrictions

$$g(\pi) > 0$$

for all π in the range $0 < \pi < \sqrt{2}$, and

(7.3) $$g(\pi) = 0$$

for $\pi = 0$ and $\pi = \sqrt{2}$. These restrictions ensure that the Lorenz curve lies below the egalitarian line.

If the density function $f(x)$ as defined in (2.2) is continuous, the derivatives of $F(x)$ and $F_1(x)$ exist; $dF/dx = f(x)$ and $dF_1/dx = xf(x)/\mu$ where μ is the mean income. Substituting these values into (7.1) yields

$$\frac{d\pi}{dx} = \frac{1}{\sqrt{2}}\left[f(x) + \frac{xf(x)}{\mu}\right]$$

$$\frac{d\eta}{dx} = \frac{1}{\sqrt{2}}\left[f(x) - \frac{xf(x)}{\mu}\right],$$

which give the derivatives of η with respect to π as

(7.4) $$\frac{d\eta}{d\pi} = \frac{\mu - x}{\mu + x}$$

and

(7.5) $$\frac{d^2\eta}{d\pi^2} = -\frac{2\sqrt{2}\,\mu^2}{f(x)(\mu + x)^3} < 0.$$

Thus η will be maximum at $x = \mu$.

If the Lorenz curve represented by (7.2) is symmetric,[4] the value of η at π and $(\sqrt{2} - \pi)$ should be equal for all values of π, which implies that

(7.6) $$g(\pi) = g(\sqrt{2} - \pi)$$

for all π in the range $0 \leq \pi \leq \sqrt{2}$.

The curve will be skewed toward $(1, 1)$ if $g(\pi) > g(\sqrt{2} - \pi)$ for $\pi < 1/\sqrt{2}$, and it will be skewed toward $(0, 0)$ if $g(\pi) < g(\sqrt{2} - \pi)$

---

4. The symmetry of the Lorenz curve is defined in chapter 3. The idea of the symmetry of the Lorenz curve has been applied to test Kuznets' (1955) hypothesis relating to the international comparison of income distributions (see chapter 17).

for $\pi < 1/\sqrt{2}$. For example, assume that the equation of the curve is

$$(7.7) \qquad\qquad \eta = a\pi^\alpha(\sqrt{2} - \pi)^\beta$$

where $a > 0$, $\alpha > 0$ and $\beta > 0$. The restriction $a > 0$ implies that $g(\pi) \geq 0$ for all values of π in the range 0 to $\sqrt{2}$; that is, the Lorenz curve lies below the egalitarian line. Further, $\alpha > 0$ and $\beta > 0$ mean that $g(\pi)$ assumes value zero when $\pi = 0$ or $\pi = \sqrt{2}$. Using (7.6), it can be seen that the curve is symmetric if $\alpha = \beta$, skewed toward $(1, 1)$ if $\beta > \alpha$, and skewed toward $(0, 0)$ otherwise. Further, the restriction (7.5) means that for all values of x, the second derivative $g''(\pi)$ should be negative. For equation (7.7),

$$g''(\pi) = -\eta \left[\frac{\alpha(1 - \alpha)}{\pi^2} + \frac{\beta(1 - \beta)}{(\sqrt{2} - \pi)^2} + \frac{2\alpha\beta}{\pi(\sqrt{2} - \pi)} \right],$$

which shows that the sufficient conditions for $g''(\pi)$ to be always nonpositive are $0 < \alpha \leq 1$ and $0 < \beta \leq 1$. These conditions rule out the possibility of points of inflexion on the curve, which are, of course, not permissible in this case.

An alternative class of equations of the Lorenz curve, similar to the well-known constant elasticity of substitution (CES) production function proposed by Arrow, Chenery, Minhas, and Solow (1961), is given by

$$(7.8) \qquad\qquad \eta = a[\delta\pi^{-\rho} + (1 - \delta)(\sqrt{2} - \pi)^{-\rho}]^{-\nu/\rho}$$

where the parameters a, δ, ρ, and ν are all greater than zero. Rearranging (7.8) yields

$$(7.9) \qquad \eta = a\pi^\nu(\sqrt{2} - \pi)^\nu[\delta(\sqrt{2} - \pi)^\rho + (1 - \delta)\pi^\rho]^{-\nu/\rho},$$

which clearly shows that η assumes value zero when $\pi = 0$ and $\pi = \sqrt{2}$. The curve is symmetric if $\delta = \frac{1}{2}$, skewed toward $(1, 1)$ if $\delta < \frac{1}{2}$, and skewed toward $(0, 0)$ if $\delta > \frac{1}{2}$. Further, the limit of (7.9) as ρ approaches zero becomes

$$\eta = a\pi^{\delta\nu}(\sqrt{2} - \pi)^{\nu(1-\delta)},$$

which is the same class of equations as (7.7), with $\alpha = \delta\nu$ and $\beta = \nu(1 - \delta)$. Finally, the sufficient condition stated in (7.5) is always satisfied for this class of equations, that is, (7.8), if $0 < \delta < 1$ and $0 < \nu < 1$.

Derivation of the Density Function from the Lorenz Curve

The income density function underlying equation (7.2) can be obtained as follows:

$$F(x) = \frac{1}{\sqrt{2}} (\pi + \eta)$$

where use has been made of (7.1). Differentiating this equation with respect to x yields

$$(7.10) \qquad f(x) = \frac{1}{\sqrt{2}} \left[\frac{d\pi}{dx} + \frac{d\eta}{dx} \right] = \frac{1}{\sqrt{2}} \left[1 + \frac{d\eta}{d\pi} \right] \frac{d\pi}{dx},$$

which, by means of (7.4), becomes

$$(7.11) \qquad f(x) = \frac{\sqrt{2}\mu}{(\mu + x)} \frac{d\pi}{dx}.$$

Equation (7.4), written as

$$(7.12) \qquad g'(\pi) = \frac{\mu - x}{\mu + x},$$

gives the relationship between π and x. Under the sufficient conditions discussed above, $g''(\pi) < 0$ for all π in the range $0 < \pi < \sqrt{2}$, which implies that $g'(\pi)$ is a monotonically decreasing function of π and, therefore, (7.12) can always be solved for π in terms of x. Substituting the value of π for a given value of x into (7.2) gives the value of η. Further, substituting these values of π and η into (7.1) yields the distribution functions $F(x)$ and $F_1(x)$. Differentiating (7.12) with respect to x yields

$$(7.13) \qquad g''(\pi) \frac{d\pi}{dx} = \frac{-2\mu}{(\mu + x)^2},$$

which implies that $d\pi/dx > 0$, that is, that π increases as x increases. Substituting the value of π from (7.12) into (7.13) yields the value of $d\pi/dx$ in terms of x, which, on substituting into (7.11), gives the density function $f(x)$. Thus, if the condition that $g''(\pi) < 0$ is satisfied for the given equation for the Lorenz curve, it is always possible to derive the income density function underlying this equation.

The income density function derived from the Lorenz curve (7.2) must satisfy the following two conditions:

$$(7.14) \qquad \int_0^\infty f(x)\,dx = 1,$$

and

$$(7.15) \qquad \int_0^\infty xf(x)\,dx = \mu.$$

In order to show that these conditions hold, write (7.10) as

$$(7.16) \qquad f(x)\,dx = \frac{1}{\sqrt{2}}\left[1 + g'(\pi)\right]d\pi,$$

which, on integrating into the whole income range, becomes

$$\int_0^\infty f(x)\,dx = \frac{1}{\sqrt{2}}\int_0^{\sqrt{2}}\left[1 + g'(\pi)\right]d\pi$$

$$= 1 + \frac{1}{\sqrt{2}}\left[g(\sqrt{2}) - g(0)\right],$$

which obviously is equal to unity in view of (7.3). Thus condition (7.14) is always satisfied.

Write x in terms of π from (7.12) as

$$(7.17) \qquad x = \frac{\mu\left[1 - g'(\pi)\right]}{\left[1 + g'(\pi)\right]},$$

which, by means of (7.16), gives

$$xf(x)\,dx = \frac{\mu}{\sqrt{2}}\left[1 - g'(\pi)\right].$$

Integrating this into the whole income range yields

$$\int_0^\infty xf(x)\,dx = \frac{\mu}{\sqrt{2}}\int_0^{\sqrt{2}}\left[1 - g'(\pi)\right]d\pi = \mu - \frac{\mu}{\sqrt{2}}\left[g(\sqrt{2}) - g(0)\right],$$

which, by means of (7.3), indicates that condition (7.15) is also satisfied.

Equation (7.12) implies that as $x \to 0$, $g'(\pi) \to 1$. Also, if $x \to \infty$, $g'(\pi) \to -1$. As $x \to 0$, $\pi \to 0$, and as $x \to \infty$, $\pi \to \sqrt{2}$; therefore,

$g'(\pi)$ should satisfy the following restrictions:

(7.18) $$\lim_{\pi \to 0} g'(\pi) = 1$$

and

(7.19) $$\lim_{\pi \to \sqrt{2}} g'(\pi) = -1.$$

The density function implied by the equation of the Lorenz curve (7.7) is used in several economic applications in the following chapters. It is, therefore, worthwhile to investigate here whether this particular Lorenz curve satisfies conditions (7.18) and (7.19). If it does not, any attempt to derive values for $f(x)$ by numerical methods, as suggested above, may lead to erroneous values for very large or very small x. The next step, therefore, is to differentiate (7.7) with respect to π:

(7.20) $$g'(\pi) = a\alpha\pi^{\alpha-1}(\sqrt{2} - \pi)^\beta - a\beta\pi^\alpha(\sqrt{2} - \pi)^{\beta-1},$$

which gives $g'(\pi) \to \infty$ as $\pi \to 0$, and $g'(\pi) \to -\infty$ as $\pi \to \sqrt{2}$ for $0 < \alpha < 1$ and for $0 < \beta < 1$. Both limiting conditions (7.18) and (7.19) are, therefore, violated by the Lorenz curve (7.7). In order to investigate the question whether this matters in practice, it was necessary to compute the values of the function $g'(\pi)$ for a large number of alternative sets of values of α and β in the ranges $0 < \alpha < 1$ and $0 < \beta < 1$. The actual calculations clearly show that for almost all cases, the function $g'(\pi)$ varies from $+1$ to -1 for π varying from 1.2×10^{-7} (approximately zero) to $\sqrt{2} - 10^{-8}$ (approximately $\sqrt{2}$), but it has asymptotes at $\pi = 0$ and $\pi = \sqrt{2}$. This suggests that the singularities at the extreme ends should not affect the empirical results. The fact is that this function does provide good fit to a wide range of observed income distributions for different countries up to at least the 99th percentile.[5]

Derivation of Inequality Measures from the New Coordinate System of the Lorenz Curve

This section focuses on the derivation of different inequality measures by means of the new coordinate system of the Lorenz

---

5. See chapter 17.

curve. First, the Gini index, which is equal to twice the area between the Lorenz curve and the egalitarian line, is considered.[6] If the Lorenz curve is, therefore, formulated in terms of π and η, the Gini index becomes

$$G = 2 \int_0^{\sqrt{2}} g(\pi) \, d\pi,$$

which, for the specific curve (7.7), is

$$(7.21) \quad G = 2 \int_0^{\sqrt{2}} a\pi^\alpha (\sqrt{2} - \pi)^\beta \, d\pi = 2a(\sqrt{2})^{1+\alpha+\beta} B(1 + \alpha, 1 + \beta)$$

where $B(1 + \alpha, 1 + \beta)$ is again the Beta function. If $\hat{a}$, $\hat{\alpha}$, and $\hat{\beta}$ are consistent estimators of a, α, and β, respectively, the asymptotic variance of an estimator of the Gini index based on (7.21) will be[7]

$$\mathrm{Var}(G) = \left(\frac{\partial G}{\partial a}\right)^2 \mathrm{var}(\hat{a}) + \left(\frac{\partial G}{\partial \alpha}\right)^2 \mathrm{var}(\hat{\alpha}) + \left(\frac{\partial G}{\partial \beta}\right)^2 \mathrm{var}(\hat{\beta})$$

$$+ 2\left(\frac{\partial G}{\partial a}\right)\left(\frac{\partial G}{\partial \alpha}\right) \mathrm{cov}\,(\hat{a}, \hat{\alpha}) + 2\left(\frac{\partial G}{\partial a}\right)\left(\frac{\partial G}{\partial \beta}\right) \mathrm{cov}\,(\hat{a}, \hat{\beta})$$

$$(7.22) \qquad + 2\left(\frac{\partial G}{\partial \alpha}\right)\left(\frac{\partial G}{\partial \beta}\right) \mathrm{cov}\,(\hat{\alpha}, \hat{\beta})$$

where var and cov stand for variance and covariance, respectively. The partial derivative of G with respect to a is straightforward and given by

$$\frac{\partial G}{\partial a} = \frac{G}{a}.$$

In order to find the partial derivatives $\partial G/\partial \alpha$ and $\partial G/\partial \beta$, it is necessary to evaluate the partial derivatives of $B(1 + \alpha, 1 + \beta)$ with respect to α and β. The Beta function is given by

$$B(1 + \alpha, 1 + \beta) = \int_0^1 x^\alpha (1 - x)^\beta \, dx,$$

6. See lemma 5.4.
7. See Cramer (1969) and Kakwani and Podder (1973).

the partial derivative of which can be evaluated by differentiating under the integral sign:[8]

$$(7.23) \qquad \frac{\partial B(1 + \alpha, 1 + \beta)}{\partial \alpha} = \int_0^1 x^\alpha (1 - x)^\beta \log x \, dx.$$

The above integral can be evaluated by putting $r = 1$ in Formula 4.2531 of Gradsheteyn and Ryshik (1965). Thus (7.23) becomes

$$\frac{\partial B(1 + \alpha, 1 + \beta)}{\partial \alpha} = B(1 + \alpha, 1 + \beta)[\psi(1 + \alpha) - \psi(2 + \alpha + \beta)]$$

where $\psi(1 + \alpha)$ is Euler's psi function, which can be numerically computed by making use of the following relationship:[9]

$$\psi(1 + \alpha) - \psi(2 + \alpha + \beta) = \sum_{k=0}^{\infty} \left(\frac{1}{2 + \alpha + \beta + k} - \frac{1}{1 + \alpha + k} \right).$$

Thus

$$\frac{\partial G}{\partial \alpha} = [\log \sqrt{2} + \psi(1 + \alpha) - \psi(2 + \alpha + \beta)]G$$

$$\frac{\partial G}{\partial \beta} = [\log \sqrt{2} + \psi(1 + \beta) - \psi(2 + \alpha + \beta)]G.$$

By means of these partial derivatives in (7.22), the asymptotic variance of G can now be obtained from the estimated variances and covariances of the parameter estimates $\hat{a}$, $\hat{\alpha}$, and $\hat{\beta}$. The estimation of the variances and covariances of $\hat{a}$, $\hat{\alpha}$, and $\hat{\beta}$ is discussed in the following two sections of this chapter.

Now consider the estimation of the relative mean deviation (R), which was defined in (5.27). Lemma 5.9 demonstrates that R is equal to the maximum discrepancy between $F(x)$ and $F_1(x)$, which is equal to $\sqrt{2}$ times the maximum value of η. To obtain the maximum value of η, (7.7) must be differentiated with respect to π and equated to zero. Then, solving for π, the maximum value of η can be obtained from the equation of the Lorenz curve. If the equation

---

8. See Theorem 9.37 of Apostol (1958).
9. See Gradsheteyn and Ryshik (1965), p. 943.

of the Lorenz curve is (7.7), its derivative is

$$\frac{d\eta}{d\pi} = a\alpha\pi^{\alpha-1}(\sqrt{2} - \pi)^\beta - a\beta\pi^\alpha(\sqrt{2} - \pi)^{\beta-1} = 0.$$

Equating this to zero yields

$$\pi = \frac{\sqrt{2}\alpha}{\alpha + \beta},$$

and, therefore, the relative mean deviation will be

$$R = (\sqrt{2})^{1+\alpha+\beta} \frac{a\alpha^\alpha\beta^\beta}{(\alpha + \beta)^{\alpha+\beta}}.$$

Again, if the variances and covariances of $\hat{a}$, $\hat{\alpha}$, and $\hat{\beta}$ are known, it is possible to compute the asymptotic variance of T by means of an equation similar to (7.22) where

$$\frac{\partial R}{\partial a} = \frac{R}{a}$$

$$\frac{\partial R}{\partial \alpha} = R \log \frac{\sqrt{2}\alpha}{(\alpha + \beta)}$$

$$\frac{\partial R}{\partial \beta} = R \log \frac{\sqrt{2}\beta}{(\alpha + \beta)}.$$

Next consider the estimation of three inequality measures proposed by Elteto and Frigyes (1968), which have been discussed in chapter 5.

Equations (7.4) and (7.5) indicate that the value of η is maximum at $x = \mu$. Let η^* be the maximum value of η, and suppose that this maximum occurs at $\pi = \pi^*$. Then, (7.1) yields

$$F(\mu) = p_\mu = \frac{1}{\sqrt{2}} [\pi^* + \eta^*]$$

$$F_1(\mu) = L(p_\mu) = \frac{1}{\sqrt{2}} [\pi^* - \eta^*].$$

Substituting the values of p_μ and $L(p_\mu)$ into (5.32), the inequality measures u', v', and w' can be written as follows:

$$u' = \frac{2\eta^*}{\pi^* + \eta^*}$$

$$v' = 1 - \frac{(\sqrt{2} - \pi^* - \eta^*)}{(\sqrt{2} - \pi^* + \eta^*)} \frac{(\pi^* - \eta^*)}{(\pi^* + \eta^*)}$$

$$w' = 1 - \frac{(\sqrt{2} - \pi^* - \eta^*)}{(\sqrt{2} - \pi^* + \eta^*)} \, .$$

If the equation of the Lorenz curve is (7.7), π^* and η^* will be given by

$$\pi^* = \frac{\sqrt{2}\alpha}{(\alpha + \beta)} \quad \text{and} \quad \eta^* = (\sqrt{2})^{\alpha+\beta} \frac{a\alpha^\alpha\beta^\beta}{(\alpha + \beta)^{\alpha+\beta}} \, .$$

The asymptotic standard errors of these inequality measures can now be computed by using an equation similar to (7.22).

Furthermore, the estimated Lorenz curve (7.7), in conjunction with (7.1), can be used to compute any percentile of the distribution. To illustrate this point, the estimated shares of income going to the poorest and richest 5 and 10 percents have been computed in "Some Empirical Results," which follows. Jain (1975) employed equation (7.7) to compute the income shares of each decile of the population for about five hundred income distributions observed in seventy countries. A discussion of these results will be provided in chapter 16, where the international comparisons of income inequality and poverty will be made.

Finally, consider the estimation of inequality measures that, in the previous analysis, could not be obtained directly from the equation of the Lorenz curve. These measures could be written as[10]

$$\int_0^\infty v(x)f(x)\,dx$$

where $v(x)$ is a function of x. This integral for the Lorenz curve (7.2)

---

10. See equation (6.44) in chapter 6.

can be written as

$$\frac{1}{\sqrt{2}} \int_0^{\sqrt{2}} v \left[\frac{\mu \{1 - g'(\pi)\}}{\{1 + g'(\pi)\}} \right] [1 + g'(\pi)] d\pi$$

where use has been made of (7.16) and (7.17).

Estimation of the New Coordinate System from Grouped Observations

Consider a sample of N income units from a population with the probability density function $f(x)$. These N income units are grouped into $(T + 1)$ income classes, $(x_0$ to $x_1)$, $(x_1$ to $x_2)$, ..., $(x_T$ to $x_{T+1})$. If $f_t = n_t/N$ is the sample relative frequency of the tth income class, it can be seen that f_t is a consistent estimator of the probability ϕ_t of an income unit belonging to the tth class. Obviously, ϕ_t is given by

$$\phi_t = \int_{x_{t-1}}^{x_t} f(x) dx.$$

Denote $F(x_t)$ as the population distribution function, which is written as

$$F(x_t) = \int_0^{x_t} f(x) dx = \sum_{r=1}^{t} \phi_r.$$

Then the sample function

(7.24) $$p_t = \sum_{r=1}^{t} f_r$$

will clearly be a consistent estimator of $F(x_t)$.

Further, denote Q_t as the sample mean for the tth income class, which is a consistent estimator of the population mean μ_t. Then the population first-moment distribution function $F_1(x_t)$, given by

$$F_1(x_t) = \frac{1}{\mu} \int_0^{x_t} xf(x) dx = \frac{1}{\mu} \sum_{r=1}^{t} \phi_r \mu_r,$$

will have its consistent estimator

$$(7.25) \qquad q_t = \frac{1}{Q} \sum_{r=1}^{t} f_r Q_r$$

where $t = 1, 2, \ldots, T$ and $Q = \sum_{r=1}^{T+1} f_r Q_r$. The sample mean income is Q, and is obviously a consistent estimator of the population mean μ.

Now, by means of (7.1), the consistent estimators of π_t and η_t are

$$(7.26) \qquad z_t = \frac{p_t + q_t}{\sqrt{2}} \quad \text{and} \quad y_t = \frac{p_t - q_t}{\sqrt{2}},$$

respectively. Because the estimators z_t and y_t are consistent, they may be written as differing from π_t and η_t only by some random error terms. By means of (7.26), the equation of the Lorenz curve (7.7), in terms of the sample observations on z_t and y_t, can be written as

$$(7.27) \quad \log y_t = a' + \alpha \log z_t + \beta \log (\sqrt{2} - z_t) + w_{1t}$$

where $a' = \log a$ and w_{1t} is a random disturbance, which, in the following section, will be shown to be of order $N^{-1/2}$ in probability.

In what follows, it will be useful to write the above equation in vector and matrix notation as

$$(7.28) \qquad Y_1 = Z_1 \delta + W_1$$

where Y_1 is a $T \times 1$ vector of T observations on $\log y_t$, and Z_1 is a $T \times 3$ matrix of T observations on the right-hand side variables of (7.27). The first column of Z_1 consists of T unit elements. W_1 is the column vector of T observations on the disturbance term, and δ is the column vector consisting of three elements, a', α, and β. An estimator of δ will lead to the estimates of all the parameters of the Lorenz curve (7.7). The least-squares estimator of δ is

$$\hat{\delta} = (Z_1' Z_1)^{-1} Z_1' Y_1,$$

which will be referred to as Method I in subsequent discussions.

It will be shown in the next section that $\hat{\delta}$ is a consistent estimator of δ, and that its asymptotic variance-covariance matrix is given by[11]

$$\text{Var} (\hat{\delta}) = (Z_1' Z_1)^{-1} Z_1' \Omega_{11} Z_1 (Z_1' Z_1)^{-1}$$

---

11. See Goldberger (1964), Theil (1971), or Johnston (1963). This is, in fact, a well-known result in econometrics literature.

where

$$E(W_1 W_1') = \Omega_{11}$$

is the variance-covariance matrix of W_1. The asymptotically more efficient estimator of δ is, however,

$$\hat{\hat{\delta}} = (Z_1' \Omega_{11}^{-1} Z_1)^{-1} Z_1' \Omega_{11}^{-1} Y_1,$$

which can also be shown to be consistent. Its asymptotic variance-covariance matrix would be

$$\mathrm{Var}\ (\hat{\hat{\delta}}) = (Z_1' \Omega_{11}^{-1} Z_1)^{-1}.$$

Note that $\hat{\hat{\delta}}$ is the well-known generalized least-squares estimator of δ. This method of estimation will be referred to as Method II. Furthermore, information on income ranges is available for most income distributions that can be effectively utilized to improve the precision of the estimates. In this regard, consider (7.4), which for the Lorenz curve (7.7) can be written as

$$(7.29) \qquad \frac{(\mu - x_t)}{(\mu + x_t)} \frac{\pi_t(\sqrt{2} - \pi_t)}{\eta_t} = (\sqrt{2} - \pi_t)\alpha - \pi_t\beta.$$

Substituting the estimates of π_t, η_t, and μ, the above equation becomes

$$(7.30) \qquad \frac{(Q - x_t)}{(Q + x_t)} \frac{z_t(\sqrt{2} - z_t)}{y_t} = (\sqrt{2} - z_t)\alpha - z_t\beta + w_{2t}$$

where w_{2t} is the random error that will be shown to be of order $N^{-1/2}$ in probability.

From (7.27) and (7.30), eliminate β, and estimate a' and α from the resulting equation by the ordinary least-squares method (Method I), or the generalized least-squares method (Method II). Similarly, after eliminating α from (7.27) and (7.30), estimate β from the resulting equation. In this way, the extra information on income ranges is being utilized and, therefore, should lead to more efficient estimators of the parameters. One problem still remains, however; this procedure does not provide the covariance of the estimators of α and β that is required for computing the standard errors of the inequality measures. Alternatively, equations (7.27) and (7.30) can be combined, and a', α, and β estimated from the combined equation. This procedure is similar to the one suggested by Theil (1963) in connection with mixed estimation, and by Zellner (1962) in connection with seemingly unrelated regressions. To demonstrate this, write (7.30) in vector and matrix notation as

(7.31) $$Y_2 = Z_2\delta + W_2$$

where Y_2 is the column vector of T observations on the left-hand, dependent variable in (7.30), Z_2 the $T \times 3$ matrix, the first column of which consists of zeros, and the second and third columns of which consist of T observations on the right-hand, explanatory variables $(\sqrt{2} - z_t)$ and $-z_t$, respectively. The vector of stochastic disturbances is W_2.

Equations (7.28) and (7.31) can now be combined as

(7.32) $$Y = Z\delta + W$$

where

$$Y = \begin{bmatrix} Y_1 \\ Y_2 \end{bmatrix}, \quad Z = \begin{bmatrix} Z_1 \\ Z_2 \end{bmatrix}, \quad \text{and} \quad W = \begin{bmatrix} W_1 \\ W_2 \end{bmatrix},$$

W being the vector of $2T$ disturbances with zero mean and covariance matrix as

$$EWW' = \Omega = \begin{bmatrix} \Omega_{11} & \Omega_{12} \\ \Omega_{21} & \Omega_{22} \end{bmatrix},$$

The coefficient vector δ can now be estimated from (7.32) by direct least-squares:

$$\hat{\delta}^* = (Z'Z)^{-1}Z'Y,$$

the variance-covariance matrix of which will be

$$\text{Var}(\hat{\delta}^*) = (Z'Z)^{-1}Z'\Omega Z(Z'Z)^{-1}.$$

This method will be referred to as Method III. The asymptotically most efficient estimator of δ will, however, be

$$\hat{\hat{\delta}}^* = (Z'\Omega^{-1}Z)^{-1}Z'\Omega^{-1}Y,$$

with its asymptotic variance-covariance matrix

$$\text{var}(\hat{\hat{\delta}}^*) = (Z'\Omega^{-1}Z)^{-1}.$$

The estimator $\hat{\hat{\delta}}^*$ will be referred to as Method IV.

It still remains to be shown that $\hat{\hat{\delta}}^*$ is more efficient than $\hat{\delta}$. To demonstrate this, write[12]

$$(7.33) \qquad \Omega^{-1} = \begin{bmatrix} \Omega_{11}^* & \Omega_{12}^* \\ \Omega_{21}^* & \Omega_{22}^* \end{bmatrix}$$

where

$$\Omega_{11}^* = \Omega_{11}^{-1}(I + \Omega_{12}\Omega_{22}^*\Omega_{21}\Omega_{11}^{-1})$$
$$\Omega_{12}^* = -\Omega_{11}^{-1}\Omega_{12}\Omega_{22}^*$$
$$\Omega_{22}^* = [\Omega_{22} - \Omega_{21}\Omega_{11}^{-1}\Omega_{12}]^{-1}.$$

Now write

$$(Z'\Omega^{-1}Z) = Z_1'\Omega_{11}^*Z_1 + 2Z_1'\Omega_{12}^*Z_2 + Z_2'\Omega_{22}^*Z_2,$$

which, by means of (7.33), simplifies to

$$(Z'\Omega^{-1}Z) = (Z_1'\Omega_{11}^{-1}Z_1) + [\Omega_{21}\Omega_{11}^{-1}Z_1 - Z_2]'\Omega_{22}^*[\Omega_{21}\Omega_{11}^{-1}Z_1 - Z_2].$$

The second term in the right-hand side of this expression is, of course, nonnegative definite, which implies that[13]

$$(Z_1'\Omega_{11}^{-1}Z_1)^{-1} - (Z'\Omega^{-1}Z)^{-1}$$

is nonnegative definite. Thus, the estimator $\hat{\delta}^*$ is asymptotically more efficient than $\hat{\delta}$.

The derivation of the consistent estimator of the covariance matrix Ω is discussed in the following section.

Standard Errors of the Estimates

The standard errors of the estimators discussed in the preceding section can be obtained only if a consistent estimator of the co-variance matrix Ω can be found. In order to find such an estimator, it must be assumed that the absolute frequencies $(n_1, n_2, \ldots, n_{T+1})$ follow a multinomial distribution, so that the means, variances, and

12. See Goldberger (1964), p. 38.
13. Ibid.

covariances of the relative frequencies are given by[14]

$$E(f_t) = \phi_t, \quad \text{var } (f_t) = \frac{1}{N} \phi_t(1 - \phi_t)$$

and

$$E(f_t f'_t) = - \frac{1}{N} \phi_t \phi'_t \quad \text{if } t \neq t'$$

where $t = 1, 2, \ldots, T + 1$. One can always write

(7.34) $$f = \phi + \epsilon$$

where $f' = (f_1, f_2, \ldots, f_{T+1})$, $\phi' = (\phi_1, \phi_2, \ldots, \phi_{T+1})$, and $\epsilon' = (\epsilon_1, \epsilon_2, \ldots, \epsilon_{T+1})$ is a disturbance vector such that

(7.35) $$E(\epsilon) = 0, \quad \text{and} \quad E(\epsilon\epsilon') = \frac{1}{N} \Sigma,$$

Σ being the $(T + 1) \times (T + 1)$ matrix given by

$$\Sigma = \begin{bmatrix} \phi_1 & 0 \cdots\cdots\cdots\cdots\cdots 0 \\ \cdot & & \cdot \\ \cdot & & \cdot \\ \cdot & & \cdot \\ 0 & 0 \cdots\cdots\cdots\cdots\cdots \phi_{T+1} \end{bmatrix} - \phi\phi'.$$

Using (7.24) and (7.34) yields

(7.36) $$p_t = \sum_{r=1}^{t} \phi_r + \sum_{r=1}^{t} \epsilon_r = F(x_t) + u_t$$

where $$F(x_t) = \sum_{r=1}^{t} \phi_r, \quad \text{and} \quad u_t = \sum_{r=1}^{t} \epsilon_r.$$

Expression (7.36) can also be written in vector notations as

$$p = F + u$$

---

14. See Aigner and Goldberger (1970), and Kakwani and Podder (1973).

where

$$p = \begin{bmatrix} p_1 \\ p_2 \\ \cdot \\ \cdot \\ \cdot \\ p_T \end{bmatrix}, \quad F = \begin{bmatrix} F(x_1) \\ F(x_2) \\ \cdot \\ \cdot \\ \cdot \\ F(x_T) \end{bmatrix}, \quad \text{and} \quad u = A\epsilon,$$

A being the $T \times (T + 1)$ matrix of constants as given by[15]

$$A = \begin{bmatrix} 1 & 0 & 0 \cdots\cdots\cdots 0 & 0 \\ 1 & 1 & 0 \cdots\cdots\cdots 0 & 0 \\ 1 & 1 & 1 \cdots\cdots\cdots 0 & 0 \\ \vdots & & \vdots & \vdots \\ \cdot & & \cdot & \cdot \\ \vdots & & \vdots & \vdots \\ \vdots & & \vdots & \vdots \\ 1 & 1 & 1 \cdots\cdots\cdots 1 & 0 \end{bmatrix}.$$

It is now assumed that the total number of income classes is so large that the population mean income in any income class μ_t is approximately equal to its sample estimate Q_t for all $t = 1, 2, \ldots, T + 1$. Under this assumption the sample mean is given by

$$(7.37) \qquad\qquad Q = \mu + \ell$$

where $\mu^{*'} = (\mu_1, \mu_2, \ldots, \mu_{T+1})$ and $\ell = \mu^{*'}\epsilon$. Substituting (7.34) and (7.37) into (7.25) yields

$$(7.38) \qquad q_t = F_1(x_t) + v_t - \frac{F_1(x_t)\cdot\ell}{\mu} + O_p\left(\frac{1}{N}\right)$$

where $v_t = 1/\mu \sum_{r=1}^{t} \mu_r\epsilon_r$, and $O_p(1/N)$ includes all the remainder terms that are of order $1/N$ or less in probability.[16]

---

15. See Kakwani and Podder (1973).

16. The order of a term in probability is a widely used concept in econometric literature. For details, see Mann and Wald (1943), Dhrymes (1970), and Theil (1971).

Let v be a column vector of T elements $v_1, v_2, \ldots, v_T$; then

$$v = \frac{1}{\mu} M \epsilon$$

where

$$M = \begin{bmatrix} \mu_1 & 0 & 0 \cdots\cdots 0 & 0 \\ \mu_1 & \mu_2 & 0 \cdots\cdots 0 & 0 \\ \vdots & & & \vdots \\ \vdots & & & \vdots \\ \vdots & & & \vdots \\ \mu_1 & \mu_2 & \mu_3 \cdots\cdots \mu_T & 0 \end{bmatrix}$$

is of order $T \times (T + 1)$. Substituting (7.36) and (7.38) into (7.26) and using (7.1) yields

$$y_t = \eta_t + \frac{1}{\sqrt{2}} \left(u_t - v_t + \frac{F_{1t}\ell}{\mu} \right) + O_p\left(\frac{1}{N}\right),$$

$$z_t = \pi_t + \frac{1}{\sqrt{2}} \left(u_t + v_t - \frac{F_{1t}\ell}{\mu} \right) + O_p\left(\frac{1}{N}\right).$$

If these equations are substituted into (7.7), the equation of the Lorenz curve becomes

(7.39) $\log y_t = a' + \alpha \log z_t + \beta \log (\sqrt{2} - z_t) + w_{1t}$

where

(7.40) $w_{1t} = k_{1t}u_t + k_{2t}v_t + k_{3t}\dfrac{\ell}{\mu},$

$$k_{1t} = \frac{1}{\sqrt{2}\eta_t} + \frac{\beta}{\sqrt{2}(\sqrt{2} - \pi_t)} - \frac{1}{\sqrt{2}}\frac{\alpha}{\pi_t},$$

$$k_{2t} = \frac{\beta}{\sqrt{2}(\sqrt{2} - \pi_t)} - \frac{\alpha}{\sqrt{2}\pi_t} - \frac{1}{\sqrt{2}\eta_t},$$

and

$$k_{3t} = \left[\frac{1}{\sqrt{2}\eta_t} - \frac{\beta}{\sqrt{2}(\sqrt{2} - \pi_t)} + \frac{\alpha}{\sqrt{2}\pi_t} \right] F_{1t}.$$

Note that u_t, v_t, and ℓ are random variables with zero mean and variance of order $1/N$. It follows that w_{1t}, which is a linear homogeneous function of u_t, v_t, and ℓ, would be of order $N^{-1/2}$ in probability. The remaining terms in (7.39), which are of order $1/N$ or less in probability, have been neglected. The asymptotic properties of linear estimators will not, therefore, be affected.[17]

Equation (7.40) can be written in matrix notations as

$$W_1 = K_1 A \epsilon + \frac{1}{\mu} K_2 M \epsilon + \frac{1}{\mu} K_3 l \mu^{*\prime} \epsilon$$

where

$$K_j = \begin{bmatrix} K_{j1} & 0 \cdots\cdots 0 \\ \vdots & \vdots \\ \vdots & \vdots \\ \vdots & \vdots \\ 0 & 0 \cdots\cdots K_{jT} \end{bmatrix}.$$

Note that $j = 1, 2, 3$, and l is the $T \times 1$ vector of unit elements. The variance-covariance matrix of W_1 will be

$$EW_1 W_1' = \Omega_{11} = \frac{1}{N} K \Sigma K'$$

where

$$K = K_1 A + \frac{1}{\mu} K_2 M + \frac{1}{\mu} K_3 l \mu_*',$$

and use has been made of (7.35).

Now Ω_{11} can be estimated by means of the estimates of α and β obtained by the least-squares procedure. The consistent estimators of η_t and π_t respectively are, of course, y_t and z_t, and q_{1t} is the consistent estimator of F_{1t}. Furthermore, the covariances between the explanatory variables in (7.39) and the error term w_{1t} are of the order $1/N$ in probability, which vanish asymptotically. Thus, the estimators of a', α, and β, discussed in the preceding section, will be consistent.

Following exactly the same procedure as above for (7.30), one

17. See Aigner and Goldberger (1970), Zellner and Lee (1965), and Kakwani and Podder (1973).

can write

$$w_{2t} = L_{1t}u_t + L_{2t}v_t + L_{3t}\frac{\ell}{\mu}$$

where

$$L_{1t} = \frac{1}{\sqrt{2}}(\alpha + \beta) - \frac{1}{\sqrt{2}}\frac{(\mu - x_t)}{\mu + x_t}\frac{\pi_t(\sqrt{2} - \pi_t)}{\eta_t^2} + \frac{(\mu - x_t)}{(\mu + x_t)}\frac{(1 - \sqrt{2}\pi_t)}{\eta_t}$$

$$L_{2t} = \frac{1}{\sqrt{2}}(\alpha + \beta) + \frac{1}{\sqrt{2}}\frac{(\mu - x_t)}{(\mu + x_t)}\frac{\pi_t(\sqrt{2} - \pi_t)}{\eta_t^2} + \frac{(\mu - x_t)}{(\mu + x_t)}\frac{(1 - \sqrt{2}\pi_t)}{\eta_t}$$

$$L_{3t} = -\frac{1}{\sqrt{2}}(\alpha + \beta)F_{1t} - \frac{1}{\sqrt{2}}\frac{(\mu - x_t)}{(\mu + x_t)}\frac{\pi_t(\sqrt{2} - \pi_t)}{\eta_t^2}F_{1t}$$

$$- \frac{(\mu - x_t)}{(\mu + x_t)}\frac{(1 - \sqrt{2}\pi_t)}{\eta_t}F_{1t} + \frac{2x_t}{(\mu + x_t)^2}\frac{\pi_t(\sqrt{2} - \pi_t)}{\eta_t}\mu.$$

In the matrix notation the above equation becomes

$$W_2 = L_1 A\epsilon + \frac{1}{\mu}L_2 M\epsilon + \frac{1}{\mu}L_3 l\mu^{*'}\epsilon$$

where

$$L_j = \begin{bmatrix} L_{j1} & 0\cdots\cdots\cdots 0 \\ \cdot & & \cdot \\ \vdots & & \vdots \\ \vdots & & \vdots \\ \vdots & & \vdots \\ 0 & 0\cdots\cdots\cdots L_{jT} \end{bmatrix}.$$

The variance-covariance of W_2 will therefore be

(7.41) $$E(W_2 W_2') = \Omega_{22} = \frac{1}{N}L\Sigma L'$$

where

$$L = L_1 A + \frac{1}{\mu}L_2 M + \frac{1}{\mu}L_3 l\mu^*.$$

Similarly, the covariance of w_1 and w_2 is

$$(7.42) \qquad E(W_1 W_2') = \Omega_{12} = \frac{1}{N} K \, \Sigma \, L'.$$

Equations (7.41) and (7.42) can be used to estimate Ω_{11} and Ω_{12}. A numerical illustration of these estimates is provided in the following section.

Some Empirical Results

In this section results of the estimation of the Lorenz curve and associated inequality measures are presented. The data used for this purpose are, again, from *The Australian Survey of Consumer Expenditures and Finances*, 1966–68 (Drane and others), the nature of which was briefly discussed in chapter 5. The first of the two stages of the survey, consisting of 5,443 observations provides the data referred to here. The income considered is net of taxes but does not include imputed rent from owner-occupied houses. In addition, individual income figures made it possible to compute the actual values of the Gini index and other measures, which were useful in judging the accuracy of the new coordinate system discussed in this chapter. Income data in group form are presented in table 7.1.

In this table, the first three columns represent grades of income, number of families in each income range, and mean income within each income range, respectively. Columns four and five present a cumulative proportion of families (p) and a cumulative proportion of income received (q), respectively. In columns six and seven, z and y were calculated from columns four and five on the basis of formulas given in (7.26).

Table 7.2 presents the estimated parameters of the Lorenz curve (7.7), along with the different inequality measures. The equation was estimated by means of the four alternative methods of estimation discussed above. The last row in the table presents the actual values of the inequality measures computed on the basis of individual observations. The inequality measures computed by all four methods are very close to the actual values, and their standard errors are generally low. Method IV provides the best results because the standard errors are the lowest, and the estimated inequality measures are closest to their actual values.

Table 7.1. *Income Distribution Data, Australia, 1966–67*

Income range (Australian dollars)	Number of families	Mean income (Australian dollars)	p	q	z	y
Below 1,000	310	674.39	0.05698	0.009274	0.046849	0.03373
1,000–1,999	552	1,426.10	0.15846	0.044193	0.143297	0.080799
2,000–2,999	1,007	2,545.79	0.34357	0.157912	0.354601	0.131280
3,000–3,999	1,193	3,469.35	0.56287	0.341510	0.639493	0.156525
4,000–4,999	884	4,470.33	0.72536	0.516805	0.878343	0.147471
5,000–5,999	608	5,446.60	0.83713	0.663701	1.061248	0.122633
6,000–6,999	314	6,460.93	0.89485	0.753693	1.165696	0.099813
7,000–7,999	222	7,459.14	0.93566	0.827147	1.246493	0.076730
8,000–8,999	128	8,456.66	0.95919	0.875164	1.297084	0.059415
9,000–10,999	112	9,788.38	0.97978	0.923794	1.346030	0.039588
Over 11,000	110	15,617.69	1.00000	1.000000	1.414213	0.0

Table 7.2. *Results of Different Methods of Estimation*

Method of estimation	Coefficient estimates		Inequality measures				
			G	R	u'	v'	w'
I	$\alpha =$ 0.7542 (0.0061) $\beta =$ 0.8042 (0.0072) $a =$ 0.2728 (0.0156)		0.3203 (0.0041)	0.2250 (0.0081)	0.3772 (0.0051)	0.6002 (0.0015)	0.3579 (0.0048)
II	$\alpha =$ 0.7535 (0.0059) $\beta =$ 0.8029 (0.0067) $a =$ 0.2730 (0.0132)		0.3208 (0.0039)	0.2252 (0.0070)	0.3774 (0.0043)	0.6004 (0.0013)	0.3583 (0.0038)
III	$\alpha =$ 0.7615 (0.0042) $\beta =$ 0.8061 (0.0058) $a =$ 0.2744 (0.0121)		0.3206 (0.0038)	0.2255 (0.0022)	0.3767 (0.0041)	0.6009 (0.0009)	0.3596 (0.0037)
IV	$\alpha =$ 0.7611 (0.0009) $\beta =$ 0.8049 (0.0020) $a =$ 0.2732 (0.0091)		0.3195 (0.0008)	0.2246 (0.0018)	0.3753 (0.0009)	0.5993 (0.0008)	0.3583 (0.0029)
Inequality measures calculated from individual observations			0.3196	0.2219	0.3750	0.5951	0.3521

Note: The figures in parentheses are the asymptotic standard errors.

Next, the upper and lower bounds on the Gini index proposed by Gastwirth (1972) are computed. (The derivation of the bounds has been discussed in chapter 6.) In the present case the lower and upper bounds were computed at 0.313 and 0.322, respectively. The Gini index computed in table 7.2 lies within these bounds for all four methods of estimation. Thus, the goodness-of-fit test criterion proposed by Gastwirth and Smith (1972) is satisfied for the density function fitted here.

The equation of the curve (7.7) was also fitted to twenty income groups considered earlier by Kakwani and Podder (1973), using Method I of estimation. The G and R have been computed at 0.320

Table 7.3. *Actual and Estimated* y

Actual	Methods of estimation			
y	I	II	III	IV
0.0337	0.0349	0.0349	0.0343	0.0342
0.0808	0.0764	0.0766	0.0758	0.0755
0.1313	0.1307	0.1310	0.1306	0.1300
0.1565	0.1586	0.1588	0.1589	0.1583
0.1475	0.1498	0.1500	0.1503	0.1498
0.1226	0.1235	0.1237	0.1240	0.1236
0.0998	0.0999	0.1002	0.1004	0.1001
0.0767	0.0766	0.0769	0.0769	0.0768
0.0594	0.0592	0.0593	0.0594	0.0593
0.0396	0.0394	0.0395	0.0395	0.0395

and 0.224, respectively. These results clearly show that increasing the number of income groups from eleven to twenty improves the accuracy of the technique.

Table 7.3 presents the actual and estimated values of y by means of different methods of estimation. Clearly, the estimated values of y for all four methods are very close to the actual values. Because the graphical representations of the estimated Lorenz curves could not be visually distinguished, it was not considered worthwhile to present them here.

To obtain the estimated frequency distribution of income, it is necessary to obtain the values of π for given values of x from the following nonlinear equation:

$$(7.43) \qquad a\alpha\pi^{\alpha-1}(\sqrt{2} - \pi)^{\beta} - \beta a\pi^{\alpha}(\sqrt{2} - \pi)^{\beta-1} = \frac{\mu - x}{\mu + x}$$

where the estimates of a, α, and β are given in table 7.2. The Newton-Raphson method was used to compute π for given values of x.[18] The estimated frequency distribution for the family income thus obtained is given in table 7.4. It can be concluded from this table that the density function underlying the Lorenz curve (7.5) provides a reasonably good fit to the whole range of observed income distribution.

18. See Henrici (1967).

Table 7.4. *Actual and Estimated Frequency Distributions of Family Income*

Income range (Australian dollars)	Relative frequency		Mean income	
	Actual	Estimated	Actual (Australian dollars)	Estimated (Australian dollars)
Under 1000	0.0569	0.0403	674.39	380.47
1,000– 1,999	0.1015	0.1188	1,426.10	1,583.66
2,000– 2,999	0.1851	0.2089	2,545.79	2,515.38
3,000– 3,999	0.2193	0.2029	3,469.35	3,482.29
4,000– 4,999	0.1625	0.1527	4,470.33	4,469.68
5,000– 5,999	0.1118	0.1033	5,446.60	5,463.85
6,000– 6,999	0.0577	0.0661	6,460.93	6,451.13
7,000– 7,999	0.0408	0.0406	7,459.14	7,471.49
8,000– 8,999	0.0235	0.0245	8,456.66	8,440.27
9,000–10,999	0.0206	0.0236	9,788.38	9,868.39
Over 11,000	0.0203	0.0183	15,617.69	15,964.67

Table 7.5. *Shares of Incomes: The Poorest and Richest Five and Ten Percents*

Shares of income	Estimated from eleven groups	Estimated from twenty groups	Actual from individual observations
Poorest 5 percent	0.5857	0.623	0.767
Poorest 10 percent	2.260	2.314	2.132
Richest 5 percent	14.200	14.380	14.424
Richest 10 percent	23.600	23.780	23.757

The estimated shares of incomes going to the poorest and richest 5 and 10 percents are presented in table 7.5. The table clearly indicates that the estimated income shares are quite close to the actual shares, based on individual observations. The twenty income groups again provide more accurate results than the eleven groups.

CHAPTER 8

The Generalization of the
Lorenz Curve

IN MANY AREAS OF ECONOMICS, relations among the distributions of
different economic variables must be analyzed. For example, economic theory suggests a relation between total family expenditure
and income. It is important, therefore, to know under what conditions total expenditure is more equally distributed than income,
especially because expenditure is considered a better indicator of
the actual economic position of a family than its current income.

The Lorenz curve technique can be effectively used to solve this
problem. Mahalnobis (1960) proposed to extend and generalize the
concept of the Lorenz curve to deal with problems of consumer
behavior patterns with respect to different commodities. He suggested that generalized Lorenz curves be called concentration curves,[1]
and, in fact, used them as a convenient graphical device to describe
consumption patterns for different commodities based on data from
the *National Sample Survey of India*.

Kakwani (1977c) provided, however, a more general and rigorous
treatment of concentration curves in a study of the relationships
among the distributions of different economic variables. For example, certain theorems that provide the conditions under which the
variable y will be Lorenz superior (or inferior) to the variable x have
been proven. These theorems have many applications in economics,
particularly in the field of public finance where the effect of taxation
and public spending on income distribution is analyzed. Other areas
in which these theorems can be applied are inflation as it affects

1. The Lorenz curve is a special case of such curves, namely, concentration
curves for income.

income distribution, estimation of Engel elasticities, disaggregation of total inequality by factor components, and economic growth and income distribution.

This chapter provides a detailed discussion of concentration curves and related theorems. Some of the applications of the theorems are discussed in this chapter; others will be considered in detail in subsequent chapters.

Derivation of Concentration Curves

Suppose income X is a random variable with probability density function $f(X)$ and distribution function $F(X)$, the proportion of units having an income less than or equal to x being $F(x)$. Let $g(X)$ be a continuous function of X so that its first derivative exists, and $g(X) \geq 0$ for all $X \geq 0$. If $E[g(X)]$ exists, it follows that

$$(8.1) \qquad F_1[g(x)] = \frac{1}{E[g(X)]} \int_0^x g(X)f(X)\,dX$$

can be defined where

$$E[g(X)] = \int_0^\infty g(X)f(X)\,dX,$$

so that

$$(8.2) \qquad \lim_{x \to 0} F_1[g(x)] = 0$$

$$(8.3) \qquad \lim_{x \to \infty} F_1[g(x)] = 1.$$

The relationship between $F_1[g(x)]$ and $F(x)$ will be called the concentration curve of the function $g(x)$. The curve is obtained by inverting the functions $F_1[g(x)]$ and $F(x)$ and eliminating x if the functions are invertible. Alternatively, the curve can be plotted by generating the values of $F(x)$ and $F_1[g(x)]$ by giving some arbitrary values to x. Like the Lorenz curve, this curve is represented in a unit square. The ordinate and abscissa of the curve are $F_1[g(x)]$ and $F(x)$, respectively. Equations (8.2) and (8.3) imply that the curve passes through $(0, 0)$ and $(1, 1)$.

If $f(X)$ is continuous, the derivative of $F_1[g(x)]$ with respect to x exists and is given by

$$(8.4) \qquad \frac{dF_1[g(x)]}{dx} = \frac{g(x)f(x)}{E[g(X)]} \geq 0,$$

which implies that $F_1[g(x)]$ is a monotonic nondecreasing function of x.

By means of (2.2) and (8.4) the slope of the concentration curve is

$$(8.5) \qquad \frac{dF_1[g(x)]}{dF(x)} = \frac{g(x)}{E[g(X)]},$$

which is obviously nonnegative. If it is assumed that $g(x) > 0$ for all $x > 0$, (8.5) implies that the concentration curve is monotonically increasing.

The second derivative of the concentration curve is

$$(8.6) \qquad \frac{d^2F_1[g(x)]}{dF^2(x)} = \frac{g'(x)}{E[g(X)]} \cdot \frac{1}{f(x)},$$

which may be positive or negative depending on the sign of $g'(x)$. Clearly, if $g'(x) > 0$ for all $x \geq 0$, the concentration curve is convex to the F axis, which implies that $F_1[g(x)] < F(x)$ for all x. In this case, the concentration curve falls below the egalitarian line. If $g'(x) < 0$, the concentration curve is concave to the F-axis and $F_1[g(x)] > F(x)$, which implies that the curve lies above the egalitarian line. If, however, $g'(x) = 0$ for all x, the concentration curve coincides with the egalitarian line.

It can be seen that the Lorenz curve of income x is a special case of the concentration curve for the function $g(x)$ when $g(x) = x$.

The relationship between $F_1[g(x)]$ and $F_1(x)$ will be called the relative concentration curve of $g(x)$ with respect to x. Similarly, let $g^*(x)$ be another continuous function of x; then the graph of $F_1[g(x)]$ versus $F_1[g^*(x)]$ will be called the relative concentration curve of $g(x)$ with respect to $g^*(x)$.

The Concentration Curve for Several Well-Known Income Distributions

First consider the Pareto distribution whose probability distribution function is given by (see (2.3))

$$(8.7) \qquad F(x) = 1 - \left(\frac{x}{x_0}\right)^{-\alpha} \quad \text{when} \quad x \geq x_0.$$

If it is assumed that

$$(8.8) \qquad g(x) = Ax^\eta,$$

then

$$(8.9) \qquad F_1[g(x)] = \frac{1}{E[g(X)]} \int_0^x A\alpha x_0^\alpha X^{\eta-\alpha-1} dX$$

where use has been made of the Pareto density function $f(x)$ as given in (2.4). Equation (8.9) is evaluated as

$$(8.10) \qquad F_1[g(x)] = \frac{A\alpha x_0^\eta}{E[g(X)](\alpha - \eta)} \left[1 - \left(\frac{x_0}{x} \right)^{\alpha-\eta} \right].$$

In this equation $F_1[g(x)]$ should approach unity as x approaches infinity. It can be seen that this limit exists only if $\alpha > \eta$, which, if satisfied, yields

$$(8.11) \qquad E[g(X)] = \frac{A\alpha x_0^\eta}{(\alpha - \eta)}.$$

Now, eliminating x from (8.7) and (8.10), and using (8.11), yields

$$(8.12) \qquad 1 - F_1[g(x)] = [1 - F(x)]^{(\alpha-\eta)/\alpha},$$

which is the equation of the concentration curve for the function $g(x)$ defined in (8.8).[2] When $\eta = 1$, (8.12) reduces to the equation of the Lorenz curve for the Pareto distribution as derived in (3.12). Note that the concentration curve (8.12) is defined if, and only if, $\eta < \alpha$.

Next, the concentration curve for the lognormal distribution defined in (2.26) can be derived. Again, if the probability distribution of the lognormal distribution is denoted as

$$(8.13) \qquad F(x) = \Lambda(x \mid \mu, \sigma^2)$$

where $\Lambda(x \mid \mu, \sigma^2)$ has been defined in (3.18), then

$$F_1[g(x)] = \frac{1}{E[g(X)]} \int_0^x A X^\eta d\Lambda(X \mid \mu, \sigma^2),$$

which, by means of (3.18), simplifies to

$$(8.14) \qquad F_1[g(x)] = \Lambda(x \mid \mu + \eta\sigma^2, \sigma^2).$$

By means of the definition of the function $\phi(t)$ given in (3.20),

---

2. This result was derived by Roy, Chakravarty, and Laha (1959).

(8.13) and (8.14) can be written as

$$\frac{\log x - \mu}{\sigma} = \phi[F(x)]$$

and

$$\frac{\log x - \mu - \eta\sigma^2}{\sigma} = \phi[F_1\{g(x)\}],$$

respectively. Eliminating $\log x$ from these equations yields the equation of the concentration curve as[3]

(8.15) $$\phi[F_1\{g(x)\}] = \phi[F(x)] - \eta\sigma,$$

which depends only on the parameters, σ and η. If $\eta = 1$ is substituted into (8.15), the equation of the Lorenz curve for the log-normal distribution as given in (3.23) is obtained.

Some Useful Theorems

Let $\eta_g(x)$ be the elasticity of $g(x)$ with respect to x; then

(8.16) $$\eta_g(x) = \frac{g'(x)x}{g(x)}$$

where $g'(x)$ is the first derivative of $g(x)$. Similarly, denote $\eta_{g^*}(x)$ as the elasticity of $g^*(x)$ with respect to x. Then the following theorem, which has a wide range of economic applications, can be stated.[4]

THEOREM 8.1. *The concentration curve for the function $g(x)$ will lie above (below) the concentration curve for the function $g^*(x)$ if, and only if, $\eta_g(x)$ is less (greater) than $\eta_{g^*}(x)$ for all $x \geq 0$.*

Proof. By means of (8.5), the slope of the relative concentration curve of $g(x)$ with respect to $g^*(x)$ is

(8.17) $$\frac{dF_1[g(x)]}{dF_1[g^*(x)]} = \frac{E[g^*(X)]}{E[g(X)]} \frac{g(x)}{g^*(x)},$$

---

3. This result was derived by Iyenger (1960).
4. For this and subsequent theorems in this chapter, see Kakwani (1977c).

which implies that the relative concentration curve is monotonic increasing. Because the curve must pass through $(0, 0)$ and $(1, 1)$, a sufficient condition for $F_1[g(x)]$ to be greater (less) than $F_1[g^*(x)]$ is that the curve be convex (concave) from above. To establish the curvature, the second derivative of $F_1[g(x)]$ with respect to $F_1[g^*(x)]$ is obtained as

$$(8.18) \qquad \frac{d^2 F_1[g(x)]}{dF_1^2[g^*(x)]} = \frac{(E[g^*(X)])^2}{E[g(X)]} \frac{g(x)}{g^{*2}(x)} \frac{[\eta_g - \eta_{g^*}]}{xf(x)}$$

where use has been made of (8.6) and (8.16). The sign of the second derivative is given by $\eta_g(x) - \eta_{g^*}(x)$. Thus, the second derivative is positive (negative) if $\eta_g(x)$ is greater (less) than $\eta_{g^*}(x)$ for all x. The concentration curve for $g(x)$ lies, therefore, above (below) the concentration curve for $g^*(x)$ if $\eta_g(x)$ is less (greater) than $\eta_{g^*}(x)$ for all $x \geq 0$. This proves the sufficient condition. The necessary condition follows immediately from equation (8.18), and this completes the proof of the theorem.

Let $g^*(x)$ = the constant for $x \geq 0$; then the elasticity $\eta_{g^*}(x) = 0$ and $F_1[g^*(x)] = F(x)$, which is the equation of the egalitarian line. This leads to the following corollary.

COROLLARY 8.1.   *The concentration curve for the function $g(x)$ will be above (below) the egalitarian line if, and only if, $\eta_g(x)$ is less (greater) than zero for all $x \geq 0$.*

(The proof of corollary 8.1 is also given by Roy, Chakravarty, and Laha (1959).

Next, assume that $g^*(x) = x$ so that $\eta_{g^*}(x) = 1$, and the concentration curve for $g^*(x)$ is now the Lorenz curve for x. It follows from corollary 8.1 that the Lorenz curve for x lies below the egalitarian line, and that, therefore, the curve is concave from above. Further, corollary 8.2 follows from theorem 8.1.

COROLLARY 8.2.   *The concentration curve for the function $g(x)$ lies above (below) the Lorenz curve for the distribution of x if, and only if, $\eta_g(x)$ is less (greater) than unity for all $x \geq 0$.*

If the function $g(x)$ has unit elasticity for all $x \geq 0$, the second derivative of the relative concentration curve of $g(x)$ with respect to x will be zero, which implies that the slope of the relative concentration curve will be constant for all values of x. Because the curve must pass through $(0, 0)$ and $(1, 1)$, the relative concentration curve of $g(x)$ with respect to x coincides with the egalitarian line. Thus, $F_1[g(x)] = F_1(x)$ for all $x \geq 0$. Similarly, if $F_1[g(x)] = F_1(x)$, the slope of the relative concentration will be constant, which, from (8.17), implies that $g(x)/x$ is constant for all x. This gives $\eta_g(x)$ as unity for all x, and proves the following corollary.

COROLLARY 8.3.   *The concentration curve for $g(x)$ coincides with the Lorenz curve for x if, and only if, $\eta_g(x)$ is unity for all $x \geq 0$.*

Note that the concentration curve for $g(x)$ is not the same as the Lorenz curve for $g(x)$. Now consider the condition under which both are identical.

Let $Y = g(X)$ be a random variable with the probability density function $f^*(Y)$ and the distribution function $F^*(Y)$; if the mean of Y exists, the first-moment distribution function of Y is given by

$$(8.19) \qquad F_1^*(y) = \frac{1}{E(Y)} \int_0^y Y f^*(Y) dY.$$

Then $[F^*(y), F_1^*(y)]$ is a point on the Lorenz curve for $g(x)$. The following theorem gives the conditions under which

$$F^*[g(x)] = F(x)$$
$$(8.20) \qquad F_1^*[g(x)] = F_1[g(x)]$$

for all values of x.

THEOREM 8.2.   *If the function $g(x)$ has a continuous derivative $g'(x)$ strictly positive for all $x \geq 0$, the concentration curve for $g(x)$ coincides with the Lorenz curve for the distribution of $g(x)$.*

Proof. The condition $g'(x) > 0$ for all x implies that $g(x)$ is strictly monotonic. Further, if $g(x)$ has a continuous nonvanishing derivative in the region $x \geq 0$, the probability density function of Y is given by[5]

$$(8.21) \qquad f^*(Y) = f[h(Y)] \, | \, h'(Y) \, |$$

where $X = h(Y)$ is the solution of $Y = g(X)$.

Now consider the graph of $F(x)$ against $F^*[g(x)]$, which has the

---

5. See Wilks (1944), p. 55.

slope

$$\frac{dF^*[g(x)]}{dF(x)} = \frac{f^*(y)}{f(x)h'(y)},$$

which, by means of (8.21), becomes unity if $h'(y) > 0$. Furthermore, $g'(x) > 0$ necessarily implies that $h'(y) > 0$. Because the curve $F(x)$ versus $F^*[g(x)]$ passes through $(0, 0)$ and $(1, 1)$ and has slope unity for all x, it must coincide with the line through $(0, 0)$ and $(1, 1)$. Thus $F^*[g(x)] = F(x)$.

Similarly, it can be proved that the graph of $F_1[g(x)]$ against $F_1^*[g(x)]$ has slope unity for all $x \geq 0$. Because the curve passes through $(0, 0)$ and $(1, 1)$, it must coincide with the straight line joining $(0, 0)$ and $(1, 1)$, which implies that $F_1^*[g(x)] = F_1[g(x)]$. This proves the theorem.

The following corollaries follow immediately from theorems 8.1 and 8.2.

COROLLARY 8.4. *If the functions $g(x)$ and $g^*(x)$ have continuous derivatives strictly greater than zero for all x, $g(x)$ is Lorenz superior (inferior) to $g^*(x)$ if $\eta_g(x)$ is less (greater) than $\eta_{g^*}(x)$ for all $x \geq 0$.*

COROLLARY 8.5. *If the function $g(x)$ has a continuous derivative $g'(x) > 0$ for all x, $g(x)$ is Lorenz superior (inferior) to x if $\eta_g(x)$ is less (greater) than unity for all $x \geq 0$.*

THEOREM 8.3. *If $g(x) = \sum_{i=1}^{k} g_i(x)$ so that*

$$E[g(x)] = \sum_{i=1}^{k} E[g_i(x)]$$

where E is the expected value operator,

(8.22) $$E[g(x)]F_1[g(x)] = \sum_{i=1}^{k} E[g_i(x)]F_1[g_i(x)].$$

Proof. Substituting $g(x) = \sum_{i=1}^{k} g_i(x)$ into (8.1) and interchanging the summation and integral signs gives[6]

(8.23) $$F_1[g(x)] = \frac{1}{E[g(x)]} \sum_{i=1}^{k} \int_0^x g_i(X)f(X)\,dx.$$

6. The interchange of summation and integral signs is permissible if k is finite.

Now $F_1[g_i(x)]$ is given by

$$(8.24) \qquad F_1[g_i(x)] = \frac{1}{E[g_i(x)]} \int_0^x g_i(X)f(X)\,dX,$$

which, on substituting into (8.23), gives the result stated in the theorem.

Let $g(x) = a + bx$ so that $E[g(x)] = a + b\mu$ where $E(x) = \mu$; then $g(x)$ can be treated as the sum of two functions, a and bx. Thus, theorem 8.3 yields

$$(8.25) \qquad F_1[a + bx] = \frac{1}{(a + b\mu)} [aF(x) + b\mu F_1(x)]$$

because the concentration curve for a constant function coincides with the egalitarian line. Equation (8.25) can also be written as

$$F_1[a + bx] - F_1(x) = \frac{a}{a + b\mu} [F(x) - F_1(x)].$$

Because $F(x) \geq F_1(x)$ for all x, it is implied that the concentration curve for a linear function $(a + bx)$ lies above (below) the Lorenz curve for x if a is greater (less) than zero. Further, if $b > 0$, the function $g(x) = a + bx$ is a monotonic increasing function of x and has a continuous first derivative $g'(x)$ strictly greater than zero. Then the concentration curve for $(a + bx)$ coincides with the Lorenz curve of function $(a + bx)$. This leads to the following corollary.

COROLLARY 8.6.   *If $b > 0$, the linear function $(a + bx)$ is Lorenz superior (inferior) to x if a is greater (less) than zero.*

In the above corollary, if $a < 0$, the linear function $(a + bx)$ will be negative for $x \leq -a/b$. Consider the case in which the function $(a + bx)$ is forced to be equal to zero when $x \leq -a/b$. Under this assumption the mean value of the function is

$$E[a + bx] = \int_{-a/b}^{\infty} (a + bx)f(x)\,dx$$

$$(8.26) \qquad\qquad = a + b\mu - aF\left(\frac{-a}{b}\right) - b\mu F_1\left(\frac{-a}{b}\right),$$

and the first-moment distribution function becomes

$$F_1(a + bx) = \frac{1}{E(a + bx)} \int_{-a/b}^{x} (a + bx)f(x)\,dx$$

$$(8.27) \qquad = \frac{a}{\mu^*}\left[F(x) - F\left(\frac{-a}{b}\right)\right] + \frac{b\mu}{\mu^*}\left[F_1(x) - F_1\left(\frac{-a}{b}\right)\right]$$

for $x \geq -a/b$ where $\mu^* = E(a + bx)$. Note that $F_1(a + bx) = 0$ for $x < -a/b$.

By means of (8.26), expression (8.27) can be written as

$$F_1(a + bx) - F_1(x)$$

$$= \frac{a}{\mu^*}[F(x) - F_1(x)] - \frac{[1 - F_1(x)]}{\mu^*}[a + b\mu - \mu^*].$$

The right-hand side can be negative or positive, depending on the value of x. Thus, the Lorenz curves for x and $(a + bx)$ may intersect.

Some Applications of the Theorems

In this section three of the applications of the theorems given in the preceding section are considered.

The Engel curve

The Engel curve is the relationslip between expenditure on a commodity and total expenditure (or income). If $g(x)$ represents the equation of the Engel curve of a commodity, the elasticity of the function $g(x)$ with respect to x indicates whether the commodity is inferior, necessary, or luxury. The commodity is said to be inferior if its elasticity is negative, which implies that the expenditure on an inferior commodity decreases as income increases. The commodity is called necessary (luxury) if its elasticity is less (greater) than unity.

From corollaries 8.1 and 8.2 it follows that if the concentration curve of a commodity lies above the egalitarian line, it is an inferior commodity; if the concentration curve lies between the Lorenz curve of x and the egalitarian line, it is a necessary commodity;

Figure 6. *Concentration Curves for Commodities*

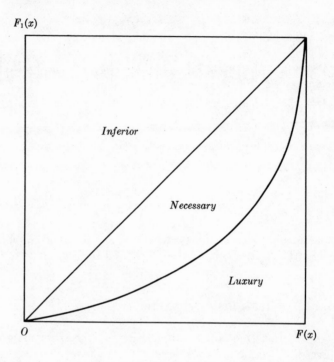

and if the concentration curve lies below the Lorenz curve, the commodity is luxury. The concentration curve of a commodity indicates, therefore, whether a particular commodity is inferior, necessary, or luxury. The curve given in figure 6 is the Lorenz curve of income. In the same figure the concentration curves of different commodities can be drawn by plotting points $F(x)$ and $F_1[g(x)]$ for different values of x. The cumulative proportion of expenditure on the commodity, when income units are arranged according to income, is denoted by $F_1[g(x)]$. The position of the concentration curve in the figure will indicate whether the commodity is inferior, necessary, or luxury.

Consumption and saving functions

In the Keynesian case, consumption is related to income either linearly or curvilinearly. First, assume that the relation is linear:

$$(8.28) \qquad c = \alpha + \beta x$$

where β is the marginal propensity to consume, x is the disposable income, and c is the consumption expenditure of an individual. Because α and β are greater than zero, it follows from corollary 8.6 that personal consumption expenditure is Lorenz superior to the personal disposable income. Personal consumption expenditure will, therefore, be more equally distributed than personal disposable income.

The saving function corresponding to (8.28) is

$$(8.29) \qquad s = -\alpha + (1 - \beta)x,$$

which, again from corollary 8.6, implies that personal savings will be more unequally distributed than personal disposable income, provided the marginal propensity is less than unity. Note that the marginal propensity to consume cannot exceed unity in this model; otherwise, savings will be negative for the whole society.

Let y be the gross income and $T(y)$ the tax function; the consumption function in (8.28) then becomes

$$c = \alpha + \beta[y - T(y)],$$

which, on differentiating with respect to y, yields

$$\frac{dc}{dy} = \beta[1 - T'(y)].$$

Note that $T'(y)$ is the marginal tax rate at income level y. Clearly, $dc/dy > 0$ when $T'(y) < 1$, which, from theorem 8.2, shows that the concentration curve for the personal consumption expenditure coincides with its Lorenz curve if the marginal tax rate is less than unity. The elasticity of c with respect to y will be

$$\eta_{cy} = \frac{\beta[1 - T'(y)]y}{\alpha + \beta[y - T(y)]},$$

which will be less than unity provided that

$$(8.30) \qquad \beta T(y)[1 - \eta_t(y)] < \alpha$$

where $\eta_t(y)$ is the elasticity of $T(y)$ with respect to y. It is well known that if $\eta_t(y) > 1$ for all y, the tax function is progressive, and if $\eta_t(y) = 1$, the tax function is proportional; otherwise, it is regressive.[7] If it is assumed that $T(y) \geq 0$ for all y, which excludes

---

7. A more detailed discussion of tax progressivity is given in chapter 12.

the possibility of negative income tax, the inequality in (8.30) will be true when the $T(y)$ function is progressive or proportional throughout the income range. Thus from corollary 8.2 it follows that personal consumption expenditure will be more equally distributed than pretax income for both proportional and progressive tax systems. If the tax system is regressive, it is impossible to make any *a priori* statement regarding the distribution of consumption expenditure.

The elasticity of personal savings with respect to gross income is

$$\eta_{sy} = \frac{(1 - \beta)[1 - T'(y)]y}{-\alpha + (1 - \beta)[y - T(y)]},$$

which will be greater than unity provided that

(8.31) $$(1 - \beta) T(y)[1 - \eta_t(y)] + \alpha > 0.$$

If $\beta < 1$ and $\eta_t(y) \leq 1$, (8.31) will hold. From corollary 8.2 it follows, therefore, that if the marginal propensity to consume is less than unity, savings will be more unequally distributed than pretax income for both regressive and proportional tax systems. If taxes are progressive, however, no statement regarding the distribution of savings can be made.

Now consider the rate of interest as an additional variable in the saving function (8.29):

$$s = -\alpha + (1 - \beta)x + \lambda r$$

where r is the rate of interest and $\lambda \geq 0$ is the corresponding parameter. The elasticity of saving with respect to disposable income x will then be

$$\eta_s(x) = \frac{(1 - \beta)x}{-\alpha + (1 - \beta)x + \lambda r}.$$

This equation clearly indicates that as r increases, $\eta_s(x)$ decreases; it follows from theorem 8.1, therefore, that the concentration curve for savings will shift upward as r increases. If the marginal propensity to consume is less than unity, s will be an increasing function of x, and the concentration curve for savings will coincide with its Lorenz curve. One can therefore conclude that the higher the interest rate, the more equal will be the distribution of savings, a conclusion based on the assumption that increases in the interest rate do not alter the distribution of disposable income.

Next consider curvilinear consumption and savings functions. If the average propensity to consume decreases as income increases, the income elasticity of consumption will be less than unity, and the income elasticity of savings will be greater than unity. It immediately follows from corollary 8.2 that the concentration of personal consumption expenditure (personal savings) will be above (below) the Lorenz curve for disposable income. Because personal consumption and savings are both increasing functions of disposable income, their concentration curves will coincide with their respective Lorenz curves. This leads to the conclusion that, if the average propensity to consume decreases as income rises, the inequality of disposable income will, for curvilinear consumption and savings functions, be greater than that of personal consumption, but less than that of personal savings.

The Stiglitz model of distribution of income and wealth among individuals

Stiglitz (1969a) considered a simple model of accumulation with a linear savings function, a constant reproduction rate, homogeneous labor, and equal division of wealth among one's heirs. He proved that in such a model, the distribution of wealth and income will tend to a state of complete equalization if the balanced growth is stable. He further demonstrated that his basic conclusions are unaltered under a variety of alternative savings assumptions. His proof of these propositions depends on the comparison of rates of growth of wealth between an arbitrary pair of rich and poor income groups. Tsuji (1972) proved some of these propositions using the variance and the Gini coefficient as measures of inequality. It is demonstrated below that the theorems presented in the preceding section can be effectively applied to prove all these propositions in terms of Lorenz preference.

Stiglitz's basic model is described as follows. Consider a society that is divided into a number of groups arranged in ascending order of wealth. Labor is homogeneous; therefore, all workers receive the same wage. In addition, all the members of any one group possess the same wealth. Under these assumptions, the per capita income of group i is given by

$$(8.32) \qquad\qquad y_i = w + rc_i$$

where c_i is the capital per person in the ith group, w is the wage rate, and r the interest rate. Let s_i be the per capita saving of this group, s_i being a linear function of per capita income in the group; it then follows that

$$(8.33) \qquad\qquad s_i = my_i + b$$

where m is the marginal propensity to save, and b the per capita saving at zero income; b can be either negative or positive.

Suppose that the population of each group is increasing at the same constant rate n, and there is no intermarriage among the groups. These assumptions ensure that the relative proportion of the population of each group, f_i, remains constant. The per capita wealth accumulation for group i is then given by

$$(8.34) \qquad\qquad \frac{1}{c_{it}} \frac{dc_{it}}{dt} = \frac{s_{it}}{c_{it}} - n$$

where the suffix t stands for time. Substituting (8.32) and (8.33) into (8.34) yields

$$\frac{dc_{it}}{dt} = (b + mw) + (mr - n)c_{it},$$

which is a first-order differential equation. Its solution is

$$(8.35) \qquad c_{it} = \frac{(b + mw)}{(n - mr)} \left[1 - e^{-(n-mr)t}\right] + e^{-(n-mr)t} c_i$$

where c_i now represents the wealth of the ith group at $t = 0$.

Consider how the distribution of wealth changes with time. The coefficient of c_i in (8.35) is always greater than zero, and, therefore (from theorem 8.2), the concentration curve for c_{it} coincides with its Lorenz curve. It immediately follows from corollary 8.6 that the distribution of c_{it} will be Lorenz superior (inferior) to the distribution of c_i if a given by

$$(8.36) \qquad\qquad a = \frac{(b + mw)}{(n - mr)} \left[1 - e^{-(n-mr)t}\right]$$

is greater (less) than zero.

Now consider the conditions of equilibrium under which a is negative or positive. For this purpose, a production function that is concave and exhibits constant returns to scale must be assumed. If y is the output per worker and k is the aggregate capital-labor ratio, it follows that

$$y = f(k), \qquad f'(k) > 0, \qquad f''(k) < 0.$$

If each factor of production is paid with its marginal product, the wage rate w and interest rate r are given by

(8.37) $$r = f'(k), \qquad w = f(k) - kf'(k).$$

If k_i is denoted as the capital in the ith group divided by the total population, then

$$k_i = f_i c_i,$$

which clearly yields

(8.38) $$k = \Sigma k_i = \Sigma f_i c_i.$$

The differential equation of the aggregate capital accumulation is, therefore,

(8.39) $$\frac{dk}{dt} = \Sigma f_i \frac{dc_i}{dt} = (b + mw) - k(n - mr)$$

where use has been made of the fact that the relative proportion of population f_i in each group remains constant.

If the economy is in balanced growth, $dk/dt = 0$, which from (8.39) yields

(8.40) $$m(w + rk) = nk - b.$$

Substituting $y = \Sigma f_i y_i$ into (8.32) and (8.38), this equation becomes

(8.41) $$mf(k) = nk - b,$$

the solution of which yields the aggregate capital-labor ratio, leading to balanced growth. If $b > 0$, there is a unique solution. If, in contrast, $b < 0$, there will be two balanced growth paths.[8] The balanced growth path is said to be stable (unstable) if $\partial(dk/dt)/\partial k$ at $dk/dt = 0$ is less (greater) than zero. Differentiating (8.39) partially with respect to k gives

(8.42) $$\frac{\partial}{\partial k}\left(\frac{dk}{dt}\right) = -(n - mr),$$

---

8. See Stiglitz (1969a). These results are based on the concavity of the production function and on the other conditions of the production function given in (8.37).

which implies that the balanced growth path will be stable (unstable) if $(n - mr)$ is greater (less) than zero.

From (8.41) note that the intersection of line $nk - b$ and curve $mf(k)$ yields the solution for the balanced growth path. If there is only one balanced growth path, the slope of line $nk - b$ at this point must be greater than the slope of curve $mf(k)$. The slope of $mf(k)$ is $mf'(k)$, which, from (8.37), is equal to mr. This gives $n > mr$, which, from (8.42), leads to the result that if there is only one balanced growth path, it is globally stable. In contrast, if there are two balanced growth paths, it can similarly be shown that the lower will be locally unstable and the upper locally stable.

If the economy is in balanced growth, equation (8.40) will be true. Substituting this equation into (8.36), a becomes

$$a = k[1 - e^{-(n-mr)t}],$$

which is clearly positive (negative) if $(n - mr)$ is greater (less) than zero. The distribution of c_{it} will, therefore, be Lorenz superior (inferior) to c_i if $(n - mr)$ is greater (less) than zero. This leads to the conclusion that the distribution of wealth must eventually become more (less) egalitarian if the economy is at a stable (unstable) balanced growth path.

Now consider the movement of the distribution of income over time. Substituting (8.32) into (8.35) yields the income of the ith group at time t as

$$y_{it} = \left[w + \frac{r(b + mw)}{(n - mr)}\right][1 - e^{-(n-mr)t}] + e^{-(n-mr)t}y_i$$

where y_i now represents the wealth of the ith group at $t = 0$. If the economy is in a balanced growth path, by means of (8.40) this equation becomes

$$y_{it} = (w + kr)[1 - e^{-(n-mr)t}] + e^{-(n-mr)t}y_i.$$

By means of corollary 8.6 the distribution of y_{it} is found to be Lorenz superior (inferior) to the distribution of y_i if $(n - mr)$ is greater (less) than zero. It can, therefore, be concluded that the distribution of income will eventually become more (less) egalitarian if the economy is at a stable (unstable) balanced growth path.

The Concentration Index

In this section the concentration index is defined and some theorems related to it are given.

DEFINITION 8.1.   *The concentration index for $g(x)$ is defined as one minus twice the area under the concentration curve for $g(x)$.*

The concentration index for $g(x)$ is given by

$$(8.43) \qquad C_g = 1 - 2 \int_0^\infty F_1[g(x)] f(x) dx,$$

which, on integration by parts, becomes

$$(8.44) \quad C_g = \frac{2}{E[g(x)]} \left[\int_0^\infty g(x) F(x) f(x) dx - \frac{E[g(x)]}{2} \right].$$

Further, integrating by parts, it can be demonstrated that

$$E[F(x)] = \int_0^\infty F(x) f(x) dx = \tfrac{1}{2},$$

which shows that the probability distribution function $F(x)$ always has a mean equal to one-half. The covariance of the functions $g(x)$ and $F(x)$ can then be written as

$$\text{cov}\,[g(x), F(x)] = \int_0^\infty [g(x) - E(g(x))][F(x) - \tfrac{1}{2}] f(x) dx,$$

which, by means of (8.44), gives

$$(8.45) \qquad C_g = \frac{2}{E[g(x)]} \text{cov}\,[g(x), F(x)].$$

The Gini index of the variable $y = g(x)$ will be

$$G_g = 1 - 2 \int_0^\infty F_1^*(y) f^*(y) dy$$

where $F_1^*(y)$ is defined in (8.19), and $f^*(y)$ is the probability density function of y. It is not difficult, then, to show that

$$(8.46) \qquad G_g = \frac{2}{E[g(x)]} \, \text{cov} \, [g(x), F^*(g(x))]$$

where $F^*(y) = F^*(g(x))$ is the probability distribution function of y.

According to (8.45) and (8.46) the relationship between C_g and G_g is

$$(8.47) \qquad C_g = \frac{\text{cov} \, [g(x), F(x)]}{\text{cov} \, [g(x), F^*(g(x))]} \, G_g.$$

If the number of income units is fixed in the population, clearly the variance of $F(x)$ will be identical to the variance of $F^*[g(x)]$.[9] Substituting this into (8.47) yields

$$(8.48) \qquad C_g = \frac{R[g(x), F(x)]}{R[g(x), F^*(g(x))]} \, G_g$$

where $R(a, b)$ is the coefficient of correlation between a and b. Note that the probability distribution function $F(x)$ is the cumulative proportion of income units when the units are arranged according to their incomes. Similarly, $F^*[g(x)]$ is the cumulative proportion of income units when the same units are arranged according to $g(x)$. The difference between $F(x)$ and $F^*[g(x)]$ will, therefore, be due to the difference in rankings of the variables x and $g(x)$. Thus, if $F(x)$ and $F^*[g(x)]$ in (8.48) are replaced by the rankings of x and $g(x)$, respectively, the correlation coefficients in the equation will remain the same. This leads to the following theorem.

THEOREM 8.4.   *The concentration index of the function $g(x)$ is related to the Gini index of $g(x)$ by*

$$(8.49) \qquad C_g = \frac{R[g(x), r(x)]}{R[g(x), r(g(x))]} \, G_g$$

where $r(x)$ stands for the rank of x, and $r(g(x))$ the rank of $g(x)$.[10]

9. In fact, all the moments of $F(x)$ and $F^*(g(x))$ will be identical.

10. Pyatt (1975) proved a similar theorem in connection with the decomposition of total income inequality by factor components. A discussion of this will follow.

Note that if $g(x)$ remains constant, the concentration index coincides with the egalitarian line so that $C_g = 0$. If $g(x) = \alpha x$ where α is any positive constant, the concentration index is equal to the Gini index of x. Furthermore, if $g'(x) \geq 0$ for all x, x and $g(x)$ will have exactly the same ranking, in which case the correlation between $g(x)$ and $r[g(x)]$ will be equal to the correlation between $g(x)$ and $r(x)$. From the above theorem it follows, therefore, that C_g is always positive and will be equal to the Gini index of the function $g(x)$. In addition, if $g'(x) < 0$ for all x, x and $g(x)$ will have exactly opposite ranking, and the correlations $R[g(x), r(x)]$ and $R[g(x), r(g(x))]$ will be of the same magnitude but opposite sign. In this case, C_g will be equal to minus one times the Gini index G_g. Finally, if $g(x)$ is not a monotonic function, C_g will lie between $-G_g$ and $+G_g$. This leads to the following corollary.

COROLLARY 8.7.

$$-G_g \leq C_g \leq G_g$$

where C_g and G_g are the concentration and Gini indexes, respectively, for any function $g(x)$.

THEOREM 8.5.   If $g(x) = \sum_{i=1}^{k} g_i(x)$ so   that $E[g(x)] = \sum_{i=1}^{k} E[g_i(x)]$, then

(8.50)
$$E[g(x)]C_g = \sum_{i=1}^{k} E[g_i(x)]C_{g_i}$$

where C_g and C_{g_i} are concentration indexes for $g(x)$ and $g_i(x)$, respectively.

Proof.   Substituting (8.22) into (8.43) gives

$$C_g = 1 - \frac{2}{E[g(x)]} \int_0^\infty \sum_{i=1}^{k} E[g_i(x)]F_1[g_i(x)]f(x)\,dx,$$

which, on interchanging the summation and integral sign, becomes

(8.51) $$C_g = 1 - \frac{2}{E[g(x)]} \sum_{i=1}^{k} \int_0^\infty E[g_i(x)]F_1[g_i(x)]f(x)\,dx.$$

Now C_{g_i} is defined as

(8.52)
$$C_{g_i} = 1 - 2 \int_0^\infty F_1[g_i(x)]f(x)\,dx.$$

Substituting (8.52) into (8.51), and considering the fact that $E[g(x)] = \sum_{i=1}^{k} E[g_i(x)]$ yields the result stated in theorem 8.5.

Note that the result stated in theorem 8.5 does not require that functions $g(x)$ and $g_i(x)$ be monotonic. If it is assumed, however, that $g'(x) \geq 0$, that is, that $g(x)$ is a monotonic function of x, it follows from theorem 8.4 that $C_g = G_g$. Furthermore, if $g_i(x)$ is any function of x (not necessarily monotonic), it follows from corollary 8.7 that $C_{g_i} \leq G_{g_i}$ where G_{g_i} is the Gini index of $g_i(x)$. Substituting these results into (8.50) immediately leads to the following corollary.

COROLLARY 8.8.

$$E[g(x)]G_g \leq \sum_{i=1}^{k} E[g_i(x)]G_{g_i}$$

where G_g and G_{g_i} are Gini indexes for $g(x)$ and $g_i(x)$, respectively.

Again assume that $g(x) = a + bx$ so that $E[g(x)] = a + b\mu$. If $b > 0$, $g'(x)$ is strictly greater than zero. The concentration index for $g(x)$ will, therefore, be the same as the Gini index of the function.

From the fact that the Gini index of a constant is zero, and the Gini index of bx is the same as the Gini index of x, it follows from theorem 8.5 that

$$(a + b\mu)G^* = b\mu G$$

where G is the Gini index of x, and G^* is the Gini index of the linear function $(a + bx)$. This leads to the following corollary.

COROLLARY 8.9.   *If G is the Gini index of a random variable x, the Gini index G^* of a linear function $(a + bx)$ for $b > 0$ is given by*

$$G^* = \frac{b\mu G}{a + b\mu}$$

where $E(x) = \mu$.

In the above corollary, if $a = 0$, $G^* = G$, which implies that if all incomes are multiplied by the same constant, the income inequality remains unchanged. Furthermore, G^* is less (greater) than G if a is greater (less) than zero.

Next consider the case where $a < 0$, and the function $(a + bx)$ is forced to be equal to zero for all values of $x \leq -a/b$.

Now denote $G(-a/b)$ as the Gini index of the units that have income less than or equal to $-a/b$. If P is the point on the

Figure 7. *Calculation of the Gini Index from the Lorenz Curve*

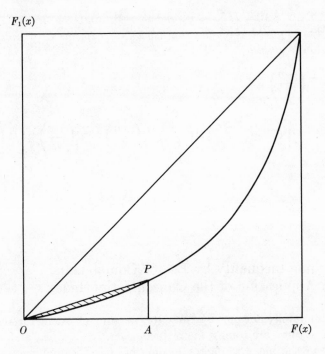

Lorenz curve for $x = -a/b$ so that its coordinates are $[F(-a/b), F_1(-a/b)]$, the Gini index $G(-a/b)$ is given by the shaded area in figure 7 divided by the area of the triangle OAP. Thus,

$$(8.52) \qquad G\left(\frac{-a}{b}\right) = 1 - \frac{2\displaystyle\int_0^{-a/b} F_1(x)f(x)\,dx}{F\left(\dfrac{-a}{b}\right)F_1\left(\dfrac{-a}{b}\right)}.$$

When the Gini index of the linear function $(a + bx)$ is forced to equal zero for $x \leq -a/b$, it is given by

$$(8.53) \qquad G^* = 1 - 2\int_{-a/b}^{\infty} F_1(a + bx)f(x)\,dx$$

where $F_1(a + bx)$ is defined in (8.27).

Now, substituting (8.27) into (8.53) gives the result stated in the following corollary.

COROLLARY 8.10. *If* $a < 0$ *and* $b > 0$, *and the linear function* $(a + bx)$ *is forced to equal zero when* $x \leq -a/b$, *the Gini index* G^* *of* $(a + bx)$ *is given by*

$$G^* = F\left(\frac{-a}{b}\right)$$

$$+ \frac{b\mu}{\mu^*}\left[G - G\left(\frac{-a}{b}\right)F\left(\frac{-a}{b}\right)F_1\left(\frac{-a}{b}\right) - F\left(\frac{-a}{b}\right) + F_1\left(\frac{-a}{b}\right)\right]$$

where

$$\mu^* = a + b\mu - b\mu F_1\left(\frac{-a}{b}\right) - aF\left(\frac{-a}{b}\right).$$

Income Inequality by Factor Components: An Application of the Concentration Index

Total family income is equal to the sum of all factor incomes. Suppose there are total n factor incomes x_1, x_2, . . . , x_n, and $g_i(x)$ is equal to the mean i^{th} factor income of the units having the same total income x. Then,

$$(8.54) \qquad\qquad x = \sum_{i=1}^{n} g_i(x).$$

If families are arranged according to their total income x, $F_1[g_i(x)]$, as defined in (8.24), will be interpreted as the proportion of the ith factor income of families having total income less than or equal to x. Applying theorem 8.5 to (8.54) yields the Gini index of total family income as equal to

$$(8.55) \qquad\qquad G = \frac{1}{\mu}\sum_{i=1}^{n} \mu_i Cg_i$$

where Cg_i is the concentration index of the ith factor income $g_i(x)$, and μ_i is the mean of the ith factor income of all the families. Note that use has been made of the fact that the concentration index of x is equal to its Gini index.

Equation (8.55) expresses the Gini index of total family income as the weighted average of the concentration indexes of each factor income component, the weights being proportional to the mean of each factor income. The factor income $g_i(x)$ is not necessarily an increasing function of x; therefore, corollary 8.7 yields

(8.56) $$Cg_i \leq G_i$$

for all $i = 1, 2, \ldots, n$ where G_i denotes the Gini index of the ith factor income. Substituting (8.56) into (8.55) yields

(8.57) $$G \leq \frac{1}{\mu} \sum_{i=1}^{n} \mu_i G_i,$$

which shows that the weighted average of the factor income Gini indexes provides only the upper bound of the Gini index of the total income.[11] The exact relationship between the Gini indexes of the total income and its factor components was derived by Pyatt (1975). His result can readily be obtained by substituting (8.49) into (8.55), yielding

$$G = \frac{1}{\mu} \sum_{i=1}^{n} \mu_i \frac{R[g_i(x), r(x)]}{R[g_i(x), r(g_i(x))]} G_i$$

where $R[a, b]$ is the coefficient of correlation between a and b, $r(x)$ stands for the rank of x, and $r(g_i(x))$ the rank of the ith factor income $g_i(x)$.

Equation (8.55) can be used to analyze the relationship between functional and size distributions of income. The total family income consists of wages, salaries, property income, profits, capital gains, and other miscellaneous components of income. This equation provides the quantitative framework to analyze the contribution of each of these components to the inequality of total family income. To illustrate this numerically, the data obtained from *The Australian Survey of Consumer Expenditures and Finances, 1966–68* (Drane and others), are used. (The data are from the second stage of the survey, consisting of a sample of 2,757 families. A brief description of the survey is provided in chapter 6.)

The original observations are grouped into twelve classes according to total family income, and the arithmetic mean of each factor

11. The result given in (8.57) was derived earlier by Rao (1969).

income is given for each income class. The concentration index of each factor income was computed by fitting the new coordinate system of the Lorenz curve proposed by Kakwani and Podder (1976). (This system was discussed in chapter 7.)

Note that, because the families are ranked only according to total income, only the concentration indexes can be computed for each factor income from the grouped data. The computations of the Gini indexes require ranking of families according to each factor income, which is generally unavailable. To analyze the contribution of each factor income to total inequality, only the concentration indexes are required. The Gini indexes of factor incomes do not serve the purpose because they provide only the upper bound, as shown in (8.57).

The numerical results giving the contribution of each factor income to total inequality are presented in table 8.1. The second column gives the mean income of each factor income. (The figures in parentheses are the percentage shares of each factor.) The third column gives the concentration indexes of each factor income, and the fourth presents the contribution of each factor income to total income inequality. Finally, the fifth column expresses these contributions in percentages.

Several interesting points emerge from the numerical results given in the table. Income from employment, including wages and salaries, is the major functional component, contributing 87.38 percent of total income. Income from unincorporated business forms the second major functional component and has a share of 7.09 percent in total income. All other components of income have shares of less than 6 percent. The concentration index of employment income is 0.34, which is quite close to the Gini index of total income, 0.36. This implies that income from employment is quite evenly distributed over the total income and constitutes an important finding because it casts doubt on the commonly held belief that the larger the family's average income, the smaller the proportion derived from employment. The concentration index of the capital gains is 0.77, implying that capital gains are heavily concentrated at high income levels. It can, therefore, be concluded that larger incomes are more likely to have larger proportions of capital gains than smaller incomes. The concentration index of the property income is 0.43, relatively much smaller than the concentration indexes of unincorporated business income (0.58) and capital gains (0.77). Thus, the higher proportion of property income can be observed among low income families.

Table 8.1. *Income Inequality by Factor Components*

Sources of income	Mean income (Australian dollars)	Concen-tration index	Contribution of each factor income to total income inequality	Percentage contribution
Employment	3399 (87.38)	0.3449	0.3014	82.67
Unincorporated business income	276 (7.09)	0.5852	0.0415	11.38
Property [a]	106 (2.72)	0.4322	0.0117	3.21
Regular annuity [b]	37 (0.95)	0.0544	0.00052	.15
Capital items [c]	18 (0.46)	0.3737	0.0017	.46
Capital gains [d]	39 (1.04)	0.7737	0.0080	2.19
Miscellaneous	14 (0.36)	0.2922	0.0010	.27
Total income [e]	3890 (100.00)	0.3645	0.3645	100.00

a. Property income includes interest, dividend, and rent.

b. Regular annuity includes regular payments from superannuation and trust funds.

c. Capital items includes lump-sum payments from private trust funds, annuity and lump-sum superannuation payments, insurance policy bonuses cashed, insurance policy matured or surrendered.

d. Capital gains includes gifts and other capital receipts.

e. Total income does not include government cash benefits such as pensions, unemployment benefits, child endowment, etc.

The figures in the last column of the table indicate that employment income contributes as much as 82.67 percent to total income inequality. It would seem, then, that any policy that increases the labor share of the functional distribution may not significantly decrease the inequality of the size distribution of total income. For example, if the concentration indexes of factor incomes remain constant, but the share of income from employment increases by 1 percent, total income inequality will reduce by only .43 percent, and the contribution of employment income to total inequality will increase from 82.67 percent to 83.99 percent, an increase of 1.32 percent.

PART FOUR

Expenditure Systems and Income Inequality

CHAPTER 9

Linear Expenditure Systems and Income Inequality: Some Applications

THE RELATIONS between the consumption of different commodities and disposable income (or total expenditure), generally estimated from household surveys, play a central role in the models of income distribution and growth. In his 1957 study of family budgets, Ernst Engel, a German economist and pioneer in this field, arrived at the conclusion that the proportion of expenditure devoted to food decreases as the standard of living of a household increases. This observation, now regarded as universally true, has become known as Engel's law.

Engel's empirical investigations suggest that the expenditure on a given commodity varies with income in accordance with a certain underlying mathematical relationship. This relationship is generally termed the Engel curve, and Engel curves of all commodities put together are called expenditure systems. This chapter focuses, in general, on some income distribution models based on linear expenditure systems, and, in particular, on the utilization of linear expenditure systems in evaluating the effect of relative price changes on real income inequality.

The Linear Expenditure System

Demand equations of the linear expenditure system (LES) are given by

$$(9.1) \qquad p_i q_i = p_i \gamma_i + \beta_i \left(v - \sum_{i=1}^{n} p_i \gamma_i \right)$$

where q_i is the per capita demand for the ith commodity and p_i is its price. There are n commodities, and v is the per capita total expenditure. If $v_i = p_i q_i$ is denoted as the per capita expenditure on the ith commodity, and $a = \sum_{i=1}^{n} p_i \gamma_i$, equation (9.1) becomes

$$(9.2) \qquad v_i = p_i \gamma_i + \beta_i (v - a)$$

where β_i and γ_i are the parameters.

The above system of demand equations is derived by maximizing the Klein and Rubin (1947) form of the utility function,[1]

$$(9.3) \qquad u = \sum_{i=1}^{n} \beta_i \log (q_i - \gamma_i),$$

subject to the budget restriction

$$v = \sum_{i=1}^{n} p_i q_i$$

where the parameters β_i and γ_i satisfy the restrictions

$$0 < \beta_i < 1, \qquad \gamma_i \geq 0 \quad (i = 1, 2, \ldots, n).$$

$$\sum_{i=1}^{n} \beta_i = 1$$

Note that function (9.3) is defined only for

$$0 < (q_i - \gamma_i).$$

Equation (9.2) can be interpreted as follows.[2] Given total expenditure v and prices $p_1, p_2, \ldots, p_n$, the consumer first purchases minimum required quantities of each good: γ_1 of good 1, $\ldots$, γ_n of good n. The total expenditure on these minimum required quantities is

$$a = \sum_{i=1}^{n} p_i \gamma_i,$$

which is called the subsistence expenditure. The income remaining

---

1. This utility function is also widely known as the Stone-Geary utility form.
2. See Goldberger (1967).

after the subsistence expenditure is called the supernumerary income or expenditure, and is distributed among n goods in the proportions $\beta_i, \beta_2, \ldots, \beta_n$, which are called marginal budget shares.

Let η_i be the elasticity of demand for the ith good with respect to total expenditure, and η_{ij} the price elasticity of the ith good with respect to the price of the jth good; these elasticities are then derived from (9.2) as

$$\eta_i = \frac{\beta_i}{w_i}$$

(9.4)
$$\eta_{ij} = -\frac{\beta_i}{v_i} p_j \gamma_j \quad \text{if} \quad i \neq j$$

$$\eta_{jj} = -\frac{\beta_j}{v_j}(p_j \gamma_j + v - a)$$

where $w_i = v_i/v$ is the ith budget share.

Further, let G_i be the Gini index for the distribution of expenditure on the ith commodity, and G^* the Gini index of total expenditure. Applying corollary 8.9 to (9.2) then yields

(9.5)
$$G_i = \frac{\beta_i \mu^* G^*}{\mu_i}$$

where

$$\mu_i = p_i \gamma_i + \beta_i(\mu^* - a)$$

is the mean expenditure on the ith commodity and μ^* is the mean of total expenditure. Substituting (9.4) into (9.5) gives

(9.6)
$$G_i = \bar{\eta}_i G^*$$

where $\bar{\eta}_i$ is the expenditure elasticity of the ith commodity at the mean expenditures. Thus this equation proves that the expenditure elasticity of the ith commodity at the mean expenditures is equal to the ratio of the Gini indexes of the distributions of the ith commodity expenditure and the total expenditure, respectively. If the elasticity is greater (less) than unity, expenditure on the ith commodity is more (less) unequally distributed than the total expenditure.

If data on expenditures on different commodities are available in grouped form, the Gini indexes G_i and G^* can be estimated quite

accurately.[3] Then equations (9.5) and (9.6) can be used to estimate the marginal budget shares β_i and also the elasticities $\bar{\eta}_i$.

Income Inequality and Relative Price Changes

In this section the linear expenditure system is used to evaluate
the effect of relative price changes on the inequality of real income.
Substituting (9.1) into (9.3) yields the indirect utility function as

$$u = \sum_{i=1}^{n} \beta_i \log \beta_i + \log (v - a) - \sum_{i=1}^{n} \beta_i \log p_i.$$

Suppose the prices p_i change to p_i^* where $i = 1, 2, \ldots, n$, and the
total expenditure v changes to v^*; the resulting change in the utility
function will then be

$$\Delta u = \log (v^* - a^*) - \log (v - a) - \sum_{i=1}^{n} \beta_i (\log p_i^* - \log p_i)$$

where

$$a^* = \sum_{i=1}^{n} p_i^* \gamma_i.$$

If the change in utility is set at zero, the total expenditure of family
v^* is such that the family maintains the same level of utility:

$$(9.7) \qquad v^* = a^* + (v - a) \prod_{i=1}^{n} \left(\frac{p_i^*}{p_i}\right)^{\beta_i}$$

where v^* is the total expenditure of the family, which will buy the
same level of utility as before, but at new prices $p_1^*, p_2^*, \ldots, p_n^*$.

Let G_R be the Gini index of the real expenditure v^* at new prices;
then, applying corollary 8.9 to equation (9.7) yields

$$(9.8) \qquad G_R = \frac{\displaystyle\prod_{i=1}^{n} \left(\frac{p_i^*}{p_i}\right)^{\beta_i} \mu^* G^*}{a^* + (\mu^* - a) \displaystyle\prod_{i=1}^{n} \left(\frac{p_i^*}{p_i}\right)^{\beta_i}}$$

---

3. See chapters 6 and 7 on the estimation of Gini indexes.

where μ^* and G^* are the mean and the Gini index of total expenditure, respectively, in the base year.

It is obvious from (9.8) that if all prices change in the same proportion, $G_R = G^*$, that is, the inequality of the distribution of money expenditure in the base year is the same as the inequality of real expenditure.

The ratio v^*/v is the true cost of living index.[4] It compares the cost of living in two periods. For example, if v^* exceeds v by, say, 10 percent, the cost of living has gone up by this percentage. The real expenditure in the current period is obtained by dividing the money expenditure in the current period by the true cost of living index (v^*/v). Thus, the true cost of living index converts money expenditure into real expenditure. In the spirit of the true cost of living index, use the ratio G_R/G^* as an index of income inequality to take into account the effect of relative price changes. This index converts the inequality of household money expenditure distribution into the inequality of real household expenditure. If this index is less (greater) than unity, it is implied that the relative price changes are making the expenditure distribution more (less) unequal. Consider the following hypothetical example to illustrate the use of this index.

Suppose in the base year the Gini index of money expenditure is 0.30, and at the end of the first year changes to 0.32. If the income inequality index for this year is, say, 0.95, the true income inequality will be 0.32 divided by 0.95, which is equal to 0.337. This means that because of relative price changes, real expenditure inequality has increased by 12.3 percent instead of 6.7 percent.

The numerical results on the new index of income inequality, based on United Kingdom data, are presented in table 9.1. A detailed description of the data is given by Muellbauer (1974a) where the linear expenditure system was estimated by means of nine major commodity groups. The inequality index was then computed for nine years covering the period 1964 to 1972.

The second and third columns in the table give the relevant parameter estimates, which are derived from the actual annual relative price changes. The fourth column presents the true cost of living index, and the fifth column, our calculations of the new income

---

4. See Klein and Rubin (1947), Samuelson (1947), Geary (1949), Kloek (1966), and Theil (1975).

Table 9.1. *Index of Income Inequality, United Kingdom, 1964–72*

Fiscal year	More than nine commodity goods		True cost of living index	Index of income inequality
	a^*/a	$\Pi_i (p_i^*/p_i)^{\beta i}$		
1964	1.000	1.000	1.000	1.000
1965	1.048	1.041	1.046	0.9952
1966	1.090	1.074	1.085	0.9898
1967	1.118	1.100	1.112	0.9892
1968	1.168	1.156	1.164	0.9931
1969	1.229	1.210	1.223	0.9894
1970	1.296	1.278	1.290	0.9907
1971	1.399	1.375	1.391	0.9885
1972	1.481	1.443	1.469	0.9823

inequality index. The table indicates that the true cost of living has increased uniformly every year and about 47 percent during the period 1964–72. The index of inequality has decreased during the same period from 1.000 to 0.982, which, because of changes in relative prices, has the effect of increasing income inequality. The 1971–72 change is particularly marked. Thus, the Gini index of real expenditure in 1972 will be higher than the Gini index of actual money expenditure by about 1.018 percent, a figure obtained by dividing 1 by 0.982.

Income Inequality and Relative Price Changes: An Alternative Approach

If the price of the jth commodity changes by α_j percent, the demand for the ith commodity will change by $\eta_{ij}\alpha_j$ percent, and the resulting demand for the ith commodity will be

$$q_i^* = q_i(1 + \eta_{ij}\alpha_j).$$

The expenditure on the ith commodity now becomes

(9.9) $$v_i^* = v_i(1 + \eta_{ij}\alpha_j)$$

where $\tilde{v}_i^* = p_i q_i^*$, v_i being the expenditure on the ith commodity without price change.

By means of (9.4), equation (9.9) becomes

$$\tilde{v}_i^* = v_i \left(1 - \frac{\beta_i}{v_i} p_j \gamma_j \alpha_j \right) \quad \text{if} \quad i \neq j$$

$$\tilde{v}_j^* = v_j \left[1 - \frac{\beta_j \alpha_j}{v_j} (p_j \gamma_j + v - a) \right].$$

The total real expenditure then obtained is

(9.10) $$\tilde{v}^* = v - \alpha_j \gamma_j p_j - \alpha_j \beta_j (v - a)$$

where $\tilde{v}^* = \sum_{i=1}^{n} \tilde{v}_i^*$, and the restriction $\sum_{i=1}^{n} \beta_i = 1$ has been utilized.

It is worth noting that the real expenditure $\tilde{v}^*$ has a different interpretation from the one given in (9.7). That is, $\tilde{v}^*$ is the expenditure that will be incurred after price change, but this expenditure is calculated at the original prices. If there were no price change, v would be the total expenditure. If α_j is positive, that is, if the increase in price of a commodity should reduce the real total expenditure, $\tilde{v}^*$ will be less than v. In contrast, v^* as given in (9.7) will be more than v because the family income has to increase with increased prices in order to maintain the same utility level.

If $\tilde{G}_R$ is the Gini index of the real expenditure $\tilde{v}^*$, applying corollary 8.9 to equation (9.10) yields

(9.11) $$\tilde{G}_R - G^* = \frac{\alpha_j (\beta_j a - p_j \gamma_j) G^*}{\mu^* - \alpha_j p_j \gamma_j - \alpha_j \beta_j (\mu^* - a)}$$

where G^* is the Gini index of the total expenditure v and $\mu^* = E(v)$ is the mean total expenditure before any price change. Equation (9.11) provides the percentage change in the Gini index of real expenditure when the price of the jth commodity changes by α_j percent, other prices remaining constant.

Data from the *Mexico Household Survey*, conducted by the Bank of Mexico in 1968, were used to illustrate the above results numerically. The families considered were headed by urban entrepreneurs. The parameters and the linear expenditure system were estimated by the usual least-squares method by means of individual observa-

Table 9.2. *Parameter Estimates of the Linear Expenditure System*

	β_i		$p_i\gamma_i$ (in pesos per month)	
Commodity	Estimate	SE[a]	Estimate	SE[a]
Food	0.12569	0.003767	174.40913	7.34878
Clothing	0.10883	0.003790	50.53256	6.70168
Housing	0.20907	0.003884	83.08426	11.78322
Durables	0.08329	0.002164	24.94211	4.62963
Others	0.47311	0.007859	111.10675	31.75128

Note: The total mean expenditure = μ^* = 671.5, in pesos per month.
a. SE = Standard error.

Table 9.3. *Percentage of Change in Gini Index with Price Increase of Ten Percent by Commodity*

Commodity	Percentage of change in Gini index
Food	1.76
Clothing	0.03
Housing	−0.15
Durables	−0.18
Others	−1.57

tions. These parameters, along with their standard errors, are provided in table 9.2.[5]

Table 9.3 presents numerical results of the percentage change in the Gini index of real expenditure when the price of each commodity increases by 10 percent at a time.

5. All the parameters of the linear expenditure system are not identifiable from the expenditure data alone; the Lluch (1973) extended linear expenditure system was used to identify these parameters. A discussion of the extended linear expenditure system is given in the following section.

The Extended Linear Expenditure System

In this section the relationship between the parameters of the extended linear expenditure system (ELES) and the Gini indexes of various expenditures and income is discussed, as well as a new method of estimating this system.

Developed by Lluch in 1973, the ELES introduces savings into the linear expenditure system (LES). The consumer problem is formulated as follows. Choose $q(t)$, $0 \leq t \leq \infty$, so that

$$\int_0^\infty e^{-\delta t} \, u[q(t)] dt$$

is maximized, subject to

$$\frac{dw(t)}{dt} = \rho w(t) + y(t) - \sum_{i=1}^n p_i q_i(t)$$

where

$q(t)$, n vector of commodity flows;
$w(t)$, nonhuman wealth at time t;
$y(t)$, exogenous flow of labor income at time t;
ρ, interest rate or rate of reproduction of nonhuman wealth;
δ, subjective rate of discount;
$u(\cdot)$, instantaneous utility function.

Note that in the above formulation the present value of the future utility is maximized, subject to an expected wealth constraint. If the instantaneous utility function $u(\cdot)$ is of the Stone-Geary form, as given in (9.3), the demand equations for the ELES at time $t = 0$ are obtained as

(9.12) $$v_i = p_i \gamma_i + \beta_i^*(x - a)$$

where $v_i = p_i q_i$, $a = \sum_{i=1}^n p_i \gamma_i$ is again the subsistence expenditure, and x is the permanent income

$$x = \rho w + y + L(\dot{y})$$

where $w(0) = w$, $y(0) = y$, and

$$L(\dot{y}) = \int_0^\infty e^{-\rho t} \frac{dy(t)}{dt} \, dt$$

is the present value of the expected change in labor income. Assuming that $L(\dot{y})$ is zero, x will be the same as the measured income and equal to income from nonhuman wealth, plus labor income. The parameters in (9.12) satisfy the following restrictions:

$$\beta_i^* = \alpha \beta_i, \qquad 0 < \beta_i < 1, \qquad \alpha = \delta/\rho, \quad \text{and} \quad \sum_{i=1}^n \beta_i = 1.$$

Adding equation (9.12) gives the consumption function

(9.13) $$v = (1 - \alpha)a + \alpha x$$

where α is the marginal propensity to consume. Equation (9.13) yields an expression for x in terms of v, which, on substituting into (9.12), gives the LES:

$$v_i = p_i \gamma_i + \beta_i(v - a).$$

Thus, the ELES contains the LES and the aggregate consumption function (9.13).

The following interpretation of the ELES seems useful. Given the total income x and prices $p_1, p_2, \ldots, p_n$, the consumer first purchases the minimum required of each good: γ_1 of good 1, γ_2 of good 2, $\ldots$, γ_n of good n. At the given prices, this costs $a = \sum_{i=1}^n p_i \gamma_i$, which is equal to the subsistence expenditure. The income remaining after the subsistence expenditure $(x - a)$ is then distributed among n goods and savings in the proportions $\beta_1^*, \beta_2^*, \ldots, \beta_n^*$ and β_{n+1}^*, respectively, where $\beta_{n+1}^* = (1 - \alpha)$ is the marginal propensity to save.

Let $\tilde{\eta}_i$, $\tilde{\eta}_{ij}$ denote income and price elasticities in ELES; then[6]

$$\tilde{\eta}_i = \frac{\alpha \beta_i x}{v_i}$$

(9.14) $$\tilde{\eta}_{ij} = -\frac{\alpha \beta_i p_i \gamma_i}{v_i}$$

$$\tilde{\eta}_{jj} = -\frac{\alpha \beta_i}{v_i} [p_i \gamma_i + (x - a)]$$

6. See Lluch, Powell, and Williams (1975).

where $i, j = 1, 2, \ldots, n$, and

(9.15) $$\eta = \alpha + \frac{(1 - \alpha)(v - a)}{v}$$

is the elasticity of total expenditure with respect to income x.

Let G be the Gini index of income x, and μ the mean income; then, applying corollary 8.9 to (9.13) yields

(9.16) $$G^* - G = - \frac{(1 - \alpha)aG}{\mu^*}$$

where G^* is the Gini index of total expenditure and μ^* the mean total expenditure. This equation clearly shows that total expenditure is more equally distributed than income. Furthermore, μ and μ^* are related by

(9.17) $$\mu^* = (1 - \alpha)a + \alpha\mu,$$

which, on substituting into (9.16), gives

(9.18) $$\alpha = \frac{\mu^* G^*}{\mu G}.$$

This equation can also be written as

(9.19) $$\bar{\eta} = \frac{G^*}{G}$$

where $\bar{\eta}$ is the value of η as given in (9.15) at $v = \mu^*$. Equation (9.19) implies that the elasticity of total expenditure with respect to income is equal to the ratio of the Gini indexes of total expenditure and income, respectively.

Applying corollary 8.9 to (9.12) yields

(9.20) $$G_i = \frac{\beta_i^* \mu G}{\mu_i}$$

where μ_i is the mean expenditure on the ith commodity and is given by

(9.21) $$\mu_i = p_i \gamma_i + \beta_i^* (\mu - a).$$

Equation (9.20) can also be written as

$$\tilde{\eta}_i = \frac{G_i}{G}$$

where $\tilde{\eta}_i$ is the income elasticity at the mean income as defined in (9.14). This equation shows that the income elasticity of the ith commodity is equal to the ratio of the Gini indexes of the distributions of the ith commodity expenditure and income. Substituting (9.20) and (9.18) into (9.17) and (9.21) gives

$$a = \frac{\mu\mu^*(G - G^*)}{(\mu G - \mu^* G^*)}$$

and

$$p_i\gamma_i = \mu_i - \frac{\mu_i G_i(\mu - \mu^*)}{\mu G - \mu^* G^*} .$$

This completes the expression of all the parameters of the ELES in terms of the Gini indexes of the expenditures and income. The Gini indexes can, in turn, be accurately estimated from the grouped observations by means of the techniques discussed in chapters 6 and 7. This, then, constitutes an alternative method of estimating the complete ELES from the grouped observations.

Again, by means of the *Mexico Household Survey* data as well as the Gini indexes, the parameters of the ELES can be estimated. The numerical estimates are given in table 9.4. The Gini indexes were computed by fitting the new coordinate system of the Lorenz curve

Table 9.4. *Estimates of the* ELES *Using the New Method of Estimation Based on Grouped Data, and the Least-Squares Method Based on Individual Observations*

Commodity	Mean (pesos per month)	Gini indexes	β_i^* Grouped data	LSE[a]	$p_i\gamma_i$ (pesos per month) Grouped data	LSE[a]
Food	203	0.3327	0.1492	0.0943	152.8	174.4
Clothing	75	0.5447	0.0906	0.0816	43.2	50.5
Housing	131	0.5587	0.1612	0.1568	73.9	83.1
Durables	44	0.6299	0.0610	0.0625	21.9	24.9
Others	219	0.6765	0.3268	0.3549	102.8	111.1
Total expenditure	671	0.5312	0.788	.75	394.6	444.1
Income	747	0.6058				

a. LSE = Least-Squares Estimates obtained on the basis of individual observations.

to the grouped observations, and the least-squares estimates were obtained on the basis of the individual observations.

Distribution of Savings

If savings S is defined as the difference between income and total expenditure v, the ELES yields the savings function as

$$S = x - v = (1 - \alpha)(x - a)$$

where use has been made of (9.13). Applying corollary 8.9 to this equation yields

$$(9.22) \qquad\qquad G_s = \frac{\mu}{(\mu - a)} G$$

where G_s is the Gini index of savings. Now, a is the subsistence expenditure, which will be less than the mean income μ. Equation (9.22) implies, therefore, that savings are more unequally distributed than income.

If small changes in relative prices do not affect the distribution of income, the elasticity of G_s with respect to p_j is obtained from (9.22) as

$$\frac{\partial G_s}{\partial p_j} \frac{p_j}{G_s} = \frac{p_j \gamma_j}{(\mu - a)} ,$$

which implies that an increase in price of the jth commodity will increase the inequality of savings.

The numerical values of these elasticities were computed by means of data from the *Mexico Household Survey*, and the results are presented in table 9.5, which indicates that the increase in food prices has the maximum effect on the distribution of savings.

Table 9.5. *Elasticities of the Gini Index of Savings with Respect to Prices*

Commodity	Elasticity
Food	0.576
Clothing	0.167
Housing	0.274
Durables	0.082
Others	0.367

CHAPTER 10

Estimation of Engel Elasticities from the Lorenz Curve

THIS CHAPTER concerns the analysis of nonlinear Engel curves by means of the Lorenz curve. A number of statistical problems arise in estimating elasticities of these Engel curves from grouped data. In this chapter, the new coordinate system of the Lorenz curve discussed in chapter 7 is utilized to tackle these problems.

To estimate Engel elasticities, it is first necessary to specify the forms of the Engel function. Allen and Bowely (1935) based their analysis of consumer behavior on the linear Engel curve. Later, Prais and Houthakker (1955) investigated several nonlinear forms of the Engel function and concluded that a semi-logarithmic form is best suited to describe the demand for necessities, and that a double logarithmic form best describes the demand for luxuries. Seven alternative forms of the Engel function were considered for the present investigation; these are semi-log, linear, hyperbolic, semi-log-inverse, double-log, log-inverse, and double-log-inverse. All these forms can be estimated by simple regression techniques after appropriate transformations.

A rigorous treatment of the estimation of regression equations from grouped data was provided by Prais and Aitchison (1954), who demonstrated that, whatever the method of grouping, the generalized least-squares method applied to the grouped means will result in unbiased estimators of the regression coefficients. Their conclusion is correct, however, only for those Engel functions that are linear in the original variables. If, in contrast, the nonlinear Engel functions, in which the original variables are transformed to logarithms or reciprocals, are estimated, application of generalized least-squares requires the geometric and harmonic means of the original variables within each income class; these, however, are seldom available. The usual procedure, therefore, is to use the arithmetic means as proxy for the geometric and harmonic means, a process that invariably introduces bias into the estimates of the parameters of the nonlinear Engel functions.

Kakwani (1977b) estimated the geometric and harmonic means of various expenditures within each income group in order to obtain the unbiased estimates of the parameters of the Engel functions. The new coordinated system of Lorenz curves was used for this purpose. The empirical results indicate that the magnitude of bias in the elasticity estimates of different commodities depends on the form of the Engel function. In general, the percentage bias was small for semi-log, double-log, and double-log-inverse forms, whereas the hyperbolic and log-inverse forms gave consistently large bias.

It was mentioned in chapter 8 that Mahalnobis (1960) used concentration curves to describe the consumption pattern for different commodities. It was also demonstrated that the concentration index of a commodity is closely related to its elasticity. By means of these concentration indexes, Kakwani (1977b) introduced a new index of the elasticity (inelasticity) of a commodity. This index indicates the extent to which elasticity deviates from unity over the whole income range. In the same paper, he also proposed an alternative method of estimating Engel elasticities from concentration indexes.

This chapter provides a detailed discussion of these results on the estimation of Engel elasticities by means of the concentration curves. In addition, a new equation of the Engel curve, which is based on a new coordinate system for the Lorenz curve discussed in chapter 7, is considered. The Lorenz curve is fitted to the expenditure data, and the expenditure elasticities are derived in terms of the estimated parameters of the Lorenz curve for total expenditure as well as for expenditure on each commodity. On the basis of the empirical results, it is demonstrated that the proposed equation of the Engel function performs better than the other well-known forms of the Engel function, according to two criteria: goodness of fit and the adding-up criterion (emphasized by Nicholson in 1957).

Throughout this chapter, empirical results are based on Indonesian data, available in grouped form for both urban and rural sectors, and obtained from the *National Social and Economic Survey* carried out during the period October–December 1969. Original observations were grouped into ten classes according to the total per capita expenditure of the families; only the arithmetic mean expenditures for the ten expenditure classes were provided in the survey report.[1]

Elasticity Index of a Commodity

Let x be the total per capita expenditure of a family, which is a random variable with probability distribution function $F(x)$. If $F_1(x)$ is the proportion of the total per capita expenditure of families having total per capita expenditure less than or equal to x, the relationship between $F(x)$ and $F_1(x)$ will be the Lorenz curve of the distribution of x. Further, if $v_i(x)$ is denoted as the Engel function of the ith commodity, the function $F_1[v_i(x)]$, as defined in (8.1), will be interpreted as the proportion of per capita expenditure on the ith commodity of families having a total per capita expenditure less than or equal to x. The relationship between $F_1[v_i(x)]$ and $F(x)$ will be the concentration curve of the ith commodity.

Corollary 8.2 indicates that the concentration curve of the ith commodity lies above (below) the Lorenz curve for x if $\eta_i(x)$ is less (greater) than unity for all $x \geq 0$, $\eta_i(x)$ being the elasticity of the ith commodity. Further, it follows from theorem 8.1 (page 157) that the larger the absolute difference $|\eta_i(x) - 1|$ for all x, the more the area between the concentration curve of the ith commodity and the Lorenz curve for x. The area between the two curves can be used, therefore, as a measure of elasticity, or inelasticity, of the commodity under consideration. Thus, the elasticity index of the ith commodity is defined as

$$(10.1) \qquad E_i = C_i - G$$

where G is the Gini index of the per capita total expenditure and C_i is the concentration index of the ith commodity when the families are arranged according to their per capita total expenditure. Clearly, E_i is equal to twice the area between the two curves. The ith commodity will be elastic (inelastic) if E_i is greater (less) than zero.

The elasticity of a commodity generally varies with the total per capita expenditure, and E_i is a single measure of elasticity, or inelasticity, of a commodity. It should, therefore, be used with caution.

---

1. For further discussion, see Gupta (1975).

Because the magnitude of E_i merely indicates how much the elasticity of the ith commodity deviates from unity over the whole range of income, the index can be used only for comparative purposes. The attractive feature of the index is, however, that it can be computed from grouped observations on expenditures without specifying the form of the Engel function.

If per capita expenditure on a family's food is expressed as the sum of per capita expenditures on k food items, it follows from theorem 8.5 that

$$(10.2) \qquad C_f = \frac{1}{Q_f} \sum_{i=1}^{k} Q_i C_i$$

where C_f is the concentration index of the total food expenditure and C_i the concentration index for the ith food item. In addition, Q_f and Q_i are the mean per capita expenditures on total food and on the ith food item, respectively. Substituting (10.1) into (10.2) yields

$$E = \frac{1}{Q_f} \sum_{i=1}^{k} Q_i E_i \,,$$

which expresses the elasticity index of total food as the weighted average of the elasticity indexes of all food items, the weights being proportional to the expenditure share of each food item.

Again, theorem 8.5 yields

$$G = \frac{1}{\mu} \sum_{i=1}^{n} Q_i C_i$$

where n is the total number of commodity groups and μ is the mean total per capita expenditure. Substituting (10.1) into this equation gives

$$\frac{1}{\mu} \sum_{i=1}^{n} Q_i E_i = 0,$$

which proves that the weighted average of the elasticity indexes of all commodities equals zero, the weights being proportional to the expenditures on commodities. Thus, the elasticity index satisfies the adding-up criterion, which says that the weighted average of the elasticities of all commodities must be equal to one at all income levels.

Computation of Elasticity Indexes by Means of Indonesian Data

For the purpose of computing the elasticity indexes, data were obtained from the Indonesian *National Social and Economic Survey*, which covered the period October 1969–April 1970, and was carried out in two four-month periods: October–December 1969 and January–April 1970.

To compute the concentration indexes from the grouped data, the new coordinate system for the Lorenz curve, as defined in (7.7), was fitted to each expenditure distribution. The concentration indexes were then computed by means of (7.21), which was derived in chapter 7.

Table 10.1 presents the estimates of the parameters of the new coordinate system for the Lorenz curve (7.7) as well as the elasticity index for each commodity in the combined urban and rural sectors of Indonesia. The square of the correlation between the actual and estimated values of η is R^2, and is given in the fourth column. The fifth column gives estimates of the concentration index for each commodity computed from the Lorenz curve, and the sixth column reports the values of the proposed elasticity index. Note that the values of R^2 are consistently high for all the commodity expenditures. The actual and estimated values of η are not reported here, but they were close to two decimal places for the entire expenditure range. The estimates of the elasticity index indicates that cereal and cassava are highly inelastic, whereas meat, eggs, and milk products are highly elastic. In addition, total food is inelastic. Among nonfood commodities, durables and semidurables are highly elastic, whereas the expenditure on housing is inelastic.

The proposed elasticity index was also computed for each of these commodities separately in the urban and rural sectors, but space does not permit reporting the numerical results here. They did indicate, however, that the elasticity index for most commodities was higher for the rural sector than for the urban sector. The only exception was expenditure on housing, which had more inelastic demand in the rural sector than in the urban. Because urban sector households have a higher average income than those of the rural sector, the results confirm the hypothesis that income elasticity diminishes with the household income level.

Table 10.1. *Estimates of the Lorenz Function and the Elasticity Index by Commodity, Indonesia (Urban and Rural), 1969*

Commodity	a	α	β	R^2	Concentration index	Elasticity index
Cereal and cassava	0.1748	0.7854	0.8617	0.9990	0.196	-0.151
Sea food	0.4286	0.9219	0.9517	0.9995	0.430	0.083
Meat	0.6692	0.9940	1.0308	0.9996	0.623	0.276
Eggs and milk	0.6773	1.0013	1.0437	0.9998	0.625	0.278
Vegetables	0.2767	0.9164	0.8353	1.0000	0.295	-0.052
Fruit and peas	0.4535	0.9232	0.8486	0.9995	0.479	0.132
Other foods	0.3777	0.9213	0.9153	0.9997	0.386	0.039
Total food	0.2988	0.8750	0.8296	0.9999	0.326	-0.021
Tobacco and alcohol	0.3866	0.9145	0.8868	1.0000	0.402	0.055
Housing	0.2933	0.8766	0.8064	0.9999	0.324	-0.023
Miscellaneous goods	0.5488	0.9667	0.9305	0.9999	0.544	0.197
Clothing	0.3728	0.9066	0.8695	1.0000	0.392	0.045
Durables and semi-durables	0.6031	0.9773	0.9220	1.0000	0.598	0.251
Other expenditures	0.3625	0.9112	0.7909	1.0000	0.397	0.050
Total expenditure	0.3186	0.8848	0.8234	0.9999	0.347	0.000

Table 10.2. *Decomposition of the Elasticity Index of Total Food in Terms of Elasticity Indexes by Commodity, Indonesia (Urban and Rural), 1969*

Commodity	Percentage of expenditure by commodity	Elasticity index	Contribution to total food by commodity	Percentage of contribution
Cereal and cassava	44.54	−0.151	−0.0672	−319
Sea food	7.93	0.083	0.0065	31
Meat	4.80	0.276	0.0132	63
Eggs and milk	1.62	0.278	0.0045	21
Vegetables	5.62	−0.052	−0.0029	−14
Fruit and peas	10.27	0.132	0.0135	64
Tobacco and alcohol	8.42	0.055	0.0046	22
Other foods	16.79	0.039	0.0065	31
Total food	100	−0.021	−0.021	−100

Table 10.2 gives the decomposition of the elasticity index of total food in terms of the elasticity indexes of each food item. If the elasticity index of total food is set at −100, the contribution of cereal and cassava is as much as −319. Vegetables, which are also inelastic, contribute only −14. All other food items are elastic, their contributions varying from +22 to +64. This indicates that cereal and cassava together is a dominant item in total food expenditure. If this item is excluded, total food will become highly elastic. From this it can be inferred that for any future projections, it would be erroneous to use the aggregate elasticity of the food group, and that disaggregation of the food group is much needed in this situation.

Estimation of Engel Functions from Grouped Observations

In this section the estimation of expenditure elasticities is considered by specifying the various forms of the Engel functions. The nonlinear Engel functions present a special problem when estimated from grouped observations. An attempt is made here to solve this problem by means of the estimated equation of the Lorenz function considered in chapter 7.

The following seven forms of the Engel function were chosen for the purpose of estimating the expenditure elasticities:

(a) Semi-log $\qquad q_i = \alpha_{0i} + \alpha_{1i} \log x;$
(b) Linear $\qquad\quad q_i = \alpha_{0i} + \alpha_{1i} x;$
(c) Hyperbolic $\quad\ \ q_i = \alpha_{0i} + \alpha_{1i}/x;$
(d) Semi-log-inverse $\quad q_i = \alpha_{0i} + \alpha_{1i} \log x + \alpha_{2i}/x;$
(e) Double-log $\quad\ \ \text{Log } q_i = \alpha_{0i} + \alpha_{1i} \log x;$
(f) Log-inverse $\quad\ \ \text{Log } q_i = \alpha_{0i} + \alpha_{1i}/x;$
(g) Double-log-inverse $\text{Log } q_i = \alpha_{0i} + \alpha_{1i} \log x + \alpha_{2i}/x.$

The per capita expenditure on the ith commodity is denoted by q_i, and x is the total per capita expenditure. As mentioned above, all these forms can be estimated by simple regression techniques after appropriate transformation. The two-parameter forms (a), (b), (c), (e), and (f) were investigated by Prais and Houthakker (1955), using United Kingdom data. The two additional forms that are included here, (d) and (g), are simply the combinations of semi-log and hyperbolic, and the double-log and log-inverse forms, respectively.

A multivariate regression equation representing the above forms of the Engel function can be written as

$$(10.3) \qquad\qquad y = X\beta + u$$

where y is a vector of n individual observations on the dependent variable of the particular Engel function, and X is the $n \times \Lambda$ matrix of n observations on the Λ independent variables, Λ being equal to 2 for the forms (a), (b), (c), (e), and (f), and 3 for the forms (d) and (g). The first column of X has all elements equal to one. The coefficient vector is β, and u is a vector of n disturbances.

It is assumed that the disturbances in (10.3) have a zero mean, constant variance, and are independently distributed; this implies that

$$Eu = 0, \qquad Euu' = \sigma^2 I.$$

If the n individual observations were available, the least-squares method could be applied to (10.3) to obtain the best linear unbiased estimates of the parameters of the Engel functions. Because these observations are not available for Indonesia, the parameters must be estimated from the grouped data.

Assume that the original n observations are grouped into k expenditure classes, giving arithmetic means of different expenditures in each class. The regression equation (10.3), in terms of grouped means, can then be written as

(10.4) $$\bar{y} = \bar{X}\beta + \bar{u}$$

where $\bar{y} = Gy$, $\bar{X} = GX$, and $\bar{u} = Gu$, G being the grouping matrix introduced by Prais and Aitchison (1954). Thus

$$(GG')^{-1} = \begin{bmatrix} f_1 & \cdots\cdots\cdots\cdots\cdots\cdots & 0 \\ \vdots & & \vdots \\ \vdots & f_2 & \vdots \\ \vdots & & \vdots \\ \vdots & \cdot & \vdots \\ \vdots & \cdot & \vdots \\ \vdots & \cdot & \vdots \\ \vdots & \cdot & \vdots \\ \vdots & \cdot & \vdots \\ \vdots & \cdot & \vdots \\ \vdots & \cdot & \vdots \\ 0 & \cdots\cdots\cdots\cdots\cdots & f_k \end{bmatrix}$$

where $f_1, f_2, \ldots, f_k$ are the relative frequencies in each group.

It can be shown that $E(\bar{u}\bar{u}') = \sigma^2 (GG')$, which justifies the application of Aitken's (1934) generalized least-squares method to (10.4) in order to obtain the most efficient estimates of the parameters. Prais and Aitchison (1954) demonstrated that, whatever the method of grouping, the generalized least-squares estimators are unbiased, although they have a larger variance than estimates based on individual observations.

Premultiplying equation (10.4) by $(GG')^{-\frac{1}{2}}$ yields

(10.5) $$y^* = X^*\beta + u^*$$

where

$$y^* = (GG')^{-\frac{1}{2}}\bar{y}, \qquad X^* = (GG')^{-\frac{1}{2}}\bar{X}, \quad \text{and} \quad u^* = (GG')^{-\frac{1}{2}}\bar{u},$$

$(GG')^{-\frac{1}{2}}$ being the diagonal matrix with its elements equal to the square root of the frequencies in each expenditure class. Note that this transformation is equivalent to multiplying each class mean by the square root of the corresponding relative frequency in the class. It is clear that

(10.6) $$Eu^* = 0, \quad \text{and} \quad Eu^*u'^* = \sigma^2 I.$$

Thus, the ordinary least-squares procedure, when applied to transformed equation (10.5), will yield

(10.7) $\hat{\beta} = [\bar{X}'(GG')^{-1}\bar{X}]^{-1}[\bar{X}'(GG')^{-1}\bar{y}],$

which is the same as the generalized least-squares estimator derived by Prais and Aitchison (1954). From a practical point of view, this is a useful result because it allows the use of an ordinary least-squares computer program to obtain the most efficient estimates of the Engel parameters.

It should now be noted that the elements of $\bar{y}$ and $\bar{X}$ in (10.4) are the means of the relevant variables of the Engel function in each income class. If the relevant variables in the Engel function are the logarithms, or the reciprocal of expenditures, as is the case for most of the Engel forms, the geometric and harmonic means of the individual observations will be needed for each income class in order to derive $\bar{y}$ and $\bar{X}$ in (10.7). The available grouped data give, in practice, only the arithmetic means of the observations. The usual procedure is to compute $\hat{\beta}$ on the basis of the available arithmetic means for each income class. This will, of course, introduce bias into the estimates of the Engel parameters. (The usual method will be referred to as Method I.)

To obtain unbiased estimators of the Engel parameters, estimate the geometric and harmonic means of various expenditures within each income class from the estimated equation of the Lorenz curve given in (7.7). This procedure is as follows:

If $\eta = g(\pi)$ denotes the equation of the new coordinate system for the Lorenz curve of x, from (7.16) the density function of x will be given by

(10.8) $$f(x)dx = \frac{1}{\sqrt{2}}[1 + g'(\pi)]d\pi$$

(10.9) $$\pi = \frac{1}{\sqrt{2}}[F(x) + F_1(x)]$$

(10.10) $$\eta = \frac{1}{\sqrt{2}}[F(x) - F_1(x)].$$

Similarly, if $\eta_i = g_i(\pi_i)$ denotes the equation of the concentration curve for the ith commodity, π_i and η_i will be given by

(10.11) $$\pi_i = \frac{1}{\sqrt{2}}[F(x) + F_1(v_i(x))]$$

(10.12) $$\eta_i = \frac{1}{\sqrt{2}}\left[F(x) - F_1(v_i(x))\right],$$

where $v_i(x)$ denotes the Engel function for the ith commodity.

Now, differentiating (10.11) and (10.12) with respect to x yields

(10.13) $$\frac{d\eta_i}{d\pi_i} = \frac{Q_i - v_i(x)}{Q_i + v_i(x)},$$

which, on solving for $v_i(x)$, gives

(10.14) $$v_i(x) = \frac{Q_i(1 - g_i'(\pi_i))}{(1 + g_i'(\pi_i))}.$$

Let G_{it} and M_{it} be the geometric and harmonic means of the expenditure on the ith commodity in the tth expenditure class, then, (10.8) and (10.14) yield

$$\log G_{it} = \frac{1}{\sqrt{2}} \int_{\pi_{t-1}}^{\pi_t} \log\left[\frac{Q_i(1 - g_i'(\pi_i))}{(1 + g_i'(\pi_i))}\right](1 + g'(\pi))d\pi$$

$$\frac{1}{H_{it}} = \frac{1}{\sqrt{2}} \int_{\pi_{t-1}}^{\pi_t} \frac{(1 + g_i'(\pi_i))}{Q_i(1 - g_i'(\pi_i))}(1 + g'(\pi))d\pi.$$

To evaluate these integrals, the following relation was used:

$$\pi_i + g_i(\pi_i) = \pi + g(\pi).$$

It was derived from equations (10.9), (10.10), (10.11), and (10.12) by eliminating $F_1(x)$ and $F_1(v_i(x))$. The numerical results were obtained by assuming that $g(\pi)$ and $g_i(\pi_i)$ are of the form (7.7), the parameter estimates of which are reported in table 10.1. On the basis of the geometric and harmonic means for each income class, $\bar{y}$ and $\bar{X}$ were constructed for each of the Engel functions specified above, which can be used in (10.7) to obtain parameter estimates. This method will be referred to as Method II.

A Comparison of Elasticities

The results of the applications of the statistical techniques discussed in the preceding section are presented below. The first step involves the estimation of Engel functions by means of applying the least-squares technique to the transformed equation (10.5).

The first column of X^* consists of the square root of the relative frequencies in each expenditure class. It was necessary to modify the standard regression program so that the regression equation always passes through the origin. For each item of consumer expenditure, all seven Engel functions were fitted to the urban and rural sectors, both separately and combined. In all, ninety-eight regressions were fitted, and the expenditure elasticities were computed at the mean values of the total expenditure. This method of estimation is referred to as Method I.

To estimate the elasticities by Method II, it is necessary to compute, through the standard computer program for numerical integration, the geometric and harmonic means of different expenditures in each income range. Once these means have been computed, the procedure of computing the Engel coefficients by Method II is the same as that followed for Method I.

Note that for the nonlinear Engel functions, the estimated expenditure on a particular item at the mean value of the total expenditure differs slightly from the actual mean expenditure. This difference is a result of the fact that the logarithm (or the reciprocal) of mean expenditures is unequal to the mean of the logarithm (or reciprocal) of expenditures. The estimated expenditures have been used here to compute the elasticities at the mean value of the total expenditure.

It was mentioned above that the usual method (Method I) introduces bias into the estimates of the Engel parameters. The difference between the elasticities computed by the two methods of estimation should give some indication of the extent of bias introduced. The percentage bias, defined as the difference between the two elasticities divided by the elasticity computed by Method II, is computed for the different forms of the Engel function. The results are presented in table 10.3.

For the linear form, the two methods of estimation give the same elasticity estimates. The table clearly indicates that the magnitude of bias depends on the form of the Engel function. For example, the percentage bias is generally small for semi-log, double-log, and double-log-inverse forms, and consistently large for hyperbolic and log-inverse forms. In addition, bias is generally positive for semi-log, hyperbolic, semi-log-inverse, and log-inverse forms, indicating that method I overestimates the elasticities for these forms. The double-log form gives negative bias in eight out of fourteen cases, and the double-log-inverse form gives negative bias for most cases. It may

Table 10.3. *Sample Estimate of Percentage Bias in Estimates of Expenditure Elasticities Computed by Method I, Indonesia (Urban and Rural), 1969*

| | Forms of the Engel function | | | | | |
Commodity	Semi-log	Hyper-bolic	Semi-log-inverse	Double-log	Log-inverse	Double-log-inverse
Cereal and cassava	0.2	10.9	−2.9	−3.7	5.5	−2.6
Sea food	1.5	11.7	1.9	−1.6	9.8	−2.8
Meat	2.4	11.9	7.9	−1.3	14.1	−7.4
Eggs and milk	2.6	12.1	8.5	−2.7	10.0	−5.4
Vegetables	0.9	11.9	.4	0.1	12.6	−1.6
Fruit and peas	2.2	12.2	5.5	0.4	9.8	1.9
Other foods	1.3	12.0	1.4	−0.9	11.6	−3.1
Total food	1.1	12.0	0.8	−0.9	9.9	−0.9
Tobacco and alcohol	1.5	11.9	2.2	−1.1	10.3	−2.0
Housing	1.1	11.8	0.9	0.0	10.5	0.1
Miscellaneous goods	2.4	12.1	7.1	0.7	12.8	−0.9
Clothing	1.4	12.1	2.2	−0.9	10.0	−1.3
Durables and semi-durables	2.8	12.2	9.5	1.5	12.8	1.3
Other expenditures	1.9	12.4	4.1	2.2	13.2	−1.7

be concluded, therefore, that the elasticities based on the double-log and double-log-inverse forms are likely to be underestimated when Method I is used.

The expenditure elasticities estimated by Method II are presented in table 10.4.

Note that the elasticity estimates based on different forms of the Engel curve differ considerably. Among the two-parameter Engel curves, the double-log form gives the highest estimate, and the hyperbolic form the lowest estimate. (This observation was originally made by Prais and Houthakker (1955) on the basis of a British study.) The linear form gives the second highest estimates, but in Prais and Houthakker's investigation it was the semi-log form that gave the second highest estimates.

The expenditure elasticities were computed for urban and rural sectors separately, and, again, because of space restrictions, the numerical results are not reported here. The comparison of these elasticities indicated, however, that for the semi-log, hyperbolic, semi-log-inverse, and log-inverse forms, the rural sector elasticities were higher than the urban sector elasticities for most of the com-

Table 10.4. *Estimates of Expenditure Elasticities for Forms of the Engel Function Computed by Method II, Indonesia (Urban and Rural), 1969*

Forms of the Engel function

Commodity	Semi-log	Linear	Hyperbolic	Semi-log-inverse	Double-log	Log-inverse	Double-log-inverse
Cereal and cassava	0.51	0.47	0.26	0.56	0.62	0.38	0.54
Sea food	1.02	1.22	0.46	1.39	1.36	0.77	1.33
Meat	1.40	2.03	0.59	2.28	2.22	1.26	2.15
Eggs and milk	1.40	2.05	0.59	2.28	2.18	1.20	2.19
Vegetables	0.75	0.82	0.34	0.97	0.82	0.44	0.87
Fruit and peas	1.14	1.52	0.49	1.70	1.39	0.78	1.37
Other foods	0.94	1.09	0.42	1.25	1.15	0.63	1.17
Total food	0.82	0.92	0.38	1.06	0.96	0.53	0.95
Tobacco and alcohol	0.98	1.17	0.44	1.34	1.19	0.66	1.20
Housing	0.82	0.92	0.38	1.07	0.93	0.51	0.93
Miscellaneous goods	1.26	1.76	0.53	1.96	1.62	0.88	1.67
Clothing	0.96	1.14	0.43	1.31	1.16	0.64	1.16
Durables and semi-durables	1.37	2.02	0.57	2.24	1.76	0.96	1.80
Other expenditures	0.98	1.23	0.43	1.40	1.07	0.58	1.11

modities. The double-log and double-log-inverse forms did not show such patterns.

Now consider the problem of making a choice among alternative forms of the Engel function on the basis of goodness of fit. The multiple correlation coefficient, R^2, is widely used for this purpose, but there are two problems associated with it. One is the comparison of the correlation coefficients of the first four forms with those of the last three forms. For the first four forms, the multiple correlation coefficient measures the degree of "explanation" of the variance of q_i, whereas for the last three forms, it measures the degree of explanation of the variance of log q_i; the two are, of course, incomparable. The second problem concerns the grouping of observations. This was considered by Prais and Aitchison (1954), and later by Cramer (1964). These authors demonstrated that the correlation coefficient based on grouped data is an unsatisfactory estimate of the correlation in the population, and, therefore, of little statistical interest.

In view of the limitations of the multiple correlation, the following distance function was used here as a selection criterion:[2]

$$D_i^2 = \frac{1}{(k - \Lambda)} \sum_{j=1}^{k} f_i (q_{ij} - \hat{q}_{ij})^2$$

where q_{ij} is the observed level of consumer expenditure on the ith commodity in the jth expenditure class, and $\hat{q}_{ij}$ the expenditure on the ith commodity in the jth expenditure class, as estimated from a given form of the Engel curve. The number of expenditure classes is k, and Λ is the number of explanatory variables in the given Engel curve.

The computed values of the distance function for the various forms of the Engel function are presented in table 10.5; the Engel function giving the minimum value of the distance function was chosen for each commodity. The results are reported in table 10.6, which gives the coefficient estimates along with the standard errors of the selected Engel functions.

On the basis of the distance function criterion, the linear form was most preferred and was selected in seven out of fourteen cases.

---

2. This function was used by Jain and Tendulkar (1973). Because they were comparing the goodness-of-fit of only two-parameter curves, however, they did not divide it by degrees of freedom.

Table 10.5. *Computed Values of the Distance Function for Forms of the Engel Function, Indonesia (Urban and Rural), 1969*

				Forms of the Engel function			
Commodity	Semi-log	Linear	Hyperbolic	Semi-log-inverse	Double-log	Log-inverse	Double-log-inverse
Cereal and cassava	49.90	360.15	996.78	14.05	138.798	367.058	9.581
Sea food	112.35	0.92	366.46	41.80	7.588	244.983	2.377
Meat	219.76	24.62	467.88	111.61	25.612	384.663	6.990
Eggs and milk	27.34	3.04	56.92	14.56	1.186	49.566	1.976
Vegetables	21.79	0.88	79.46	7.59	2.671	60.742	0.492
Fruit and peas	500.81	51.83	1,097.05	289.58	80.29	923.25	112.51
Other foods	379.51	4.62	7,282.15	139.60	5.14	925.60	8.94
Total food	8,639.54	103.33	30,612.09	3,602.39	335.501	21,405.42	529.82
Tobacco and alcohol	128.19	0.68	388.76	52.78	2.40	290.22	1.40
Housing	103.83	1.54	346.64	44.67	9.51	255.72	10.18
Miscellaneous goods	234.16	24.39	493.63	131.40	23.96	442.48	9.66
Clothing	89.45	0.46	269.23	38.30	3.08	200.75	2.90
Durables and semi-durables	99.63	16.07	188.86	61.02	19.48	179.24	14.77
Other expenditures	46.08	2.85	108.38	25.87	14.58	94.32	10.82

Table 10.6. Expenditure Elasticities and Coefficient Estimates of Forms of the Engel Function by Residual Variance Estimates, Indonesia (Urban and Rural), 1969

Commodity	Form of the Engel function	Coefficient estimates α_{0i}	α_{1i}	α_{2i}	Elasticity
Cereal and cassava	Double-log-inverse	3.76 (0.03)	0.37 (0.004)	−247.98 (3.74)	0.545
Sea food	Linear	−19.22 (1.68)	0.07 (0.001)	—	1.223
Meat	Double-log-inverse	−10.85 (1.13)	2.01 (0.14)	−201.42 (125.88)	2.151
Eggs and milk	Double-log	−13.33 (0.56)	2.18 (0.08)	—	2.180
Vegetables	Double-log-inverse	− 3.14 (0.11)	0.99 (0.01)	156.51 (12.57)	0.874
Fruit and peas	Linear	−55.68 (12.66)	0.12 (0.007)	—	1.516
Other foods	Linear	−16.63 (3.78)	0.14 (0.0002)	—	1.091
Total food	Linear	90.70 (17.87)	0.70 (0.01)	—	0.917
Tobacco and alcohol	Linear	−15.37 (1.45)	0.08 (0.001)	—	1.168
Housing	Linear	8.93 (2.18)	0.07 (0.001)	—	0.921
Miscellaneous goods	Double-log-inverse	− 9.23 (0.42)	1.79 (0.05)	166.11 (47.03)	1.674
Clothing	Linear	−11.12 (1.19)	0.06 (0.0006)	—	1.142
Durables and semi-durables	Double-log-inverse	−10.72 (0.56)	1.90 (0.07)	127.49 (62.44)	1.805
Other expenditures	Linear	− 9.91	0.04	—	1.230

Note: The figures in parentheses are standard errors.

214

The double-log-inverse form was selected in five cases. The semi-log form, which was found by Prais and Houthakker (1955) to be the best on the multiple correlation criterion, was unacceptable according to the present criterion. The double-log form performed well in only one case.

Among food items, that of cereal and cassava has the lowest elasticity, whereas eggs and milk have the highest elasticity. Total food is inelastic, which is a result of the fact that cereal and cassava together form a dominant item in total food expenditure. Among nonfood items, only expenditure on housing is inelastic. The expenditure on durables and semi-durables has the highest elasticity.

For the double-log-inverse form, the expenditure elasticity η_i is expressed as

$$\eta_i = \alpha_{1i} - \frac{\alpha_{2i}}{x} ,$$

which implies that elasticity increases (decreases) with income, provided α_{2i} is greater (less) than zero. As income increases, elasticity approaches α_{1i}. The rate at which elasticity changes with income is

$$\frac{d\eta_i}{dx} = \frac{\alpha_{2i}}{x^2} ,$$

which depends on the magnitude of the coefficient α_{2i}, and on the level of income. The rate at which the proportional expenditure on the ith commodity changes with income is given by

$$(10.15) \qquad \frac{d}{dx}\left(\frac{q_i}{x}\right) = \frac{q_i(\eta_i - 1)}{x^2} ,$$

which implies that the proportional expenditure on the ith commodity increases (decreases) if the commodity is elastic (inelastic). Similarly, it can be seen that for the linear form, elasticity decreases (or increases) with income if the intercept α_{0i} is negative (or positive). The semi-log form implies that elasticity always decreases with income. In view of these properties of the different Engel functions, further implications of the results given in table 10.6 can be discussed.

Note that for most of the commodities, elasticity decreases with income. There are, however, a few exceptions. Elasticity increases with income for expenditures on vegetables, housing, durables, and total food, and the expenditure on eggs and milk displays almost constant elasticity. The double-log-inverse form gives the maximum negative value of the coefficient α_{2i} for cereal and cassava, implying a faster decline in expenditure elasticity for this item. Because this item is highly inelastic, the proportional expenditure on it will also decline at a faster rate, which may lead to an increase in the proportional expenditure on elastic food items.

Because cereal and cassava are a dominant expenditure item, they have considerable effect on total food elasticity. Thus two factors determine whether total food elasticity increases or decreases with income: the decline in elasticity of cereal and cassava, and the increase in proportional expenditure on elastic food items. Because the expenditure elasticity on total food increases with income (which follows from the positive intercept of the linear form), the second factor dominates. Furthermore, total food elasticity is close to unity and has a tendency to increase with income. It follows from (10.15), then, that the proportion of expenditure on total food may not decline with the rising per capita total expenditure, which is a proxy for income. This is an important conclusion, implying that, for future planning, food needs have to be given careful attention.

Finally, the weighted average of the elasticities of all the commodities was computed as 1.026. This implies that the adding-up criterion is approximately satisfied at the mean expenditure level.

An Alternative Method of Estimating Elasticities

It was mentioned in "Elasticity Index of a Commodity" that the concentration index of a commodity is closely related to its elasticity, and that the expenditure on an elastic commodity will have a higher value of the concentration index than that on a relatively inelastic commodity. By means of the concentration indexes for various items of consumer expenditure, this section presents an alternative method of estimating the Engel elasticities.

Iyenger (1960) estimated Engel elasticities from concentration curves by means of Indian data obtained from the *National Sample Survey of India*, 1955–56. His method rests on two basic assumptions: the log-normality of income (or expenditure) distribution, and the constancy of Engel elasticity. These assumptions are, however, rather restrictive. The log-normality assumption implies that the Lorenz curve for income (or total expenditure) is symmetric, which may not be true. Second, the constant elasticity Engel function may not necessarily be the best for estimating elasticities. The method of estimation developed in this section relaxes both these assumptions.

Let $y_i^* = E(y_i|x)$ be the conditional expectation of y_i for a given value of x; the equation of a two-parameter Engel curve as listed in "Estimation of Engel Functions from Grouped Observations" can be written as

$$(10.16) \qquad y_i^* = a + bz(x)$$

where y_i is either q_i, the expenditure on the ith commodity, or log q_i, depending on the form of the curve; $z(x)$ is a function of x, which is the per capita total expenditure; and x is a random variable with mean μ. Obviously, $z(x)$ will also be a random variable, which has, say, mean μ_z and the concentration index C_z. It is then clear from (10.16) that y_i^* is a random variable with mean $(a + b\mu_z)$. By means of corollary 8.9, it follows that

$$(10.17) \qquad (a + b\mu_z)C_{y_i}^* = b\mu_z C_z$$

where $C_{y_i}^*$ is the concentration of y_i^*.

Note that only the variable y_i for a given x was observed. To estimate parameters a and b, replace the mean, the concentration index of y_i^* by the mean, and the concentration index of observed variable y_i, respectively. Thus according to (10.17), the estimates of a and b are

$$(10.18) \qquad \hat{a} = \mu_{y_i} - \hat{b}\mu_z$$

$$(10.19) \qquad \hat{b} = \frac{\mu_{y_i}C_{y_i}}{\mu_z C_z}$$

where μ_{y_i} and C_{y_i} are the mean and the concentration index of y_i, respectively.

For the different forms of the Engel function, the estimates of α_{0i} and α_{1i} are derived from (10.18) and (10.19):

Engel curve	*Estimate of* α_{0i}	*Estimate of* α_{1i}
Semi-log	$Q_i - \hat{\alpha}_{1i} \log G$	$\dfrac{Q_i C_i}{\log G \cdot C_l}$
Linear	$Q_i - \hat{\alpha}_{1i}\mu$	$\dfrac{Q_i C_i}{\mu G}$
Hyperbolic	$Q_i - \dfrac{\hat{\alpha}_{1i}}{H}$	$\dfrac{Q_i C_i H}{C_R}$
Double-log	$\log G_i - \hat{\alpha}_{1i} \log G$	$\dfrac{C_{li} \log G_i}{C_l \log G}$
Log-inverse	$\log G_i - \dfrac{\hat{\alpha}_{1i}}{H}$	$\dfrac{\log G_i C_{li} H}{C_R}$

where G_i = the geometric mean of the expenditure on the ith commodity,

G = the geometric mean of the total expenditure,

H = the harmonic mean of the total expenditure,

C_i = the concentration index of the expenditure on the ith commodity,

C_{li} = the concentration index of the logarithm of the expenditure on the ith commodity,

C_l = the concentration index of the logarithm of the total per capita expenditure,

C_R = the concentration index of the reciprocal of the per capita expenditure.

Note that C_R will always be negative. This method of estimation will be referred to as Method III.

The equation of the new coordinate system for the Lorenz curve as given in (7.7) was fitted to the logarithms and the reciprocal of the mean expenditures in each income class. Equation (7.21) was then used to compute the various concentration indexes. The elasticity estimates obtained by means of Method III are presented in table 10.7.

Table 10.7 clearly shows that the elasticity estimates obtained by means of Method III are quite close to the corresponding estimates obtained by Method II for the semi-log, linear, and double-log forms. Between the two methods, there are, however, considerable

Table 10.7. *Estimates of Expenditure Elasticities for Forms of the Engel Function Computed by Method III, Indonesia (Urban and Rural), 1969*

Commodity	Forms of the Engel function				
	Semi-log	Linear	Hyper-bolic	Double-log	Log inverse
Cereal and cassava	0.515	0.566	0.516	0.618	0.437
Sea food	1.005	1.238	1.664	1.364	0.965
Meat	1.334	1.796	3.938	2.238	1.584
Eggs and milk	1.337	1.800	3.974	2.247	1.590
Vegetables	0.737	0.850	0.898	0.834	0.590
Fruit and peas	1.094	1.379	2.056	1.381	0.978
Other foods	0.921	1.112	1.373	1.163	0.823
Total food	0.801	0.939	1.044	0.954	0.675
Tobacco and alcohol	0.952	1.158	1.473	1.196	0.847
Housing	0.797	0.932	1.034	0.924	0.654
Miscellaneous goods	1.206	1.568	2.731	1.641	1.161
Clothing	0.933	1.131	1.410	1.159	0.821
Durables and semi-durables	1.295	1.722	3.493	1.787	1.265
Other expenditures	0.943	1.143	1.441	1.078	0.763

differences in the estimates for the remaining two forms, hyperbolic and log-inverse. These differences may be a result of the fact that both forms have large residual variances.

A New Specification of the Engel Curve

In this section an alternative specification of the Engel curve is considered; one proposed by Kakwani (1978b). This specification is derived from the new coordinate system for the Lorenz curve.

Again denote $\eta = g(\pi)$ as the equation of the Lorenz curve for the distribution of total per capita expenditure. Note that π and η are defined in (10.9) and (10.10). The derivatives of η with respect to π are

$$(10.20) \qquad g'(\pi) = \frac{\mu - x}{\mu + x}$$

$$(10.21) \qquad g''(\pi) = \frac{-2\sqrt{2}\mu^2}{f(x)(\mu + x)^3} < 0$$

where $f(x)$ is the probability density function of x.

Again, writing $\eta_i = g_i(\pi_i)$ as the equation of the concentration curve for the ith commodity, the first derivative of η_i with respect to π_i, that is, $g_i'(\pi_i)$, is derived in (10.13). The second derivative will be

$$(10.22) \qquad g_i''(\pi_i) = -\frac{2\sqrt{2}Q_i^2 v_i'(x)}{f(x)[Q_i + v_i(x)]^3}.$$

Now combining (10.20), (10.13), (10.21), and (10.22) yields the income elasticity of the ith commodity as

$$(10.23) \quad \eta_i(x) = \frac{v_i'(x)x}{v_i(x)} = \frac{g_i''(\pi_i)[1 + g'(\pi)]^2[1 - g'(\pi)]}{g''(\pi)[1 + g_i'(\pi_i)]^2[1 - g_i'(\pi_i)]}.$$

If data are available in grouped form and arranged according to total per capita expenditure, this equation can be used to compute expenditure elasticities at the endpoint of each expenditure class. To compute elasticity at any income level, the following relation must be used:

$$(10.24) \qquad \pi + g(\pi) = \pi_i + g_i(\pi_i),$$

which is derived from

$$F(x) = \frac{1}{\sqrt{2}}[\pi + \eta] = \frac{1}{\sqrt{2}}[\pi_i + \eta_i].$$

Equation (10.24) gives the values of the π_i for any given value of π. For any given value of x, (10.20) gives the value of π, which, on substituting into (10.24), gives the value of π_i. Furthermore, substituting the computed values of π and π_i into (10.23) yields the expenditure on income elasticity at any given level of income. Similarly, substituting π_i into (10.14) gives the expenditure on the ith commodity for any given level of income. Thus, there is a new specification Engel curve, based on the new coordinate system of the Lorenz curve, which fits extremely well to observed expenditure distributions.

A numerical illustration follows by means of Indonesian data.

Again assume that functions $g(\pi)$ and $g_i(\pi_i)$ are of the form (7.7), the parameter estimates of which are given in table 10.1, along with the square of the correlation between actual and estimated η and η_i for $i = 1, 2, \ldots, n$.

The expenditure elasticities estimated from (10.23) are presented in table 10.8 at various income levels, including the mean. The last

Table 10.8. *Elasticities by Commodity with Respect to Various Levels of per Capita Total Expenditure, Indonesia (Urban and Rural), 1969*

Commodities	Per capita expenditure levels in rupees									Mean
	300	500	750	1000	1250	1500	2000	2500	3000	
Cereal and cassava	1.1125	0.8859	0.7032	0.6215	0.5711	0.5359	0.4844	0.4505	0.4348	0.558
Sea food	1.2709	1.4923	1.5020	1.4132	1.3786	1.3541	1.3000	1.2424	1.1707	1.379
Meat	5.6562	2.6165	2.4663	2.1994	2.0826	2.0628	2.004	2.0217	2.0213	2.005
Eggs and milk	1.5324	2.2579	2.6264	2.2873	2.1599	2.0350	2.0191	2.0559	2.1054	2.035
Vegetables	0.4790	0.6314	0.7969	0.8661	0.8917	0.8994	0.8983	0.8630	0.8611	0.891
Fruit and peas	1.3591	1.4337	1.4394	1.3662	1.3341	1.3136	1.4014	1.3776	1.3648	1.348
Other foods	0.8536	1.0679	1.2238	1.2295	1.2187	1.2022	1.1499	1.1092	1.0668	1.216
Total food	1.0281	0.9880	0.9664	0.9542	0.9498	0.9446	0.9357	0.9252	0.9210	0.948
Tobacco and alcohol	1.0561	1.1259	1.2118	1.2369	1.2325	1.2208	1.1979	1.1697	1.1374	1.220
Housing	0.9668	0.9158	0.9051	0.9276	0.9183	0.9242	0.9362	0.9417	0.9278	0.921
Miscellaneous goods	0.9579	1.5543	1.7460	1.7100	1.6500	1.6221	1.6348	1.6551	1.6440	1.632
Clothing	1.1146	1.0825	1.1736	1.1857	1.1890	1.1786	1.1505	1.1356	1.1168	1.172
Durables and semi-durables	1.1803	1.6905	1.9558	1.8396	1.7749	1.7411	1.7204	1.7274	1.7266	1.729
Other expenditures	0.8582	0.9291	1.0267	1.070	1.0853	1.1014	1.1284	1.1436	1.1684	1.088
Weighted averages of elasticities	1.0206	0.9985	1.0537	1.0055	0.9960	0.9976	1.0000	0.9982	1.0000	1.009

Table 10.9. *Income Elasticities Based on Alternative Engel Curves (At Mean Values), Indonesia (Urban and Rural), 1969*

Commodity	Semi-log	Linear	Hyper-bolic	Semi-log-inverse	Double-log	Log-inverse	Double-log-inverse	New curve
				Alternative Engel curves				
Cereal and cassava	0.5130	0.471	0.294	0.5395	0.60	0.4012	0.5334	0.5586
Sea food	1.0365	1.221	0.514	1.4184	1.33	0.8418	1.2902	1.3797
Meat	1.4361	2.041	0.657	2.4591	2.19	1.4345	1.9954	2.0051
Eggs and milk	1.4413	2.092	0.658	2.4781	2.12	1.3241	2.0769	2.0351
Vegetables	0.7579	0.823	0.385	0.9783	0.82	0.4906	0.8628	0.8918
Fruit and peas	1.1671	1.487	0.550	1.7917	1.40	0.8565	1.3943	1.3481
Other foods	0.9492	1.091	0.475	1.2724	1.14	0.7018	1.138	1.2160
Total food	0.8266	0.916	0.421	1.0671	0.95	0.5745	0.9408	0.9483
Tobacco and alcohol	0.9904	1.168	0.489	1.3669	1.18	0.7234	1.1769	1.2206
Housing	0.8248	0.921	0.417	1.0786	0.93	0.5669	0.9288	0.9219
Miscellaneous goods	1.2941	1.760	0.600	2.1028	1.63	0.9890	1.662	1.6324
Clothing	0.9724	1.142	0.481	1.3370	1.15	0.7034	1.1471	1.1727
Durables and semi-durables	1.4051	2.019	0.636	2.4601	1.79	1.0843	1.8298	1.7293
Other expenditures	0.9998	1.233	0.481	1.4551	1.10	0.6524	1.1420	1.0888
Weighted averages of elasticities	0.8726	0.9998	0.4382	1.1701	1.0118	0.6124	1.0080	1.0098

Table 10.10. *Weighted Residual Sum of Squares for Forms of Engel Function, Indonesia (Urban and Rural), 1969*

Commodity	Semi-log	Linear	Hyperbolic	Semi-log-inverse	Double-log	Log-inverse	Double-log-inverse	New curve
Cereal and cassava	141.98	2,881.19	6,204.61	9.96	1,508.2	2,247.8	11.2	42.52
Sea food	746.99	7.35	2,640.07	152.25	296.3	1,567.6	82.1	2.90
Meat	1,572.57	196.99	3,521.06	502.58	1,159.0	2,346.1	55.0	6.08
Eggs and milk	194.89	24.35	428.60	65.59	66.4	332.1	28.3	0.07
Vegetables	143.32	7.01	568.10	27.00	5.1	404.8	6.8	0.20
Fruit and peas	3,526.95	414.67	8,185.59	1,371.84	136.4	6,411.5	131.5	23.48
Other foods	2,504.56	36.95	9,208.75	497.81	256.5	5,974.2	228.9	9.04
Total food	56,147.3	826.61	218,534.92	13,649.36	607.5	141,676.1	52.5	34.46
Tobacco and alcohol	864.39	5.48	2,823.81	203.69	29.6	1,930.7	31.4	0.30
Housing	688.03	12.31	2,492.83	178.38	9.7	1,706.9	9.3	1.46
Miscellaneous goods	1,657.75	195.12	3,702.83	605.28	3.6	3,009.6	29.6	0.59
Clothing	602.4	3.67	1,956.29	149.67	11.2	1,345.2	12.1	0.47
Durables and semi-durables	715.31	128.57	1,431.06	294.08	6.4	1,238.3	1.1	0.14
Other expenditures	319.72	22.8	803.16	117.45	31.3	646.3	6.1	0.08

row in the table gives the weighted averages of the elasticities, the weights being proportional to the expenditures on the commodities.

If the adding-up criterion is to be satisfied, the weighted average of elasticities must be equal to one at all levels of income.[3] Clearly, the adding-up criterion is approximately satisfied at all income levels. The maximum error is about 5 percent at the expenditure level of Rs 750. For cereal and cassava, the expenditure elasticity decreases monotonically as income increases. But for other commodities, the elasticities are not monotonic. The forms of the Engel curve considered by Prais and Houthakker (1955), semi-log, linear, hyperbolic, double-log, and log-inverse, imply that either the elasticities are monotonic (increasing or decreasing) or constant. These curves may not, therefore, be considered suitable for all the commodities.

Table 10.9 presents the elasticity estimates at mean per capita total expenditure, based on alternative forms of the Engel curve; the estimation of Method I is used. The last row of table 10.9, which gives the weighted average of elasticities, shows that the additivity criterion is definitely not satisfied for semi-log, hyperbolic, semi-log-inverse, and log-inverse. On the basis of this criterion, the new curve performs better than all the other curves, with the exception of the double-log-inverse and linear models. The additivity condition is, of course, exactly satisfied for the linear Engel function.

To compare the goodness-of-fit of the new form of Engel curve considered here with other well-known forms, the weighted residual sum of squares (WRSS) is presented in table 10.10.[4] Note that the new curve performs better than all other curves on the basis of the minimum weighted residual sum of squares criterion. There is, however, one exception. For cereal and cassava, semi-log-inverse and double-log-inverse forms give a lower value of the (WRSS) than the proposed new curve.

3. See Nicholson (1957).

4. Note that table 10.5 gives the values of the distance function, which is equal to the weighted residual sum of squares divided by degrees of freedom.

PART FIVE

Policy Applications

CHAPTER 11

Redistribution through Taxation: Some Miscellaneous Applications

THE EFFECT OF DIRECT TAXES on income distribution is taken up in this section. If x is the pretax income of an individual and $T(x)$ the tax function, the disposable income is given by

(11.1) $$d(x) = x - T(x),$$

the first derivative of which will be

$$d'(x) = 1 - T'(x).$$

Clearly, $d'(x) > 0$ when $T'(x) < 1$, which implies that the concentration curve of the disposable income coincides with its Lorenz curve if the marginal tax rate is less than unity. Applying theorem 8.3 to (11.1) yields

(11.2) $$\mu_d F_1[d(x)] = \mu F_1(x) - Q F_1[T(x)]$$

where μ and μ_d are the mean pretax and posttax incomes, respectively, and Q is the average tax yield. The equation (11.2) can also be written as

(11.3) $$F_1[d(x)] - F_1(x) = \frac{e}{1-e}[F_1(x) - F_1(T(x))]$$

where $e = Q/\mu$ is the average tax rate for the entire society.

If the tax function $T(x)$ is such that the average tax rate increases as income increases, the tax elasticity will be greater than unity for all x. Following corollary 8.2, this implies that $F_1(x) > F_1[T(x)]$ for all x. Equation (11.3) shows, therefore, that posttax income is

Lorenz superior to pretax income. The conclusion, then, is that posttax income will be more equally distributed than pretax income if the average tax rate increases with income. Note that the marginal tax rate need not increase with income for this result to hold, and, obviously, an increasing marginal tax rate is a stronger condition than an increasing average tax rate.

If $T_1(x)$ is any other tax function with disposable income $d_1(x)$ and the average tax rate e_1, (11.3) yields

$$F_1[d(x)] - F_1[d_1(x)] = \frac{(e - e_1)F_1(x)}{(1 - e)(1 - e_1)}$$

$$+ \frac{e_1 F_1[T_1(x)]}{(1 - e_1)} - \frac{e F_1[T(x)]}{(1 - e)},$$

which, from theorem 8.1, implies that if there are two tax functions yielding the same average tax rate, the tax function with uniformly higher tax elasticity will give a more equal posttax income distribution than a tax function of lower tax elasticity. Similarly, if the tax functions have the same tax elasticity, the tax function with a higher average tax rate gives a more equal posttax income distribution than the tax function with a lower tax rate, provided both functions have elasticities greater than unity, that is, provided both are progressive. If, however, the tax elasticities are equal but less than unity, that is, regressive, the tax function with a lower average tax rate will give a more equal posttax distribution than the one with a higher average tax rate.

Effect of Indirect Taxes on Income Distribution

In this section the extended linear expenditure system (ELES) is used to measure the effect of indirect taxes on income distribution.

Suppose there are n commodities and $t_1, t_2, \ldots, t_n$ are the corresponding indirect tax rates on them. Further, assume that the indirect tax is partly paid by producers and partly by consumers. If h_i denotes the proportion of the indirect tax on the ith commodity, which is passed on to the consumers, the observed price of the ith commodity will be given by

$$p_i = \bar{p}_i + h_i t_i$$

where $\bar{p}_i$ is the price of the ith commodity in the absence of indirect taxes. Note that if $h_i = 1$, the consumers bear the burden of all the taxes on the ith commodity. If, however, $h_i = 0$, the producers pay for all the indirect taxes on this commodity. In practice, h_i will lie between zero and unity, its actual value depending on the supply and demand elasticity of the ith commodity.

The expenditure on the ith commodity by a family with income x will be

$$v_i = \bar{p}_i q_i + h_i t_i q_i$$

where q_i is the quantity of the ith commodity consumed by the family. The second quantity on the right-hand side is the indirect tax paid by the family on the ith commodity. After the indirect taxes have been paid, the family income will be

$$d(x) = x - \sum_{i=1}^{n} h_i t_i q_i,$$

which, by means of the demand equation for the ELES as given in (9.12), becomes

$$(11.4) \qquad d(x) = \left[1 - \sum_{i=1}^{n} \alpha_i \beta_i^* \right] x + \sum_{i=1}^{n} \alpha_i (a\beta_i^* - p_i \gamma_i)$$

where

$$\alpha_i = \frac{h_i t_i}{p_i}$$

is the indirect tax per dollar spent on the ith commodity. After the indirect taxes have been paid, the mean income becomes

$$(11.5) \qquad \mu_d = \mu - \sum_{i=1}^{n} \alpha_i p_i \gamma_i - \sum_{i=1}^{n} \alpha_i \beta_i^* (\mu - a).$$

The second term on the right-hand side of (11.5) is the tax paid on the subsistence expenditure, and the third term is the mean tax paid on the expenditure above the subsistence expenditure.

Differentiating (11.4) with respect to x gives

$$d'(x) = 1 - \sum_{i=1}^{n} \alpha_i \beta_i^*,$$

which will be strictly greater than zero if

$$(11.6) \qquad \sum_{i=1}^{n} \alpha_i \beta_i^* < 1.$$

Now $\sum_{i=1}^{n} \beta_i^*$ is equal to the marginal propensity to consume, which is less than unity. In addition, α_i is the indirect tax per dollar spent on the ith commodity, which will also be less than unity. Therefore, the sum $\sum_{i=1}^{n} \alpha_i \beta_i^*$ will certainly be less than unity, which shows that condition (11.6) will always be true. According to theorem 8.2, then, it is implied that the concentration curve for $d(x)$ coincides with its Lorenz curve. Thus applying corollary 8.9 to (11.4) gives

$$G_d = \frac{1}{\mu_d} [1 - \sum_{i=1}^{n} \alpha_i \beta_i^*] \mu G$$

where G_d is the Gini index of the distribution of family income after indirect taxes have been paid.

Differentiating this equation with respect to t_j yields

$$\frac{t_j}{G_d} \frac{\partial G_d}{\partial t_j} = \frac{\alpha_j p_j \gamma_j}{\mu_d} - \frac{\mu G \alpha_j (1 - \alpha_j) \beta_j^* (a - \sum_{i=1}^{n} \alpha_i p_i \gamma_i)}{\mu_d^2 G_d} ,$$

which is the elasticity of the Gini index of income with respect to tax rate after indirect tax. This elasticity measures the effect of change in the indirect tax rate of a commodity on the distribution of income after indirect tax.

Taxation in an Inflationary Economy[1]

Consider an economy in which prices and productivity are rising at an annual rate of $100p$ and $100s$ percent, respectively. Let x be the initial income of a unit, which, after t years, becomes

$$x_t = (1 + p)^t (1 + s)^t x.$$

This equation implies that the distribution of pretax income remains unaffected by changes in prices and productivity, whereas the real income of every unit increases at the same rate as productivity. Let the tax function be

(11.7) $$T(x) = \alpha x^\delta$$

---

1. This application is based on Kakwani (1978a).

where α and δ are parameters. This function gives a rather good fit to the Australian personal income tax data provided in the numerical illustration discussed in this section.

Equation (11.7) gives a progressive (regressive) tax system if δ is greater (less) than unity, and proportional if δ is equal to unity.

The average tax rate of the society at time t is

$$e_t = [(1 + p)(1 + s)]^{(\delta-1)t}e$$

where e is the average tax rate in the base year. This equation implies that if the taxes are progressive, that is, if $\delta > 1$, the average tax rate will increase (decrease) in time if p and s are greater (less) than zero. The disposable income at time t of a unit having initial income x is

$$d_t(x) = x_t - \alpha x_t^{\delta};$$

the result, therefore, of applying theorem 8.3 to this equation is

(11.8) $$F_t^*(x) = \frac{e_t}{(1 - e_t)} [F_1(x) - q(x)]$$

where $F_t^*(x)$ is the proportion of disposable income of units having an initial income less than or equal to x, and where $q(x)$ given by

$$q(x) = \frac{1}{Q} \int_0^x \alpha x^{\delta} f(x) dx$$

is the proportion of tax paid by income units having income less than or equal to x at time zero. In addition, Q is equal to the average tax revenue in the base year.

Differentiating (11.8) with respect to p yields

(11.9) $$\frac{\partial F_t^*(x)}{\partial p} = \frac{(\delta - 1)te_t}{(1 + p)(1 - e_t)^2} [F_1(x) - q(x)].$$

Corollary 8.5, indicates that if the tax system is progressive, $\delta > 1$ and $F_1(x) > q(x)$, which implies that the right-hand side of (11.9) is positive for all x; therefore, as p increases, the Lorenz curve for posttax income distribution will shift upward. Similarly, if the tax system is regressive, $\delta < 1$ and $F_1(x) < q(x)$; the right-hand side of (11.9) is again positive, and the Lorenz curve again shifts upward as p increases. Thus inflation decreases the posttax income inequality for both progressive and regressive tax systems, provided pretax income distribution is unaffected by inflation.

This conclusion is valid only if the taxes are not adjusted to inflation. If the tax function is changed every year by keeping δ constant, and the parameter α is changed so that the ratio of tax to income remains constant, then α at time t is equal to

$$\alpha_t = \frac{\alpha}{[(1+p)(1+s)]^{(\delta-1)t}},$$

which means that α is reduced (increased) every year if the tax function is progressive (regressive). Further, note that if δ does not change from year to year, $[F_1(x) - q(x)]$ also remains unchanged. It follows from (11.8), therefore, that the Lorenz curve of posttax income distribution does not shift with inflation. Thus if the tax function is adjusted every year so that the tax-income ratio remains constant, inflation will not change the posttax income distribution for any progressive or regressive tax system.

Theorem 8.5 indicates that the Gini index of the posttax income at t is equal to

$$G_t^* = G - \frac{e_t}{(1-e_t)}(C-G)$$

where G is the Gini index of pretax income and C is the concentration index of the taxes. The elasticity of the Gini index of posttax income with respect to inflation rate is

$$\frac{p}{G_t^*}\frac{\partial G_t^*}{\partial p} = \frac{-pt(\delta-1)e_t(C-G)}{(1+p)(1-e_t)^2 G_t^*}.$$

The Gini index and the elasticity of the Gini index with respect to the inflation rate can now be computed by means of data from the Australian *Taxation Statistics* for the assessment year 1971–72. The data were available only in grouped form, and the income considered is the actual income of individual taxpayers less the expenditure incurred in gaining that income. The Gini index of pretax income was computed at 0.346. The concentration index for the taxes paid was computed at 0.542,[2] and the tax function was estimated from the grouped data by means of the weighted regression method,

$$\log T = -6.8068 + 1.588 \log x,$$

2. These indexes were computed by fitting the new coordinate system of the Lorenz curve discussed in chapter 7.

Table 11.1. *Gini Index of Posttax Income and Its Elasticity with Respect to Inflation Rate, Australia, 1971–74*

Rate of inflation	Fiscal 1972		Fiscal 1973		Fiscal 1974	
	Gini index	Elasticity	Gini index	Elasticity	Gini index	Elasticity
−10	0.3141	0.0076	0.3157	0.0143	0.3171	0.0201
− 5	0.3129	0.0038	0.3134	0.0074	0.3138	0.0109
− 3	0.3124	0.0022	0.3124	0.0015	0.3125	0.0067
0	0.3117	0.0000	0.3110	0.000	0.3103	0.0000
3	0.3110	−0.0022	0.3096	−0.0047	0.3081	−0.0071
5	0.3106	−0.0037	0.3086	−0.0080	0.3065	−0.0128
10	0.3094	−0.0074	0.3061	−0.0165	0.3024	−0.0279
15	0.3083	−0.0110	0.3035	−0.0258	0.2981	−0.0455

where x represents income and T represents taxes. The squared correlation between the estimated and actual values of T was computed at 0.98.

Table 11.1 presents the Gini index of posttax income and its elasticity with respect to the rate of inflation. The productivity is assumed to rise at an annual rate of 3 percent; the income year 1970–71 is considered the base year; and the Gini index of posttax income for this year is computed as equal to 0.312. Thus, in Australia personal income tax reduces income inequality by about 9 percent. The table indicates that the Gini index is affected by inflation, and that the magnitude of effect is sensitive to the rate of inflation, as indicated by the numerical values of the elasticity. For the given rate of inflation the numerical value of the elasticity increases with time.

Tax Evasion and Income Distribution[3]

There is considerable income that is understated in individual income tax returns. This phenomenon, which appears to be widespread, has two serious consequences. First, it leads to a loss in tax revenue for the Government, which could otherwise be utilized for

3. This and the following section are based on Kakwani (1978c).

useful purposes. Second, it may reduce the progressivity of the tax system, thus altering the posttax income distribution.

The problem of illegal income tax evasion has been considered by several authors. Allingham and Sandmo (1972) presented a tax evasion model that analyzes the individual taxpayer's decision whether, and to what extent, to avoid taxes by deliberately understating his income. In their model, the taxpayer maximizes his cardinal utility function, which is assumed to be a function of income only. Further, the marginal utility of the taxpayer is assumed to be everywhere positive and strictly decreasing, which implies that the taxpayer is risk-averse. Their analysis is limited to the case of a proportional tax system.[4]

Srinivasan (1973) proposed an alternative model of tax evasion, which is more general because it allows for a progressive tax system. In his model, the taxpayer is assumed to maximize his posttax expected income instead of his cardinal utility function. This assumes that the taxpayer is risk-neutral, rendering this model less general than the one considered by Allingham and Sandmo.

Singh (1973) analyzed the policy implications of Srinivasan's model in the context of the Indian situation, but the technique that he adopted can be modified to any situation. He computed the probability of detection at different levels of income so that tax evasion may be completely eliminated. His numerical results, based on the Indian tax structure, indicate that the probability of detection has to be greater than one-third to eliminate tax evasion.

The purpose of this and the following sections is to investigate the effect of tax evasion on income distribution. Although this problem is important from a policy point of view, it has not been theoretically explored. In this section the discussion is limited to the framework of Srinivasan's model.

Let x be the true income of a taxpayer, and assume that it is a random variable. In addition, suppose that this income is known to the taxpayer, but not to the taxation department, and suppose the taxpayer knows that π is the probability of his being detected if he understates his income. Let λ be the proportion by which he understates his income. His declared income will then be

$$(11.10) \qquad\qquad y = (1 - \lambda)x.$$

---

4. See also Kolm (1973) for further analysis of this model.

The tax is levied on the declared income provided he is not detected. If, however, he is detected, he pays tax on his true income and also a penalty on the understated income. If $P(\lambda)$ is the penalty multiplier, $P(\lambda)\lambda x$ is the penalty on the understated income λx. If $T(x)$ is the tax function, the expected income of a taxpayer with true income x will be, after paying taxes and penalty,

$$(11.11) \quad Z(x) = \pi[x - T(x) - \lambda P(\lambda)x] + (1 - \pi)[x - T(y)].$$

He will now choose λ so as to maximize $Z(x)$. The first-order condition for a maximum of (11.11) will then be given by

$$(11.12) \quad \frac{\partial Z(x)}{\partial \lambda} = -\pi[P(\lambda) + \lambda P'(\lambda)]x + (1 - \pi)T'(y)x = 0$$

where (11.10) has been utilized. The second-order condition

$$D = -\pi[2P'(\lambda) + \lambda P''(\lambda)]x - (1 - \pi)T''(y)x^2 < 0$$

will always be satisfied if it is assumed that the tax system is progressive, that is, if $T''(x) > 0$ and for all $\lambda \geq 0$, $P(\lambda) \geq 0$, $P'(\lambda) > 0$, and $P''(\lambda) \geq 0$. This means that the penalty multiplier is a positive, increasing, and convex function of λ.

With the additional assumptions that $P(0) = 0$, that is, that the penalty multiplier is zero when there is no understatement of income, and $T'(0) = 0$, that is, the marginal tax rate is zero at zero income, it can be seen that

$$\left.\frac{\partial Z(x)}{\partial \lambda}\right|_{\lambda=0} = (1 - \pi)T'(x)x > 0$$

and

$$\left.\frac{\partial Z(x)}{\partial \lambda}\right|_{\lambda=1} = -\pi[P(1) + P'(1)]x < 0.$$

Together, these two inequalities imply that there exists a unique solution of λ in the interior of $(0, 1)$, which maximizes the expected income after taxes and penalties.

If $\epsilon = (\partial \pi/\partial x)(x/\pi)$ is denoted as the elasticity of the probability of detection with respect to income, differentiating (11.12) with respect to x, and solving for $\partial \lambda/\partial x$, yields

$$(11.13) \quad \frac{\partial \lambda}{\partial x} = -\frac{(1 - \pi)(1 - \lambda)T''(y)x - \epsilon T'(y)}{D},$$

which is positive for a progressive tax system if $\epsilon \leq 0$. In addition, $\epsilon = 0$ implies that the probability of detection π is independent of income x. If $\epsilon < 0$, it is implied that the probability of detection actually falls as income rises. This corresponds to a situation in which the richer class of taxpayer succeeds in buying greater immunity from detection because of the greater resources for corrupt gratification that are at his disposal. Equation (11.13) leads, therefore, to the conclusion that given a progressive tax function, the richer a person, the larger the optimal proportion by which he will understate his income, provided the probability of detection π is either independent of x or a decreasing function of x.

Differentiating (11.10) and using (11.13) yields the elasticity of the declared income y with respect to true income x as

$$(11.14) \qquad \eta_y(x) = 1 + \frac{(1 - \pi) T''(y) x^2}{D} - \frac{x^2 \epsilon T'(y)}{Dy}.$$

The second term in (11.14) is negative, and its magnitude is less than unity. If $\epsilon = 0$, the elasticity $\eta_y(x)$ will be positive. From theorem 8.2 it follows, therefore, that the concentration curve of the declared income coincides with its Lorenz curve. Further, the elasticity $\eta_y(x)$ is strictly less than unity for a progressive tax system. From corollary 8.5 it follows, then, that the distribution of the declared income will be Lorenz superior to the distribution of true income. From this it can be concluded that the declared income is more equally distributed than the true income, provided the tax system is progressive and the probability of detection π is independent of x.

Next, consider the distribution of the expected posttax income when there is tax evasion. Differentiating $Z(x)$ in (11.11) with respect to x and using (11.12) yields

$$\frac{\partial Z}{\partial x} = \pi [1 - T'(x) - \lambda P(\lambda)] + (1 - \pi)[1 - (1 - \lambda) T'(y)]$$

$$- \frac{\pi \epsilon}{x} [T(x) - T(y) + \lambda P(\lambda) x].$$

(11.15)

It is not clear whether the sign $\partial Z / \partial x$ is unambiguously positive or negative. To determine the sign, consider the value of this derivative at $\lambda = 0$. Thus,

$$\left.\frac{\partial Z}{\partial x}\right|_{\lambda=0} = 1 - T'(x),$$

which is positive if the marginal tax rate is less than unity for all values of x. Differentiating (11.15) with respect to λ yields

(11.16) $\quad \dfrac{\partial}{\partial \lambda}\left(\dfrac{\partial Z}{\partial x}\right) = (1 - \pi)yT''(y) - \epsilon T'(y)$

where (11.12) has been utilized. The right-hand side of (11.16) is always positive for $\epsilon \leq 0$. This equation implies, therefore, that $\partial Z/\partial x$ is a monotonic increasing function of λ. Because $\partial Z/\partial x$ is positive at $\lambda = 0$, $\partial Z/\partial x$ will also be positive for all values of x. Thus applying theorem 8.2 leads to the conclusion that the concentration curve of the posttax income distribution coincides with its Lorenz curve, provided the tax system is progressive and $\epsilon \leq 0$.

Elasticity of $Z(x)$ with respect to x is obtained from (11.15) as

(11.17) $\quad \eta_z(x) = 1 - \dfrac{1}{Z}\big[\pi T(x)\{\eta_t(x) - 1\}$

$\qquad\qquad + (1 - \pi)T(y)\{\eta_t(y) - 1\} + \pi\epsilon\{T(x) - T(y) + \lambda P(\lambda)x\}\big]$

where $\eta_t(x)$ is the elasticity of the tax function $T(x)$ with respect to x. For a progressive tax system, $\eta_t(x)$ is clearly greater than unity for all values of x. If $\epsilon = 0$, equation (11.17) implies, therefore, that the elasticity $\eta_z(x)$ will always be less than unity for all values of x. From corollary 8.5 it follows, then, that the distribution of the posttax income will be Lorenz superior to the distribution of the true pretax income. From this it can be concluded that if the tax system is progressive, the posttax distribution will be more equally distributed than the pretax income distribution, even if there is tax evasion, and provided the probability of detection is independent of income x.

If the tax system is proportional, the tax elasticity $\eta_t(x)$ will be unity for all values of x, which from (11.17) implies that if $\epsilon < 0$, $\eta_z(x)$ will be greater than unity for all x. Again, from corollary 8.5, it follows that the distribution of posttax income will be Lorenz inferior to the distribution of the true pretax income. From this it can be concluded that if the tax system is proportional, the posttax distribution will be more unequally distributed than the pretax income distribution, provided the probability of detection is a decreasing function of income. Further, it can be seen that if $\epsilon = 0$, $\eta_z(x)$ will be unity for all x. This result immediately leads to the conclusion that if the tax system is proportional and the probability of detection is independent of income, the inequality of both pre- and posttax incomes will be identical, even if there is tax evasion.

Substituting $\lambda = 0$ into (11.17), $\eta_z(x)$ becomes

$$\eta_d(x) = 1 - \frac{T(x)[\eta_t(x) - 1]}{x - T(x)},$$

which is the elasticity of posttax income when there is no tax evasion. The difference between the two elasticities,

(11.18) $\qquad\qquad \eta_z(x) - \eta_d(x),$

will, therefore, be zero when $\lambda = 0$. Differentiating (11.18) with respect to λ gives

(11.19) $\quad \dfrac{\partial}{\partial \lambda}\big[\eta_z(x) - \eta_d(x)\big] = \dfrac{x(1 - \pi)yT''(y) - \epsilon x T'(y)}{Z}$

where use has been made of (11.16). The right-hand side of (11.19) is positive if the tax system is progressive and if $\epsilon \leq 0$. This shows that $\eta_z(x) - \eta_d(x)$ is a monotonic increasing function of λ, and that at $\lambda = 0$, this function is equal to zero. Thus $\eta_z(x) \geq \eta_d(x)$ must be true for any λ in the interior of $(0, 1)$. Theorem 8.2 implies that the distribution $Z(x)$ will be Lorenz inferior to the distribution of $d(x)$. Note that $d(x)$ is the posttax income when there is no tax evasion. From this it can be concluded that given a progressive tax function and probability of detection π, either independent of income x or a decreasing function of x, the posttax income will be more unequally distributed in the presence of understatement than in its absence.

Now consider the way in which the distribution of the posttax income depends on the probability of detection.

Differentiating (11.12) with respect to π and solving for $\partial\lambda/\partial\pi$ yields

(11.20) $\qquad\qquad \dfrac{\partial \lambda}{\partial \pi} = \dfrac{xT'(y)}{\pi D},$

which is always negative. This leads to corollary 1 of Srinivasan, which states that, *ceteris paribus*, the optimal proportion λ by which income is understated decreases as the probability of detection π increases.

Differentiating the elasticity $\eta_z(x)$ with respect to π gives

$$\frac{\partial \eta_z(x)}{\partial \pi} = -\frac{T(x)}{Z} [\eta_t(x) - \eta_z(x)] + \frac{T(y)}{Z} [\eta_t(y) - \eta_z(x)]$$

$$(11.21) \qquad -\frac{x\lambda P(\lambda)}{Z} [1 - \eta_z(x)] + x(1 - \pi)yT''(y) \frac{\partial \lambda}{\partial \pi}.$$

Now, examine the sign of the expression on the right-hand side of (11.21). It was indicated earlier that $\eta_z(x) < 1$ for all x if the tax system is progressive and $\epsilon = 0$. Further, for a progressive tax system the tax elasticities $\eta_t(x)$ and $\eta_t(y)$ will always be greater than unity for all values of x and y. The first term on the right-hand side of (11.21) will, therefore, be negative, whereas the second term will be positive. Because the tax system is progressive and $x \geq y$, $T(x) \geq T(y)$ and $\eta_t(x) \geq \eta_t(y)$. These two conditions together imply that the first term in (11.21) will be of higher magnitude than the second term. The third and fourth terms on the right-hand side of (11.21) are clearly negative because $\eta_z(x) < 1$; $\partial \lambda / \partial \pi$ was shown to be negative in (11.20). Clearly, then, the elasticity $\eta_z(x)$ decreases as π increases. Corollary 8.4 implies that as π increases, the Lorenz curve of the posttax income distribution shifts upward toward the egalitarian line. Thus, it can be concluded that the inequality of the expected income, after taxes and penalties have been paid, decreases as the probability of detection π increases.

This result is important from a policy point of view. An increase in probability of detection not only increases the tax revenue for the government, but also renders the posttax income distribution more egalitarian. Srinivasan (1973) and Singh (1973) considered the problem of allocation of resources for detection of income understatement. Srinivasan arrived at the conclusion that as long as the marginal increase in expected revenue (net of cost) to the government remains positive, resources should be allocated to the detection of tax evasion. Both Srinivasan and Singh ignored the egalitarian implications of increasing the probability of detection. In their model, the amount of expenditure on detection is determined by maximizing the difference between the cost of scrutiny and the expected revenue and penalties. To incorporate the egalitarian aspect of probability of detection. Srinivasan's model must be extended so that the amount of expenditure on detection is determined by maximizing the social welfare function instead of the expected tax revenue.

Tax Evasion Model Incorporating Risk-Aversion Behavior of Taxpayers

In this section an alternative model of tax evasion, which was outlined by Allingham and Sandmo in 1972, and incorporates the observed phenomenon of risk-aversion in the behavior of taxpayers, is considered. By means of the framework of this model, the effect of tax evasion on income inequality is discussed.

Following Allingham and Sandmo, assume that the taxpayer's behavior conforms to the Von Neumann-Morgenstern axioms on behavior under uncertainty. The taxpayer's cardinal utility $u(x)$ is a function of income x only, and the marginal utility is assumed to be everywhere positive and strictly decreasing, so that the taxpayer is risk-averse.

Assume that tax is levied at the constant rate θ on the declared income y. Again, λ is the proportion by which he understates his income, and α is the additional penalty on his undeclared income λx, if caught. Note that the penalty rate α is higher than θ. The taxpayer will choose λ so as to maximize

$$(11.22) \qquad E[u(x)] = (1 - \pi)u(X) + \pi u(Y)$$

where

$$(11.23) \qquad X = x - \theta(1 - \lambda)x$$

$$(11.24) \qquad Y = x - \theta(1 - \lambda)x - \alpha\lambda x.$$

The first-order condition for the maximum of (11.22) can be written as

$$(11.25) \qquad \frac{\partial E[u(x)]}{\partial \lambda} = (1 - \pi)u'(X)\theta x - \pi u'(Y)x(\alpha - \theta) = 0.$$

The second-order condition

$$(11.26) \qquad \frac{\partial^2 E[u(x)]}{\partial \lambda^2} = D = (1 - \pi)u''(X)\theta^2 x^2$$
$$+ \pi u''(Y)x^2(\alpha - \theta)^2 < 0$$

will always be satisfied because of the assumption of the concave utility function.

Now consider the conditions under which the optimal solution of λ lies in the interior of $(0, 1)$. If $\lambda > 0$, $\partial E[u(x)]/\partial\lambda$ must increase with λ in the neighborhood of $\lambda = 0$. This gives

(11.27) $\left.\dfrac{\partial E[u(x)]}{\partial\lambda}\right|_{\lambda=0} = x(\theta - \alpha\pi)u'((1 - \theta)x) > 0.$

Similarly, for $\lambda < 1$, $\partial E[u(x)]/\partial\lambda$ must decrease with λ in the neighborhood of $\lambda = 1$. This gives

(11.28) $\left.\dfrac{\partial E[u(x)]}{\partial\lambda}\right|_{\lambda=1} = (1 - \pi)u'(x)\theta x$

$$- \pi u'((1 - \alpha)x)x(\alpha - \theta) < 0.$$

The conditions (11.27) and (11.28) can be written as

$$\theta > \pi\alpha$$

$$\pi\alpha > \theta\left[\pi + (1 - \pi)\dfrac{u'(x)}{u'((1 - \alpha)x)}\right],$$

which, if satisfied, will guarantee a unique optimal solution of λ in the interior of $(0, 1)$.

It will be useful to introduce here the measures of risk-aversion in order to evaluate the results on income distribution. The well-known Pratt-Arrow measures of risk-aversion are:

Absolute risk-aversion:

$$R_A(x) = -\dfrac{u''(x)}{u'(x)}$$

Relative risk-aversion:

(11.29) $$R_R(x) = -\dfrac{u''(x)\cdot x}{u'(x)}.$$

An illuminating discussion of these concepts is found in Arrow (1965). In addition, they have been used in the analysis of taxation and risk-taking by Mossin (1968), Stiglitz (1969b), and Ahsan (1974). The following hypotheses on risk-aversion have been advanced by Arrow (1965):

(a) Decreasing absolute risk-aversion, that is, $R_A(x)$ is a decreasing function of x.

(b) Increasing relative risk-aversion, that is, $R_R(x)$ is an increasing function of x.

By means of the above definitions of risk-aversion, D, defined in (11.26), can be written as

$$D = - (1 - \pi)\theta x^2 u'(X)[\theta R_A(X) + (\alpha - \theta)R_A(Y)].$$

Further, differentiating (11.25) with respect to x and solving for $\partial\lambda/\partial x$ yields

$$(11.30) \qquad \frac{\partial\lambda}{\partial x} = \frac{(1 - \pi)\theta u'(X)}{D} [R_R(X) - R_R(Y)]$$

where use has been made of (11.29). Because D is unambiguously negative, the sign of $\partial\lambda/\partial x$ depends on whether the relative risk-aversion is an increasing or decreasing function of x. Because $X > Y$, $R_R(X) > R_R(Y)$ implies the hypothesis of increasing relative risk-aversion. From this it can be concluded that the richer a person, the larger (smaller) the optimal proportion by which he will understate his income if the relative risk-aversion is a decreasing (increasing) function of income.

The declared income of a taxpayer is given by (11.10), which, when differentiated with respect to x and by means of (11.30), becomes

$$(11.31) \qquad \frac{\partial y}{\partial x} = (1 - \lambda) - x\frac{\partial\lambda}{\partial x}.$$

Now, $\partial\lambda/\partial x$ is negative under the hypothesis of increasing relative risk-aversion, which makes the derivative $\partial y/\partial x$ unambiguously positive. From this it can be concluded that given the hypothesis of increasing relative risk-aversion, the richer a person, the larger his declared income. Allingham and Sandmo (1972) arrived at the same conclusion under the assumption that $\alpha \geq 1$, which is rather restrictive.

Theorem 8.2 clearly indicates that the concentration curve of the declared income will coincide with its Lorenz curve. To compare the inequality of declared income with that of true income, the elasticity of y with respect to x must be derived. This is determined from (11.31) as

$$\eta_y(x) = 1 - \frac{x^2}{y} \frac{\partial \lambda}{\partial x}$$

where use has been made of (11.10). The elasticity will be greater than unity for all x if $\partial \lambda / \partial x$ is negative for all x. Indeed, $\partial \lambda / \partial x$ is negative under the assumption of increasing relative risk-aversion. From corollary 8.5 it immediately follows, therefore, that the distribution of y will be Lorenz inferior to the distribution of x. Thus, it can be concluded that the declared income will be more unequally distributed than the true income, provided the relative risk-aversion is an increasing function of income.

Next, consider the distribution of the posttax expected income, which is given by

$$Z(x) = (1 - \pi)X + \pi Y.$$

The first derivative of $Z(x)$ with respect to x is derived from (11.23) and (11.24) as

$$(11.32) \quad \frac{\partial Z(x)}{\partial x} =$$

$$- \frac{(1 - \pi)\theta x^2 u'(X)[\theta Y + (\alpha - \theta)X][\pi R_A(X) + (1 - \pi)R_A(Y)]}{Dx},$$

which is unambiguously positive. This implies that the larger the true income before tax, the larger the expected income after tax. From theorem 8.2 it immediately follows that the concentration curve for $Z(x)$ will coincide with its Lorenz curve.

The elasticity of $Z(x)$ with respect to x is obtained from (11.32) as

$$\eta_z(x) = \frac{[\theta Y + (\alpha - \theta)X][\pi R_A(X) + (1 - \pi)R_A(Y)]}{Z[\theta R_A(X) + (\alpha - \theta)R_A(Y)]},$$

which simplifies to

$$\eta_z(x) = 1 - \frac{(\theta - \alpha\pi)[R_R(X) - R_R(Y)]}{Z[\theta R_A(X) + (\alpha - \theta)R_A(Y)]}.$$

This equation implies that the elasticity $\eta_z(x)$ will be less (greater) than unity for all x if the relative risk-aversion is an increasing (decreasing) function of x. From corollary 8.5 it follows that the distribution of $Z(x)$ will be Lorenz superior (inferior) to the distribution of x if the elasticity of $Z(x)$ is less (greater) than unity for all x. Thus, it can be concluded that expected income after paying taxes and penalties will be more (or less) equally distributed than the pretax true income if relative risk-aversion is an increasing (or decreasing) function of income.

CHAPTER 12

Measurement of Tax Progressivity and Built-in Flexibility: An International Comparison

THE PROGRESSIVITY OF A TAX SYSTEM is generally defined in terms of the average rate of tax along the income scale. A tax system is said to be (a) progressive when the average rate of tax rises with income, (b) proportional when the average tax rate remains constant, and (c) regressive when it falls with rising income. A measure of progression indicates the extent to which a given tax system deviates from proportionality at a given level of income. Obviously, progression of tax changes with income and does not provide a single index to represent an overall progressivity of a tax system. In contrast, a single measure of *progressivity* indicates the extent of overall deviation of a tax system from proportionality. Although a number of alternative measures of tax progression have been proposed,[1] there seems little agreement among economists as to which measure is the most appropriate.

Any tax system incorporates two distinct factors, the average tax rate and the degree of progressivity, both of which influence the distribution of income. A new measure of tax progressivity proposed by Kakwani clearly brings out the individual effects of these factors on the distribution of income,[2] and can also be used in the context of progressivity of the whole fiscal system.

---

1. Among the important contributions in this field are those of Pigou (1947), Slitor (1948), Dalton (1955), and Musgrave and Thin (1948).
2. See Kakwani (1977d).

In this chapter several issues concerning the measurement of tax progressivity are discussed. Particular attention is paid to a new measure of tax progressivity, a measure derived from the notion of concentration curves, which was discussed in chapter 7. Empirical analysis is carried out on data from four developed countries—Australia, Canada, the United States, and the United Kingdom.

The second problem considered in this chapter is the measurement of built-in flexibility, which refers to the sensitivity of tax yield to changes in national income. With a progressive tax system, an increase in the level of national income leads to a more than proportional increase in tax revenue. The effect of built-in flexibility is to stabilize income by reducing the multiplier.

The problem of estimating alternative measures of built-in flexibility is also considered here. It is demonstrated that the new coordinate system for the Lorenz curve can be effectively utilized to obtain reliable estimates of built-in flexibility. Further, a method is provided to investigate the effects of income redistribution on built-in flexibility. Again, empirical analysis is based on data from the four above-mentioned countries.

Measurement of Tax Progressivity

Let $T(x)$ be the tax paid by an individual with income x. This tax system is defined as proportional when the average tax rate $T(x)/x$ is constant for all x. The tax system will be progressive (regressive) when the average tax rate increases (decreases) with income. This concept of progressivity implies that a tax system is progressive, proportional, and regressive when the marginal tax rate is greater, equal, or less than the average tax rate, respectively. Using this definition, Slitor (1948) proposed the following measure of progression:[3]

$$(12.1) \qquad \frac{de(x)}{dx} = \frac{m(x) - e(x)}{x}$$

3. The derivation of the relationship (12.1) is as follows:

$$\frac{de(x)}{dx} = \frac{d}{dx}\left[\frac{T(x)}{x}\right] = \frac{1}{x^2}\left[x\frac{dT(x)}{d(x)} - T(x)\right]$$

$$= \frac{1}{x}\left[\frac{dT(x)}{dx} - \frac{T(x)}{x}\right] = \frac{1}{x}[m(x) - e(x)].$$

where $e(x) = T(x)/x$ is the effective tax rate at the income level x and $m(x) = dT(x)/dx$ is the marginal tax rate at the same level of income. This measure of progression is generally referred to as average rate progression.[4]

An alternative measure of progression, suggested by Pigou (1947) and subsequently considered by Musgrave and Thin (1948), is the marginal rate progression, which is defined as

$$\frac{dm(x)}{dx} = \frac{d^2T(x)}{dx^2} \, ,$$

and which is equal to the rate of change in the marginal tax rate. The marginal rate progression is equal to zero when the tax is proportional, positive when the tax is progressive, and negative when the tax is regressive. Thus, the tax system is progressive (regressive) if the marginal tax rate increases (decreases) with income.

In chapter 8, it was shown that posttax income will be more equally distributed than pretax income if the average tax rate increases with income. But the marginal tax rate need not increase with income for this result to hold. The increasing marginal tax rate is, in fact, a stronger condition than the increasing average tax rate, and the former necessarily implies the latter but not vice versa. From this, it may be concluded that the definition of progressivity in terms of rising average tax rate is compatible with the definition of progressivity in terms of rising marginal tax rate only under the condition that the marginal tax rate is continuously rising.[5]

Two other measures of progression were proposed by Musgrave and Thin (1948). One is referred to as liability progression and defined as the ratio of the percentage change in tax liability to the concurrent percentage change in income. This measure is, in fact, equivalent to the elasticity of $T(x)$ with respect to x. If this elasticity is denoted as $\eta_t(x)$, the liability progression can be written as

$$(12.2) \qquad \eta_t(x) = \frac{dT(x)}{dx} \frac{x}{T(x)} = \frac{m(x)}{e(x)} \, ,$$

4. See Pigou (1947) and Musgrave and Thin (1948).

5. In this connection, Musgrave and Thin (1948) noted that the marginal tax rate does not, in general, rise continuously, but steps up by income brackets. There are certain ranges for which the rate structure is proportional, according to the marginal rate progression, but progressive, according to the average rate progression. If the brackets are disregarded in favor of the "marginal rate trend," this difficulty disappears.

which is the ratio of the marginal to the average tax rate at income level x.

The tax system is proportional when the liability progression is equal to unity for all x, and progressive (regressive) when the liability progression is greater (less) than unity. Equation (12.2) clearly shows that the definition of liability progression is compatible with the definition of progression (regression) in terms of rising (falling) average tax rate.

The other measure of progression proposed by Musgrave and Thin is referred to as residual income progression and defined as the elasticity of income after tax with respect to income before tax. If this elasticity is denoted as $\eta_d(x)$, it follows that

$$\eta_d(x) = \frac{x}{x - T(x)} \frac{d}{dx} [x - T(x)]$$

(12.3)
$$= \frac{1 - m(x)}{1 - e(x)}.$$

A proportional rate of tax will give the residual income progression as unity for all x. In contrast, the tax system will be progressive (regressive) if the residual income progression is less (greater) than unity at all levels of income. Equation (12.3) clearly shows that this measure of progression (regression) is also fully compatible with our basic definition of progression (regression) in terms of the rising (falling) average tax rate.

All the measures of progression discussed so far belong to the same family. They relate to progression at a given point in the income scale and, therefore, do not give a single index of overall tax progressivity. To arrive at a single measure of progressivity, Musgrave and Thin (1948) proposed comparing the Lorenz curves of the pre- and posttax income distributions. Their measure indicates the extent to which a given tax system results in a shift in the distribution of income toward equality: A progressive tax system is associated with a decrease in income inequality, whereas the regressive tax structure leads to an increase in income inequality. Thus if the Gini index is used as a measure of inequality, the difference or ratio of the Gini index of the posttax income to that of the pretax income provides a single measure of tax progressivity.

The Musgrave-Thin measure of tax progressivity appears intuitively appealing and is widely used. It will be demonstrated below, however, that by simply comparing the Lorenz curves of pretax and posttax incomes, a suitable measure of progressivity cannot be derived.

Comparison of Alternative Measures of Tax Progressivity

In this section numerical estimates of the alternative measures of tax progression at different levels of income are compared. Data used for this purpose are from the *Australian Taxation Statistics* for the assessment year 1971–72. They are available only in grouped form, and the individual taxpayers are classified according to the size of their net income, which is defined as the actual income less expenditure incurred in gaining that income.

It should be pointed out that the estimation of tax progression measures discussed in the preceding section requires the specification of the form of the tax function that fits well to the entire income range. The alternative forms of the tax function have not been empirically investigated. Recall that in chapter 11 the tax function given in equation (11.7) was fitted to the Australian data. The main drawback of this function is that it gives the same tax elasticity for the entire income range, which implies that the coefficient of liability progression defined in (12.2) would indicate the same progressivity at all levels of income. Because progressivity varies with income, the tax function (11.7) is not suitable for comparing the progressivity of one tax system with that of another.

In this section an alternative specification of the tax function is used to estimate the elasticities at different levels of income. This specification is derived from the new coordinate system for the Lorenz curve and was used in chapter 10 to estimate the Engel elasticities.

The new coordinate system for the Lorenz curve as defined in (7.7) is fitted to income as well as to the tax liability of the taxpayers. The tax elasticities are then estimated by means of equation (10.23) at different levels of income, and the effective average tax rates directly obtained from the data for each income group. The marginal tax rates are computed by multiplying the elasticities by their corresponding average tax rates; the numerical results are presented in table 12.1.

Table 12.1 *Measures of Degree of Progression by Income Class, Australia, Fiscal 1971*

Income class (Australian dollars)	Average tax rate	Marginal tax rate	Liability progression	Average rate progression $(10^{-4} \times)$	Residual income progression
417 – 599	0.0183	0.0364	1.9823	0.302	0.9816
600 – 799	0.0275	0.0550	2.0026	0.344	0.9717
800 – 999	0.0377	0.0741	1.9646	0.364	0.9622
1,000– 1,199	0.0461	0.0883	1.9161	0.351	0.9558
1,200– 1,399	0.0538	0.1003	1.8650	0.332	0.9508
1,400– 1,599	0.0603	0.1097	1.8184	0.308	0.9474
1,600– 1,799	0.0672	0.1191	1.7735	0.288	0.9444
1,800– 1,999	0.0748	0.1294	1.7283	0.273	0.9410
2,000– 2,199	0.0818	0.1381	1.6878	0.256	0.9387
2,200– 2,399	0.0884	0.1463	1.6547	0.241	0.9365
2,400– 2,599	0.0944	0.1537	1.6283	0.228	0.9345
2,600– 2,799	0.0991	0.1595	1.6088	0.215	0.9329
2,800– 2,999	0.1026	0.1639	1.5968	0.204	0.9317
3,000– 3,199	0.1053	0.1676	1.5917	0.194	0.9304
3,200– 3,399	0.1081	0.1720	1.5918	0.187	0.9283

3,400— 3,599	0.1113	0.1776	1.5957	0.184	0.9254
3,600— 3,799	0.1146	0.1838	1.6029	0.182	0.9218
3,800— 3,999	0.1184	0.1909	1.6125	0.181	0.9178
4,000— 4,249	0.1227	0.1997	1.6273	0.181	0.9122
4,250— 4,499	0.1277	0.2099	1.6443	0.182	0.9058
4,500— 4,749	0.1325	0.2202	1.6625	0.184	0.8989
4,750— 4,999	0.1373	0.2307	1.6810	0.186	0.8917
5,000— 5,249	0.1418	0.2410	1.6995	0.188	0.8844
5,250— 5,499	0.1460	0.2507	1.7177	0.190	0.8774
5,500— 5,749	0.1503	0.2608	1.7349	0.192	0.8699
5,750— 5,999	0.1548	0.2710	1.7505	0.193	0.8625
6,000— 6,499	0.1608	0.2858	1.7770	0.192	0.8510
6,500— 6,999	0.1692	0.3039	1.7962	0.192	0.8379
7,000— 7,499	0.1772	0.3204	1.8081	0.190	0.8260
7,500— 7,999	0.1850	0.3354	1.8131	0.188	0.8155
8,000— 8,999	0.1968	0.3554	1.8059	0.176	0.8025
9,000— 9,999	0.2126	0.3789	1.7821	0.166	0.7888
10,000—14,999	0.2531	0.4018	1.5875	0.099	0.8009
15,000—19,999	0.3251	0.4515	1.3888	0.063	0.8127
20,000—29,999	0.4039	0.4858	1.2027	0.027	0.8626
30,000—49,999	0.4925	0.5923	1.2026	0.019	0.8033
50,000—99,999	0.5674	0.6599	1.163	0.009	0.7862
Over 100,000	0.6076	—	—	—	—

The first column in the table gives the income ranges. The second and third columns report the average and the marginal tax rate, respectively. The numerical values of the alternative measures of tax progression are presented in the last three columns. These values have been obtained by means of equations (12.1), (12.2), and (12.3).

The second column indicates that the average tax rate increases monotonically with income, which implies that Australian income taxes are progressive for the entire income range. The third column shows that the marginal tax rate also increases monotonically with income, which demonstrates that the Australian tax system is progressive even on the basis of marginal rate progression.

The numerical results given in the last three columns indicate that the various measures applied to the same distribution of income and taxes give different degrees of change in progression when moving up the income scale. For example, the coefficient of liability progression shows an increase in progressivity to the income level of $799, and then a decrease in progressivity to the income level of $3,199. In contrast, the coefficient of residual income progression shows a monotonic increase in progressivity to the income level $9,999. The average rate progression shows almost continuous declining progressivity throughout the income range, which is clearly incompatible with the other two measures of progressivity.

From these observations, it can be concluded that the alternative measures of tax progressivity give conflicting results. Statements about changes in the pattern of progression should, therefore, be made strictly in the context of specific measures.

Axioms of Tax Progressivity

Consider two basic axioms that should be satisfied by a measure of tax progressivity, and that conform to the intuitive notion of tax progressivity.

Axiom 12.1. *Progressivity (regressivity) is always displayed by an increasing (decreasing) average tax rate.*

Axiom 12.2. *The magnitude of progressivity is unaffected if the tax liability of every individual is increased or decreased in the same proportion.*

Clearly, axiom 12.1 needs no explanation because it follows immediately from the basic definition of tax progressivity. Axiom 12.2 can be justified on the grounds that a measure of tax progressivity shows the deviation of a given tax system from proportionality. Increasing or decreasing the tax rates at all income levels should not, therefore, affect the deviation of a given tax system from proportionality.

Of all the measures of tax progression discussed in "Measurement of Tax Progressivity," liability progression is the only measure that satisfies both these axioms and is equal to the tax elasticity. Because the tax elasticity is always unity for the proportional taxes, the magnitude of the difference of tax elasticity from unity measures the deviation of a given tax system from proportionality.

In the next section a single, overall measure of tax progressivity that satisfies both above axioms is introduced.

Derivation of a New Measure of Tax Progressivity

Suppose that the pretax income x of an individual is a random variable with mean μ and probability distribution function $F(x)$. The relationship between $F(x)$ and $F_1(x)$ is the Lorenz curve for x. If $F_1[T(x)]$ denotes the proportion of taxes paid by taxpayers having an income less than or equal to x, the relationship between $F(x)$ and $F_1[T(x)]$ will be the concentration curve of taxes.

The vertical distance between the curves $F_1(x)$ and $F_1[T(x)]$, depends on the tax elasticity. If this elasticity is unity at all income levels, the two curves coincide. It follows from theorem 8.1 that the larger the difference between tax elasticity and unity, the greater the distance between $F_1(x)$ and $F_1[T(x)]$.

It was pointed out in the preceding section that the measure of liability progression satisfies both axioms of tax progressivity. In addition, this measure is related to the concept of tax elasticity. Clearly, a suitable measure of tax progressivity should depend only on the magnitude of the difference between tax elasticity and unity, which suggests that such a measure should be based on the area between the curves $F_1(x)$ and $F_1[T(x)]$. If C is denoted as the concentration index of taxes, and G the Gini index of the pretax income, it is possible that

$$P = C - G$$

may be a suitable measure of tax progressivity. It is obvious that P

is equal to twice the area between the curves $F_1(x)$ and $F_1[T(x)]$. Moreover, P is positive (negative) if the tax elasticity is greater (less) than unity for all x and assumes value zero when the tax elasticity is unity for all incomes. Thus, the positive value of P implies a progressive tax system, and the negative value implies a regressive tax system. Further, it can be seen that P increases (decreases) with the increase (decrease) in tax elasticity at all income levels. Finally, note that this measure satisfies axioms 12.1 and 12.2.

The posttax income of a unit with income x is given by

$$(12.4) \qquad d(x) = x - T(x),$$

which is an increasing function of x if the marginal tax rate is strictly less than unity for all incomes. Theorem 8.2 indicates that the concentration curve for $d(x)$ coincides with its Lorenz curve. Applying theorem 8.5 to (12.4) yields

$$(12.5) \qquad \mu_d G^* = \mu G - QC$$

where $\mu_d = \mu - Q$ is the mean posttax income, and Q is the mean tax revenue. In addition, G and G^* are the Gini indexes of pre- and posttax incomes, respectively. The expression (12.5) can also be written as

$$(12.6) \qquad G^* = G - \frac{Pe}{(1-e)}$$

where $e = Q/\mu$ is the average tax rate of the society in question.

Equation (12.6) indicates that posttax income inequality is a function of three quantities: inequality of income before tax, average tax rate, and tax progressivity. Note that the average tax rate can change without changing the tax progressivity. The elasticities of the Gini index of the posttax income with respect to the average tax rate and the progressivity can, therefore, be written as

$$(12.7) \qquad \eta_e = - \frac{Pe}{(1-e)^2 G^*}$$

$$(12.8) \qquad \eta_p = - \frac{Pe}{(1-e) G^*}.$$

Equations (12.7) and (12.8) show that for a progressive (regressive) tax system, income inequality decreases (increases) with increases in e and P. Further, note that the ratio of the two elasticities η_e

and η_p exceeds one in absolute terms. From this it can be concluded that posttax income inequality is more sensitive to average tax rate than to tax progressivity.

Differentiating (12.6) totally yields

$$\frac{dG^*}{G^*} = \frac{G}{G^*} \frac{dG}{G} + \eta_p \frac{dP}{p} + \eta_e \frac{de}{e} ,$$

which gives a decomposition of the percentage change in posttax income inequality in terms of the percentage changes in pretax income inequality, average tax rate, and tax progressivity.

The Musgrave-Thin measure of effective progression is given by $(G - G^*)$, which will be identical to the above-described measure of progressivity P if, and only if, the average tax rate of the society is 0.5. Equation (12.7) indicates that the larger (smaller) the average tax rate for a given tax elasticity or progressivity, the more equal (unequal) the posttax income distribution. If it is assumed that the change in average tax rate does not affect the pretax income distribution, the Musgrave-Thin measure may show increase or decrease in progressivity even if the tax elasticity has remained constant at all income levels.

This implies that by doubling tax rates at all income levels, tax progressivity will increase according to the Musgrave-Thin measure, thereby violating axiom 12.2; in fact, Musgrave and Thin measured the redistributive effects of taxes, which have been shown to be a function of the average tax rate in addition to progressivity.

Now, suppose that the total tax function $T(x)$ is equal to the sum of n individual taxes $T_1(x)$, $T_2(x), \ldots, T_n(x)$; then, by means of theorem 8.5, it follows that

(12.9) $$C = \sum_{i=1}^{n} \frac{e_i}{e} C_i$$

where C_i is the concentration index of the ith type of tax, and e_i the average tax rate of the same type of tax. From (12.9) it follows that

(12.10) $$P = \sum_{i=1}^{n} \left(\frac{e_i}{e}\right) P_i$$

where P_i is the tax progressivity of the ith type of taxes. This equation shows that the progressivity of all the taxes together is equal to the weighted average of the progressivity of each tax, the weights being proportional to their average tax rates. Equation (12.10) can be used to analyze the percentage contribution of each kind of tax to total tax progressivity.

Substituting (12.10) into (12.6) yields

$$\frac{G^* - G}{G} = - \frac{\sum_{i=1}^{n} p_i e_i}{(1 - e)G},$$

which provides the decomposition of the percentage change in inequality (due to the tax system as a whole) in terms of the contribution of each kind of tax. If P_i is positive, the contribution of the ith kind of tax is negative, and if P_i is negative, the contribution is positive.

Intercountry Comparison of Factors Affecting Inequalities of Disposable Incomes

In this section changes in degrees of posttax income inequalities in four countries (Australia, the United Kingdom, Canada, and the United States) are discussed.[6] (Posttax income inequality refers to the inequality of disposable income.) The discussion is limited to the effects of personal income tax.

The published data are available in grouped form, which is based on the size of pretax income. For each income class, the source publications report data on the number of taxpayers, the total income, and the total income tax paid.

To calculate the tax progressivity, it was necessary to compute the Gini index of pretax income and the concentration index of the total amounts of personal income tax paid. The equation of the new coordinate system for the Lorenz curve discussed in chapter 7

6. The data for this section were obtained from the official income tax statistics of the countries in question. The publications referred to are: (for Australia) *Taxation Statistics*, 1961–62 to 1972–73, The Government Printer of Australia, Canberra; (for Canada) *Taxation Statistics*, 1966–72, Department of National Revenue, Taxation Division; (for the United Kingdom) *Report of the Commissioners of Her Majesty's Inland Revenue*, 1958–59 to 1966–67, Great Britain's Board of Inland Revenue; (for the United States) *Trends in the Income of Families and Persons in the United States*, 1958–70, U.S. Government Printing Office.

was fitted separately to income and taxes paid, and the concentration indexes were then computed by integrating the area under the concentration curve (see equation (7.21)).

It must be emphasized that there are limitations in a comparison of tax progressivity by means of taxation statistics from different countries. First, these data refer to earners or individual income recipients, not to families. Second, not everyone who receives income is required to file returns, the proportion of earners not filing tax returns depending on the exemptions allowed and varying from country to country. Third, each country has a different definition of income. Fourth, inaccuracies in the data resulting from tax evasion and tax avoidance are not of the same magnitude in all countries.

The numerical results of the comparison of tax progressivity in the different countries are presented in tables 12.2, 12.3, 12.4, and 12.5. The first column gives the Gini index of pretax income. The second and the third columns present the tax progressivity index P and the average tax rate e, respectively. The posttax Gini index is computed in the fourth column by means of formula (12.6). Elasticities of the posttax Gini index are presented in the fifth and sixth columns. Columns 7, 8, 9, and 10 provide the decomposition of the percentage change in the posttax income inequality.

Several interesting findings emerge from the numerical results given in the first four tables. First, the intercountry comparison shows that there are relatively small differences in the degrees of pre- and posttax income inequality, but that these differences are markedly higher in the United States than in other countries. Second, the degree of tax progressivity shows considerable variations in the countries studied. Ranking the countries in descending order of progressivity, the United Kingdom is followed by Australia, Canada, and the United States. Third, there are yearly fluctuations in the average tax rate in all the countries, but the intercountry differences are relatively small for the periods studied.

The empirical results clearly indicate the appreciable declines over a period of time in the degree of tax progressivity in all four countries, especially in the United Kingdom, where it is the highest. This decrease would have accentuated the income inequalities in the different countries, but its effect was offset by the upward trend in the average tax rates. The relative contributions of changes in different factors to the changes in posttax income inequality are shown in columns 8, 9, and 10.

Table 12.2. Progressivity Index for Personal Income Tax, Australia

Fiscal year	Gini index of pretax income (G)	Progressivity index (P)	Average tax rate (e)	Gini index of posttax income (G*)	η_p	η_e	Percentage change in posttax Gini index	Percentage change resulting from changes in pretax Gini index	Percentage change resulting from changes in progressivity	Percentage change resulting from changes in tax rate
1961	0.3627	0.2437	0.1025	0.3349	−0.0831	−0.0926	—	—	—	—
1962	0.3594	0.2421	0.0982	0.3331	−0.0791	−0.0877	−0.54	−0.98	0.05	0.39
1963	0.3681	0.2393	0.1014	0.3411	−0.0792	−0.0881	2.40	2.60	0.09	−0.29
1964	0.3540	0.2434	0.1091	0.3242	−0.0919	−0.1032	−4.92	−4.12	−0.14	−0.66
1965	0.3471	0.2307	0.1185	0.3161	−0.0981	−0.1113	−2.53	−2.12	0.48	−0.89
1966	0.3475	0.2293	0.1245	0.3149	−0.1036	−0.1183	−0.40	0.11	0.06	−0.57
1968	0.3514	0.2150	0.1332	0.3183	−0.1038	−0.1198	1.07	1.25	0.65	−0.83
1969	0.3564	0.2052	0.1396	0.3231	−0.1031	−0.1198	1.48	1.59	0.47	−0.58
1970	0.3571	0.2029	0.1476	0.3220	−0.1092	−0.1281	−0.36	0.21	0.11	−0.68
1971	0.3520	0.1975	0.1445	0.3186	−0.1047	−0.1224	−1.03	−1.59	0.29	0.27
1972	0.3515	0.1893	0.1570	0.3163	−0.1114	−0.1322	−0.77	−0.15	0.44	−1.06

Table 12.3. *Progressivity Index for Personal Income Tax, Canada*

Fiscal year	(G)	(P)	(e)	(G*)	η_p	η_e	Percentage change in posttax Gini index	Percentage change resulting from changes in pretax Gini index	Percentage change resulting from changes in progressivity	Percentage change resulting from changes in tax rate
1964	0.3322	0.1920	0.1080	0.3090	-0.0752	-0.0843	—	—	—	—
1965	0.3377	0.1861	0.1016	0.3167	-0.0664	-0.0740	2.51	1.78	0.23	0.50
1966	0.3466	0.1919	0.1033	0.3245	-0.0681	-0.0760	2.46	2.79	-0.21	-0.12
1967	0.3506	0.1997	0.1156	0.3245	-0.0805	-0.0910	0.07	1.26	-0.28	-0.91
1968	0.3571	0.2001	0.1260	0.3283	-0.0879	-0.1006	1.16	1.99	-0.01	-0.82
1969	0.3659	0.1741	0.1175	0.3427	-0.0676	-0.0767	4.49	2.67	1.14	0.68
1970	0.3754	0.1692	0.1225	0.3518	-0.0672	-0.0766	2.64	2.78	0.19	-0.33

Table 12.4. *Progressivity Index for Personal Income Tax, United Kingdom*

Fiscal year	(G)	(P)	(e)	(G*)	η_p	η_e	Percentage change in posttax Gini index	Percentage change resulting from changes in pretax Gini index	Percentage change resulting from changes in progressivity	Percentage change resulting from changes in tax rate
1959	0.3411	0.3236	0.1212	0.2964	-0.1505	-0.1712	—	—	—	—
1960	0.3496	0.3182	0.1145	0.3085	-0.1334	-0.1506	4.07	2.88	0.25	0.94
1961	0.3571	0.3135	0.1225	0.3133	-0.1397	-0.1592	1.57	2.43	0.20	-1.06
1962	0.3522	0.2979	0.1210	0.3112	-0.1318	-0.1500	-0.68	-1.56	0.69	0.19
1963	0.3589	0.2860	0.1226	0.3190	-0.1253	-0.1428	2.50	2.17	0.52	-0.19
1964	0.3379	0.2984	0.1180	0.2979	-0.1341	-0.1520	-6.62	-6.61	-0.54	0.53
1965	0.3455	0.2821	0.1284	0.3040	-0.1367	-0.1569	1.97	2.57	0.73	-1.33
1966	0.3518	0.2762	0.1447	0.3051	-0.1531	-0.1790	0.37	2.07	0.29	-1.99
1967	0.3454	0.2540	0.1449	0.3024	-0.1423	-0.1664	-0.89	-2.09	1.23	-0.03

Note: The fiscal year in the United Kingdom is from April 5 to April 4 of the following year.

Table 12.5. *Progressivity Index for Personal Income Tax, United States*

Fiscal year	(G)	(P)	(e)	(G^*)	η_p	η_e	Percentage change in posttax Gini index	Percentage change resulting from changes in pretax Gini index	Percentage change resulting from changes in progressivity	Percentage change resulting from changes in tax rate
1958	0.4379	0.1956	0.1217	0.4108	-0.0660	-0.0751	—	—	—	—
1959	0.4430	0.1899	0.1267	0.4155	-0.0663	-0.0759	1.13	1.25	0.19	-0.31
1960	0.4409	0.1820	0.1251	0.4149	-0.0627	-0.0717	-0.15	-0.51	0.27	0.09
1961	0.4453	0.1298	0.1280	0.4262	-0.0447	-0.0513	2.68	1.05	1.80	-0.17
1963	0.3874	0.1554	0.1376	0.3626	-0.0683	-0.0792	-14.83	-13.57	-0.88	-0.38
1964	0.3819	0.0851	0.1254	0.3697	-0.0330	-0.0378	2.26	-1.53	3.09	0.70
1965	0.3928	0.1651	0.1210	0.3701	-0.0614	-0.0699	-0.00	2.97	-3.10	0.13
1966	0.3978	0.1600	0.1246	0.3750	-0.0607	-0.0694	1.31	1.33	0.19	-0.21
1967	0.4082	0.1573	0.1291	0.3849	-0.0606	-0.0695	2.64	2.79	0.10	-0.25
1968	0.4135	0.1642	0.1424	0.3862	-0.0706	-0.0823	0.38	1.36	-0.27	-0.71
1969	0.4196	0.1563	0.1472	0.3926	-0.0687	-0.0805	1.65	1.59	0.34	-0.28
1970	0.3772	0.1561	0.1373	0.3524	-0.0705	-0.0817	-10.24	-10.79	0.01	0.54

Distributional Effects of Taxes and Public Expenditures

In this section detailed empirical findings on the breakdown of the distributional effects of taxation and public spending into individual components are presented. The fact that the data have been obtained from different studies on the incidence of taxes and expenditures renders intercountry comparisons difficult because of the differences in concepts, methods, and assumptions employed by different authors. For reasons of space, comments on intercountry divergencies are limited, and the interested reader is referred to the original studies. The Australian data are from Bentley, Collins, and Drane (1974); Canadian data from Dodge (1975); and United States data from two studies, one conducted by the Tax Foundation (1966) and the other by Reynolds and Smolensky (1974).

Empirical results are presented in tables 12.6 to 12.11. The formats of the tables are identical. There are six columns, the first giving the percentages of each individual tax or expenditure item to the total revenues and total expenditures, respectively. The second and third columns give concentration indexes (C) and progressivity indexes (P), respectively. The fourth column contains the relative contributions of individual items to progressivity indexes in percentage terms. And the last two columns summarize the distributive effects of individual taxes and expenditure items.

Table 12.6, which displays Australian data, demonstrates the dominant role played by personal income tax in reducing income inequality. Secondary roles are fulfilled by company tax, state probate, and succession duties. In contrast, income inequality is increased by some of the taxes, the largest increase resulting from indirect taxes. In addition, local government taxes as a whole are significantly regressive, second in importance only to indirect taxes, and the overall tax system reduces income inequality by 5.48 percent. Table 12.7 provides a further breakdown of the comprehensive distributional effects of the indirect taxes given in table 12.6; each individual commodity tax is shown to be regressive. This result casts doubt on the commonly held belief that indirect taxes can be made progressive by making a distinction between luxuries and necessities.

Table 12.8, displaying Canadian data, provides calculations on

Table 12.6. *Distributional Effects of Different Taxes, Australia, Fiscal 1967*

Tax	Percentage of total taxes	Concen-tration index C	Progres-sivity index P	Contribution to total progressivity	Change in total income inequality resulting from taxes	Contribution to total percentage of change in income inequality
Personal income tax	37.02	0.4460	0.1375	125.68	-0.0213	-6.9
Company tax	13.45	0.4288	0.1203	40.0	-0.0068	-2.2
Estate gifts duties	0.90	0.9755	0.6670	15.56	-0.0026	-0.84
Indirect taxes	30.77	0.2116	-0.0969	-73.58	0.0125	4.05
State motor taxes	3.22	0.2098	-0.0987	-7.90	0.0013	0.42
State probate and succession duties	2.05	0.9374	0.6289	31.85	-0.0054	-1.75
Other state taxes	7.16	0.2346	-0.0739	-13.09	0.0022	0.71
Total local government taxes	5.34	0.1683	-0.1402	-18.52	0.0031	1.00
Total tax	100.00	0.3489	0.0404	100.00	-0.0169	-5.48

Table 12.7. *Distributional Effects of Indirect Taxes by Individual Commodity, Australia, Fiscal 1967*

Indirect tax by commodity	Percentage of total taxes	Concentration index C	Progressivity index P	Contribution to total progressivity	Change in total income inequality resulting from different indirect taxes	Contribution to total percentage of change in income inequality resulting from taxes
Durables and minor durables	14.32	0.2576	−0.0509	−6.30	0.0009	0.29
Household overhead	10.16	0.0065	−0.3020	−26.49	0.0038	1.23
Food	7.95	0.0958	−0.2127	−14.58	0.0021	0.68
Tobacco and alcohol	32.67	0.1918	−0.1167	−32.87	0.0047	1.52
Personal care	1.34	0.1191	−0.1894	−2.16	0.0003	0.10
Clothing	3.11	0.2135	−0.095	−2.59	0.0004	0.13
Education	2.26	0.1793	−0.1292	−2.50	0.0004	0.13
Taxes, fines, and legal costs	6.01	0.3072	−0.0013	−0.09	0.0001	0.003
Motor vehicle expenses and fares	8.05	0.2029	−0.1056	−7.33	0.0011	0.36
Recreation	14.13	0.2670	−0.0415	−5.09	0.0007	0.23
All commodities	100.00	0.1926	−0.1159	100.00	0.0144	4.67

Table 12.8. *Distributional Effects of Taxes and Public Expenditures, Canada, Fiscal 1970*

Tax and expenditure	Percentage of total taxes or expenditures	Concentration index C	Progressivity index P	Contribution to total progressivity	Change in total income inequality resulting from taxes and expenditures	Contribution of taxes and government expenditure to total percentage of change in income inequality
Federal tax	49.80	0.4078	0.0410	91.97	−0.0085	−2.32
Provincial and local tax	50.20	0.3704	0.0036	8.13	−0.0007	−0.19
Total government tax	100	0.3890	0.0222	100	−0.0092	−2.51
Federal expenses	52.58	0.1206	−0.2462	−62.60	−0.0587	−16.00
Provincial and local expenditure	47.42	0.2038	−0.1630	−37.40	−0.0351	−9.57
Total government expenditure	100	0.1600	−0.2068	−100	−0.0938	−25.27
Total net effect	—				−0.1030	−28.08

Table 12.9. *Distributional Effects of Taxes and Public Expenditures, United States, Fiscal 1961*

Tax and expenditure	Percentage of total taxes or expenditures	Concentration index C
Tax		
Personal income tax	44.54	0.5387
Estate and gift tax	1.89	0.9801
Corporate income tax	22.71	0.4447
Excise and customs	14.41	0.2949
Social security tax	16.45	0.3206
Total federal income tax	100.00	0.4547
Personal income tax	5.42	0.5332
Estate and gift tax	1.00	0.9801
Corporate income tax	2.77	0.4456
Excise and sales tax	42.44	0.2846
Property tax	36.73	0.2640
Social insurance	11.64	0.2967
Total state and local tax	100.00	0.3033
Expenditure		
National defense	52.56	0.1806
Other general expenditures	9.47	0.1806
Elementary education	0.31	0.1545
Higher education	0.21	0.5381
Public assistance	2.93	−0.5667
Labor	0.61	0.3972
Veterans' benefits	6.28	0.0468
Highways	2.80	0.2914
Agriculture	4.07	0.0184
Net interest	6.51	0.2942
Social security	14.25	−0.2361
Total federal expenditure	100.00	0.0968
General expenditures	34.68	0.1806
Elementary education	32.01	0.1518
Higher education	5.78	0.5357
Public assistance	4.35	−0.5669
Streets and highways	12.33	0.2920
Agriculture	1.03	0.2076
Net interest	1.50	0.2946
Social insurance	8.32	−0.2361
Total state and local expenditure	100.00	0.1404
Total net effect		

Progressivity index P	Contribution to total progressivity	Change in total income inequality resulting from taxes and expenditures	Contribution of taxes and expenditures to total percentage of change in income inequality
0.1775	84.5	−0.0215	−5.95
0.6189	12.5	−0.0032	−0.88
0.0835	20.3	−0.0051	−1.43
−0.0663	−10.2	+0.0026	+0.72
−0.0406	−7.1	+0.0018	+0.50
0.0935	100.00	−0.0254	−7.04
0.1720	+16.1	−0.0013	−0.36
0.6189	+10.7	−0.0009	−0.24
0.0844	+4.0	−0.0003	−0.09
−0.0766	−56.1	+0.0045	+1.25
−0.0972	−61.7	+0.0050	+1.37
−0.0645	−13.0	+0.0010	+0.29
−0.0579	−100.0	+0.0080	+2.22
−0.1806	−35.9	−0.0264	−7.30
−0.1806	−6.5	−0.0047	−1.32
−0.2067	−0.2	−0.0002	−0.05
0.1769	+−0.1	+0.0001	+0.03
−0.9279	−10.3	−0.0075	−2.09
0.0360	+−0.1	+0.0001	+0.02
−0.3144	−7.5	−0.0055	−1.52
−0.0698	−0.7	−0.0005	−0.15
−0.3428	−5.3	−0.0039	−1.07
−0.0670	−1.6	−0.0012	−0.33
−0.5973	−32.2	−0.0237	−6.55
−0.2644	−100.00	−0.0734	−20.33
−0.1806	−28.4	−0.0091	−2.51
−0.2094	−30.4	−0.0097	−2.69
0.1745	−4.6	+0.0015	+0.40
−0.9281	−18.3	−0.0059	−1.62
−0.0692	−3.9	−0.0012	−0.34
−0.1536	−0.7	−0.0002	−0.06
−0.0666	−0.4	−0.0001	−0.04
−0.5973	−22.5	−0.0072	−1.99
−0.2208	−100.00	−0.0319	−8.85
		−0.1227	−34.00

Table 12.10. *Distributional Effects of Taxes and Public Expenditures, United States, Fiscal 1970*

Tax and expenditure	Percentage of total taxes or expenditures	Concentration index C
Tax		
Personal income tax	46.42	0.5157
Estate and gift tax	1.96	0.9630
Corporate income tax	16.12	0.4934
Excise and customs	9.58	0.3378
Social security tax	25.91	0.3477
Total federal income tax	100	0.4601
Personal income tax	10.08	0.5157
Estate and gift tax	0.98	0.9630
Corporate income tax	3.17	0.4921
Excise and sales tax	45.05	0.3361
Property tax	33.19	0.2691
Social insurance	7.53	0.3477
Total state and local tax	100	0.3439
Expenditure		
National defense	48.27	0.1981
Other general expenditures	7.68	0.1981
Social security	22.82	0.2852
Unemployment compensation	2.17	0.0679
Veterans' benefits	5.46	0.0410
Other transfers	1.68	0.2315
Net interest	8.13	0.2698
Agriculture	2.55	0.1691
Elementary education	0.67	0.1531
Higher education	0.19	0.5790
Highways	0.11	0.2169
Labor	0.27	0.4518
Total federal expenditure	100	0.0832
General expenditures	33.43	0.1981
Public assistance	12.52	−0.4931
Elementary education	32.28	0.1525
Higher education	8.51	0.5770
Streets and highways	11.65	0.2207
Agriculture	0.96	0.1795
Labor	0.65	0.4490
Total state and local expenditure	100	0.1332
Total net effect		

Progressivity index P	Contribution to total progressivity	Change in total income inequality resulting from taxes and expenditures	Contribution of taxes and expenditures to total percentage of change in income inequality
0.1181	87.7	−0.0116	−2.92
0.5654	17.7	−0.0023	−0.58
0.0958	24.7	−0.0033	−0.83
−0.0598	−9.2	+0.0012	+0.30
−0.0499	−20.7	0.0027	+0.68
0.0625	100.0	−0.0132	−3.32
0.1181	+22.1	−0.0014	−0.35
0.5654	+10.3	−0.0007	−0.18
0.0945	+5.6	−0.0004	−0.10
0.0615	−51.6	+0.0034	+0.85
−0.1285	−79.4	+0.0052	+1.31
0.0499	−7.0	+0.0005	+0.12
−0.0537	−100.00	0.0066	1.66
−0.1995	−30.6	−0.0193	−4.87
−0.1995	−4.9	−0.0031	−0.77
−0.6828	−49.6	−0.0313	−7.87
−0.3297	−2.3	−0.0014	−0.36
−0.3566	−6.2	−0.0039	−0.98
−0.1661	−0.9	−0.0006	−0.14
−0.1278	−3.3	−0.0021	−0.52
−0.2285	−1.8	−0.0012	−0.29
−0.2445	−0.5	−0.0003	−0.08
0.1814	+0.1	+0.0001	+0.01
−0.1807	−0.1	−0.00004	−0.01
0.0542	+0.1	+0.00003	+0.01
−0.3144	−100.00	−0.0631	−15.87
−0.1995	25.2	−0.0099	−2.48
−0.8907	42.2	−0.0165	−4.14
−0.2451	29.9	−0.0117	−2.94
0.1794	−5.8	+0.0028	+0.57
−0.1769	7.8	−0.0030	−0.77
−0.2181	0.8	−0.0003	−0.08
0.0514	−0.1	+0.0001	+0.01
−0.2644	−100.00	−0.0391	−9.83
		−0.1088	−27.36

the distributional effects of federal, provincial, and local taxes and expenditures. Results indicate that the effect of the fiscal policy at both levels of government are favorable to the goal of reducing income inequality, although a significant difference appears in the magnitude of effects of public expenditures and taxes at the two levels. Fiscal operations at the federal level are more progressive than those at the provincial and local levels, both in regard to taxes and expenditures. Moreover, expenditures at both levels are more redistributive than are taxes.

Tables 12.9 and 12.10 give a detailed picture of the distributional effects of the fiscal operations of federal, state, and local governments in the United States. They reveal important features of the fiscal system. For example, whereas federal taxes, overall, contributed to the reduction in income inequality, the system of taxation prevailing at the state and local levels resulted in an increase in income inequality in both years studied, 1961 and 1970. In contrast, public expenditures at the federal level as well as at state and local levels contributed to a reduction in income inequality both in 1961 and in 1970. A significant finding that emerges from a comparison of the numerical values in tables 12.9 and 12.10 is that fiscal operations at the federal level became less progressive in 1970 than they had been in 1961, both with respect to taxes and expenditures. During the same period, however, fiscal operations at the state and local levels became more progressive. Thus, whereas taxes became less regressive, expenditures became more progressive. These changes imply that the federal government deviated from egalitarianism, and that state and local governments moved closer to egalitarian policies. The change is most striking in the area of personal income tax at the federal level where the influence toward a reduction in income inequality declined from 5.95 percent to 2.92 percent. The net effect of fiscal operations at both levels of government was less progressive in 1970 than in 1961. During this period, moreover, the contribution of fiscal operations at all levels of government to the reduction in inequality declined from 34 percent to a little over 27 percent.

Finally, table 12.11 provides international comparison of the total distributional effects of different kinds of tax systems on income distribution. The data indicate that the Australian tax system is more egalitarian than those of Canada and the United States; that the totality of Australian government taxes reduces income inequality by about 5.51 percent, whereas the corresponding figure for Canada

Table 12.11. International Comparisons of Distributional Effects of Different Taxes and Public Expenditures

Tax	Percentage of total taxes or expenditures	Concentration index C	Progressivity index P	Contribution to total progressivity and expenditures	Change in total income inequality resulting from taxes and expenditures	Contribution of taxes and expenditures to total percentage of change in income inequality
	Australia, Fiscal 1967					
Federal taxes	82.14	0.3612	0.0527	108.49	−0.0182	−5.89
State and local taxes	17.86	0.2895	−0.0190	−8.51	+0.0012	0.38
Total government taxes	100.00	0.3484	0.0399	100.00	−0.0170	−5.51
	Canada, Fiscal 1970					
Federal taxes	49.80	0.4078	0.0410	91.97	−0.0085	2.32
State and local taxes	50.20	0.3704	0.0036	8.13	−0.0007	−0.19
Total government taxes	100.00	0.3890	0.0222	100.00	−0.0092	−2.51
Federal expenditures	52.58	0.1206	−0.2462	−62.60	−0.0587	−16.00
State and local expenditures	47.42	0.2038	−0.1630	−37.40	−0.0351	−9.57
Total government expenditure	100.00	0.1600	−0.2068	−100.00	−0.0938	−25.57
Net effect of taxes and expenditures	—			—	−0.1030	−28.08
	United States, Fiscal 1970					
Federal taxes	63.24	0.4601	0.0625	199.63	−0.0132	−3.32
State and local taxes	36.76	0.3439	−0.537	−99.63	+0.0066	+1.66
Total government taxes	100.00	0.4174	0.0198	100.00	−0.0066	−1.66
Federal expenditures	57.63	0.0832	−0.3144	−61.80	−0.0631	−15.87
State and local expenditures	42.37	0.1332	−0.2644	−38.20	−0.0391	−9.83
Total government expenditure	100.00	0.1044	−0.2932	−100.00	−0.1022	−25.70
Net effect of taxes and expenditures	—			—	−0.1088	−27.36

is 2.51 percent and 1.66 percent for the United States; and that
state and local taxes are regressive both in Australia and in the
United States, whereas in Canada the taxes are progressive at both
local and national levels. A comparison of the effects of government
expenditure on income distribution indicates that the difference
between Canada and the United States is relatively small. Moreover, the progressivity of government expenditure is considerably
higher in the United States than in Canada. This would have resulted in more egalitarian distribution of income in the United States
than in Canada, had this effect not been offset by higher average
government expenditure in Canada.

Measurement of Built-in Flexibility and Its Stabilizing Effect

Several measures of built-in flexibility have been suggested. Vickrey (1949), for example, defined built-in flexibility as the ratio of
tax yield in prosperity to tax yield in depression. Musgrave and
Miller (1948) proposed the elasticity of tax yield with respect to
total income; this measure is generally referred to as effective tax
revenue elasticity. An alternative measure of built-in flexibility is
the effective marginal tax rate,[7] defined as the change in tax revenue
following a unit change in total income. This measure has been
used by Clement (1960), Pechman (1956), Cohen (1959), Pearse
(1962), and Dorrington (1974), among others.

To measure the stabilizing effect of built-in flexibility, Musgrave
and Miller (1948) proposed the γ coefficient, which is defined as

$$(12.11) \qquad \gamma = 1 - \frac{\Delta Y}{\Delta Y_a}$$

where ΔY refers to the change in income in the particular tax system
under study, ΔY_a refers to the potential change in income that
would occur in the absence of any tax-yield sensitivity, and γ is

---

7. Note that the terms "effective tax revenue elasticity" and "effective marginal
tax rate" refer to the sensitivity of the tax yield to the changes in total income. The
terms "tax elasticity" and "marginal tax rate" used in the context of tax progression in "Measurement of Tax Progressivity" relate the changes in the tax liability of an individual to the changes in his taxable income.

interpreted as the fraction of the change in income that is prevented because of the existence of built-in flexibility.

Musgrave and Miller considered the following aggregative model to establish the relationship between built-in flexibility and its stabilizing effect:

$$\Delta Y = \Delta C + \Delta A$$

$$\Delta C = c(\Delta Y - \Delta T)$$

$$\Delta T = m\Delta Y$$

where

Y = income,
C = consumption,
T = taxes,
A = autonomous components of expenditure,
c = marginal propensity to consume,
m = effective marginal tax rate.

It follows that

(12.12)
$$\Delta Y = \frac{\Delta A}{1 - c + cm}.$$

In the absence of built-in flexibility, $m = 0$, in which case

(12.13)
$$\Delta Y_a = \frac{\Delta A}{(1 - c)}.$$

As c and m are generally positive and less than unity, the presence of built-in flexibility reduces the multiplier. Substituting (12.12) and (12.13) into(12.11) gives the γ coefficient:

(12.14)
$$\gamma = \frac{cm}{1 - c + cm}.$$

If the marginal propensity to consume is known, (12.14) gives the relationship between built-in flexibility in the tax system and the extent to which fluctuations in total income are thereby prevented.

The Empirical Estimation of Built-in Flexibility

The data used for the purpose of estimating built-in flexibility were again obtained from Australia, Canada, the United States, and the United Kingdom.

The estimation of the measures of built-in flexibility requires the specification of the tax function that fits well to the entire income range. In this case, the tax function based on the new coordinate system of the Lorenz curve is used. Recall that this function was used in "Comparison of Alternative Measures of Tax Progressivity" to estimate the tax elasticity at different levels of income. A detailed description of it is provided in the last section of chapter 10 in connection with the estimation of Engel elasticities. The method of estimation described in chapter 10 must be modified to estimate the effective tax revenue elasticity. A suggested modification follows.

Denote $\eta = g(\pi)$ as the equation of the Lorenz curve of pretax income; π and η are defined in (7.1). Then the pretax income denoted by x will be

$$(12.15) \qquad x = \frac{\mu[1 - g'(\pi)]}{[1 + g'(\pi)]}$$

where μ is the mean of pretax income. Note that (7.4) has been used to derive this equation. If Q denotes the mean tax yield, then

$$(12.16) \qquad Q = \int_0^\infty T(x)f(x)\,dx$$

where $f(x)$ is the probability density function of x. Substituting (7.16) into (12.16) yields

$$(12.17) \qquad Q = \frac{1}{\sqrt{2}} \int_0^{\sqrt{2}} T(x)[1 + g'(\pi)]d\pi$$

where x is given by (12.15). Differentiating (12.17) with respect to μ gives the effective tax revenue elasticity as

$$(12.18) \qquad \frac{\partial Q}{\partial \mu} \cdot \frac{\mu}{Q} = \frac{\mu}{\sqrt{2}\,Q} \int_0^{\sqrt{2}} T'(x)[1 - g'(\pi)]d\pi$$

where use has been made of the fact that $g(\pi)$ is independent of μ.

Let $\eta^* = g^*(\pi^*)$ be the equation of the concentration curve for the tax function $T(x)$; then (10.14) yields

$$T(x) = \frac{Q[1 - g^{*\prime}(\pi^*)]}{[1 + g'^*(\pi^*)]},$$

which, in conjunction with (12.15) and (10.22), gives the first derivative of $T(x)$ as

(12.19) $$T'(x) = \frac{Q}{\mu} \frac{g^{*\prime\prime}(\pi^*)[1 + g'(\pi)]^3}{g''(\pi)[1 + g'^*(\pi^*)]^3} .$$

Substituting (12.19) into (12.18) gives the effective tax revenue elasticity as

(12.20) $$\frac{\partial Q}{\partial \mu} \cdot \frac{\mu}{Q} = \frac{1}{\sqrt{2}} \int_0^{\sqrt{2}} \frac{g^{*\prime\prime}(\pi^*)}{g''(\pi)} \frac{[1 + g'(\pi)]^3}{[1 + g'^*(\pi^*)]^3} [1 - g'(\pi)]d\pi$$

where π and π^* from (10.24) are related by

(12.21) $$\pi + g(\pi) = \pi^* + g^*(\pi^*),$$

which gives the value of π^* for any given value of π.

Suppose now that the individual taxpayers are arranged into $(T + 1)$ income classes, $(x_0$ to $x_1)$, $(x_1$ to $x_2)$, ..., $(x_T$ to $x_{T+1})$. Let f_t and μ_t be the relative frequency and the mean of the pretax income in the tth class, respectively; the mean for all the taxpayers will then be

$$\mu = \sum_{t=1}^{T+1} \mu_t f_t.$$

If Q_t denotes the mean tax revenue in the tth income class, the mean tax yield from all the taxpayers will be

$$Q = \sum_{t=1}^{T+1} Q_t f_t,$$

which gives the average tax rate as equal to Q/μ.

By means of the observations on f_t, μ_t, and Q_t, the observations on (π_t, η_t) for income and (π_t^*, η_t^*) for taxes can be derived. These in turn are used for the least-squares estimates of the functions $g(\pi)$ and $g^*(\pi^*)$. It is assumed that these functions are of the form

(12.22) $$g(\pi) = a\pi^\alpha(\sqrt{2} - \pi)^\beta$$

(12.23) $$g^*(\pi^*) = a^*\pi^{*\alpha^*} (\sqrt{2} - \pi^*)^{\beta^*}.$$

Substituting the estimated values of $g(\pi)$ and $g^*(\pi^*)$ into (12.20) gives the effective tax-revenue elasticity.

The integral given in (12.20) was evaluated numerically in conjunction with equation (12.21). The effective average tax rates

Table 12.12. *Intercountry Comparison of Built-in Flexibility and Its Stabilizing Effect for the United Kingdom, Australia, Canada, and the United States, Fiscal 1959–72*

Fiscal year	Effective average tax rate	Effective marginal tax rate	Effective tax revenue elasticity	γ
United Kingdom				
1959	0.1211	0.2351	1.9412	0.4136
1960	0.1145	0.2180	1.9037	0.3954
1961	0.1225	0.2292	1.8709	0.4074
1962	0.1210	0.2225	1.8388	0.4003
1963	0.1226	0.2188	1.7845	0.3963
1964	0.1180	0.2165	1.8345	0.3937
1965	0.1284	0.2266	1.7649	0.4047
1966	0.1447	0.2520	1.7413	0.4305
1967	0.1449	0.2446	1.6881	0.4232
Australia				
1961	0.1025	0.1760	1.7166	0.3455
1962	0.0981	0.1701	1.7337	0.3379
1963	0.1014	0.1720	1.6961	0.3404
1964	0.1091	0.1849	1.6948	0.3568
1965	0.1185	0.1995	1.6837	0.3744
1966	0.1245	0.2082	1.6720	0.3845
1968	0.1332	0.2180	1.6367	0.3954
1969	0.1396	0.2227	1.5952	0.4005
1970	0.1476	0.2362	1.6005	0.4147
1971	0.1445	0.2299	1.5908	0.4082
1972	0.1570	0.2470	1.5733	0.4256

were directly obtained from the grouped data for the four countries, and the effective marginal tax rates were then computed by multiplying the computed values of the effective tax-revenue elasticity by the effective average tax rates. The values of γ as defined in (12.14) were obtained by assuming the marginal propensity to consume to be 0.75 for all countries. Because this assumption is unrealistic, the comments on intercountry comparisons of the effectiveness of built-in flexibility must be qualified. The numerical results are presented in table 12.12.

Note that the degree of built-in flexibility, measured by both the effective marginal tax rate and the effective tax-revenue elasticity, shows considerable variation in the four countries. Ranking the

Table 12.12 (Continued)

Fiscal year	Effective average tax rate	Effective marginal tax rate	Effective tax revenue elasticity	γ
Canada				
1964	0.1080	0.1726	1.5980	0.3411
1965	0.1016	0.1589	1.5644	0.3228
1966	0.1033	0.1650	1.5970	0.3311
1967	0.1156	0.1841	1.5926	0.3558
1968	0.1260	0.2016	1.6001	0.3769
1969	0.1175	0.1759	1.4970	0.3452
1970	0.1225	0.1789	1.4608	0.3492
United States				
1958	0.1217	0.1914	1.5729	0.3647
1959	0.1267	0.1949	1.5381	0.3690
1960	0.1251	0.1785	1.4271	0.3487
1961	0.1280	0.1762	1.3763	0.3458
1963	0.1376	0.1987	1.4439	0.3735
1964	0.1254	0.1550	1.2359	0.3174
1965	0.1210	0.1706	1.4100	0.3385
1966	0.1246	0.1708	1.3710	0.3388
1967	0.1291	0.1745	1.3514	0.3436
1968	0.1424	0.1923	1.3503	0.3658
1969	0.1472	0.1963	1.3339	0.3706
1970	0.1373	0.1928	1.4043	0.3664

countries in descending order of effective marginal tax rate, the United Kingdom is followed by Australia, the United States, and Canada. In addition, the ranking of the countries is altered if the effective tax-revenue elasticity is used as a measure of built-in flexibility. According to this measure Canada shows a higher built-in flexibility than the United States, the reason being that the average tax rate is slightly higher in the United States than in Canada, which offsets the ranking. The higher built-in flexibility in the United Kingdom and Australia indicates that these economies are relatively slow to respond to any increase or decrease in government expenditure. For example, in Australia during 1970–71, the value of α was equal to 0.408, which implies that about 40 percent of an increase in income would be prevented because of built-in flexibility. In the same year, the figure for Canada was only 34 percent, and 36 percent for the United States.

Comparing yearly fluctuations, note that effective tax-revenue elasticity declined in all four countries during the period studied. In contrast, the effective marginal tax rate increased in Australia during the same period, whereas for the other three countries, there was no appreciable change. The conclusion is that the two widely used measures of built-in flexibility may lead to conflicting results; this, in turn, poses the problem of choosing one measure over the other.

The measurement of built-in flexibility is important because of its stabilizing effect on income, indicated by the α coefficient, which, as can be seen from (12.14), depends on two factors: the effective marginal tax rate and the marginal propensity to consume. If the marginal propensity to consume is fixed, the effective marginal tax rate will contain sufficient information regarding the stabilizing effect of built-in flexibility. From this it may be argued that the effective marginal tax rate should be preferred to the measure of effective tax-revenue elasticity as a measure of built-in flexibility. Musgrave and Miller (1948) analyzed the degree of built-in flexibility in terms of both effective average tax rate and elasticity.

On the basis of the effective marginal tax rate, as well as the γ coefficient, it may be inferred that built-in flexibility did not show appreciable change in the United Kingdom, the United States, or Canada during the period studied. In Australia, however, built-in flexibility increased gradually during 1960–61 and 1970–71. Thus, the Australian economy is becoming increasingly sluggish because of built-in flexibility, a conclusion, however, which assumes that other factors affecting the multiplier do not offset the effect of built-in flexibility.

Effect of Income Redistribution on Built-in Flexibility

The degree of built-in flexibility depends both on the level and the inequality of income. If the tax system is progressive, an increase in the level of national income leads to an increase in both effective average and marginal tax rates. This occurs frequently during inflationary periods when the tax structure is not automatically adjusted for inflation. The result is an increase in built-in flexibility, which, in turn, stabilizes the income.

This section focuses on the effect of income redistribution on built-in flexibility. Usually, it is impossible to determine whether a more equal or unequal distribution of pretax income will lead to a higher or lower built-in flexibility. This is an empirical question, which will be investigated here by means of the Australian data. The procedure adopted is as follows.

The Gini index of income based on the Lorenz curve (12.22) was derived in (7.21). This equation gave a partial derivative of the Gini index with respect to a as equal to

$$\frac{\partial G}{\partial a} = \frac{G}{a},$$

which implies that as a increases (decreases) by 1 percent, the Gini index of income also increases (decreases) by 1 percent, provided α and β do not change. This result provides a method of redistributing income without affecting the skewness of the Lorenz curve, which depends on α and β.

Assume that the mean income of society changes by $100\,\epsilon$ percent, and that the income inequality measured by the Gini index by $100\,\delta$ percent. If the skewness of the Lorenz curve remains unchanged, the mean income μ changes to $(1 + \epsilon)\,\mu$, and the parameter a changes to $(1 + \delta)a$. The remaining parameters of the Lorenz curve, α and β, remain unchanged. Suppose that this increase in the level and inequality of income changes f_t and μ_t in each income class to $\tilde{f}_t$ and $\tilde{\mu}_t$, respectively. Clearly, $\tilde{f}_t$ and $\tilde{\mu}_t$ must satisfy

$$(12.24) \qquad \sum_{t=1}^{T+1} \tilde{f}_t = 1$$

$$(12.25) \qquad \sum_{t=1}^{T+1} \tilde{\mu}_t \tilde{f}_t = (1 + \epsilon)\mu.$$

Equation (7.16) indicates that

$$(12.26) \qquad f_t = \frac{1}{\sqrt{2}} \int_{\pi_{t-1}}^{\pi_t} [1 + g'(\pi)]d\pi,$$

which can also be written as

$$(12.27) \qquad f_t = \frac{1}{2}\left[f_t + \frac{\mu_t f_t}{\mu} \right] + \frac{1}{\sqrt{2}} \int_{\pi_{t-1}}^{\pi_t} g'(\pi)\,d\pi$$

where use has been made of

$$\Delta \pi_t = \frac{1}{\sqrt{2}} \left[\Delta F(x_t) + \Delta F_1(x_t) \right]$$

(12.28)
$$= \frac{1}{\sqrt{2}} \left[f_t + \frac{\mu_t f_t}{\mu} \right],$$

$\Delta \pi_t$ being equal to $\pi_t - \pi_{t-1}$. Equation (7.20) indicates that if a changes to $a(1 + \delta)$, $g'(\pi)$ will change to $(1 + \delta)g'(\pi)$. Following (12.26), this yields

$$\tilde{f}_t = \frac{1}{\sqrt{2}} \int_{\pi_{t-1}}^{\pi_t} \left[1 + (1 + \delta)g'(\pi) \right] d\pi,$$

which, by means of (12.27), becomes

(12.29)
$$\tilde{f}_t = f_t \left(1 + \frac{\delta}{2} \right) - \frac{\delta}{2\mu} \mu_t f_t.$$

Note that $\tilde{f}_t$ depends only on δ and not on ϵ. Further, (12.29) shows that $\tilde{f}_t$ satisfies (12.24).

Again, using (7.16) in conjunction with (12.15) yields

$$\mu_t = \frac{1}{f_t} \int_{x_{t-1}}^{x_t} x f(x) \, dx$$

(12.30)
$$= \frac{\mu}{\sqrt{2} f_t} \int_{\pi_{t-1}}^{\pi_t} \left[1 - g'(\pi) \right] d\pi,$$

which, by means of (12.28), yields

(12.31)
$$\int_{\pi_{t-1}}^{\pi_t} g'(\pi) \, d\pi = \frac{f_t}{\sqrt{2}} \frac{(\mu - \mu_t)}{\mu}.$$

If μ and a change to $\mu(1 + \epsilon)$ and $a(1 + \delta)$, respectively, (12.30) yields

$$\tilde{\mu}_t = \frac{(1 + \epsilon)\mu}{\sqrt{2} \tilde{f}_t} \int_{\pi_{t-1}}^{\pi_t} \left[1 - (1 + \delta)g'(\pi) \right] d\pi,$$

which, by means of (12.31), simplifies to

(12.32)
$$\tilde{\mu}_t = \frac{(1 + \epsilon)f_t}{2 \tilde{f}_t} \left[\mu + \mu_t - (1 + \delta)(\mu - \mu_t) \right].$$

Note that $\tilde{\mu}_t$ depends on both δ and ϵ. Further, it can be seen from (12.32) that $\tilde{\mu}_t$ satisfies (12.25).

In "Comparison of Alternative Measures of Tax Progressivity," the tax elasticity for each income group was computed by means of the new coordinate system for the Lorenz curve. These elasticities are used here to compute the changes in the mean tax yield caused by changes in the level and inequality of income. If the tax elasticity in the tth income class is denoted by ω_t, then

$$\frac{\tilde{Q}_t - Q_t}{Q_t} = \omega_t \frac{(\tilde{\mu}_t - \mu_t)}{\mu_t}$$

where $\tilde{Q}_t$ denotes the mean tax yield in the tth income class after the mean income of all the taxpayers has changed by ϵ percent and inequality of income has changed by δ percent. The mean tax yield from all the taxpayers will now be equal to

$$\tilde{Q} = \sum_{t=1}^{T+1} \tilde{Q}_t \tilde{f}_t,$$

which gives the average tax rate as

(12.33) $$\tilde{e} = \tilde{Q}/(1 + \epsilon)\mu,$$

which can be computed for different values of ϵ and δ.

The new parameters of the function $g(\pi)$ defined in (12.22) are $(1 + \delta)a$, α, and β with mean income $(1 + \epsilon)\mu$. The parameter estimates of $g^*(\pi^*)$ defined in (12.23) can be estimated by the least-squares method and the new series $\tilde{f}_t$ and $\tilde{Q}_t$. These new estimates of the function $g(\pi)$ and $g^*(\pi^*)$ in (12.20) and (12.21) give the effective tax revenue elasticity when the mean and inequality of income have changed by ϵ and δ percent, respectively. The effective marginal tax rate can then be obtained by multiplying this elasticity by the effective average tax rate given in (12.33). The numerical estimates are presented in table 12.13. The stabilizing effect of the built-in flexibility measure by γ coefficient has been computed by assuming that the marginal propensity to consume is 0.75.

Table 12.13 shows that both the effective average and marginal tax rates increase with the increase in the mean income of society. But these results are intuitively obvious. In addition, note that the effective tax revenue elasticity does not show such a pattern.

Table 12.13. *Calculation of Built-in Flexibility with Postulated Changes in Income Distribution, Australia, Fiscal 1971*

Percentage change in the mean income		Percentage change in the Gini index of pretax income					
		-15 percent	-10 percent	-5 percent	0 percent	5 percent	10 percent
Zero	Effective tax revenue elasticity	1.665	1.639	1.614	1.591	1.570	1.553
	Effective average tax rate	0.138	0.140	0.142	0.145	0.147	0.149
	Effective marginal tax rate	0.2300	0.2295	0.2292	0.2307	0.2308	0.2314
	γ	0.4083	0.4077	0.4074	0.4090	0.4091	0.4097
5 percent	Effective tax revenue elasticity	1.672	1.643	1.615	1.589	1.566	1.547
	Effective average tax rate	0.142	0.144	0.146	0.149	0.151	0.153
	Effective marginal tax rate	0.2372	0.2366	0.2358	0.2368	0.2365	0.2367
	γ	0.4157	0.4151	0.4143	0.4153	0.4150	0.4152
10 percent	Effective tax revenue elasticity	1.678	1.646	1.616	1.588	1.563	1.543
	Effective average tax rate	0.146	0.148	0.150	0.153	0.155	0.157
	Effective marginal tax rate	0.2450	0.2436	0.2424	0.2430	0.2423	0.2422
	γ	0.4236	0.4222	0.4210	0.4216	0.4209	0.4208
15 percent	Effective tax revenue elasticity	1.683	1.649	1.616	1.587	1.561	1.538
	Effective average tax rate	0.150	0.152	0.154	0.156	0.158	0.161
	Effective marginal tax rate	0.2524	0.2506	0.2489	0.2476	0.2466	0.2476
	γ	0.4391	0.4291	0.4275	0.4262	0.4252	0.4262

When the income inequality is increased, this elasticity, in fact, decreases with the increase in mean income.

The second important finding of these results concerns the effective average tax rate, which increases (decreases) with the increase (decrease) in pretax income inequality. The effective marginal tax rate, in contrast, does not show a similar pattern. Thus generalizations regarding the direction of the change in built-in flexibility with respect to income redistribution are not possible.

CHAPTER 13

Redistributive Effects of Alternative Negative Income Tax Plans

NEGATIVE INCOME TAX and guaranteed annual income are the two commonly suggested fiscal measures to transfer income from the rich to the poor in order to reduce poverty.[1] The objective of negative income tax proposals is to extend the income tax rates beyond zero to negative levels so that families having an income below a break-even level obtain an allowance from the government. A break-even level of income is the level at which a family neither pays an income tax nor receives a cash allowance from the government.

The guaranteed income scheme, which is also referred to as social dividend taxation, pays a cash subsidy to every family, depending on the family composition; in turn, each family is subjected to a proportional tax on income, excluding cash benefits.

One of the first formulas for negative income tax was proposed by Friedman (1962). Under his plan, the break-even level of income is determined by the total value of exemptions and deductions allowed under existing tax laws to a family of a given size. The plans proposed by Lampman (1964) and Green (1966) are identical and differ only slightly from the Friedman plan. All three determine the break-even level of income on the basis of the poverty standard for a family of a given size. In addition, these plans have the same marginal tax rate,

---

1. This chapter is based on Kakwani (1977e).

although the Friedman plan provides more benefits to larger families than the Lampman and Green plans.

Among several guaranteed income plans, the Smith (1965) plan is the only one that provides for the differing needs of children and adults within a family. In contrast, the Tobin (1965) plan gives the same allowance to every family member; the Rolph (1967) plan is similar to the Tobin plan, except that it applies a lower tax rate on family income other than allowance.

This chapter concerns the distributional effects of the alternative income maintenance plans mentioned above. The Gini index of the disposable family income is used as a measure of inequality to compare the different plans, and the effect of changes in the parameters of the negative income tax plans on income inequality is analyzed in terms of elasticities. The present analysis does not include the effect of taxes on the work incentive. In other words, it is assumed that the proposed plans do not alter the distribution of actual earned income, that is, income before taxes and transfers.

Because the income maintenance plans mentioned above are basically similar, a general framework incorporating all the plans is provided. This framework is discussed in the following section, and a brief summary of the different plans is given.

Alternative Negative Income Tax Plans

Suppose there are N families, and x_i is the total income of the ith family, which is of size n_i; then $R(n_i)$ can be defined as the break-even level of that family. (As mentioned above, this is the level of income at which the net allowance and net tax are equal to zero.) If a family of size n_i has an income less than $R(n_i)$, the family receives a cash allowance from the government; if the family income is greater than $R(n_i)$, it pays a positive tax to the government.

Assuming that the marginal tax rate β is the same for both positive and negative income tax, the net tax paid by the ith family is given by

$$T_i = -\beta[R(n_i) - x_i] \quad \text{if } x_i \leq R(n_i)$$

(13.1) $$= \beta[x_i - R(n_i)] \quad \text{if } x_i \geq R(n_i),$$

which can also be written as

(13.2) $$T_i = \beta x_i - \beta R(n_i).$$

If it is specified that

$$R(n_i) = a + \beta n_i,$$

then (13.2) becomes

(13.3) $$T_i = \beta x_i - a\beta - b\beta n_i.$$

If μ is the mean family income before taxes and transfers, and μ_n is the mean family size, the average tax rate of all the families will be

(13.4) $$e = \beta[\mu - a - b\mu_n]/\mu,$$

which is nonnegative if $\mu \geq a + b \mu_n$. Further, the average tax rate will always be less than unity if the marginal tax rate is less than unity.

The disposable income of the ith family is given by

(13.5) $$d_i = (1 - \beta)x_i + a\beta + b\beta n_i,$$

which will always be positive if the marginal tax rate is less than unity. Note that the pretax income is always assumed to be non-negative.

If $a\beta = a^*$ and $b\beta = b^*$, the tax paid (received) by the ith family will be

$$T_i = -a^* - b^* n_i + \beta x_i,$$

which is obtained from (13.2). In effect, this equation implies that the above negative income tax plan gives a cash subsidy to every family depending on its size, when it becomes subject to a β percent tax rate on income other than allowance. The cash subsidy given to a family whose size is n_i is equal to $a^* + b^* n_i$ where a^* is the lump sum subsidy, and b^* is the size of the credit per member of the family, assuming uniformity for each member.

This plan does not provide for the differing needs of children and adults within the families. One method of doing so is to specify the break-even level of a family as

$$R(n_i) = a + b_1 n_{i_1} + b_2 n_{i_2}$$

where n_{i_1} is the number of children (say, under 18) in the ith family, and n_{i_2} is the number of adults in the same family. Then (13.1) becomes

(13.6) $$T_i = \beta x_i - a\beta - \beta b_1 n_{i_1} - \beta b_2 n_{i_2},$$

and the average tax rate of all the families is, therefore, given by

$$(13.7) \qquad e = \frac{\beta[\mu - a - b_1\mu_{n_1} - b_2\mu_{n_2}]}{\mu}$$

where μ_{n_1} is the mean number of children in the families, and μ_{n_2} is the mean number of adults. The average tax rate will be nonnegative if $\mu \geq a + b_1\mu_{n_1} + b_2\mu_{n_2}$. Now, the disposable income of the ith family will be given by

$$(13.8) \qquad d_i = (1 - \beta)x_i + a\beta + \beta b_1 n_{i_1} + \beta b_2 n_{i_2};$$

this too will always be positive if $0 < \beta < 1$.

Again, if $a\beta = a^*$, $b_1\beta = b_1^*$ and $b_2\beta = b_2^*$ are denoted, this negative income tax plan, in effect, gives a cash subsidy to every family that is subject to a β percent tax rate on income other than allowance. This subsidy to the ith family is equal to $a^* + b_1^* n_{i_1} + b_2^* n_{i_2}$ where b_1^* is the size of the credit per child in the family, and b_2^* is the credit for each adult. Again, a^* is the lump sum cash subsidy to each family and does not depend on family size.

The alternative negative income tax plans that have been described are summarized below.

The Friedman plan

Under this plan the break-even level of a family is determined by the total value of exemptions and deductions allowed to a family of a given size. According to the 1964 U.S. tax laws, each member of a family has a $600. exemption and a $100. deduction. The head of the family is allowed a deduction of $300. A tax rate of 50 percent is applied for both positive and negative income tax. Thus under this plan, $\beta = 0.5$, $a = 200$, and $b = 700$.

The Lampman-Green plan

Here, a rate, say, of 50 percent, is applied to the amount by which the poverty standard differs from the actual income of a family. According to Lampman and Green, the poverty level could be reasonably approximated by $1,500. for the family head plus $500. for each dependent. Thus under this plan, $\beta = 0.5$, $a = \$1,000.$, and $b = \$500.$

The Tobin plan

Under this plan a basic allowance of $500. is paid to every member of a family, which is then subject to a $33\frac{1}{3}$ percent tax rate on income other than allowance. Tobin, in fact, merges the negative tax with the present positive tax system, but this will not be considered here. Thus under this plan, $\beta = 0.333$, $a = 0$, and $b\beta = 500$, which means that b is equal to $1,500.

The Rolph plan

This plan is similar to Tobin's plan except that a tax rate of 30 percent instead of $33\frac{1}{3}$ percent is applied.

The Smith plan

This is the only plan that provides for the differing needs of children and adults within a family. The plan pays $1,000. a year to each adult and $200. a year to each child. Each family is then subject to a tax rate of 40 percent. Thus under this plan, $\beta = 0.40$, $a = 0$, $\beta b_1 = $200.$, and $\beta b_2 = $1,000.$, which means that $b_1 = $500.$, and $b_2 = $2,500.

Progressivity of a Negative Income Tax Plan

Suppose that the families are arranged according to their incomes, $x_1 < x_2 < \ldots, < x_N$; the ordinate of the concentration curve of the family size at $p = i/N$ for $i = 0,1,2,\ldots, N$ will be

$$C_n(0) = 0$$

$$C_n\left(\frac{i}{N}\right) = \sum_{k=1}^{i} n_k / \sum_{k=1}^{N} n_k$$

where $i \leq N$. Let C_n be the concentration index of the family size, which is equal to one minus twice the area under the concentration curve of the family size; then, applying theorem 8.5 to (13.3), the concentration index of taxes yielded is [2]

2. Note that theorem 8.5 was proved under the assumption that the distribution of income is continuous. It is not difficult to demonstrate that this theorem is also valid for a discrete distribution of income, as is the case here.

(13.9) $$C = (\beta\mu G - \beta b\mu_n C_n)/\mu e$$

where G is the Gini index of family income, and e is the average tax rate, which was defined in (13.4). Note that in the derivation of (13.9), the following facts were used: the concentration index of a constant is zero; the Gini index of βx_i is the same as the Gini index of x_i, and the concentration index of $b\beta n_i$ is equal to the concentration index of n_i.

The new progressivity index, introduced in the preceding chapter, for the tax function (13.3) will then be given by

(13.10) $$P = \frac{\beta}{\mu e} [aG + b\mu_n(G - C_n)],$$

which will be positive if $G \geq C_n$. It follows from corollary 8.2 that $G > C_n$ if the family size elasticity with respect to x is less than or equal to unity for all values of x. In practice, it is unlikely that this elasticity will exceed unity because the proportional increase in family size is generally less than the proportional increase in income. Thus it follows from (13.10) that the negative income tax plan (13.3) will be progressive.

Differentiating P in (13.10) partially with respect to β gives $\partial P/\partial \beta = 0$, which implies that the tax progressivity is unaffected by the change in the marginal tax rate.

Denote η_a and η_b as the elasticities of the progressivity index P with respect to a and b, respectively; then,

(13.11) $$\eta_a = \frac{a\beta}{\mu e} \frac{(P + G)}{P}$$

$$\eta_b = \frac{\beta\mu_n b}{\mu e} \frac{(G - C_n + P)}{P}.$$

These equations imply that the tax progressivity increases as a and b increase.

Now substitute $a\beta = a^*$ and $b\beta = b^*$ into (13.10), with a^* being the lump-sum subsidy, and b^* the size of credit per family member. This yields

$$P = \frac{a^*G + b^*\mu_n(G - C_n)}{\beta\mu - a^* - b^*\mu_n},$$

which gives the elasticities of P with respect to β, a^*, and b^* as

$$(13.12) \qquad\qquad \eta_\beta = -\frac{\beta}{e}$$

$$(13.13) \qquad\qquad \eta_{a^*} = \frac{(G+P)a^*}{\mu e P}$$

$$(13.14) \qquad\qquad \eta_{b^*} = \frac{\mu_n b^*(G - C_n + P)}{\mu e P}.$$

Equation (13.12) implies that tax progressivity decreases as the marginal tax rate increases, provided the cash subsidy a^* and the size of credit per family member b^* are kept constant. In contrast, (13.13) and (13.14) show that the tax progressivity increases as a^* and b^* increase.

Next, consider the Smith plan, which provides for the differing needs of children and adults within a family. If theorem 8.5 is applied to (13.6), the result is

$$C = \frac{1}{\mu e} \left[\beta \mu G - \beta b_1 \mu_{n_1} C_{n_1} - \beta b_2 \mu_{n_2} C_{n_2} \right]$$

where C_{n_1} and C_{n_2} are the concentration indexes of the children and adults within a family, and e is given in equation (13.7). The progressivity index for the tax function (13.6) will, therefore, be

$$(13.15) \qquad P = \frac{\beta}{\mu e} \left[aG + b_1 \mu_{n_1}(G - C_{n_1}) + b_2 \mu_{n_2}(G - C_{n_2}) \right],$$

which will be positive (indicating progressive tax function) if the elasticities, with respect to family income, of the children and adults within a family are less than unity at all levels of income. The elasticities of P with respect to β, a, and b can be obtained from equation (13.15).

Negative Income Tax and Income Inequality

The concentration curve for the disposable income d_i as defined in (13.5) coincides with the Lorenz curve for d_i if the ranking of families according to their disposable income is identical to their ranking according to their pretax income. It can be seen from (13.5) that this condition is satisfied if

(13.16) $$\frac{\partial n_i}{\partial x_i} > -(1 - \beta)/b\beta.$$

In practice, $\partial n_i/\partial x_i$ is generally positive, implying that larger families have higher income. It seems reasonable, therefore, to assume that condition (13.16) will be satisfied. The Gini index of the disposable income will then be the same as its concentration index. Thus, applying theorem 8.5 to (13.5) yields the Gini index of the disposable income as

(13.17) $$G^* = [(1 - \beta)\mu G + b\beta\mu_n C_n]/(1 - e)\mu,$$

which can also be written as

$$G^* = G - \beta[aG + b\mu_n(G - C_n)].$$

Now $G > C_n$ because of the assumption that family size elasticity is less than unity. It follows, then, from (13.17) that the Gini index of disposable income will be less than the Gini index of pretax income.

Denote η_β^*, η_a^*, and η_b^* as the elasticities of G^* with respect to β, a, and b, respectively; then, equation (13.17) yields

(13.18) $$\eta_\beta^* = \frac{-(G - G^*)}{(1 - e)G^*}$$

(13.19) $$\eta_a^* = -\frac{a\beta}{(1 - e)\mu}$$

(13.20) $$\eta_b^* = -\frac{b\beta\mu_N(G^* - C_N)}{(1 - e)\mu G^*},$$

which are related as

(13.21) $$\eta_a^* + \eta_b^* = (1 - \beta)\eta_\beta^*.$$

Equation (13.18) implies that if a and b are kept constant, posttax income inequality decreases as β increases. It was noted in the preceding section that the tax progressivity P remains constant as β changes. Because posttax income inequality depends on two factors, tax progressivity and average tax rate, an increase in the average tax rate causes posttax income inequality to decrease as β increases. Further, equation (13.19) implies that the Gini index of posttax income decreases as a increases. Equation (13.11) indicates that tax progressivity increases as a increases, which, in effect, reduces income inequality. In contrast, however, an increase in a reduces the average tax rate, which, in effect, increases income inequality. Equation (13.19) implies that the effect of an increase in tax progressivity dominates the effect of decreasing the average tax rate so that the net effect of the two factors reduces the posttax income inequality as a increases. Finally, equation (13.20) does not indicate whether income inequality increases or decreases as b increases. It is impossible to say, therefore, whether the effect of increasing tax progressivity dominates the effect of decreasing the average tax rate as b increases. If, however, it is assumed that $a = 0$, the elasticity η_b^* becomes

$$\eta_b^* = -\frac{b\beta(1 - \beta)\mu\,\mu_n(G - C_n)}{(1 - e)^2\mu^2 G^*},$$

which implies that income inequality decreases as b increases. From (13.21) it immediately follows that the ratio of the two elasticities, η_b^* and η_β^*, is less than unity in absolute terms. Thus, income inequality is more sensitive to the tax rate β than to the parameter b, provided $a = 0$, that is, when the break-even level of income is proportional to the family size. Similarly, if it is assumed that $b = 0$, it follows from (13.21) that

$$|\eta_a^*| = (1 - \beta)|\eta_\beta^*|,$$

which implies that $|\eta_a^*| < |\eta_\beta^*|$. Thus, income inequality is more sensitive to the tax rate than to the break-even level of income provided the break-even level of income does not depend on the size of the family.

If $a\beta = a^*$ and $b\beta = b^*$ are substituted into (13.17), a^* being the lump-sum subsidy, and b^* the size of credit per family member, the elasticities of G^* with respect to β, a^*, and b^* are

$$(13.22) \qquad \eta_\beta^* = -\frac{\mu\beta(G - G^*)}{(1 - e)\mu G^*}$$

$$(13.23) \qquad \eta_{a*}^* = -\frac{a^*}{(1 - e)\mu}$$

$$(13.24) \qquad \eta_{b*}^* = -\frac{\mu_n b^*(G^* - C_n)}{(1 - e)\mu G^*},$$

which are related as

$$(13.25) \qquad \eta_{a*}^* + \eta_{b*}^* = \frac{(1 - \beta)}{\beta}\eta_\beta.$$

Equations (13.22) and (13.23) imply that income inequality decreases as β and a^* increase. Equation (13.24) does not indicate whether income inequality increases or decreases as b^* increases. Note that, according to (13.12), the tax progressivity decreases as β increases, which causes income inequality to increase. Clearly, an increase in the average tax rate dominates a decrease in tax progressivity, which results in the decrease in equality.

Assume that $b^* = 0$, that is, every family is getting a lump-sum subsidy a^* but no credit for family size; then, (13.25) yields

$$|\eta_{a^*}^*| = \frac{(1 - \beta)}{\beta} |\eta_{\beta}^*|,$$

that is, the ratio of the two elasticities $\eta_{a^*}^*$ and η_{β}^* exceeds unity in absolute terms if $0 < \beta < \frac{1}{2}$. Thus, it can be concluded that over a range of values $0 < \beta < \frac{1}{2}$, income inequality is more sensitive to a cash subsidy than to the tax rate. Similarly, if it is assumed that $a^* = 0$, that is, that the cash subsidy to a family is strictly proportional to its size, then again it can be shown that income inequality is more sensitive to credit size than to tax rate, provided the tax rate is less than 50 percent.

Next consider the Smith plan, which provides for the differing needs of the children and adults within a family. Using theorem 8.5 in connection with (13.8) yields

$$(13.26) \qquad G^* = \frac{1}{(1 - e)\mu} \left[(1 - \beta)\mu G + b_1^* \mu_{n_1} C_{n_1} + b_2^* \mu_{n_2} C_{n_2} \right]$$

where C_{n_1} and C_{n_2} are the concentration indexes of the children and adults within a family. Further, $b_1^* = \beta b_1$, $b_2^* = \beta b_2$, and e, as defined in (13.7), is given by

$$e = \frac{\beta \mu - a^* - b_1^* \mu_{n_1} - b_2^* \mu_{n_2}}{\mu}$$

where $a^* = a\beta$. Note that a^* is the cash subsidy, and b_1^* and b_2^* are the credit sizes given to each child and adult, respectively, within a family. The elasticities of G^* with respect to β, a^*, b_1^* and b_2^* can be obtained from equation (13.26).

A Numerical Illustration

In this section a numerical illustration, based on 1964 income data from *Current Population Reports* of the U.S. Bureau of the Census,

Department of Commerce, Series P-60, No. 47, is provided. Income includes money wages or salary, net income from nonfarm self-employment, net income from farm self-employment, social security, interest (on savings or bonds), dividends and income from estates or trusts, rent, unemployment compensation, and all other sources, such as private or government pensions.

The data were arranged in groups consisting of seventeen income classes. The midpoint of each income class was used as an approximation of the mean income for each of the income classes below $15,000. A value of $19,000. was used as the mean income for the $15,000. to $24,999. interval. For the $25,000. and over interval, the Pareto curve was fitted to estimate the mean income. Information on average family size and average number of children and adults within families in each income class was extracted from the first five tables of *Current Population Reports.* Table 13.1 gives the basic data used to compare the redistributive effects of the alternative negative income tax plans. The last row gives the Gini indexes and the concentration indexes of different variables, which were computed by fitting the equation of the new coordinate system for the Lorenz curve discussed in chapter 7.

The family size has a concentration index of 0.115, which is much smaller than the Gini index of the total income, 0.407. This implies that family members are more evenly distributed across the income ranges than family income. Similarly, the concentration index of the adults is 0.100, which is smaller than the concentration index of the children, 0.141. This implies that adults within families are more evenly distributed across income ranges than are children.

Table 13.2 presents the computed values of the Gini index for disposable income and the index of tax progressivity for the alternative negative income tax plans. The parameter values of the alternative plans are reported in the first three columns. The fourth column gives the average tax rates, which have been computed from (13.4) and (13.7). The fifth column reports the numerical values of tax progressivity based on (13.10) and (13.15). The computed values of the Gini index are given in the sixth column. These are based on (13.17) and (13.26).

The positive values of the average tax rate indicate that these plans generate revenue to the government to finance expenditures other than allowances. Thus, the effects of these alternative plans are not purely redistributive.

The values of the Gini index for disposable income indicate that

Table 13.1. *Distribution of Income and Family Composition Data for the United States, 1964*

Income (U.S. dollars)	Number of families (thousands)	Estimated mean income (U.S. dollars)	Average family size	Average number of children in families	Average number of adults in families
Under 1,000	4,672	500	1.776	0.490	1.286
1,000– 1,499	3,354	1,250	1.909	0.455	1.454
1,500– 1,999	2,515	1,750	2.298	0.662	1.636
2,000– 2,499	2,815	2,250	2.588	0.838	1.750
2,500– 2,999	2,515	2,750	2.710	0.883	1.827
3,000– 3,499	2,635	3,250	2.857	1.027	1.830
3,500– 3,999	2,456	3,750	3.094	1.158	1.936
4,000– 4,999	5,151	4,500	3.100	1.172	1.928
5,000– 5,999	5,510	5,500	3.373	1.347	2.026
6,000– 6,999	5,270	6,500	3.579	1.501	2.078
7,000– 7,999	4,791	7,500	3.788	1.549	2.239
8,000– 8,999	3,893	8,500	3.675	1.461	2.214
9,000– 9,999	3,114	9,500	3.854	1.537	2.317
10,000–11,999	4,672	11,000	3.762	1.381	2.381
12,000–14,999	3,354	13,500	3.787	1.241	2.546
15,000–24,999	2,575	19,000	3.910	1.239	2.671
Over 25,000		36,041	3.644	1.158	2.486
Total	59,892	6,603	3.167	1.158	2.008
Concentration indexes	—	0.40686[a]	0.11507	0.1414	0.0999

Source: Current Population Reports, U.S. Bureau of the Census, Series P-60, No. 47, "Income in 1964 of Families and Persons in the United States," 1965.

a. This figure is the Gini index of income.

Table 13.2. *Tax Progressivity and Income Inequality under Alternative Negative Income Tax Plans, United States, 1964*

Plan	Cash subsidy a* (U.S. dollars)	Credit per family member b* (U.S. dollars)	Marginal tax rate (percent)	Average tax rate (percent)	Tax progressivity	Gini index for disposable income
Friedman	100	350	50	31.7	0.174	0.3261
Lampman and Green	500	250	50	30.4	0.216	0.3122
Tobin	0.0	500	33	9.0	0.775	0.3301
Rolph	0.0	500	30	6.0	1.162	0.3327
Smith	0.0	200[a] 1,000[b]	40	6.1	1.68	0.2975

a. $200. is the credit per child.
b. $1,000. is the credit per adult.

all these plans substantially reduce the inequality of earned income, and that their redistributive effect is considerably stronger than that of the existing tax system in the United States, which is based on the increasing marginal tax rates of income.[3]

The first two plans have the same marginal tax rate, but Friedman's plan provides more benefits to larger families than the Lampman-Green plan. Note, however, that the Lampman-Green plan results in more equal distribution of income than Friedman's plan. It can be inferred, therefore, that giving more benefits to larger families does not lead to a more equal distribution of income. The Smith plan results in the most equal distribution of disposable income, the reason being that it gives a higher allowance to an adult than to a child within a family. Because adults in families are more equally distributed across the income ranges than children, the larger credit size to adults tends to distribute the income more evenly.

The index of tax progressivity, presented in the fifth column, differs considerably under different plans. The Friedman plan is the least progressive, whereas Smith's is the most progressive. The progressivity index for the last two plans, Rolph and Smith, exceeds unity, which indicates that a larger proportion of lower income earners are paying negative taxes.

Note, in addition, that the average tax rate also differs considerably under different plans. A comparison of these plans would be more meaningful if they yielded the same average tax rates. It was assumed, therefore, that if the minimum guaranteed incomes of the families differing in size were predetermined, depending on the plan (that is, a^* and b^* are given), the marginal tax rate could be computed so that all the plans yield the same average tax rate. The income inequality and tax progressivity are then computed for each plan. These numerical results are presented in table 13.3.

Table 13.3 shows that for each negative income tax plan, the tax progressivity decreases and the marginal tax rate increases as the average tax rate increases from 5 to 20 percent. Although the decrease in progressivity should cause an increase in income inequality, the latter decreases because the effect of increase in the average tax rate dominates the effect of decreasing progressivity. Further,

3. The numerical values that would show the redistributive effect of the existing tax system are not reported here, but it is well known that the existing system does not reduce the Gini index by as much as 20 percent, as is the case here.

Table 13.3. *Tax Progressivity and Income Inequality under Alternative Negative Income Tax Plans for Given Average Tax Rates, United States, 1964*

	Average tax rates											
	5 percent			10 percent			15 percent			20 percent		
Plan	P	G*	β	P	G*	β	P	G*	β	P	G*	β
Friedman	1.103	0.34881	0.23303	0.551	0.34559	0.28302	0.368	0.34198	0.33302	0.276	0.33793	0.38302
Lampman and Green	1.316	0.33760	0.24563	0.624	0.33753	0.29563	0.438	0.32945	0.34563	0.329	0.32461	0.39563
Tobin	1.399	0.33320	0.28982	0.699	0.32911	0.33982	0.466	0.32453	0.38982	0.350	0.31939	0.43982
Smith	2.053	0.29881	0.38918	1.026	0.29281	0.43918	0.684	0.28610	0.48918	0.512	0.27855	0.53918

Table 13.4. *Elasticities of Income Inequalities and Tax Progressivity with Respect to Negative Income Parameters, United States, 1964*

Plan	Negative Income Tax Parameters		
	β	a^*	b^*
Friedman	-0.18130	-0.02217	-0.15906
	$(-1.577\ \ )$	$(\ 0.159\ \ )$	$(\ 0.405\ \ )$
Lampman and Green	-0.21782	-0.10880	-0.10878
	$(-1.644\ \ )$	$(\ 0.718\ \ )$	$(\ 1.854\ \ )$
Tobin	-0.08542	0.0	-0.17207
	$(-3.66\ \ )$		$(0.0\ \ \ \ \ )$
Rolph	-0.06672	0.0	-0.17268
	$(-5.00\ \ )$		$(\ 0.0\ \ \ )$
Smith	-0.1566	0.0	-0.0196[a]
	$(-6.558\ \ )$		-0.2151[b]

a. Elasticity with respect to the size of credit per child.
b. Elasticity with respect to the size of credit per adult.

although the plans yield the same average tax rate, they differ considerably in their progressivity as well as in their redistributive effect. Although the Smith plan gives the highest value of progressivity and the least value of the Gini index, it requires the highest marginal tax rate in order to yield a given average tax rate. In selecting a particular plan, there must be a trade-off between the income inequality and the marginal tax rate because low income inequality requires a higher value of the marginal tax rate.

Table 13.4 presents the computed elasticities of the Gini index with respect to the three parameters β, a^*, and b^*. The figures in parentheses are the elasticities of the tax progressivity. Note that the elasticities of the tax progressivity index are generally higher than those of the Gini index, which implies that the tax progressivity index is more sensitive to changes in parameters than income inequality. Under the Friedman and Lampman-Green plans, income inequality is more sensitive to the marginal tax rate than either cash subsidy a^* or the size of the credit per family member b^*. These plans differ considerably, however, in their relative sensitivity of inequality with respect to cash subsidy and credit size. Under the Friedman plan, income inequality is more sensitive to the per member credit size than to the cash subsidy, which is independent of family size. The reverse is the case under the Lampman-Green plan. Under the Tobin and

Rolph plans, income inequality is considerably more sensitive to the size of the credit per member than to the marginal tax rate. Under the Smith plan, the sensitivity of income inequality with respect to the marginal tax rate is higher with respect to the credit size per child, but lower with respect to the credit size per adult.

Some Comments

In this chapter a method of comparing the redistributive effect and the progressivity of alternative negative income tax plans was provided. Although the emphasis was placed on the well-known negative income tax plans, the method is general enough to be used in investigating any plan, and the framework provided here can be useful in evolving a plan that would be suitable for any country.

The analysis given above did not include the problem of choice between work and leisure, a choice that can considerably affect the progressivity of the tax system. This problem will be considered in the following chapter. Further, it was assumed that the tax rate is the same for both positive and negative income tax. It will be interesting for future research to relax this assumption so that a wide range of negative income tax plans can be investigated.

CHAPTER 14

Negative Income Tax, Work Incentive, and Income Distribution

THE PURPOSE OF THIS CHAPTER is to evaluate the effect of different negative income tax proposals on the level and distribution of income through their effects on the individual's choice between income and leisure. The model considered here assumes that every individual has the same utility function, which depends on consumption and leisure, and that an individual allocates his time between work and leisure so that his utility function is maximized.

Recent literature on negative income tax concerns the problem of determining the optimal tax structure.[1] The debate was initiated in 1971 by Mirrlees, whose analysis was based on a particular form of the utility function and a specific density function. He demonstrated that the optimal tax structure would be approximately linear with negative income tax at low incomes. Sheshinski (1972a) continued the debate by working with more general assumptions regarding the form of the utility function, but restricting himself to linear tax functions. He arrived at a conclusion similar to that of Mirrlees, that is, that the optimal tax structure will always be progressive, in other words, a linear tax function with a lump-sum subsidy.

This chapter does not concern the problem of optimal tax structure, but rather the effects of changes in parameters of given nega-

---

1. The optimal tax structure is one that is associated with the maximum social welfare.

tive income tax plans on the mean income and the degree of inequality. The Cobb-Douglas utility function is used to incorporate the work-leisure choice in the model. The degree of inequality is again measured by the Gini index. And the elasticities of the mean income and the Gini index with respect to tax parameters, as well as the parameter of the utility function, are derived to study these effects.

The Choice between Work and Leisure

Suppose that wage rate of an individual is determined by an index of his productive ability n. Further, assume that n is a random variable with a given density function $f(n)$. If y is the number of hours that an individual works, his earned (labor) income z is given by $z = ny$. Assuming that the tax function is linear, his consumption,[2] or posttax income, is

$$(14.1) \qquad x = \alpha + (1 - \beta)z$$

where α is the positive lump-sum subsidy, and β the marginal tax rate that lies in the range $0 < \beta < 1$.

Each individual treats the parameters α and β as given and determines his labor supply so as to maximize his utility function, subject to the budget constraint (14.1). Assume that each individual in the society has an identical utility function[3]

$$(14.2) \qquad u = \log x + a \log(1 - y),$$

which is the Cobb-Douglas function considered earlier by Mirrlees (1971), Atkinson (1973), Wesson (1972), Romer (1975), and Itsumi (1974). Note that y is normalized so that its upper limit is unity. The value of a measures the extent to which the individual values leisure over consumption. If $a < 1$, it is implied that the individual values consumption more than leisure. As a increases, the value given to leisure relative to consumption increases.

2. Consumption includes saving. This terminology is used throughout the present chapter.

3. The assumption that each individual has an identical utility function implies interpersonal comparisons of utility. This assumption, although restrictive, is widely used by economists. It would be useful to generalize this model, but such an exercise is outside the scope of the present study.

The first-order condition for a maximum of u in (14.2) is given by

$$\frac{\partial u}{\partial y} = \frac{(1-\beta)n}{x} - \frac{a}{(1-y)} = 0,$$

which, by means of (14.1), gives

$$(14.3) \qquad z = \frac{-at}{(1+a)} + \frac{n}{(1+a)} \quad \text{if } n > at$$

$$= 0 \qquad\qquad\qquad \text{if } n \leq at$$

where $t = \alpha/(1-\beta)$. The second-order condition

$$\frac{\partial^2 u}{\partial y^2} = -\frac{(1-\beta)^2 n^2}{x^2} - \frac{a}{(1-y)^2} < 0$$

is always satisfied if $a > 0$. It follows from (14.3) that the pretax income depends on the tax structure. Further, note that an individual who has ability less than, or equal to, at will have maximum utility if he does not work at all.

Equation (14.1) gives the posttax income as

$$x = \frac{\alpha}{(1+a)} + \frac{n(1-\beta)}{(1+a)} \quad \text{if } n > at$$

$$= \alpha \qquad\qquad\qquad \text{if } n \leq at.$$

The above results are valid even if an increasing monotonic transform of the utility function (14.2) is used. The probability distribution function $F(n)$ given by

$$(14.4) \qquad F(n) = \int_0^n f(n)\,dn$$

is interpreted as the proportion of individuals in the population who have ability less than, or equal to, n. If $\bar{n}$ is the mean level of ability of the population, the first-moment distribution function is defined as

$$(14.5) \qquad F_1(n) = \frac{1}{\bar{n}} \int_0^n nf(n)\,dn,$$

which is the cumulative proportion of ability of individuals whose ability is less than, or equal to, n.

Now, substituting (14.4) and (14.5) into (14.3) gives the pretax mean income of the society as

$$(14.6) \quad \mu_z = \frac{-at}{(1 + a)} [1 - F(at)] + \frac{\bar{n}}{(1 + a)} [1 - F_1(at)],$$

and the posttax mean income is obtained from (14.1) as

$$(14.7) \qquad \mu_x = \alpha + (1 - \beta)\mu_z.$$

If $a = 0$, equation (14.3) indicates that z becomes n, which implies that $y = 1$, that is, that every individual works the maximum possible number of hours. This is so because individuals do not give any value to leisure. In this situation, (14.6) shows that $\mu_z = \bar{n}$ and yields

$$\mu_z - \bar{n} = \frac{-at}{(1 + a)} [1 - F(at)] - \frac{\bar{n}}{(1 + a)} [a + F_1(at)],$$

which is always negative. The difference $(\bar{n} - \mu_z)$ therefore, is the average loss of income to the society resulting from the work-leisure choice. Further, if $\alpha = 0$, $\mu_z = \bar{n}/(1 + a)$; this implies that even if the tax system is proportional, the mean income of the society is reduced because of the work-leisure choice, although the reduction in the mean income is less for the proportional tax system than for a progressive tax system, that is, when $\alpha > 0$.

The derivative of μ_z with respect to t may be obtained by means of $dF(at)/dt = af(at)$, and $dF_1(at)/dt = a^2t f(at)/\bar{n}$. Thus

$$(14.8) \qquad \frac{d\mu_z}{dt} = - \frac{a[1 - F(at)]}{(1 + a)} .$$

Now, if η_α and η_β are denoted as the elasticities of μ_z with respect to α and β, respectively, (14.8) gives

$$(14.9) \qquad \eta_\alpha = - \frac{at[1 - F(at)]}{(1 + a)\mu_z}$$

$$(14.10) \qquad \eta_\beta = - \frac{\beta at[1 - F(at)]}{(1 + a)\mu_z} ,$$

which are related as

$$(14.11) \qquad |\eta_\beta| = \frac{\beta}{(1 - \beta)} |\eta_\alpha|.$$

Equations (14.9) and (14.10) imply that the mean pretax income of the society decreases as α or β increases. Equation (14.11) implies that the ratio of the two elasticities η_α and η_β exceeds unity in absolute terms if $0 < \beta < \frac{1}{2}$. Thus it can be concluded that for $0 < \beta < \frac{1}{2}$, the mean pretax income of the society is more sensitive to tax subsidy than to marginal tax rate.

If η_α^* and η_β^* are denoted as the elasticities of the posttax mean income with respect to α and β, respectively, (14.7) gives

$$\eta_\alpha^* = \frac{[1 + a\,F(at)]\alpha}{(1 + a)\mu_x}$$

$$\eta_\beta^* = -\frac{\bar{n}\beta[1 - F_1(at)]}{(1 + a)\mu_x},$$

which leads to the conclusion that the posttax mean income of the society increases with the increase in α, but decreases with the increase in β.

The mean tax revenue of the government is clearly the difference between pre- and posttax mean incomes, which is obtained from (14.7) as

$$\mu_z - \mu_x = -\alpha + \beta\mu_z.$$

This equation shows that the mean tax revenue can be of either sign, depending on the values of α, β, a, and the distribution of ability. Recent literature on optimal taxation specifies that the government revenue be zero so that the only function of the linear tax system is to redistribute income.[4] This restriction is clearly equivalent to

(14.12) $\alpha = \beta\,\mu_z$

where μ_z is given in (14.6). Now, eliminating α from (14.6) and (14.12) and differentiating μ_z with respect to β yields

$$\frac{\partial\mu_z}{\partial\beta}\frac{\beta}{\mu_z} = -\frac{a\beta[1 - F(at)](1 - \beta)^{-1}}{(1 + a)(1 - \beta) + a\beta[1 - F(at)]},$$

which is the elasticity of μ_z with respect to β, subject to restriction (14.12). Note that $t = \beta\mu_z/(1 - \beta)$. The negative value of this

---

4. Note that the well-known negative income tax plans considered in the preceding chapter do not consider any such restriction.

elasticity implies that the mean income of the society decreases as the marginal tax rate β increases. Further, if $\beta \leq \frac{1}{2}$, this elasticity is always less than unity in absolute value. This means that if β increases by 1 percent, the mean income will decrease by less than 1 percent provided the marginal tax rate β is less than one half.

Work-Leisure Choices and Income Inequality

As tax parameters change, individuals are likely to adjust the number of their working hours, which, in turn, changes both pre- and posttax income distributions. These effects are analyzed below.

Applying corollary 8.10 to (14.3), the Gini index of pretax income is

$$(14.13) \quad G_z = F(at) + \frac{\bar{n}}{(1+a)\mu_z},$$

$$[G - G(at)F(at)F_1(at) - F(at) + F_1(at)]$$

where G is the Gini index of ability of the whole population and $G(at)$ is the Gini index of ability of only those individuals with an ability less than, or equal to, at. Further, $G(at)$ is given by

$$(14.14) \qquad G(at) = 1 - \frac{2 \displaystyle\int_0^{at} F_1(n)f(n)\,dn}{F(at)F_1(at)},$$

which, on differentiating partially with respect to t, gives

$$(14.15) \quad \frac{\partial}{\partial_t}\left[G(at)F(at)F_1(at)\right] = \frac{af(at)}{\bar{n}}\left[at\,F(at) - \bar{n}\,F_1(at)\right].$$

This result will be useful in evaluating the elasticities of the Gini index with respect to tax parameters.

Note that if $\alpha = 0$ is inserted into (14.13), and (14.6) is used, G_z becomes equal to G. This implies that if the tax system is proportional, the Gini index of the pretax income will be equal to the Gini index of ability. This, in turn, leads to the conclusion that in the case of a proportional tax system, the work-leisure choice has no effect on income inequality. The difference between G_z and G would, therefore, represent the redistributive effect of negative income tax through the work-leisure choice.

Using (14.15) in conjunction with (14.8) yields the derivative of G_z with respect to t as

$$(14.16) \qquad \frac{\partial G_z}{\partial t} = \frac{a[1 - F(at)][G_z - F(at)]}{(1 + a)\mu_z}.$$

Now, if ϵ_α and ϵ_β are denoted as the elasticities of G_z with respect to α and β, respectively, equation (14.16) immediately gives

$$(14.17) \qquad \epsilon_\alpha = \frac{at[1 - F(at)][G_z - F(at)]}{(1 + a)\mu_z G_z}$$

$$\epsilon_\beta = \frac{at\,\beta[1 - F(at)][G_z - F(at)]}{(1 - \beta)(1 + a)\mu_z G_z},$$

which are related by

$$\epsilon_\beta = \frac{\beta}{(1 - \beta)}\,\epsilon_\alpha.$$

The following diagram will assist in determining the sign of these elasticities.

In figure 8 $ODEB$ is the Lorenz curve of the pretax income. The point D corresponds to the ability level at, and, therefore, $OD = F(at)$. The Gini index G_z is equal to one minus twice the area under the curve $ODEB$, which is also equal to twice the area $ODEB$. Clearly, the area $ODEB$ is equal to the sum of the area of the triangle ODB and the area DEB. The area of the triangle ODB is given by

$$\Delta ODB = \Delta OAB - \Delta ADB = \tfrac{1}{2}F(at),$$

which gives

$$(14.18) \qquad G_z = F(at) + 2\text{area } DEB.$$

The area DEB is $\tfrac{1}{2}[1 - F(at)]$ times the Gini index of the individuals whose ability is greater than at, which will obviously be positive. It follows from (14.18), therefore, that $[G_z - F(at)]$ will be positive. Using this result in (14.17), it becomes clear that both the elasticities ϵ_α and ϵ_β are positive, which means that pretax income inequality increases as the lump-sum subsidy or the marginal tax rate increases. The ratio of the two elasticities ϵ_β and ϵ_α is a function of β only, this ratio clearly being less than unity for $0 <$

Figure 8. *Lorenz Curve for Pretax Income*

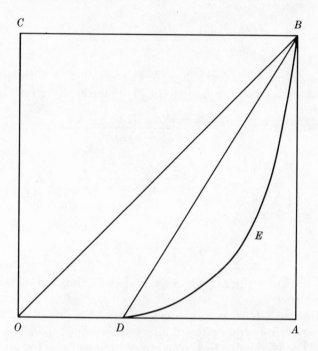

$\beta < \frac{1}{2}$. From this, it can be concluded that over the range of values $0 < \beta < \frac{1}{2}$, pretax income inequality is more sensitive to the subsidy than to the marginal tax rate.

Now, differentiating G_z partially with respect to the parameter a gives

$$\frac{\partial G_Z}{\partial a} = \frac{t}{\mu_z(1+a)} [G_z - F(at)][1 - F(at)],$$

from which it follows that if all the individuals give more value to leisure than to consumption, pretax income inequality increases.

Now, impose the restriction that pre- and posttax mean incomes are equal. Then, substituting for α from (14.12) into (14.13), and differentiating with respect to β, gives

$$(14.19) \quad \frac{\partial G_z}{\partial \beta} \frac{\beta}{G_z} = \frac{a\beta[1 - F(at)][G_z - F(at)]}{(1-\beta)[(1+a)(1-\beta) + a\beta\{1 - F(at)\}]G_z}.$$

It may be mentioned that the derivation of this result is considerably simplified by using (14.16) and

$$\frac{\partial t}{\partial \beta} = \frac{\mu_z(1 + a)}{(1 - \beta)[(1 + a)(1 - \beta) + a\beta\{1 - F(at)\}]}$$

where t, after substituting for α, is given by

$$t = \frac{\beta\mu_z}{(1 - \beta)}.$$

The elasticity given in (14.19) is clearly positive, which implies that pretax income inequality increases with an increase in the marginal tax rate.

Posttax Income Inequality

Let G_x be the Gini index of the posttax income. Then, applying corollary 8.9 to (14.1) yields

$$(14.20) \qquad G_x = \frac{(1 - \beta)\mu_z G_z}{\mu_x},$$

which can also be written as

$$(14.21) \qquad G_x = G_z - \frac{\alpha G_z}{\mu_x}.$$

This implies that if $\alpha > 0$, the posttax income inequality is always less than that of pretax income. The second term on the right-hand side of (14.21) can be regarded as the direct effect of the tax system on posttax inequality. This effect will vanish when the tax system is proportional.

It is useful to write (14.21) as

$$(14.22) \qquad \frac{G_x - G}{G} = \frac{(G_z - G)}{G} - \frac{\alpha G_z}{G\mu_x},$$

which suggests an interesting interpretation. It can be seen from (14.13) and (14.20) that if $\alpha = 0$, $G_x = G$, which means that if the tax system were proportional, the inequality of the distribution of income would be equal to the inequality of the distribution of ability. The left-hand side of (14.22) represents, therefore, the percentage change in the Gini index resulting from the presence of progressive taxes. This change consists of two components: the indirect effect of the taxes through their effect on pretax income inequality, and the direct effect of taxes on posttax income inequality. The first term on the right-hand side of (14.22) is the percentage contribution of the indirect effect, which can be of any sign. As mentioned above, the preceding section indicated that if $\alpha = 0$, $G_z = G$. Further, (14.17) implies that

$$\frac{\partial}{\partial \alpha} (G_z - G) > 0$$

for all values of α, meaning that $(G_z - G)$ is a monotonically increasing function of α and, therefore, cannot be negative for $\alpha > 0$. From this, it may be concluded that the influence of the indirect effect of a progressive tax system is always positive. In contrast, the percentage contribution of the direct effect, which is the second term on the right-hand side of (14.22), is always negative for $\alpha > 0$. To see which of the two effects dominates, differentiate (14.22) with respect to α:

$$\frac{\partial (G_x - G)}{\partial \alpha} =$$

$$- \frac{1}{\mu_x(1 + a)} \left[aF(at)\{1 - F(at)\} + G_x\{1 + aF(at)\} \right],$$

which implies that $(G_x - G)$ is a monotonic decreasing function of α. Because $(G_x - G)$ is equal to zero for $\alpha = 0$, $(G_x - G)$ cannot be positive for $\alpha > 0$. From this it follows that the net result of direct and indirect effects is negative, that is, the direct effect dominates the indirect effect. Thus any scheme of negative income tax reduces the ultimate income inequality. This dynamics prevails even when the constraint of a net government tax revenue of zero is imposed.

The elasticity of G_x with respect to α and β are derived as equal to

$$\epsilon_\alpha^* = \frac{-\alpha}{\mu_x G_x(1 + a)} \left[aF(at)\{1 - F(at)\} + G_x\{1 + aF(at)\} \right]$$

$$\epsilon_\beta^* = \frac{-\alpha\beta}{(1 - \beta)\mu_x} - \frac{\beta at[1 - F(at)]}{\mu_x G_x(1 + a)} \left[F(at) + \frac{\beta}{(1 - \beta)} G_x \right],$$

respectively. These equations imply that posttax income inequality decreases as α and β increase.

The derivative of G_x with respect to a is

$$\frac{\partial G_x}{\partial a} = -\frac{aF(at)}{\mu_x(1+a)}[G_x + 1 - F(at)],$$

which is clearly negative. This implies that as individuals value leisure more than consumption, posttax income inequality decreases. It was noted in the preceding section that pretax income inequality increases with a. The reason for this asymmetry is that the rate of change of the direct effect of taxes on income inequality, as given in (14.22), is higher than the rate of change of the indirect effect of taxes.

In the early stages of the growth of an economy, it may be expected that a will decline: that is, the members of a society whose economy is growing value consumption more than leisure. The pretax income inequality is, therefore, likely to decline, whereas the posttax income inequality will increase. When the overall standard of living of the society has increased to a reasonable level, a would be expected to increase because, at that level of living standard, preferences with respect to consumption and leisure shift in favor of leisure. This will give rise to an increase in pretax income inequality, but to a decrease in posttax income inequality.

If the constraint of a net government tax revenue of zero is imposed, G_x given in (14.20) becomes

$$G_x = (1 - \beta)G_z,$$

which gives the elasticity of G_x with respect to β as

$$\frac{\beta}{G_x}\frac{\partial G_x}{\partial \beta} = -\frac{\beta G_x[1 + aF(at)] + a\beta F(at)[1 - F(at)]}{G_x[(1+a)(1-\beta) + a\beta\{1 - F(at)\}]}.$$

This implies that the posttax Gini index decreases with an increase in the marginal tax rate β. In the preceding section it was shown that pretax income inequality increases with an increase in β. Again, the reason for this asymmetry is that the change in the direct effect of taxes dominates the change in the indirect effect.

A Numerical Illustration

This section presents a numerical illustration of the results derived in the preceding sections. The data on the frequency distribu-

Table 14.1. *Frequency Distribution of Wage Rate of Nonfarm Wage and Salary Workers, United States, May 1974*

Hourly wage (U.S. dollars)	Frequency	Mean hourly wage (U.S. dollars)	Pretax mean income with no leisure (U.S. dollars)
0–2.00	0.0459	1.33	2,766.
2–2.99	0.2155	2.65	5,512.
3–3.99	0.2260	3.35	6,968.
4–4.99	0.1662	4.64	4,651.
5–6.99	0.2280	6.09	12,667.
over 7	0.1184	7.58	15,766.
Total	1.0000	4.446	9,248.

tion of the hourly wage rate were taken from the *Monthly Labor Review*, U.S. Department of Labor, April 1975. The data were collected in the May 1973 and May 1974 supplements to the *Current Population Survey* (CPS), which consisted of a sample of 47,000 households. The sample was of nonfarm and salary workers only.

Table 14.1 presents the frequency distribution of the hourly wages. The mean wage given in the third column was estimated by fitting a Pareto curve to the first and the last intervals, and a linear density function to the remaining intervals.[5] It was assumed that the maximum an individual could work was eight hours a day, five days a week, fifty-two weeks a year. The fourth column gives the pretax mean income with no leisure under the assumption that every individual works the maximum number of hours a year, that is, 2,080 hours.

The equation of the new coordinate system for the Lorenz curve was fitted to the above distribution; it is $\eta = k\pi^\gamma(\sqrt{2} - \pi)^\delta$ where $\eta = 1/\sqrt{2}\,[F - F_1]$, and $\pi = 1/\sqrt{2}\,[F + F_1]$. In addition, k, γ, and δ were estimated by the least-squares method, and their values computed as equal to $\gamma = 0.828$, $\beta = 0.988$, and $k = 0.225$. The square of the correlation coefficient R^2 between the estimated and actual values of η was 0.996.

The Gini index was computed by integrating the area under the Lorenz curve; its value, with everyone working the same number

5. See chapter 6 for details on fitting the linear density function and the Pareto curve.

Table 14.2. *Actual and Estimated Values of η by Range of Hourly Wage Rates*

Hourly wage (U.S. dollars)	Actual η	Fitted η	Residual
0–2	0.0227	0.0224	0.00037
2–2.99	0.0843	0.0899	0.00559
3–3.99	0.1237	0.1195	0.00421
4–4.99	0.1186	0.1153	0.00327
5–6.99	0.0590	0.0598	−0.00088

of hours, is 0.233. Equation (7.43) was used to compute the value of π at the ability level $n = at$. If this value of π is denoted by $\pi(at)$, substituting $\pi(at)$ into the equation of the Lorenz curve $\eta = k\pi^\gamma(\sqrt{2} - \pi)^\delta$ gives the value of η at $n = a\,t$, which is denoted by $\eta(at)$. The values of $F(at)$ and $F_1(at)$ are then computed by

$$(14.23) \qquad F(at) = \frac{1}{\sqrt{2}}\left[\pi(at) + \eta(at)\right]$$

$$(14.24) \qquad F_1(at) = \frac{1}{\sqrt{2}}\left[\pi(at) - \eta(at)\right]$$

for different values of a and t. Because $t = \alpha/(1 - \beta)$, equations (14.23) and (14.24) give values of $F(at)$ and $F_1(at)$ for different values of a, α, and β.

To compute $G(at)$ as given in (14.14), it was necessary to evaluate the integral

$$\int_0^{at} F_1(n)f(n)\,dn,$$

which, in terms of the new coordinate system for the Lorenz curve, is given by

$$\tfrac{1}{2}\int_0^{\pi(at)} \left[\pi - g(\pi)\right]\left[1 + g'(\pi)\right]d\pi$$

where $g(\pi) = k\pi^\gamma(\sqrt{2} - \pi)^\delta$ is the equation of the Lorenz curve, and $g'(\pi)$ its first derivative. This integral is evaluated numerically. The numerical values of the mean income and the Gini index of the pre- and posttax incomes, as well as their elasticities, are presented in tables 14.3, 14.4, and 14.5 for alternative values of the parameters

(*text continues on page 322*)

Table 14.3. *Mean Income, Pre- and Post-Income Gini Indexes, and Their Elasticities for Alternative Values of Cash Subsidy and Marginal Tax Rates When $a = 0.5$, United States, 1974*

	Marginal tax rates							
	20 percent				30 percent			
	Cash subsidy (U.S. dollars)				Cash subsidy			
	500	1,000	1,500	2,000	500	1,000	1,500	2,000
Pretax mean income	5,957	5,749	5,541	5,333	5,927	5,690	5,452	5,215
Elasticities								
η_α	−0.035	−0.072	−0.113	−0.156	−0.040	−0.084	−0.131	−0.182
η_β	−0.009	−0.018	−0.029	−0.039	−0.017	−0.036	−0.056	−0.078
Posttax mean income	5,266	5,599	5,932	6,267	4,649	4,983	5,316	5,650
Elasticities								
η_α^*	0.063	0.119	0.169	0.213	0.072	0.134	0.188	0.237
η_β^*	−0.234	−0.220	−0.208	−0.197	−0.398	−0.371	−0.343	−0.327
Average tax revenue per person	150	−392	−933	691	1,278	707	136	−435
Gini index of pretax income	0.242	0.250	0.260	0.270	0.243	0.253	0.264	0.276
Elasticities								
ϵ_α	0.035	0.072	0.111	0.153	0.04	0.083	0.129	0.178
ϵ_α	0.035	0.072	0.111	0.153	0.04	0.083	0.129	0.178
ϵ_β	0.009	0.018	0.028	0.038	0.017	0.036	0.055	0.076
Gini index of posttax income	0.219	0.206	0.194	0.184	0.217	0.202	0.189	0.178
Elasticities								
ϵ_α^*	−0.00005	−0.0004	−0.001	−0.003	−0.0001	−0.0006	−0.002	−0.004
ϵ_α^*	−0.063	−0.119	−0.170	−0.216	−0.072	−0.134	−0.19	−0.240
ϵ_β^*	−0.026	−0.048	−0.069	−0.087	−0.053	−0.098	−0.139	−0.175
Percentage of persons not working	0.027	0.107	0.239	0.422	0.035	0.139	0.311	0.550

Note: The first, fourth, and seventh rows are given in U.S. dollars.

	Marginal tax rates							
	50 percent				60 percent			
	Cash subsidy				Cash subsidy			
	(U. S. dollars)							
	500	1,000	1,500	2,000	500	1,000	1,500	2,000
Pretax mean income	5,832	5,499	5,168	4,837	5,749	5,333	4,920	4,508
Elasticities								
η_α	−0.057	−0.121	−0.192	−0.273	−0.072	−0.156	−0.252	−0.364
η_β	−0.057	−0.121	−0.192	−0.273	−0.109	−0.233	−0.377	−0.545
Posttax mean income	3,416	3,750	4,084	4,419	2,800	3,133	3,468	3,803
Elasticities								
η_α^*	0.098	0.178	0.246	0.303	0.119	0.313	0.290	0.354
η_β^*	−0.902	−0.822	−0.754	−0.697	−1.321	−1.180	−1.065	−0.970
Average tax revenue per person	2,416	1,749	1,084	413	2,949	2,200	1,452	705
Gini index of pretax income	0.247	0.262	0.278	0.297	0.250	0.270	0.292	0.317
Elasticities								
ϵ_α	0.057	0.120	0.188	0.263	0.072	0.153	0.244	0.344
ϵ_α	0.057	0.120	0.188	0.263	0.072	0.153	0.244	0.344
ϵ_β	0.057	0.120	0.188	0.263	0.108	0.230	0.365	0.517
Gini index of posttax income	0.211	0.192	0.178	0.162	0.206	0.184	0.166	0.150
Elasticities								
ϵ_α^*	−0.0002	−0.001	−0.005	−0.011	−0.0004	−0.003	−0.009	−0.022
ϵ_α^*	−0.098	−0.179	−0.250	−0.313	−0.119	−0.216	−0.298	−0.373
ϵ_β^*	−0.195	−0.357	−0.493	−0.612	−0.402	−0.721	−0.982	−1.205
Percentage of persons not working	0.069	0.271	0.606	1.073	0.107	0.422	0.944	1.670

Note: The first, fourth, and seventh rows are given in U. S. dollars.

Table 14.4. Mean Income, Pre- and Post-Income Gini Indexes, and Their Elasticities for Alternative Values of Cash Subsidy and Marginal Tax Rates When a = 1.0, United States, 1974

	Marginal tax rates							
	20 percent				30 percent			
	Cash subsidy				Cash subsidy			
	(U.S. dollars)							
	500	1,000	1,500	2,000	500	1,000	1,500	2,000
Pretax mean income	4,312	4,000	3,690	3,381	4,267	3,911	3,557	3,206
Elasticities								
η_α	−0.072	−0.156	−0.252	−0.363	−0.084	−0.182	−0.297	−0.182
η_β	−0.018	−0.039	−0.063	−0.091	−0.036	−0.078	−0.127	−0.187
Posttax mean income	3,949	4,200	4,452	4,705	3,487	3,738	3,990	4,244
Elasticities								
η_α^*	0.063	0.120	0.170	0.216	0.072	0.135	0.190	0.241
η_β^*	−0.234	−0.220	−0.207	−0.196	−0.398	−0.371	−0.347	−0.325
Average tax revenue per person	362	−200	−762	−1,324	780	173	−433	−1,038
Gini index of pretax income	0.250	0.270	0.292	0.317	0.253	0.276	0.302	0.334
Elasticities								
ϵ_α	0.072	0.153	0.244	0.344	0.083	0.178	0.285	0.407
ϵ_α	0.072	0.153	0.244	0.344	0.083	0.178	0.285	0.407
ϵ_β	0.018	0.038	0.061	0.086	0.036	0.076	0.122	0.175
Gini index of posttax income	0.219	0.205	0.193	0.182	0.217	0.202	0.187	0.176
Elasticities								
ϵ_α^*	−0.0004	−0.003	−0.010	−0.023	−0.001	−0.004	−0.014	−0.034
ϵ_α^*	−0.064	−0.122	−0.178	−0.235	−0.072	−0.138	−0.202	−0.269
ϵ_β^*	−0.036	−0.068	−0.097	−0.124	−0.075	−0.141	−0.200	−0.256
Percentage of persons not working	0.107	0.422	0.944	0.167	0.139	0.550	1.230	2.177

	Marginal tax rates							
	50 percent				60 percent			
	Cash subsidy				Cash subsidy			
	(U. S. dollars)							
	500	1,000	1,500	2,000	500	1,000	1,500	2,000
Pretax mean income	4,125	3,628	3,136	2,653	4,000	3,381	2,773	2,197
Elasticities								
η_α	-0.121	-0.273	-0.467	-0.722	-0.156	-0.363	-0.651	-0.990
η_β	-0.121	-0.273	-0.467	-0.722	-0.233	-0.545	-0.977	-1.485
Posttax mean income	2,562	2,814	3,068	3,326	2,100	2,352	2,609	2,878
Elasticities								
η_α^*	0.098	0.180	0.250	0.313	0.120	0.216	0.489	0.392
η_β^*	-0.902	-0.820	-0.750	-0.687	1.321	-1.176	1.053	-0.911
Average tax revenue per person	1,562	814	68	-673	1,900	1,029	164	-682
Gini index of pretax income	0.262	0.297	0.341	0.397	0.270	0.317	0.381	0.462
Elasticities								
ϵ_α	0.120	0.263	0.434	0.645	0.153	0.344	0.587	0.713
ϵ_α	0.120	0.263	0.434	0.645	0.153	0.344	0.587	0.713
ϵ_β	0.120	0.263	0.434	0.645	0.230	0.517	0.891	1.069
Gini index of posttax income	0.211	0.191	0.174	0.158	0.205	0.182	0.162	0.141
Elasticities								
ϵ_α^*	-0.001	-0.012	-0.039	-0.09	-0.003	-0.023	-0.074	-0.323
ϵ_α^*	-0.099	-0.189	-0.283	-0.391	-0.122	-0.235	-0.362	-0.670
ϵ_β^*	-0.294	-0.541	-0.760	-0.966	-0.628	-1.137	-1.581	-2.139
Percentage of persons not working	0.271	1.073	2.398	4.244	0.422	1.670	3.734	12.96

Note: The first, fourth, and seventh rows are given in U. S. dollars.

Table 14.5. *Mean Income, Pre- and Post-Income Gini Indexes, and Their Elasticities for Alternative Values of Cash Subsidy and Marginal Tax Rates When a = 2.0, United States, 1974*

	Marginal tax rates							
	20 percent				30 percent			
	Cash subsidy (U. S. dollars)				Cash subsidy			
	500	1,000	1,500	2,000	500	1,000	1,500	2,000
Pretax mean income	2,666	2,254	1,848	1,465	2,607	2,137	1,679	1,265
Elasticities								
η_α	-0.156	-0.363	-0.651	-0.990	-0.182	-0.436	-0.787	-1.210
η_β	-0.039	-0.091	-0.163	-0.247	-0.078	-0.187	-0.337	-0.518
Posttax mean income	2,633	2,803	2,979	3,171	2,325	2,496	2,675	2,886
Elasticities								
η_α^*	0.064	0.123	0.180	0.265	0.072	0.139	0.215	0.322
η_β^*	-0.234	-0.219	-0.205	-0.184	-0.397	-0.369	-0.366	-0.291
Average tax revenue per person	33	-349	-1,130	-1,707	282	-359	-996	-1,620
Gini index of pretax income	0.270	0.317	0.381	0.462	0.276	0.334	0.415	0.513
Elasticities								
ϵ_α	0.153	0.344	0.587	0.7126	0.178	0.407	0.644	0.747
ϵ_α	0.153	0.344	0.587	0.713	0.178	0.407	0.644	0.747
ϵ_β	0.038	0.086	0.147	0.178	0.076	0.175	0.276	0.320
Gini index of posttax income	0.218	0.204	0.189	0.171	0.216	0.200	0.182	0.157
Elasticities								
ϵ_α^*	-0.003	-0.023	-0.076	-0.332	-0.004	-0.034	-0.171	-0.553
ϵ_α^*	-0.066	-0.142	-0.244	-0.542	-0.076	-0.168	-0.358	-0.784
ϵ_β^*	-0.056	-0.109	-0.162	-0.250	-0.120	-0.232	-0.365	-0.563
Percentage of persons not working	0.422	1.67	3.73	13.00	0.550	2.177	7.532	19.62

Note: The first, fourth, and second … mean income is in U. S. dollars

Table 14.5. (Continued)

	Marginal tax rates							
	50 percent				60 percent			
	Cash subsidy (U. S. dollars)				Cash subsidy			
	500	1,000	1,500	2,000	500	1,000	1,500	2,000
Pretax mean income	2,418	1,768	1,190	741	2,254	1,465	841	420
Elasticities								
η_α	−0.273	−0.722	−1.303	2.061	0.363	−0.990	−1.850	−3.142
η_β	−0.273	−0.722	−1.303	−2.061	0.545	−1.485	−2.77	−4.713
Posttax mean income	1,709	1,884	2,095	2,370	1,402	1,586	1,836	2,168
Elasticities								
η_α^*	0.100	0.192	0.346	0.521	0.123	0.265	0.478	0.679
η_β^*	−0.900	−0.808	−0.654	−0.478	−1.316	−1.103	−0.783	−0.482
Average tax revenue per person	709	−116	−905	−1,629	−852	−121	−993	−1,748
Gini index of pretax income	0.297	0.397	0.535	0.720	0.317	0.462	0.665	0.823
Elasticities								
ϵ_α	0.263	0.645	0.755	0.838	0.344	0.713	0.799	1.386
ϵ_α	0.263	0.645	0.755	0.838	0.344	0.713	0.799	1.386
ϵ_β	0.263	0.645	0.755	0.838	0.517	1.069	1.198	2.079
Gini index of posttax income	0.210	0.186	0.152	0.112	0.204	0.171	0.122	0.084
Elasticities								
ϵ_α^*	−0.012	−0.092	−0.655	−1.463	−0.023	−0.332	−1.257	−2.127
ϵ_α^*	−0.109	−0.269	−0.893	−1.744	−0.142	−0.542	−1.530	−2.435
ϵ_β^*	−0.495	−0.947	−1.633	−2.389	−1.090	−2.185	−3.564	−4.565
Percentage of persons not working	1.073	4.244	22.47	42.70	1.670	12.96	37.78	60.39

Note: The first, fourth, and seventh rows are given in U. S. dollars.

Table 14.6. *Percentage of Influence of Direct and Indirect Effects of Taxes on the Total Effect of Taxes on Income Inequality, United States, 1974*

		Marginal tax rates							
		20 percent				30 percent			
		Cash subsidy				Cash subsidy			
		500	1,000	1,500	2,000	500	1,000	1,500	2,000
a = 0.5	Indirect effect	3.86	7.30	11.59	15.88	4.29	8.58	13.30	18.45
	Direct effect	−9.87	−18.89	−28.33	−36.91	−11.16	−21.88	−32.18	−42.05
	Total effect	−6.01	−11.59	−16.74	−21.03	−6.87	−13.30	−18.88	−23.60
a = 1.0	Indirect effect	7.30	15.88	25.32	36.05	8.58	18.45	29.61	43.35
	Direct effect	−13.31	−27.40	−42.49	−57.94	−15.45	−31.75	−49.35	−67.81
	Total effect	−6.01	−12.02	−17.17	−21.89	−6.87	−13.30	−19.74	−24.46
a = 2.0	Indirect effect	15.88	36.05	63.52	98.28	18.45	43.35	78.11	120.17
	Direct effect	−22.32	−48.50	−82.40	−124.89	−25.75	−57.51	−100.00	152.74
	Total effect	−6.44	−12.45	−18.88	−26.61	−7.30	−14.16	−21.89	−32.62

Table 14.6 (Continued)

	Marginal tax rates							
	50 percent				60 percent			
	Cash subsidy				Cash subsidy			
	500	1,000	1,500	2,000	500	1,000	1,500	2,000
$a = 0.5$ Indirect effect	6.01	12.45	19.31	27.47	7.30	15.88	25.32	36.05
Direct effect	−15.45	−30.05	−42.91	−57.94	−18.89	−36.91	−54.07	−71.67
Total effect	−9.44	−17.60	−23.60	−30.47	−11.59	−21.03	−28.75	−35.62
$a = 1.0$ Indirect effect	12.45	27.47	46.35	70.39	15.88	36.05	63.52	98.28
Direct effect	−21.89	−45.47	−71.67	−102.58	−27.90	−57.94	−93.99	−137.76
Total effect	−9.44	−18.02	−25.32	−32.19	−12.02	−21.89	−30.47	−39.48
$a = 2.0$ Indirect effect	27.47	70.39	129.61	209.01	−36.05	−98.28	−185.41	−253.22
Direct effect	37.32	90.56	164.37	260.94	−48.50	−124.89	−233.05	−317.17
Total effect	−9.87	−20.17	−34.76	−51.93	−12.45	−26.61	−47.64	−63.95

a, α, and β of the model. The following observations may be made from these tables.

First, in the presence of the work-leisure choice, the pretax mean income is reduced considerably, the magnitude of reduction depending on the values of α, β, and a. The nature of the interrelationships between these parameters and the pretax mean income is revealed by the different elasticities given in the tables.

Note that for all three values of a, the reduction in the pretax mean income of the society resulting from taxes is significantly high. The tax function with parameters $\alpha = 500$ and $\beta = 20$ percent, when $a = 0.5$, gives the minimum reduction in the pretax mean income; the reduction is of the magnitude of $3,291., approximately 35 percent of the mean income with no taxes.

Second, observe that the average tax revenue per person becomes negative for high values of a and α. This is particularly relevant for policy considerations in the developing countries. Whatever the attractions of the negative income tax plans from the viewpoint of equity, their implementation will be severely limited by considerations of adverse effects on the tax revenues that are required for financing development.

Third, the empirical results show that the Gini index of the pretax income increases appreciably with increases in values of α, which is the size of the lump-sum cash subsidy, and also increases when the values of a and β rise. The nature of the effects of changes in the values of a, α, and β on the Gini index of pretax income is demonstrated by the values of the respective elasticities reported in the tables. This is a very significant result, emphasizing the importance of the often neglected incentive-to-work effect of taxation. The increase in the pretax Gini index is a reflection of the fact that the negative income tax plans cause the lower income classes to reduce the supply of their labor proportionally more than the higher income classes. Increases in the values of α, β, and a, however, lead to a reduction in the Gini index of posttax income. The relative magnitudes of the effects of changes in the three parameters can be seen from the reported values of the respective elasticities.

The disaggregation of the total effect of taxes on income inequality into direct and indirect effects of taxes is presented in table 14.6. It is given for the different values of a, α, and β.

As noted above, the indirect effect refers to the effects of taxes on income inequality resulting from changes in allocation of time between work and leisure. This effect is always positive and increases when the values of α, β, and a rise. Moreover, the increases are substantial. The direct effect is always negative and numerically higher than the indirect effect. The net result is, therefore, always reduction in inequality.

PART SIX

Measurement of Poverty

CHAPTER 15

Alternative Measures of Poverty

THE PROBLEM OF THE MEASUREMENT OF POVERTY has two aspects. First, it is necessary to specify a poverty line, the threshold income below which one is considered poor, and which may reflect the socially accepted minimal standard of living. Second, the intensity of poverty suffered by those below the threshold income must be measured once the poverty line is specified. This chapter deals with the second aspect.

Most of the literature on poverty concerns the number of people below the poverty line. But this factor, as such, does not reflect the intensity of poverty suffered by the poor. The problem is, how poor are the poor. They may have incomes that approximate the threshold level, or they may have no incomes at all. If the deviation of a poor man's income from the poverty line is proportional to the degree of misery suffered by him, the sum total of these deviations may, theoretically, be considered a desirable measure of poverty. This index, which has been used by the United States Social Security Administration, is called the poverty gap. It indicates the aggregate shortfall of income from the poverty line of all the poor taken together. The drawback of this measure, however, is that it does not take into account inequality of income among the poor.

Sen (1976) proposed a measure of poverty that avoids the drawbacks of previous measures. The derivation of his index is based on an axiomatic approach that employs an ordinal welfare concept. Kakwani (1977a) followed the alternative approach of the transfer of income from rich to poor so that the income of every poor person is brought to the poverty line. The poverty index derived by means of this approach is similar to that proposed by Sen. Kakwani also provided a theorem that shows how the aggregate poverty index can be decomposed into different groups according to certain socioeconomic characteristics of households.

This chapter focuses on alternative measures of poverty. A general class of poverty measures is proposed, which makes use of three poverty indicators: the percentage of the poor, the aggregate poverty gap, and the distribution of income among the poor. An alternative set of axioms is also introduced, which leads to a new poverty index. Numerical illustrations are based on Malaysian and Indian data.

Headcount Ratio as a Measure of Poverty

Suppose that income X of a person is a random variable with the probability distribution function $F(X)$. If x^* is the poverty level, which is assumed to be known, $F(x^*)$ will be the proportion of poor people in the society. Further, $F(x^*)$, which has often been used as a poverty measure, may be called the headcount ratio.[1]

The headcount ratio is a crude index of poverty because of two main drawbacks: it is insensitive to decreases in income of families below the poverty line, and to transfers of income among the poor, as well as to transfers from the poor to the nonpoor. To counter these shortcomings, Sen (1976) proposed the following two axioms, which a suitable measure of poverty must satisfy.

AXIOM 15.1. (Monotonicity) *Other things remaining the same, a reduction in income of a person below the poverty line must increase the poverty measure.*

AXIOM 15.2. (Transfer) *Other things remaining the same, a pure transfer of income from a person below the poverty line to anyone who is richer must increase the poverty measure.*

The headcount ratio clearly violates both axioms. Alternative poverty indexes that satisfy them will be discussed below.

Transfer-of-Income Approach to Measuring Poverty

If μ is the mean income of a society, and μ^* the mean income of

1. See Sen (1976).

persons below the poverty line, the proposed poverty index is[2]

$$(15.1) \qquad\qquad P = F(x^*)\, \frac{(x^* - \mu^*)}{\mu}$$

where P is interpreted as the percentage of total income that must be transferred from the nonpoor to the poor so that the income of everyone below the poverty line may be raised to x^*. In addition, x^* is generally less than μ. If, however, $x^* = \mu$, P will be equal to the proportion of income that must be transferred from the group having an income more than μ to the group having an income less than μ, so that both groups have the same mean income, which is equal to μ. It immediately follows from lemma 5.10, then, that P leads to the relative mean deviation, which is a well-known measure of income inequality.

Next, divide the population into k mutually exclusive regions. Denote

μ_i as the mean income of the ith region,

f_i as the proportion of the population in the ith region,

$F_i(x^*)$ as the proportion of the poor in the ith region,

μ_i^* as the mean income of the poor in the ith region.

This leads to the following relations:

$$(15.2) \qquad\qquad F(x^*) = \sum_{i=1}^{n} F_i(x^*) f_i$$

and

$$(15.3) \qquad\qquad \mu^* = \frac{1}{F(x^*)} \sum_{i=1}^{n} F_i(x^*) \mu_i^* f_i.$$

Equation (15.2) implies that the proportion of the poor in an entire population is equal to the weighted average of the proportion of the poor in each region, the weights being proportional to the population of each region. Similarly, equation (15.3) expresses the mean income of the poor in an entire population as a weighted average of the mean income of the poor in each region, the weights being propor-

---

2. See Kakwani (1977a). The poverty index denoted by P should not be confused with the measure of tax progressivity discussed in chapter 12.

tional to the income share of the poor in each region. Substituting (15.2) and (15.3) into (15.1) gives

$$(15.4) \qquad\qquad P = \frac{1}{\mu} \sum_{i=1}^{n} \mu_i f_i P_i$$

where

$$P_i = F_i(x^*) \, \frac{(x^* - \mu_i^*)}{\mu_i}$$

is the poverty index in the ith region. This leads to the following theorem.

THEOREM 15.1.   *If a population is divided into a number of mutually exclusive groups, the poverty index in the whole population is equal to the weighted average of the poverty indexes in each group, the weights being proportional to the income share of each group.*

If a population is divided into different groups according to certain socioeconomic characteristics of households, the result would be useful in analyzing the influence of each group on total poverty.

A General Class of Poverty Measures

The poverty index P derived in the preceding section does not take into account the income inequality among the poor; that is, it is insensitive to the transfer of income between poor persons. Thus, this measure violates axiom 15.2. It can be proved that axiom 15.1 will always be satisfied by this measure.

The measure P will provide adequate information about the intensity of poverty if all the poor are assumed to have exactly the same income, which is below the poverty level. In practice, income among the poor is unequally distributed, and, therefore, P cannot be an adequate measure of the intensity of poverty. More inequality of income among the poor, with the mean income remaining unchanged, implies greater hardship to the extremely poor in a society; therefore, the value of the poverty index should be higher in this case. Axiom 15.2 implies the same thing because a pure transfer of income from poor to relatively less poor people increases the income inequality among them.

Poverty will be maximum when every person below the poverty line receives zero income, in which case μ^* will be equal to zero. Thus, the upper limit for the poverty index will be $F(x^*)x^*/\mu$. If the Gini index G^* is used as a measure of income inequality among the poor, the poverty index should satisfy the following conditions:
If

$$G^* = 0, \quad \tilde{P} = \frac{F(x^*)(x^* - \mu^*)}{\mu} \tag{1}$$

(15.5)
$$\tilde{P} \leq \frac{F(x^*)x^*}{\mu} \tag{2}$$

$$\frac{\partial \tilde{P}}{\partial G^*} > 0, \quad \text{for all } G^*. \tag{3}$$

Any poverty index that satisfies the above conditions will necessarily satisfy both axiom 15.1 and axiom 15.2.

In addition, a general class of poverty measures satisfying these conditions can be written as

(15.6)
$$P_g = \frac{F(x^*)}{\mu} \left[x^* - \mu^* g(G^*) \right]$$

where $g(G^*)$ is a monotonic function of G^* so that

(15.7)
$$0 \leq g(G^*) \leq 1$$

(15.8)
$$g(G^*) = 1 \quad \text{if} \quad G^* = 0$$

(15.9)
$$g'(G^*) < 0.$$

These restrictions on $g(G^*)$ ensure that all the conditions given in (15.5) are satisfied. Further, if $g(G^*) = 1$ for all values of G^*, the index P_g reduces to P as defined in (15.1). In contrast, if it is assumed that P_g increases with G^* at a constant rate, the function $g(G^*)$ can be of the following form:

$$g(G^*) = (1 - G^*),$$

which, on substituting into (15.6), gives a more suitable poverty index:

(15.10)
$$P_1 = \frac{F(x^*)}{\mu} \left[x^* - \mu^*(1 - G^*) \right].$$

The elasticity of the poverty index P_1 with respect to G^* is

$$\eta_1 = \frac{G^*}{P_1} \frac{\partial P_1}{\partial G^*} = \frac{\mu^* G^*}{(x^* - \mu^*) + \mu^* G^*},$$

which is, of course, less than unity. Thus if income among the poor is redistributed so that the Gini index reduces by 1 percent, the poverty index reduces by less than 1 percent. The elasticity provides the information regarding the effect on the poverty index of income inequality among the poor.

A diagrammatic representation of P_1 is provided in figure 9 where OPA is the Lorenz curve, and OA is the egalitarian line. If P is the point on the Lorenz curve corresponding to a given poverty level x^*, OE is the proportion of poor families, and EP their proportion of income. Further, LP is the tangent at point P, and its slope is equal to x^*/μ. The poverty index P is then clearly equal to the area of the triangle OPF divided by the area of the triangle OEK. Further, if only the subpopulation of poor families is considered, ONP is their Lorenz curve, and OP the egalitarian line. The Gini index G^* of poor families is, therefore, given by the shaded area ONP divided by the area of the triangle OEP. Thus, the shaded area ONP is equal to $F^2(x^*)\mu^* G^*/2\mu$, which means that the poverty index P_1 corresponds to the area $ONPF$ divided by the area of the triangle OEK.

It is clear from figure 9 that the area $ONPF$ is greater than the area OPF and less than the area $OLPF$. This provides the upper and lower bounds of the poverty index P_1 as

$$P < P_1 < P + \frac{F(x^*)\mu^*}{\mu}\left(1 - \frac{\mu^*}{x^*}\right)$$

where P is given in (15.1).

An alternative poverty index is obtained by substituting[3]

$$(15.11) \qquad g(G^*) = \frac{1}{(1 + G^*)}$$

into (15.6). If this index is denoted by P_2, then

$$(15.12) \qquad P_2 = \frac{F(x^*)}{\mu}\left[x^* - \mu^*/(1 + G^*)\right].$$

---

3. Note that the function $g(G^*)$ defined in (15.11) satisfies the restrictions (15.7), (15.8), and (15.9).

Figure 9. *A Graphic Representation of Poverty*
Measures

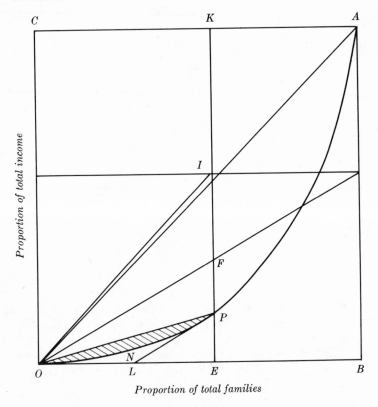

Furthermore, the elasticity of P_2 with respect to G^* is

$$\eta_2 = \frac{G^*}{P_2} \frac{\partial P_2}{\partial G^*} = \frac{\mu^* G^*}{(1 + G^*)(x^* - \mu^* + x^* G^*)} \, ,$$

which is also less than unity.

Comparing the elasticities η_1 and η_2, note that $\eta_2 < \eta_1$, which shows that the poverty index P_1 is more sensitive to the changes in inequality of income among the poor than the alternative index P_2. This result leads to a choice between the two alternative measures of poverty. If, for example, a society attaches relatively greater importance to the inequality of income among the poor, the measure

P_1 will be clearly preferred to P_2. Figure 9 indicates that

$$0 \le G^* \le 1 - \frac{\mu^*}{x^*},$$

which, on substituting into (15.12), provides the upper and lower bounds of the poverty index P_2 as

$$P \le P_2 \le P + \frac{F(x^*)\mu^*}{\mu} \frac{(x^* - \mu^*)}{(2x^* - \mu^*)},$$

where P was defined in (15.1).

Sen's Axiomatic Approach to Measuring Poverty

Sen's approach (1976) to measuring poverty is based on an ordinal welfare concept. First, define

(15.13)
$$h(x_i) = \frac{x^* - x_i}{\mu},$$

which is the poverty gap of any individual i expressed in percentage terms over the mean income. Clearly, $h(x_i)$ is nonnegative for the poor and negative for others.

Let $S(x)$ be a set of people who have an income no higher than x; the aggregate gap $H(x)$ of the set $S(x)$ is then defined as

$$H(x) = \sum_{i \in S(x)} h(x_i) v_i(x^*, \mathbf{x})$$

where $v_i(x^*, \mathbf{x})$ are nonnegative weights. Note that these weights depend on the vector of income distribution $\mathbf{x}' = (x_1, x_2, \ldots, x_n)$ and not on x_i alone (along with x^*). The index of poverty $\tilde{P}$ of a given income distribution $\mathbf{x}$ and the poverty line x^* is defined as the maximum value of the aggregate gap $H(x)$ for all x. Thus

$$\tilde{P} = \operatorname*{Max}_{x} H(x).$$

Because the weights v_i are nonnegative, and the poverty gap $h(x_i)$ is negative for the nonpoor, it is obvious that

(15.14)
$$\tilde{P} = H(x^*),$$

which is the aggregate gap of the poor only.

In this connection, the following axioms were proposed by Sen.

AXIOM 15.3. *If all the poor have the same income,*[4]

$$\tilde{P} = P.$$

AXIOM 15.4. (Relative equity). *For any pair i, j:*

$$if\ W_i(\mathbf{x}) < W_j(\mathbf{x}),\ v_i(x^*, \mathbf{x}) > v_j(x^*, \mathbf{x})$$

where $W_i(\mathbf{x})$ and $W_j(\mathbf{x})$ are the welfare levels of i and j under the income distribution $\mathbf{x}$.

AXIOM 15.5. (Monotonic welfare). *For any i and j,*

$$if\ x_i > x_j,\ then\ W_i(\mathbf{x}) > W_j(\mathbf{x}).$$

AXIOM 15.6. (Ordinal rank weights). *The weight $v_i(x^*, \mathbf{x})$ on the poverty gap of person i is proportional to the rank of i in the interpersonal welfare ordering of the poor.*

Axiom 15.3 does not require explanation because it was argued in the preceding section that the measure P provides adequate information about the extent of poverty if all the poor have exactly the same income.

Regarding axiom 15.4, note that the individual welfare $W_i(\mathbf{x})$ is taken as only ordinally measurable. This means that there is agreement as to who is poorer than who, but no agreement as to the values of the welfare differences. Axiom 15.4 implies only that the intensely poor receive higher weight than the less intensely poor, provided there is general agreement as to who is poorer than who.

Axiom 15.5 gives the relationship between income and welfare, implying that a richer person receives higher welfare than a poorer person. Axioms 15.4 and 15.5 together imply that the larger the poverty gap, the greater should be the weight attached to it. Axiom 15.6 is the most demanding. Sen justifies it by viewing deprivation as an essentially relative concept. The lower a person is on the welfare scale, the greater his sense of poverty. Moreover, his welfare rank with respect to others may represent the weight to be placed on his income gap. This axiom, in conjunction with axioms 15.4 and 15.5, means that

(15.15) $$v_i(x^*, \mathbf{x}) = k[F(x^*) - F(x_i)],$$

4. Note that this axiom differs slightly from the one proposed by Sen.

which implies that the weight attached to the poverty gap of individual i depends on the percentage of poor people who are better off than he is. Suppose that the distribution $\mathbf{x}$ is characterized by a continuous random variable x with probability distribution function $F(x)$. If $v(x^*, x)$ denotes the weight attached to the poverty gap of a person with income x, (15.15) becomes

(15.16) $$v(x^*, x) = k[F(x^*) - F(x)].$$

Note that the weight $v(x^*, x)$ is zero when $x = x^*$.

THEOREM 15.2.   *The poverty index $\tilde{P}$ satisfying axioms 15.3, 15.4, 15.5, and 15.6 is equal to P_1 where P_1 is defined in (15.10).*

Proof.   If $h(x)$ denotes the poverty gap of a person with income x, then, according to axioms 15.4, 15.5, and 15.6, $v(x^*, x)$ as defined in (15.16) will be the weight attached to the poverty gap $h(x)$. This gives the aggregate poverty gap of the poor as equal to

(15.17) $$H(x^*) = \int_0^{x^*} h(x)v(x^*, x)f(x)\,dx,$$

which has been defined in (15.14) as the poverty index $\tilde{P}$. Substituting (15.13) and (15.16) into (15.17), the poverty index $\tilde{P}$ becomes

(15.18) $$\tilde{P} = \frac{k}{\mu} \int_0^{x^*} (x^* - x)[F(x^*) - F(x)]f(x)\,dx,$$

which on integrating by parts and utilizing the result

(15.19) $$G^* = 1 - \frac{2\displaystyle\int_0^{x^*} F_1(x)f(x)\,dx}{F(x^*)F_1(x^*)}$$

simplifies to

(15.20) $$\tilde{P} = \frac{k}{\mu}\frac{F^2(x^*)}{2}[x^* - (1 - G^*)\mu^*].$$

Axiom 15.3 implies that if $G^* = 0$, $\tilde{P} = P$, which, when substituted into (15.20), gives $k = 2/F(x^*)$. Thus $\tilde{P}$ becomes

$$\tilde{P} = \frac{F(x^*)}{\mu}[x^* - (1 - G^*)\mu^*],$$

which is the poverty index P_1 as defined in (15.10). This completes the proof of theorem 15.2.

Note that Sen expresses the poverty gap as the percentage of the poverty level x^* instead of as the mean income μ of the society. His poverty index can, therefore, be written as

$$P_S = \frac{F(x^*)}{x^*} [x^* - \mu^*(1 - G^*)],$$

which in figure 9 corresponds to the area $ONPF$ divided by OEI. The upper and lower bounds for P_S are

$$F(x^*)\left(1 - \frac{\mu^*}{x^*}\right) < P_S < F(x^*)\left(1 - \frac{\mu^{*2}}{x^{*2}}\right).$$

An Alternative Set of Axioms

This section presents an alternative set of axioms, which lead to the poverty index P_2 defined in (15.12).

AXIOM 15.7.   *The total weight attached to the poverty gap of all the poor is proportional to the number of poor.*

AXIOM 15.8.   *The weight $v(x^*, x)$ on the poverty gap of a person with income x is proportional to the income of all other persons above him but below the "poverty line" x^*.*

This axiom is equivalent to

(15.21) $\qquad v(x^*, x) = \alpha[F_1(x^*) - F_1(x)],$

which implies that the weight attached to the poverty gap $h(x)$ depends on the proportion of income between x and x^*. In contrast, Sen's axiom 15.6 requires that the weight $v(x^*, x)$ depend on the proportion of persons between x and x^*. Thus there is a fundamental difference between axioms 15.8 and 15.6.

THEOREM 15.3.   *The poverty index $\tilde{P}$ satisfying axioms 15.4, 15.5, 15.7, and 15.8 is equal to P_2 where P_2 is defined in (15.12).*

Proof.   Axiom 15.7 implies that

$$\int_0^{x^*} v(x^*, x)f(x)\,dx = F(x^*),$$

which, by means of (15.21) and (15.19), yields

(15.22)
$$\alpha = \frac{2}{(1 + G^*)F_1(x^*)}.$$

Substituting (15.21) into (15.17), the poverty index $\tilde{P}$ becomes

$$\tilde{P} = \frac{\alpha}{\mu} \int_0^{x^*} (x^* - x)[F_1(x^*) - F_1(x)]f(x)\,dx,$$

which, by means of the results (15.19) and (15.22), simplifies to P_2 as defined in (15.12). This completes the proof of the theorem.

Welfare Interpretation of Poverty Measures

In this section the poverty measures P_1 and P_2 are interpreted in terms of the social welfare functions considered in chapter 5. If only the subpopulation of the poor are considered, according to theorem 5.1 their social welfare function W, defined in (5.21) and satisfying axioms 5.6, 5.7, 5.8, and 5.9, will be

$$W = F(x^*)\mu^*(1 - G^*).$$

When P percent of the income is transferred from the nonpoor to the poor, the income of every poor person is raised to x^*, and, therefore, the welfare function of the poor after the transfer becomes

(15.23)
$$W^* = F(x^*)x^*.$$

Clearly, μ is the maximum welfare of the society with a given mean income. It is then clear that the poverty measure P_1 is equal to the gain in the welfare of the poor (due to the transfer of income) expressed as a percentage of the maximum welfare of the society. If all the poor have exactly the same income, which is less than x^*, the gain in welfare, expressed as a percentage of the maximum welfare of the society, is equal to P.

The social welfare function of the poor, satisfying axioms 5.6, 5.8, 5.10, 5.11, and 5.12, is written as (see theorem 5.2)

(15.24)
$$W = \frac{F(x^*)\mu^*}{(1 + G^*)}.$$

When P percent of the income is transferred from the nonpoor to the poor, the social welfare function becomes (15.23).

The difference between (15.24) and (15.23) divided by μ clearly leads to the measure P_2. This indicates that P_2, because of the transfer of income, can also be interpreted as the gain in welfare expressed as a percentage of the maximum social welfare.

Poverty Indexes and Negative Income Tax

This section concerns the effect of negative income tax on poverty indexes. Because general framework incorporating all the well-known negative income tax plans was provided in chapter 12, only the following, simple plan is discussed here.

If a family has a per capita income above the poverty level x^*, it is taxed at a fixed rate β percent; and if the per capita income of a family falls below the poverty level, the family is given a cash subsidy, again at a fixed rate β percent on income below x^*. The disposable income of a family with pretax income x is then given by

$$(15.25) \qquad d(x) = \beta x^* + (1 - \beta)x$$

with mean disposable income

$$(15.26) \qquad \mu_d = \beta x^* + (1 - \beta)\mu.$$

Clearly, $d'(x)$ is greater than zero for $0 < \beta < 1$, which, from theorem 8.2, implies that the concentration curve for the disposable income $d(x)$ coincides with its Lorenz curve.

The mean disposable income of families below the poverty level is

$$\mu_d^* = \frac{1}{F(x^*)} \int_0^{x^*} d(x)f(x)\,dx,$$

which, by means of (15.25), simplifies to

$$(15.27) \qquad \mu_d^* = \mu^* + \beta(x^* - \mu^*).$$

Because $x^* > \mu^*$, this equation implies that the negative income tax plan always increases the mean income of poor families.

When a negative income tax is imposed, the Lorenz curve for the whole distribution shifts upward, making the posttax income distribution more equal. This is shown below.

If $F_1[d(x)]$ denotes the proportion of the disposable income of families having a pretax income less than, or equal to, x, applying theorem 8.3 to (15.25) yields

$$(15.28) \qquad F_1[d(x)] = F_1(x) + \frac{\beta x^*}{\mu_d} [F(x) - F_1(x)].$$

Because the Lorenz curve is concave from above, $F(x) > F_1(x)$, which proves that the distribution of the disposable income $d(x)$ is Lorenz superior to the distribution of x. The Gini index of the disposable income of the poor is given by

$$\tilde{G}^* = 1 - \frac{2\int_0^{x^*} F_1[d(x)]f(x)\,dx}{F(x^*)F_1[d(x^*)]},$$

which, by means of (15.19), (15.28), and

$$F_1[d(x^*)] = \frac{F(x^*)\mu_d^*}{\mu_d},$$

simplifies to

$$(15.29) \qquad \tilde{G}^* = \frac{(1 - \beta)\mu^* G^*}{\mu_d^*}.$$

Substituting (15.26), (15.27), and (15.29) into (15.10) with μ, μ^*, and G^* replaced by μ_d, μ_d^*, and $\tilde{G}^*$, respectively yields the poverty index, after the negative income tax has been imposed, as

$$\tilde{P}_1 = \frac{(1 - \beta)}{\mu_d} F(x^*)[x^* - \mu^*(1 - G^*)].$$

Therefore, the percentage change in the poverty index is given by

$$\frac{\tilde{P}_1 - P_1}{P_1} = -\frac{\beta x^*}{\beta x^* + (1 - \beta)\mu}.$$

This equation expresses the percentage change in the poverty index as a function of the two parameters x^*/μ and β. If, for example, the poverty level is specified as half the mean income of the society, that is, $x^*/\mu = 0.5$, the marginal tax rate of 18 percent will reduce the poverty index by 10 percent. The average tax rate, net of subsidy, for the entire society in this case will be about 9 percent.

In the above plan, the tax rate is equal to the subsidy rate, which does not guarantee that posttax aggregate income is equal to pretax aggregate income. Accordingly, its effects are not purely redistributive. In order to keep the total income constant, a tax rate different from the rate of subsidy is required. If it is assumed that λ is the rate of subsidy and β is the tax rate, the disposable income of a family with the pretax income x is given by

$$d(x) = x + \lambda(x^* - x) \quad \text{if } x < x^*$$

$$= x - \beta(x - x^*) \quad \text{if } x > x^*$$

where β and λ satisfy the relation

(15.30)
$$\frac{\beta}{\lambda} = \frac{P}{\left(1 - \dfrac{x^*}{\mu}\right) + P}.$$

Equation (15.1) gives the definition of P. Note that this relation has been derived from the assumption that the pretax mean income of a society is equal to the posttax (subsidy) mean income, that is, that $\mu = \mu_d$. If $\lambda = 1.0$, poverty will be completely eliminated. Equation (15.30) indicates that if $\lambda = 1.0$, β will be less than unity only if $x^* < \mu$. This demonstrates that the only necessary condition for poverty to be eliminated by interpersonal redistribution is that the poverty level be less than the mean income of a society. Further, under this plan the pre- and posttax poverty indexes are related as

(15.31)
$$\tilde{P}_1 = (1 - \lambda)P_1.$$

Therefore, λ is equal to the proportion of reduction in the poverty index resulting from the income transfer plan.

For Malaysia (see the following section), $P = 0.055$, $\mu = \$61.64$, and $x^* = \$25$. The ratio of the tax rate to the subsidy rate as computed from (15.30) is 0.084, which means that a 8.4 percent tax rate is required to eliminate poverty. To reduce the poverty index by only 50 percent, however, use equation (15.31), in which $\lambda = 0.50$, which gives $\beta = 0.042$. Thus, the marginal tax rate of 4.2 percent will reduce poverty in Malaysia by as much as 50 percent.

Poverty in Malaysia: A Numerical Illustration

The numerical illustration provided in this section is based on Malaysian data obtained from the "Post Enumeration Survey"

(PES), which was conducted in 1970 and covered approximately 135,000 individuals or 1.5 percent of the total population.[5] The per capita household income used to measure the extent of poverty in Malaysia includes wages, salaries, business, property and interest income, remittances, and transfers both in cash and kind.

The data are in grouped form, consisting of thirty-two income classes. The midpoint of each class is used as an approximation of the mean income for the fourteen income classes; for the remaining eighteen income classes, the mean income estimated by Anand (1973) was used.[6]

The poverty line is defined as twenty-five Malaysian dollars per month, per person, the figure used by Anand in 1973. In about 37 percent of the households, per capita income falls below this poverty level.

Poverty in Malaysia is analyzed by dividing the entire population into different groups according to socioeconomic and demographic characteristics of households. Detailed computations are presented in tables 15.1 to 15.5. The first column gives the proportion of the total populations in the different groups. The second column presents the per capita mean income of the entire population within each group, whereas the third column gives the per capita mean income of only the poor. The fourth column presents the numerical values of the headcount ratio, which is equal to the proportion of all households living in poverty. The computed values of the poverty index P discussed in "Transfer of Income and Poverty" are reported in column 5, whereas column 6 shows the percentage of the contribution of each group to total poverty. Equation (15.4) was used to compute the values in this column. Finally, columns 7 and 8 present the computed values of the two alternative indexes of poverty introduced in "A General Class of Poverty Measures." The figures in parentheses are the elasticities of the two indexes with respect to the Gini index of the poor.

Table 15.1 gives the computation of poverty indexes within various groups of families classified according to their race. The poverty index P of the whole population is computed at 0.055, which implies that only 5.5 percent of the total income must be transferred

---

5. See Anand (1973) for details of the survey.
6. Anand (1973) estimated the mean income in these income classes by fitting a Pareto curve.

Table 15.1. *Poverty Index by Race, Malaysia, 1970*

Race	Proportion of the population	Per capita mean income of all households (Malaysian dollars)	Per capita mean income of poor households (Malaysian dollars)	Proportion of poor households	Poverty index P	Contribution by race to total poverty (percentage)	Poverty index P_1	Poverty index P_2
Malays	55.4	41.61	15.39	0.5139	0.1187	81.2	0.1615 (0.2649)	0.15136 (0.1761)
Chinese	32.0	85.39	17.29	0.1473	0.0133	10.8	0.0201 (0.3152)	0.0188 (0.2382)
Indians	11.7	78.31	17.34	0.2480	0.0243	6.6	0.0343 (0.2929)	0.0327 (0.2173)
Others	0.9	239.86	11.76	0.4091	0.0226	1.4	0.0298 (0.2427)	0.0279 (0.1398)
Total	100.00	61.64	15.75	0.3647	0.0547	100.0	0.0752 (0.276)	0.0718 (0.1946)

Note: The figures in parentheses are the elasticities.

Table 15.2. *Poverty Index by Urban and Rural Sector, Malaysia, 1970*

Sector	Proportion of the population	Per capita mean income of all households (Malaysian dollars)	Per capita mean income of poor households (Malaysian dollars)	Proportion of poor house-holds	Poverty index P	Contribution by race to total poverty (percentage)	Poverty index P_1	Poverty index P_2
Urban	28.3	100.43	16.81	0.1572	0.0128	10.9	0.0185 (0.3059)	0.0175 (0.2207)
Rural	71.7	46.40	15.65	0.4459	0.0898	89.1	0.1232 (0.2708)	0.1171 (0.1908)
Total	100.0	61.64	15.75	0.3647	0.0547	100.0	0.0752 (0.2775)	0.0718 (0.1946)

Note: The figures in parentheses are the elasticities.

Table 15.3. *Poverty Index by State, Malaysia, 1970*

State	Proportion of the population	Per capita mean income of all households (Malaysian dollars)	Per capita mean income of poor households (Malaysian dollars)	Proportion of poor households	Poverty index P	Contribution by state to total poverty (percentage)	Poverty index P_1	Poverty index P_2
Johore	13.4	58.00	16.29	0.3290	0.0494	11.5	0.0690 (0.2844)	0.0656 (0.2103)
Kedah	11.3	44.08	15.56	0.4852	0.1039	15.5	0.1425 (0.2709)	0.1353 (0.1998)
Kelantan	9.5	31.55	14.51	0.6519	0.2167	19.5	0.2901 (0.2530)	0.2757 (0.1753)
Malacca	4.6	64.56	16.31	0.3198	0.0430	3.8	0.0618 (0.3031)	0.0583 (0.2413)
Negri Sembilan	4.7	68.02	15.89	0.3201	0.0428	4.1	0.0590 (0.2742)	0.0561 (0.2018)
Pahang	5.8	66.01	16.05	0.3061	0.0415	4.8	0.0578 (0.2819)	0.0549 (0.2219)
Penang	8.5	67.84	17.17	0.2956	0.0341	5.8	0.0481 (0.2904)	0.0459 (0.2292)
Perak	17.8	57.85	16.18	0.3450	0.0526	16.2	0.0732 (0.2814)	0.0695 (0.2319)
Perlis	1.5	28.95	14.51	0.5868	0.2127	2.8	0.2876 (0.2604)	0.2724 (0.2098)
Selangor	18.2	95.32	17.10	0.1900	0.0158	8.2	0.0221 (0.2858)	0.0211 (0.2299)
Trengganu	4.7	39.78	14.76	0.5459	0.1406	7.8	0.1886 (0.2545)	0.1794 (0.1820)
Total	100.0	61.64	15.75	0.3647	0.0547	100.0	0.0752 (0.2775)	0.0718 (0.1946)

Note: The figures in parentheses are the elasticities.

Table 15.4. *Poverty Index by Household Size, Malaysia, 1970*

Household size	Proportion of population	Per capita mean income of all households (Malaysian dollars)	Per capita mean income of poor households (Malaysian dollars)	Proportion of poor households	Poverty index P	Contribution by household to total poverty (percentage)	Poverty index P_1	Poverty index P_2
One member	8.9	135.97	17.00	0.2349	0.0138	4.9	0.0154 (0.1052)	0.0153 (0.093)
Two to three members	21.2	79.72	14.70	0.2664	0.0344	17.3	0.0487 (0.2928)	0.0455 (0.2413)
Four to five members	25.6	53.65	15.93	0.3581	0.0605	24.7	0.0850 (0.2082)	0.0804 (0.1398)
Over six	44.2	42.60	15.84	0.4418	0.0950	53.1	0.1284 (0.2602)	0.1227 (0.1609)
Total	100.0	61.64	15.75	0.3647	0.0547	100.0	0.0756 (0.2755)	0.0718 (0.1946)

Note: The figures in parentheses are the elasticities.

Table 15.5. *Poverty Index by Documented Age Group, Malaysia, 1970*

Age	Proportion of population	Per capita mean income of all households (Malaysian dollars)	Per capita mean income of poor households (Malaysian dollars)	Proportion of poor	Poverty index P	Contribution by age to total poverty (percentage)	Poverty index P_1	Poverty index P_2
Under thirty	16.8	86.34	15.06	0.2775	0.0319	13.7	0.0451 (0.2922)	0.0423 (0.2341)
Thirty to forty-nine	47.9	56.14	15.83	0.3941	0.0644	51.4	0.0886 (0.2736)	0.0843 (0.2213)
Fifty to fifty-nine	19.0	59.92	16.02	0.3434	0.0515	17.3	0.0707 (0.2723)	0.0674 (0.2110)
Over sixty	16.3	54.23	15.75	0.3923	0.0669	17.6	0.0918 (0.2711)	0.0873 (0.2019)
Total	100.0	61.64	15.75	0.3647	0.0547	100.0	0.0756 (0.2775)	0.0718 (0.1946)

Note: The figures in parentheses are the elasticities.

from the nonpoor to the poor to eliminate poverty in Malaysia. The poverty index is highest among Malays, followed by Indians and others, and finally Chinese. It shows that 81.2 percent of the contribution to total poverty comes from Malays, 10.8 percent from Chinese, 6.6 percent from Indians, and 1.4 percent from other races.

Table 15.2 gives a breakdown of families according to rural and urban areas. Although 71 percent of the population lives in rural areas, the contribution of rural areas to total poverty is 90 percent.

The poverty indexes for different states are presented in table 15.3. Four states—Kelantan, Perlis, Kedah, and Trengganu—have a mean per capita income significantly lower than the national mean income, and the values of poverty indexes shown in columns 7 and 8 are very high for these states. The richest state is Selangor, where 18.2 percent of the population lives. It contributes only 8.2 percent to total poverty.

In Table 15.4 the entire population is disaggregated according to household size. It is clear that the poverty index increases as family size increases. Note also that while the mean income of the poor does not vary significantly with household size, the proportion of the poor increases significantly when households become larger.

The breakdown of the population according to the age of the household head is provided in table 15.5. Note that the poverty index is highest among households where the age of the household head exceeds sixty years. Households where the age of the household head is less than thirty years have the least poverty. The proportion of poor among this group is 27 percent, compared to 36 percent for the entire Malaysian population.

Poverty in India: Another Numerical Illustration

The data used to measure poverty in India are from the *National Sample Survey* (NSS), 1960–61, and are available separately for the rural and urban populations. The per capita consumption expenditure was used to measure the intensity of poverty.

The poverty level is defined as Rs 18 monthly per capita expenditure, for both rural and urban populations. The Indian Planning Commission use the figure of Rs 20, but Dandekar and Rath (1971) consider this figure high for the rural population and low for the urban population. They proposed a figure of Rs 15 for the rural

Table 15.6. *Poverty Index by Urban and Rural Sector, India, 1960–61*

Sector	Proportion of population	Per capita mean expenditure of all households (rupees)	Per capita mean expenditure of poor households (rupees)	Proportion of poor households	Poverty index P	Contribution by sector to total poverty	Poverty index P_1	Poverty index P_2
Urban	18.0	29.92	13.31	0.3240	0.0508	10.5	0.0692 (0.2661)	0.0671 (0.2154)
Rural	82.0	21.76	12.53	0.5182	0.1303	89.5	0.1751 (0.2560)	0.1692 (0.1999)
Total	100.0	23.23	12.62	0.4833	0.1119	100.0	0.1508 (0.2576)	0.1458 (0.2025)

Source: National Sample Survey, Sixteenth Round, July 1960 to August 1961.
Note: Figures in parentheses are the elasticities.

poverty line, and Rs 22.5 for the urban. If one figure is to be used for both rural and urban populations, Rs 18 seems reasonable.[7]

Table 15.6 (page 349) gives the computation of poverty indexes for both the rural and urban populations. The first column provides the proportion of population in the rural and urban sections and shows that 82 percent of the population lives in rural areas. The per capita consumer expenditure of the urban population is about 38 percent higher than that of the rural population.

The poverty index P for the whole country is 0.119, which means that 11.2 percent of the total income must be transferred from the nonpoor to the poor to eliminate poverty. The values of both poverty indexes, P_1 and P_2, are much higher in rural than in urban India. Column 6 shows that the rural population, which is 82 percent of the total, contributes 89.5 percent to total poverty, whereas the urban population, which is 18 percent, contributes only 10.5 percent to total poverty. In the case of Malaysia, the contribution of the rural population, which is only 71.7 percent, is 89.1 percent, almost the same as the contribution of the rural population of India. Thus it can be concluded that the intensity of poverty in the rural population in relation to the total is higher in Malaysia than in India.

If the negative income tax plan discussed in chapter 14 were introduced in India, the marginal tax rate of 33.2 percent would be required to eliminate poverty. The corresponding figure for Malaysia is about 8 percent, which indicates that it would be much easier in Malaysia than in India to decrease poverty by interpersonal redistribution.

7. A detailed analysis of poverty in India has been provided by several authors: (Bardhan (1970), Minhas (1970), Dandekar and Rath (1971), Srinivasan, Radha Krisnan, and Vaidyanathan (1974), Vaidyanathan (1974), and Mukharji, Battacharya and Chatterjee (1972)). In all these studies the headcount ratio is used as a measure of poverty. In addition, Batty (1974), analyzed poverty in India using Sen's poverty index.

CHAPTER 16

Household Composition and Measurement of Income Inequality and Poverty

THE ECONOMIC WELFARE OF HOUSEHOLDS depends not only on income but on household size and composition as well. Because households of different compositions have different needs, it is necessary to determine their relative economic positions. Clearly, then, the measurement of income inequality or poverty should take household composition into account. To this end, attempts have been made to construct consumer-unit scales that would facilitate the comparison of different kinds of households.

The income scale measures the relative income required by families of different compositions to maintain the same level of satisfaction. In 1955 Prais and Houthakker introduced the concept of the specific consumer-unit scale, which measures the relative consumption expenditures on specific items of consumption required by different household-composition groups. Both scales may be called consumer-unit scales.

The problem, in turn, of estimating consumer-unit scales has been considered by several authors, and there are at least three approaches used for this purpose. For a brief survey of the different approaches, see Prais and Houthakker (1955), whose method, based on the Engel curve, has attracted considerable attention. They employed an iterative procedure to estimate the specific scales for food items by means of family budget data collected by the United Kingdom Ministry of Labour in 1938. Their method is, however, based on the assumption that if a good guess can be made of the income scale, it should be possible to obtain estimates of the specific scales. Forsyth (1960) continued the work of Prais and Houthakker, and concluded that separate specific and income scales cannot be estimated from the cross-section data on expenditures alone. Singh and Nagar (1973) proposed a new iterative procedure that yields the estimates of both specific and income scales independently of any such restrictions and assumptions. Although their procedure provides numerical estimates of both scales, it suffers from "a crucial identification problem," as pointed out by Muellbauer (1975c).

Barten (1964) and Muellbauer (1974b) analyzed the family-composition effect, using basic consumption theory. Muellbauer showed that the standard Engel curve method is, in general, incompatible with this theory. Because this approach also suffers from an identification problem that does not permit the estimation of family-composition parameters, an alternative model proposed by Kakwani (1977f) is considered here. The incomes of the households, in addition to their expenditures, are utilized to identify both income and specific scales from the cross-section data.

Model Used for Estimating Consumer-Unit Scales

According to Barten (1964) and Muellbauer (1974b), the household-utility function is defined as

$$(16.1) \qquad u = u\left(\frac{q_1}{m_1}, \frac{q_2}{m_2}, \ldots, \frac{q_n}{m_n}\right)$$

where q_i is the quantity consumed of commodity i, and m_i is a function of household composition that measures the effect of household composition on utility. Note that m_i is independent of the amounts of commodities consumed.

In vector and matrix notation, the utility function (16.1) can be written as

$$(16.2) \qquad u = u(\hat{m}^{-1}q)$$

where $q' = (q_1, q_2, \ldots, q_n)$ is the n vector of n commodities consumed, and $m' = (m_1, m_2, \ldots, m_n)$ is the n component vector of family-composition parameters. The symbol $(\hat{\,})$ over a vector denotes the diagonal matrix formed with the elements of that vector in the main diagonal. So that the utility in (16.2) is maximum, q is chosen, subject to the restriction

$$v = p'q$$

where v is the total household expenditure, and $p' = (p_1, p_2, \ldots, p_n)$ is the n component vector of prices.

Assume that the household-utility function is of the Stone-Geary type:

(16.3) $$u(\hat{m}^{-1}q) = \beta' \log \left[\hat{m}^{-1}q - \gamma \right]$$

where (β, γ) are n component vectors of parameters, such that $\iota'\beta = 1$, ι being a vector of unit elements, and $\log \left[\hat{m}^{-1}q - \gamma \right]$ is an n component vector with the ith element equal to $\log (q_i/m_i - \gamma_i)$. The solution of the above model then gives the following expenditure equations:

(16.4) $$\hat{p}q = \hat{p}\hat{m}\gamma + \beta(v - p'\hat{m}\gamma),$$

which implies that only the intercept terms in the expenditure equations are affected by household composition. Note that if $m = \iota$, that is, if all family-composition parameters are unity, the equation system (16.4) is identical to the well-known linear expenditure system (LES) discussed in chapter 9.

Muellbauer demonstrated that the parameters in vector m cannot be identified from the equation system as given in (16.4). The following aggregate consumption function will help to identify them:

(16.5) $$v = \alpha x + (1 - \alpha)p'\hat{m}\gamma$$

where x is the measured income, and α the marginal propensity to consume. Again, only the intercept term in the consumption function is affected by household composition. The system of $(n + 1)$ equations given in (16.4) and (16.5) leads to Lluch's extended linear expenditure system (ELES) when all the parameters in the vector m are unity.[1] The following section demonstrates that all family-composition parameters are identifiable from the combined equation system (16.4) and (16.5).

Substituting (16.4) and (16.5) into (16.3) gives the indirect

1. See "The Extended Linear Expenditure System," chapter 9.

utility function of a household as

(16.6) $u^*(x, m) = \log \alpha + \log(x - p'\hat{m}\gamma)$

$$- \beta' \log m - \beta' \log p + \beta' \log \beta$$

where $\log m$, $\log p$, and $\log \beta$ are the n component vectors with the ith element equal to $\log m_i$, $\log p_i$ and $\log \beta_i$, respectively.

Suppose that for a standard household $m = \iota$, that is, all elements of m are unity; the indirect utility function of the household then becomes

(16.7) $u^*(x^*) = \log \alpha + \log(x^* - p'\gamma) - \beta' \log p + \beta' \log \beta$

where x^* denotes the income of a standard household. Equating the utilities given in (16.6) and (16.7) yields the relationship between x and x^* as

(16.8) $$\frac{x}{x^*} = \prod_{i=1}^{n} m_i{}^{\beta_i} + \frac{1}{x^*} \left[p'\hat{m}\gamma - \left(\prod_{i=1}^{n} m_i{}^{\beta_i} \right) (p'\gamma) \right].$$

Equation (16.8) converts the income of a nonstandard household into the income of a standard household while the household remains at the same level of utility. Thus, the ratio of the two incomes x and x^* in (16.8) is the true household-income scale with reference to a standard household. The scale varies with the level of income.

Estimation of the Model

Suppose there are T households that have been divided into k groups on the basis of their age and sex composition. It is necessary to estimate $(n + 1)$ equations given in (16.4) and (16.5) within each household-composition group so that the intercept term is different in the different groups, whereas the slope has the same value for all the groups. These $(n + 1)$ equations for the jth household group are written as

(16.9) $v_j = \alpha x_j + (1 - \alpha)a_j$

and

(16.10) $v_{ij} = p_i m_{ij}\gamma_i + \beta_i(v_j - a_j)$

where v_j and v_{ij} are the total expenditure and the expenditure on the ith commodity by a household in the jth group, respectively, and

$$a_j = p'\hat{m}_j\gamma = \sum_{i=1}^{n} p_i m_{ij}\gamma_i$$

where m_j is the n-component vector of family-composition parameters for the jth group households. Then a_j can be interpreted as the subsistence expenditure of the jth group households.[2]

Estimates of α and a_j are obtained by applying the least-squares method to equation (16.9). Substituting the estimate of a_j into (16.10) and applying the least-squares method yields the estimates of $p_i m_{ij}\gamma_i$ and β_i. Suppose that δ_{ij} denotes an estimate of $p_i m_{ij}\gamma_i$ for a nonstandard household, and δ_i an estimate of $p_i m_{ij}\gamma_i$ for a standard household. Because, for a standard household, $m_{ij} = 1$ for all i, δ_i will clearly be an estimate of $p_i\gamma_i$. Further, an estimate of m_{ij} for a nonstandard household will be δ_{ij}/δ_i. The fact that estimates of δ_{ij} and δ_i can always be obtained if sufficient observations are available for each group demonstrates that all family-composition parameters can be identified.

The next step is to explore the actual estimation of (16.9) and (16.10). A typical equation representing (16.9) and (16.10) can be written as[3]

(16.11) $$Y_{ij} = \alpha_j + \beta x_{ij} + \epsilon_{ij}$$

where i varies from 1 to T_j, and j varies from 1 to k, T_j being the number of households in the jth household-composition group. Further, ϵ_{ij} is the error term. This equation implies that the intercept term is different in the different household groups, but that the slope has the same value for all the households.

The system (16.11) has $T = \sum_{j=1}^{k} T_j$ equations. Combining these equations and applying the least-squares method of estimation yields the estimates of α_j and β as

(16.12) $$\hat{\alpha}_j = \bar{Y}_j - \hat{\beta}\bar{x}_j$$

---

2. The subsistence expenditure interpretation of ELES is discussed in "Extended Linear Expenditure System" in chapter 9.

3. Note that equation (16.11) is a general form representing (16.9) and (16.10). No attempt has been made to relate the symbols in (16.11) with those in (16.9) and (16.10). In addition, β is a scalar in (16.11) but in (16.4) was defined as a vector. Note that an error term has been added in (16.11) for estimation purposes.

and

$$(16.13) \qquad \hat{\beta} = \frac{\sum\limits_{j=1}^{k} T_j \, \mathrm{cov}(x_j, Y_j)}{\sum\limits_{j=1}^{k} T_j \, \mathrm{var}(x_j)},$$

where var and cov stand for variance and covariance, respectively and are given by

$$\mathrm{var}(x_j) = (1/T_j) \left[\sum_{i=1}^{T_i} (x_{ij} - \bar{x}_j)^2 \right]$$

and

$$\mathrm{cov}(x_j, Y_j) = (1/T_j) \left[\sum_{i=1}^{T_i} (x_{ij} - \bar{x}_j)(Y_{ij} - \bar{Y}_j) \right]$$

where $\bar{x}_j = (1/T_j) \left(\sum\limits_{i=1}^{T_i} x_{ij} \right)$ and $\bar{Y}_j = (1/T_j) \left(\sum\limits_{i=1}^{T_i} Y_{ij} \right)$.

Assume that the error terms have zero means and are contemporaneously uncorrelated across the groups and over observations: that is,

$$E(\epsilon_{ij}) = 0$$

$$(16.14) \qquad E(\epsilon_{ij}\epsilon_{ij}'') = \sigma_{jj} \quad \text{if} \quad i = i' = j = j'$$

$$= 0 \quad \text{otherwise.}$$

Equation (16.14) implies that the error variance is not constant in households with different family compositions. Under these assumptions, the variances of $\hat{\beta}$ and $\hat{\alpha}_j$ are derived as equal to

$$\mathrm{var}(\hat{\beta}) = \frac{\sum\limits_{j=1}^{k} \sigma_{jj} T_j \, \mathrm{var}(x_j)}{\left[\sum\limits_{j=1}^{k} T_j \, \mathrm{var}(x_j) \right]^2}$$

and

$$\mathrm{var}(\hat{\alpha}_j) = \frac{\sigma_{jj}}{T_j} + \mathrm{var}(\hat{\beta}) \bar{x}_j^2,$$

respectively, where $\bar{x}_j = \dfrac{1}{T_j} \sum\limits_{i=1}^{T_i} x_{ij}$, and σ_{jj} is estimated by

$$\hat{\sigma}_{jj} = \text{var}(Y_j) + \hat{\beta}^2 \text{var}(x_j) - 2\hat{\beta} \text{cov}(x_j, Y_j)$$

where $\text{var}(Y_j) = (1/T_j)\left[\sum\limits_{i=1}^{T_i} (Y_{ij} - \bar{Y}_j)^2\right]$.

Because the error-term variance is different in different family-composition groups, the least-squares estimators given in (16.12) and (16.13) cannot be the best linear unbiased estimators (BLUE). The generalized least-squares estimators will, however, be BLUE. If $\tilde{\alpha}_j$ and $\tilde{\beta}$ are denoted as the generalized least-squares estimators, some algebraic manipulations yield

$$\tilde{\beta} = \frac{\sum\limits_{j=1}^{k} \dfrac{T_j \text{cov}(x_j, Y_j)}{\sigma_{jj}}}{\sum\limits_{j=1}^{k} \dfrac{T_j \text{var}(x_j)}{\sigma_{jj}}}$$

$$\tilde{\alpha}_j = \bar{Y}_j - \tilde{\beta}\bar{x}_j,$$

and their variances are given by

$$\text{var}(\tilde{\beta}) = \frac{1}{\sum\limits_{j=1}^{k} \dfrac{T_j \text{var}(x_j)}{\sigma_{jj}}}$$

$$\text{var}(\tilde{\alpha}_j) = \frac{\sigma_{jj}^2}{T_j} + \text{var}(\tilde{\beta})\bar{x}_j^2.$$

Numerical Estimates of Consumer-Unit Scales

This section focuses on the estimation of consumer-unit scales. The source of data is *The Australian Survey of Consumer Expenditures and Finances*, 1966–1968 (Drane and others), a brief description of which was provided in chapter 6.

The data were supplied by the Macquarie University Data Archive Ltd. in the form of a set of individual observations. The income considered is net of taxes but does not include imputed rent from owner-occupied houses.

The 5,459 households were divided into nine family-composition groups, the breakdown of which is:

Family-Composition Groups	Number of Households
1. Families with household head only	520
2. Household head and wife only	1,339
3. Household head, wife, and one child	998
4. Head, wife, and two children	1,199
5. Head, wife, and three children	782
6. Head, wife, and four children	375
7. Head, wife, and five children	141
8. Head, wife, and six children	61
9. All other households	44
	5,459

For the purpose of estimating the expenditure system, the commodity expenditures were divided into nine major groups, the breakdown of which follows.

Consumption-Expenditure Groups	Expenditures
1. Food	Fruit, vegetables (frozen and fresh), meat, fish, poultry, and miscellaneous groceries
2. Tobacco and alcohol	Cigarettes and alcohol
3. Clothing and personal care	Cosmetics, clothing (male and female), bed linen, and general toiletries
4. Durables, minor durables, and household overhead	Furnishings, dwelling, rent, land and water, fuel (gas, electricity), telephone, household repairs (maintenance, extensions, alterations), and property insurance
5. Motor vehicles	Operating and maintenance expenses and overhead costs
6. Medical expenses	Personal accident expenses, hospital, dental, and funeral expenses (less cash reimbursement from medical and hospital funds)
7. Recreation	Entertainment, holiday and travel expenses, food away from home

8. Education   All educational expenses
9. Other goods and   Books, stationery, chemist goods, trans-
   services   portation fares, garden, florist, legal and
                         accounting services, fees, taxes, fines, pri-
                         vate transfers, and other miscellaneous
                         expenses

Table 16.1 gives the estimates of the parameters of the extended linear expenditure system obtained by the two methods of estimation discussed in "Estimation of the Model." The second column provides the marginal budget shares β_i, and the first through the ninth columns give the estimates of $p_i m_{ij} \gamma_i$, the values of which decline as the household size increases.

The family, which consists of the household head, his wife, and two children, is assumed to be a standard family, or the unit of reference. If m_{ij} equals 100 for a standard family group of four, the specific consumer-unit scale is obtained. This scale is presented in table 16.2.

Note that there is a systematic decline in the required per capita expenditure as the household size increases. Here, the required expenditure denotes the per capita expenditure required to guarantee that the same level of utility be enjoyed by the standard household group for every household group.

The inverse relationship between the required per capita expenditure and the household size is clearly observable for every commodity group, with, however, a few exceptions. The required per capita expenditure on tobacco and alcohol, for example, declines from group 1 to group 7 but rises for the succeeding groups. Similarly, the required expenditure on medical expenses is higher for the ninth than for the eighth group.

The per capita expenditure on education declines from the one-member family to the two-member, and then increases when children are added. When the family grows larger than four, the expenditure declines again until the household size equals seven persons. For the eighth household group, it again increases.

The available data are insufficient to provide definitive explanations for such deviations. One reason may be that some of the children in the eighth group are college students who require a higher per capita expenditure on education. The same factor could explain the higher expenditure on tobacco and alcohol.

Because the specific consumer-scale estimates are almost identical

Table 16.1. *Parameter Estimates of the Expenditure System, Australia, 1967*

Item of consumption expenditure	Method of estimation	β_i	Family-composition groups								
			1	2	3	4	5	6	7	8	9
Food	I	0.08918	487.00	438.76	365.35	318.56	279.40	257.95	245.53	243.65	217.96
	II	0.094246	485.33	438.12	364.95	317.85	278.94	257.38	246.02	243.94	218.16
Tobacco and alcohol	I	0.053203	109.69	94.30	73.62	59.05	51.18	42.57	31.31	33.13	35.78
	II	0.045822	105.82	92.81	72.68	57.41	50.11	41.26	30.27	32.53	34.46
Clothing and personal care	I	0.115152	241.52	213.58	171.89	148.14	124.78	107.86	100.96	92.01	81.16
	II	0.121561	239.32	212.74	171.36	147.20	124.18	107.11	101.58	92.36	81.40
Durables, minor durables, and household overhead	I	0.334597	607.56	483.55	372.73	311.54	270.52	217.88	182.10	148.89	127.55
	II	0.34690	599.43	480.43	370.77	308.08	268.28	215.13	183.09	149.47	127.37
Motor vehicles	I	0.084365	122.13	140.56	119.89	101.85	88.53	73.85	59.16	49.3	45.55
	II	0.07928	117.82	138.91	118.86	100.02	87.35	72.38	58.37	48.84	44.37

Medical expenses	I	0.022626	47.58	40.68	36.81	31.51	26.26	23.94	20.15	13.67	18.92
	II	0.016957	45.24	39.78	36.25	30.51	25.62	23.14	19.38	13.22	18.02
Recreation	I	0.171938	259.17	189.60	144.02	123.35	101.32	84.51	72.81	60.27	61.02
	II	0.156682	249.02	185.71	141.58	119.03	98.53	81.08	70.55	58.97	57.95
Education	I	0.014447	13.85	8.78	17.43	20.91	19.57	18.99	17.90	20.77	14.84
	II	0.017781	14.28	8.94	17.53	21.09	19.68	19.14	18.30	21.00	15.22
Other goods and services	I	0.114483	247.58	159.18	124.01	104.74	87.47	78.10	72.63	62.58	59.65
	II	0.095786	238.46	135.77	121.81	100.86	84.97	75.02	70.02	61.10	56.42
Estimate of a subsistence expenditure	I		2136.08	1769.00	1425.74	1219.66	1049.03	905.64	835.79	769.58	704.75
	II		2101.61	1755.78	1417.45	1204.99	1039.56	893.97	828.78	767.41	695.21
Estimate of the marginal propensity to consume	I	0.611975									
	II	0.583686									

Table 16.2. *Estimates of the Specific Scales, Australia, 1967*

Item of consumer expenditure	Method of estimation									
		Family-composition groups								
		1	2	3	4	5	6	7	8	9
Food	I	152.87	137.73	114.69	100.00	87.71	80.97	77.07	76.48	68.42
	II	152.70	137.84	114.82	100.00	87.76	80.98	77.4	76.75	68.64
Tobacco and alcohol	I	185.76	159.70	124.67	100.00	86.67	72.09	53.03	56.1	60.59
	II	184.32	161.66	126.60	100.00	87.28	71.87	52.73	56.66	60.02
Clothing and personal care	I	163.03	144.17	116.03	100.00	84.23	72.81	68.15	62.11	54.79
	II	162.58	144.52	116.41	100.00	84.36	72.76	69.01	62.74	55.30
Durables, minor durables and household overhead	I	195.02	155.21	119.64	100.00	86.83	69.94	58.45	47.79	40.94
	II	194.57	155.94	120.35	100.00	87.08	69.83	59.43	48.52	41.34
Motor vehicles	I	119.91	138.01	117.71	100.00	86.92	72.51	58.09	48.40	44.72
	II	117.80	138.88	118.84	100.00	87.33	72.37	58.36	48.83	44.36
Medical expenses	I	151.00	129.10	116.82	100.00	83.34	75.98	63.95	43.38	60.04
	II	148.28	130.38	118.81	100.00	83.97	75.84	63.52	43.33	59.06
Recreation	I	210.11	153.71	116.76	100.00	82.14	68.51	59.03	48.86	49.47
	II	209.21	156.02	118.94	100.00	82.78	68.12	59.27	49.54	48.68
Education	I	66.24	41.99	83.36	100.00	93.59	90.82	85.60	99.33	70.97
	II	67.71	42.39	83.12	100.00	93.31	90.75	86.77	99.57	72.17
Other goods and services	I	236.38	151.98	118.40	100.00	83.51	74.57	69.34	59.75	56.95
	II	236.43	134.61	120.77	100.00	84.25	74.38	69.42	60.58	55.94

Table 16.3. *Estimated Equivalent Scales, Australia, 1967*

Per capita income level of the standard family (Australian dollars)	Family-composition groups								
	1	2	3	4	5	6	7	8	9
≤1,220	175.12	145.0	116.89	100	85.98	74.26	65.78	59.37	54.30
1,500	176.28	145.36	117.01	100	85.88	73.88	65.15	58.34	53.45
2,000	177.56	145.75	117.14	100	85.76	73.46	64.46	57.21	52.52
2,500	178.32	145.98	117.23	100	85.69	73.21	64.05	56.54	51.96
3,000	178.83	146.14	117.28	100	85.64	73.04	63.78	56.09	51.59
3,500	179.19	146.25	117.32	100	85.61	72.92	63.58	55.77	51.33
4,000	179.46	146.33	117.35	100	85.58	72.83	63.43	55.53	51.13

for the two methods of estimation (see table 16.2), it was decided to estimate the income scale by means of Method I. The income scale was computed by means of equation (16.8); the results are presented in table 16.3, which clearly indicates that, for a family to remain in the same utility level, the required per capita income declines consistently as the family size increases. A one-member family, for example, requires an almost 75 percent higher per capita income than a standard family consisting of a household head, his wife, and two children (the fourth group) in order that the two families enjoy the same level of utility. Further, the variation in income scales is negligible over the wide range of income.

For the first three family-composition groups, the differences in equivalent income scales increase slightly with higher income levels. In contrast, for households between the fifth and the ninth groups, the differences in equivalent scales diminish slightly with higher income levels. Thus it may be concluded that if the size of a family is more than four, additional children with a given income do not diminish the living standard as much as if the family existed at a lower level of income. If, however, the family size is less than four, a reduction in the standard of living will, with additional children, be higher than at higher levels of income.

Measurement of Income Inequality

This section concerns the effect of family composition on income inequality. Equation (16.8) was used to convert the income of every nonstandard household into the equivalent income of a standard household, while the two households enjoy the same level of utility. In this way, the per capita income of a standard family, corresponding to a given level of per capita household income, was obtained. This new income series is referred to as adjusted income.

Table 16.4 presents the shares of deciles and the top 5 and 1 percent of households in per capita disposable income and per capita adjusted disposable income. The shares are calculated by ranking the families according to the respective sizes of these variables.

When the families are ranked according to the size of their per capita disposable incomes, the bottom 20 percent of households receive 8.1 percent of the total income, whereas the top 20 percent receive 41.28 percent. The ranking of families according to the size

Table 16.4. *Decile Shares of per Capita Disposable Income When Families Are Ranked by Size of per Capita Disposable Income and per Capita Adjusted Income, Respectively, Australia, 1967*

	Percentage of per capita disposable income	Percentage of per capita adjusted income
1st decile	3.26	3.43
2nd decile	4.84	5.09
3rd decile	5.58	6.27
4th decile	6.40	7.22
5th decile	6.77	8.17
6th decile	8.72	9.33
7th decile	10.16	10.64
8th decile	12.27	12.35
9th decile	15.43	14.65
10th decile	25.85	22.85
Top 5 percent	16.09	14.06
Top 1 percent	5.83	5.10
Mean	A$1,207.86	A$1,041.47
Gini index	0.3312	0.2902

of their per capita adjusted incomes shows that the bottom 20 percent receive 8.5 percent of the total income, whereas the top 20 percent receive only 37.5 percent.

Figure 10 presents the Lorenz curves of per capita disposable income and per capita adjusted income. The latter is uniformly higher than the former. It can be concluded, therefore, that if the effect of family composition is considered, the resulting income distribution becomes more equal than the distribution of unadjusted money income. The Gini index was computed for both incomes by means of the following formula, which relates to individual observations:

$$ G = \frac{2}{(T-1)} \sum_{t=1}^{T} t y_t - \frac{(T+1)}{(T-1)} $$

where y_t is the proportional share in income of the tth family. The computed values of the Gini index are reported in the last row of table 16.4. When family composition is taken into account, these values indicate that there is approximately a 12 percent reduction in income inequality.

Figure 10. *Lorenz Curve of per Capita Disposable Income and per Capita Adjusted Income*

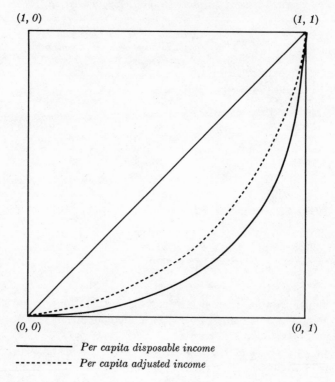

(1, 0)   *(1, 1)*

(0, 0)   *(0, 1)*

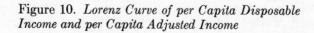

———————— *Per capita disposable income*

----------- *Per capita adjusted income*

Poverty

In this section the poverty line of a standard family will be defined. The poverty line of households of any family composition can then be established by means of the consumer-unit scale.

Assume that the poverty line for a standard family in 1966 consisted of the basic wage plus child endowment. This amounted to $32.50 a week. The round figure of $33. a week, therefore, represents the poverty line.[4] The poverty lines of households belonging to other family-composition groups were computed by means of equation (16.8). The levels are reported in the second column of table 16.5

---

4. This definition of the poverty line was adopted by Henderson, Harcourt, and Harper (1970) in order to count people with low incomes in Melbourne in 1966.

Table 16.5. *Measurement of Poverty after Correcting for Family-Composition Effect, Australia, 1967*

Family-composition group	Poverty level per capita (Australian dollars)	Percentage of families living in poverty	Percentage of poor by family-composition group	Population living in poverty	Mean per capita adjusted income of poor (Australian dollars)	Per capita disposable income of poor (Australian dollars)	Per capita poverty gap level (Australian dollars)	Cost of eliminating poverty (millions of Australian dollars)
1	751	36.54	16.74	118,687	370.61	649.06	101.94	12.1
2	622	12.47	29.43	208,659	370.43	537.27	84.73	17.7
3	501	3.12	8.19	58,067	294.84	344.66	156.35	9.1
4	429	4.50	19.03	134,923	272.21	272.21	156.79	21.1
5	369	3.71	12.77	90,539	277.76	238.9	130.10	11.8
6	319	1.86	3.70	26,233	332.99	247.26	71.75	1.9
7	282	6.38	5.55	39,349	380.84	250.6	31.4	1.2
8	255	3.28	1.41	9,997	290.81	172.69	82.31	.8
9	233	9.09	3.17	22,475	330.40	179.45	53.55	1.2
Total		9.03	100	709,000	348.54	377.96	108.5	76.9

Note: Percentage of persons living in poverty is 6.0.

in terms of the annual per capita disposable income (1966–67 Australian dollars). The percentage of families living in poverty is given in the third column, which shows that about 9 percent of the families are poor.

One-person families show the largest percentage of poor—as much as 36.54 percent. Next come two-person families, with a percentage of poor of 12.47 percent. Families with nine or more members have about 9.09 percent poor. The fourth column gives the percentage of poor in each family-composition group, and the fifth column gives the actual number of poor. Of a total population of about 12.5 million, 709,000 people live in poverty, that is, about 6 percent of the population. The mean per capita adjusted income of the poor is presented in column 6, and the per capita disposable income in column 7. Note that although the first family-composition group has the highest percentage of poor, their mean per capita adjusted income is not the lowest. The lowest mean income is, in fact, in the fifth group, consisting of households with a head, his wife, and three children. The per capita disposable income of the poor is reported in the seventh column, and the eighth column gives the per capita poverty gap, which is $108.5 for the whole nation and highest among household groups 3 and 4. Further, among one-member families, the per capita poverty gap is less than the national average. The last column gives the cost of eliminating poverty, that is, $76.9 million.

Further Analysis of Poverty

This section focuses on the results of a breakdown of aggregate poverty according to certain socioeconomic and demographic characteristics of households. Detailed computations are presented in tables 16.6 to 16.13, the formats of which are identical. There are six columns. The first column gives the percentage of families living in poverty, and the second column the percentage of individuals living in poverty. The average per capita adjusted disposable income (1966–67 Australian dollars) for the entire population of each group is presented in the third column, whereas the fourth column gives the average per capita adjusted income of only the poor. The fifth column presents the per capita poverty gap, obtained by subtracting each figure in column 4 from the common poverty level of $429 (1967 Australian dollars). The last column gives the computed

(*text continues on page 377*)

Table 16.6. *Poverty Analysis of Australia by Sex of Household Head, 1967*

Group	Percentage of families living in poverty	Percentage of population living in poverty	Per capita adjusted disposable income (Australian dollars)	Per capita adjusted disposable income of poor (Australian dollars)	Per capita poverty gap (Australian dollars)	Poverty index
Male	5.70	4.42	1,073	343	86	0.0035
Female	30.62	25.92	837	356	73	0.0227
Total	9.07	6.05	1,041			

Table 16.7. *Poverty Analysis of Australia by Marital Status of Household Head, 1967*

Group	Percentage of families living in poverty	Percentage of population living in poverty	Per capita adjusted disposable income (Australian dollars)	Per capita adjusted disposable income of poor (Australian dollars)	Per capita poverty gap (Australian dollars)	Poverty index
Never married	12.06	9.55	1,303	339	90	0.0066
Presently married	5.23	4.26	1,059	346	83	0.0033
Widowed, divorced, and separated	31.49	25.89	831	354	75	0.0235
Total	9.07	6.05	1,041	349	80	0.0046

Table 16.8. *Poverty Analysis of Australia by Age of Household Head, 1967*

Age	Percentage of families living in poverty	Percentage of population living in poverty	Per capita adjusted disposable income (Australian dollars)	Per capita adjusted disposable income of poor (Australian dollars)	Per capita poverty gap (Australian dollars)	Poverty index
Under 25 years	5.19	5.41	1,016	294	135	0.0072
25–29 years	4.35	4.67	1,056	307	122	0.0054
30–34 years	3.64	4.51	934	340	89	0.0043
35–39 years	3.46	4.07	1,055	305	123	0.0048
40–44 years	4.26	3.66	1,045	274	155	0.0054
45–49 years	4.25	3.73	1,173	275	154	0.0049
50–54 years	3.72	3.36	1,188	287	142	0.0040
55–59 years	6.67	4.22	1,219	333	96	0.0033
60–69 years	20.41	14.30	1,002	372	57	0.0081
Over 69 years	38.95	31.96	704	382	47	0.0213
Total	9.07	6.05	1,041	349	80	0.0046

Table 16.9. *Poverty Analysis of Australia by Educational Level of Household Head, 1967*

Education level	Percentage of families living in poverty	Percentage of population living in poverty	Per capita adjusted disposable income (Australian dollars)	Per capita adjusted disposable income of poor (Australian dollars)	Per capita poverty gap (Australian dollars)	Poverty index
No formal education or education to primary level	21.10	12.82	841	367	62	0.0094
Incomplete secondary (not completed to 3rd-year level)	10.19	7.15	926	355	74	0.0057
Incomplete secondary (completed 3rd-year level)	4.82	3.77	1,028	328	101	0.0037
Complete secondary and incomplete tertiary	4.47	3.11	1,226	267	162	0.0040
Complete tertiary for standard professions	5.05	4.95	1,908	396	33	0.0008
Complete general tertiary	3.28	2.69	1,709	213	216	0.0034
Technical (diploma) for nonstandard professions	2.00	1.45	1,272	293	136	0.0015
Technical for trades and crafts	3.50	4.37	1,026	343	86	0.0037
Total	9.07	6.05	1,041	349	80	0.0046

Table 16.10. *Poverty Analysis of Australia by Occupation of Household Head, 1967*

Occupation	Percentage of families living in poverty	Percentage of population living in poverty	Per capita adjusted disposable income (Australian dollars)	Per capita adjusted disposable income of poor (Australian dollars)	Per capita poverty gap (Australian dollars)	Poverty index
Executive and managerial	0.80	0.89	1,500	259	170	0.0010
Professional	0.68	0.63	1,624	214	214	0.0008
Vocational and semi-professional	2.68	3.15	1,313	285	144	0.0034
Clerical	3.30	3.55	1,129	251	178	0.0056
Sales	1.60	1.19	1,092	356	73	0.0007
Craftsmen and technical	2.72	2.87	1,034	259	170	0.0047
Semi-skilled	3.14	2.99	943	317	112	0.0035
Laborers, farmers, and unskilled	5.25	6.57	918	294	135	0.0096
Not in work force	36.37	30.09	729	371	58	0.0238
Total	9.07	6.05	1,041	349	80	0.0046

Table 16.11. *Poverty Analysis of Australia by Industry, 1967*

Industry	Percentage of families living in poverty	Percentage of population living in poverty	Per capita adjusted disposable income (Australian dollars)	Per capita adjusted disposable income of poor (Australian dollars)	Per capita poverty gap (Australian dollars)	Poverty index
Manufacturing	3.05	3.13	1,079	298	131	0.0038
Electricity, gas, water	2.29	2.43	1,027	189	240	0.0057
Transport and storage	1.75	1.78	1,031	317	112	0.0019
Finance and property	1.70	1.76	1,294	365	64	0.0009
Commerce	2.40	2.42	1,111	345	84	0.0018
Government	1.82	2.29	1,115	321	108	0.0022
Commerce and business	2.44	2.49	1,400	200	229	0.0041
Entertainment	6.51	7.94	1,057	350	79	0.0060
Other industries	6.70	8.42	1,139	193	236	0.0174
Not in work force	36.37	30.09	729	371	58	0.0238
Total	9.07	6.05	1,041	349	80	0.0046

Table 16.12. Poverty Analysis of Australia by Country of Birth of Household Head, 1967

Country of birth	Percentage of families living in poverty	Percentage of population living in poverty	Per capita adjusted disposable income (Australian dollars)	Per capita adjusted disposable income of poor (Australian dollars)	Per capita poverty gap (Australian dollars)	Poverty index
Australia and New Zealand	9.16	6.02	1,039	358	71	0.0041
Great Britain and Ireland	12.69	8.70	992	336	93	0.0081
Italy	3.29	2.06	920	306	123	0.0027
Greece and Southern Europe	6.12	7.36	919	249	180	0.0144
Netherlands and Scandinavia	5.94	5.10	1,082	266	163	0.0077
Germany and Western Europe	4.71	3.99	1,153	364	65	0.0022
Eastern Europe	3.59	2.00	1,239	289	140	0.0023
Asia	6.38	5.95	1,264	188	241	0.0113
Other countries	9.09	5.33	1,268	323	106	0.0044
Total	9.07	6.05	1,041	349	80	0.0046

Table 16.13. *Poverty Analysis of Australia by Length of Residence of Household Head, 1967*

Length of residence	Percentage of families living in poverty	Percentage of population living in poverty	Per capita adjusted disposable income (Australian dollars)	Per capita adjusted disposable income of poor (Australian dollars)	Per capita poverty gap (Australian dollars)	Poverty index
Born in Australia and New Zealand	9.16	6.02	1,039	358	71	0.0041
Under three years	19.67	20.22	918	245	184	0.0404
Three–four years	1.85	1.40	1,037	260	169	0.0023
Five–nine years	3.94	3.37	958	167	262	0.0092
Ten–thirteen years	4.09	3.38	1,026	313	116	0.0038
Fourteen–sixteen years	3.80	3.10	1,047	340	89	0.0026
Seventeen–twenty-one years	3.28	2.56	1,154	266	163	0.0036
Over twenty-one years	22.36	14.34	1,066	377	52	0.0070
Total	9.07	6.05	1,041	349	80	0.0046

values of the poverty index P, which was discussed in chapter 15. This index is obtained by multiplying column 2 by column 6, and dividing the result by column 4; it is interpreted as the percentage of the per capita adjusted income that must be transferred from rich to poor in order to eliminate poverty altogether. The poverty index P is computed at 0.0046 for the entire population, implying that only 0.46 percent of the adjusted per capita income must be transferred from the nonpoor to the poor in order to eliminate poverty in Australia.

Tables 16.6 to 16.13 show that in almost all the groups, the percentage of families living in poverty is lower than the percentage of individuals living in poverty. This indicates that the incidence of poverty is higher among small families than among large families.

Table 16.6 gives a breakdown of the households according to the sex of the household head. The result clearly shows that households headed by females are subject to a considerably higher incidence of poverty than those headed by males. The ratio of the two poverty indexes is about six, clearly indicating that women are almost certainly more susceptible to poverty than men.

The breakdown of the population according to the marital status of the household head is presented in table 16.7. It can be seen that married households have the least poverty, and that poverty among widowed, divorced, or separated individuals is significantly higher than that of the other two groups. More than 31 percent of such households live in poverty, a fact that casts doubt on the effectiveness of the present pension scheme for widowed persons.

Next, the decomposition of poverty according to the age of the household head is considered. Table 16.8 clearly indicates a high incidence of poverty among households where the age of the head is sixty years or more. The poverty among households where the age of the head is less than twenty-five years is also considerably higher than the national level. In addition, the per capita poverty gap among older households is considerably lower than that among younger households, which shows that poverty among older households can be eliminated without much cost to society. There does not appear to be a wide variation in incidence among the other age groups.

The decomposition of poverty according to the educational level of the household head is presented in table 16.9, which shows that the incidence of poverty is considerably high among households whose heads have had no formal education. The proportion of poor in this group is about 21 percent compared to 9 percent for the whole of Australia.

Table 16.10 concerns the decomposition of total poverty according to the occupation of the household head. Note that households headed by executives and managers, tertiary qualified professionals, technicians, and salesmen have relatively little poverty. In contrast, households whose heads are not in the work force have considerable poverty; about 36 percent of such households are living in poverty, and these have the lowest per capita poverty gap. This means that poverty among unemployed households can be removed without much cost to the society. Households headed by laborers, unskilled workers, self-employed workers, and farmers also show a high incidence of poverty. In this group, the percentage of individuals living in poverty (6.57 percent) is slightly higher than the percentage of households in poverty (5.25 percent). These percentages imply that the poor households in this group have a larger average size than the nonpoor households.

The distribution of poverty across broad industries (table 16.11) shows that the maximum concentration of poverty occurs among the households whose heads are not in the work force. The next group, "other industries," has a very high per capita poverty gap. There is not much variation in the incidence of poverty in the remaining groups of industries.

The distribution of poverty according to the country of birth of the household head is presented in table 16.12. Greeks and Southern Europeans appear to have a slightly higher incidence, but the overall variation of poverty is small among all groups. The percentage of Greek and Southern European families living in poverty is lower than the percentage of individuals in poverty, which may imply that the higher incidence of poverty in this group is due to large family size.

Table 16.13 focuses on the distribution of poverty according to the length of residence of the household head in Australia. It is clearly indicated that severe poverty exists among migrants who have lived less than three years in the country. This finding is important from a policy point of view; obviously, too little help is offered new migrants from the outset. Those who have lived in Australia for more than twenty-one years also have a high incidence of poverty, perhaps because of age. After twenty-one years in Australia, many migrants have reached their sixties and are, therefore, more susceptible to poverty.

CHAPTER 17

An International Comparison of
Income Inequality and Poverty

THIS CHAPTER provides an international comparison of income inequality and poverty, based on income distribution data from fifty countries. Particular attention is given to the relationship between economic growth and distribution of income by size. The skewness of the Lorenz curve is used to test Kuznets' hypothesis regarding income shares in developed and developing countries.

In the cross-country comparisons of poverty, the developed countries have been excluded. The investigation is limited to highlighting the extent of world poverty and isolating the regions of acute poverty. The poverty indexes discussed in chapter 15 are used to determine the influences of different countries or regions on world poverty.

Size Distribution of Income with Respect to Level of Development: A Review of the Literature

The search for a pattern in changes in income distribution during the course of a country's economic growth was begun by Kuznets in 1955 in his classic article, "Economic Growth and Income Inequality." His empirical investigations for three advanced countries, the United States, the United Kingdom, and Germany, indicated that "the distribution of income, as measured by annual income incidence in rather broad classes, has been moving towards equality with these trends particularly noticeable since the 1920s, but beginning perhaps in the period before the World War." In this paper, Kuznets examined income distribution in a cross-section of countries at different levels of development. Comparing five countries—India, Sri Lanka, Puerto Rico, the United Kingdom, and the United States—he concluded that income distribution in developing countries is somewhat more unequal than in the developed countries, and that the greater inequality in developing countries was primarily a result of a high concentration of income in the top income group. The share of the lower income groups was larger in the developing countries than in the developed countries, according to his findings. This means that people in intermediate income groups in developing countries have a much smaller share of the total income than those in the same groups in developed countries.

Using the same data, Kuznets further hypothesized that "in the early phases of industrialization in the underdeveloped countries, income inequality will tend to widen before the leveling forces become strong enough first to stabilize and then reduce income inequalities." This hypothesis is now popularly known as an "inverted U-shaped pattern of income inequality," [1] the inequality first increasing and then decreasing with development.

Kravis (1960) and Oshima (1962) continued the debate on the relationship between income inequality and economic growth initiated by Kuznets. Using income distribution data of the early fifties from ten countries, Kravis confirmed the Kuznets hypothesis of greater inequality in developing countries than in developed ones. He also concluded that inequality in developing countries was principally a result of the high concentration of income in the top income brackets. Oshima, however, expressed reservations about the conclusions of Kravis, because, he concluded, it is difficult to generalize about intercountry patterns in view of the vast historical, physical, regional, political, racial, and religious differences.

Kuznets returned to the debate in 1963 with a large supply of empirical evidence. Using data based on twenty distributions for eighteen countries, he again concluded that the shares of the upper income groups are distinctly larger in developing countries than in developed countries, and that the top 5 percent of families, or spending units, in most developing countries receive 30 percent of the total income or more, whereas the shares in the developed countries range from 20 to 25 percent. His conclusion regarding the shares of

1. See Ahluwalia (1974), Adelman and Morris (1971), and Chenery and Syrquin (1975).

the lower income groups differed from his 1955 results. He observed that the shares of income of the lowest 40 to 60 percent of families did not differ significantly between developing and developed countries. It still held, however, that the share of the middle income group was smaller in the developing than in the developed countries.

A number of important studies were subsequently made, among which are those of Adelman and Morris (1971), Paukert (1973), and Ahluwalia (1974). Adelman and Morris compiled data on the size distribution of income for forty-four countries. Using a stepwise analysis of variance technique, they were able to identify at least six factors that have the most significant effect on income distribution. These findings were questioned by Paukert on two accounts. First, he attacked the method of analysis of variance used and contended that other important factors influencing income distribution were overshadowed by the six factors. Second, he criticized the data and some of the computations used by Adelman and Morris. By means of an improved method of estimation, and adding information for twelve additional countries, Paukert presented income distribution data for fifty-six countries. These data supported the hypotheses proposed by Kuznets.

In his calculations of quintile shares, Paukert assumed that lower and middle incomes are lognormally distributed. Although superior to the straightforward pro rata allocation used by Adelman and Morris, this method is not entirely satisfactory because the lognormal distribution performs poorly toward the tails. In this section, the new coordinate system for the Lorenz curve is used to calculate the quintile shares; this system has been shown to produce results with a sufficient degree of precision.

In 1976 Ahluwalia reexamined the empirical basis of the inverted U-shaped pattern of the secular behavior of income inequality. His investigation was based on distributions for sixty-two countries; the multiple regression technique was used to identify the relationship between income inequality and the level of development, units of observations being the countries. He observed a statistically significant relationship between income shares and the logarithms of per capita GNP for both the upper income groups (top 20 percent) and lower income groups (lowest 60 and 40 percent). In this relationship, the logarithm of income entered in quadratic form, and, as a result, generated an inverted U-shaped curve. This seems to support Kuznets' hypothesis about the course of inequality over development. In view of the considerable importance of this problem, the next section focuses on an alternative empirical approach to test Kuznets' hypothesis, an approach based on the skewness of the Lorenz curves already discussed in considerable detail in chapters 3 and 7.

Kuznets' Hypothesis and the Skewness of the Lorenz Curve

In chapter 3 the symmetry of the Lorenz curve with respect to the diagonal perpendicular to the egalitarian line was defined. If the Lorenz curve is not symmetric, it is skewed either toward (0, 0) or toward (1, 1). It is demonstrated below that Kuznets' hypothesis about income shares can be tested by examining the skewness of the Lorenz curve. To that end, consider figure 11, which contains two Lorenz curves corresponding to income distributions I and II. These curves are clearly not symmetric with respect to the diagonal AC. Lorenz curve I is skewed toward (0, 0), whereas Lorenz curve II is skewed toward (1, 1).

Compare the shares of the lower income group (say, the bottom 20 percent units) under two income distributions. Obviously, the income share of this group is larger with Lorenz curve I than with Lorenz curve II. Similarly, comparing the shares of the upper income group (say, the top 20 percent units) under two income distributions indicates that with Lorenz curve I, this share is represented by the length BG, whereas with Lorenz curve II the share is given by BH. The share of the upper income group is, therefore, clearly larger with Lorenz curve I than with Lorenz curve II. It follows, then, that the intermediate group has a smaller income share with a Lorenz curve that is skewed toward (0, 0) than with a Lorenz curve skewed toward (1, 1), and that this group has a relatively larger share compared to the shares of the lower and upper income groups with a Lorenz curve skewed toward (1, 1).

To recapitulate, Kuznets hypothesized that as a country develops, the share of the intermediate income group increases. This implies that in the course of economic development, the Lorenz curve changes its shape with respect to its skewness from (0, 0) toward (1, 1). If two countries have Lorenz curves both skewed toward (0, 0), the one with a higher degree of skewness will obviously be less developed. In contrast, if both Lorenz curves are skewed toward (1, 1), the one with a higher degree of skewness will be more de-

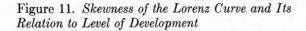

Figure 11. *Skewness of the Lorenz Curve and Its Relation to Level of Development*

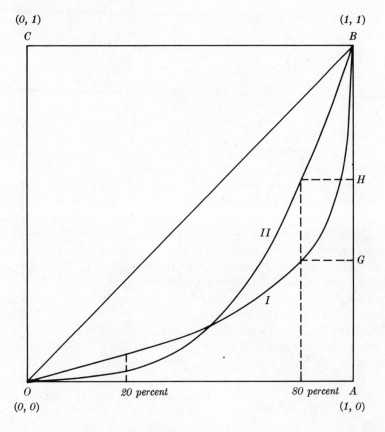

veloped. In the context of the present discussion, Kuznets' hypothesis will be sufficiently established if it can be shown that the Lorenz curves for the developing countries are, in general, skewed toward (0, 0), whereas the Lorenz curves for the developed countries are skewed toward (1, 1).

To measure the degree of skewness of a Lorenz curve, the equation

(17.1) $$\eta = a\pi^\alpha(\sqrt{2} - \pi)^\beta$$

can be fitted in the new coordinate system introduced in chapter 7. The Lorenz curve is symmetric if $\alpha = \beta$, skewed toward (0, 0) if $\alpha > \beta$, and skewed toward (1, 1) if $\alpha < \beta$. Thus the deviation of

α/β from unity can be conveniently used to measure the skewness of the Lorenz curve toward $(0, 0)$ or $(1, 1)$. If $(\alpha/\beta - 1)$ is positive (negative), the curve is skewed toward $(0, 0)$ (toward $[1, 1]$).

Intercountry Comparison of Income Inequality

What follows is an examination of the structures of income distributions for fifty countries at different stages of development indicated by their per capita incomes. The data are from a compilation of Jain (1975), who gave definitions of income and of units receiving income. Data on the per capita Gross Domestic Product (GDP) for 1970 were taken from the World Bank's data files.

There are several difficulties associated with an international comparison of income distributions, the data of which are generally subject to large errors, whose magnitude differs from country to country. In addition, the reliability of data and the definitions of income and income units are problematic. These have been widely discussed elsewhere.[2] Unavoidably, then, conclusions from international comparisons have severe limitations.

The data on the size distribution of income were, in most cases, available in the form of a frequency distribution, giving (a) the number of units with incomes in different ranges and (b) the total income in each range. Because the income ranges varied from one source to another, the distributions were not directly comparable in their original form. To ensure comparability, data were transformed into estimates of income shares accruing to different quintiles of the population. These estimates were obtained by fitting the equation of the new coordinate system of the Lorenz curve as given in (17.1). The parameters a, α, and β were estimated by using the ordinary least-squares method after transforming (17.1) into logarithms. The estimated parameter values are reported in table 17.1. The last column of the table gives the coefficient of determination (R^2), which is the correlation between the actual and estimated value of η. It can be seen that these values of R^2 are consistently high for all countries. The actual and estimated values of η, though

2. See Kuznets (1955), Titmuss (1962), Adelman and Morris (1971), and Kravis (1960).

not reported here, were very close, up to at least two decimal places. From these observations, it may be concluded that the density function underlying the new coordinate system for the Lorenz curve provides a good fit to a wide range of income distributions observed in different countries.

The relevant fractile shares, as well as the values of the Gini index and of α/β for fifty countries, are presented in table 17.2. A number of interesting findings emerge from the numerical results given in this table.

The results show considerable differences among countries with respect to the degree of income inequality, which is markedly higher in the countries reported for Africa and Latin America than elsewhere. In African countries the value of the Gini index varies from 0.446 to 0.612, with two exceptions, Chad and Uganda, where the Gini indexes are 0.369 and 0.401, respectively. The average of the Gini indexes for the ten African countries is 0.487. The countries of Latin America show still higher inequality with the average of the Gini indexes at 0.515. Among these countries the income inequality is lowest in Costa Rica and highest in Venezuela. Asian countries show a significantly lower inequality than other developing countries. The average of the Gini indexes for these countries is 0.407. In contrast, developed countries have the lowest average Gini indexes of 0.380, with France having the highest inequality of 0.518. Although these results tend to confirm Kuznets' hypothesis of greater inequality in developing countries, the differences in income inequality between the Asian and the developed countries are narrow and may be insignificant.

The second observation concerns the skewness of the Lorenz curves. The ratio α/β is greater than unity for all the developing countries, with the exception of Barbados. For most developed countries this ratio is less than unity with only two exceptions, Greece and Spain. Obviously, for the developing countries the Lorenz curves are skewed toward (0, 0), whereas for the developed countries they are skewed toward (1, 1). This observation supports Kuznets' hypothesis that the income share of the middle group is higher in the developed than in the developing countries.

Now consider the actual income shares accruing to different groups. The share of the upper income groups (top 20 percent) is distinctly larger in the developing countries than in the developed countries. This share is, in general, larger in Latin American coun-

Table 17.1. *Parameter Estimates of the New Coordinate System for the Lorenz Curve for Fifty Countries*

Country	Year	Population	GDP per capita, 1970 (U.S. dollars)	a	α	β	R^2
Asia							
Indonesia	1971	Income recipients	101	0.342	0.843	0.488	0.996
India	1964/65	Income recipients	98	0.368	0.820	0.606	0.998
Pakistan	1970/71	Households	–	0.295	0.887	0.770	0.999
Malaysia	1970	Per capita	353	0.458	0.893	0.795	0.999
Sri Lanka	1969/70	Households	174	0.370	0.974	0.869	0.999
Hong Kong	1971	Households	745	0.386	0.879	0.786	0.998
Korea	1971	Households	260	0.323	0.867	0.797	0.999
Taiwan	1964	Households	–	0.282	0.817	0.754	0.999
Philippines	1971	Households	259	0.478	0.915	0.897	0.999
Thailand	1970	Households (urban)	183	0.377	0.924	0.912	0.998
South Vietnam	1964	Households	235	0.304	0.832	0.823	0.999
Africa							
Madagascar	1960	Population	–	0.473	0.949	0.624	0.996
Ivory Coast	1959	Population	347	0.373	0.893	0.615	0.990
Dahomey	1959	Population	–	0.353	0.792	0.554	0.995
Malawi	1969	Households	74	0.411	0.913	0.715	0.999
Chad	1958	Population	–	0.315	0.878	0.701	0.988
Tanzania	1967	Households	100	0.458	0.945	0.756	0.995
Senegal	1960	Population	217	0.569	0.969	0.851	0.996
Uganda	1970	African male	135	0.369	0.888	0.829	0.999
Sierre Leone	1968/69	Households	177	0.551	0.847	0.821	0.998
Sudan	1963	Households	117	0.438	0.928	0.913	0.999

Latin America

Argentina	1961	Households	1,078	0.395	0.964	0.730	0.993
Chile	1968	Households	684	0.466	0.939	0.780	0.999
Venezuela	1971	Economically active population	999	0.606	0.977	0.853	0.998
Costa Rica	1971	Per capita	544	0.452	0.941	0.839	0.999
Colombia	1970	Economically active population	409	0.557	0.984	0.905	0.999
Brazil	1970	Households	391	0.576	0.978	0.911	0.999
Mexico	1967/68	Households	682	0.501	0.930	0.861	0.999
Dominican Rep.	1969	Households	363	0.473	0.929	0.868	0.999
Panama	1969	Economically active population	731	0.533	0.925	0.868	0.999
El Salvador	1965/67	Population	291	0.537	0.950	0.921	0.998
Ecuador	1968	Households (urban)	269	0.531	0.959	0.940	0.999
Barbados	1969/70	Economically active population	639	0.352	0.733	0.763	0.991

Developed Countries

United States	1970	Per capita	4,747	0.284	0.769	0.847	0.996
Sweden	1963	Income recipients	4,090	0.368	0.807	0.879	0.993
Canada	1965	Households	3,874	0.301	0.805	0.871	0.998
Denmark	1963	Income recipients	3,170	0.343	0.792	0.849	0.997
Germany, Fed. Rep. of	1969	Households	3,049	0.315	0.848	0.912	0.998
Australia	1967/68	Households	2,932	0.274	0.763	0.818	0.998
Norway	1963	Income recipients	2,932	0.299	0.686	0.819	0.998
France	1962	Households	2,889	0.418	0.838	0.893	0.996
Netherlands	1967	Income recipients	2,408	0.397	0.811	0.822	0.994
Finland	1962	Income recipients	2,213	0.426	0.792	0.881	0.996
New Zealand	1970/71	Income recipients	2,195	0.320	0.739	0.852	0.990
United Kingdom	1968	Households	2,139	0.315	0.828	0.910	0.995
Japan	1968	Households	1,911	0.330	0.733	0.796	0.999
Greece	1957/58	Households	1,094	0.342	0.848	0.812	0.999
Hungary	1967	Population	1,037	0.202	0.664	0.791	0.999
Yugoslavia	1968	Households	-	0.315	0.823	0.862	0.999
Spain	1964/65	Households	957	0.364	0.870	0.854	0.997

Table 17.2. *Income Shares, Gini Index, and a Measure of Skewness of the Lorenz Curve in Fifty Countries*

Country	Income share of bottom 40 percent	Income share of middle 40 percent	Income share of top 20 percent	Gini index	α/β
Asia					
Indonesia	17.3	30.7	52.0	0.462	1.725
India	15.5	32.6	51.9	0.467	1.352
Pakistan	20.6	37.9	41.5	0.33	1.152
Malaysia	12.4	32.6	55.0	0.504	1.123
Sri Lanka	17.9	36.5	45.6	0.378	1.121
Hong Kong	15.6	35.4	49.0	0.430	1.118
Korea	18.7	37.9	43.4	0.360	1.088
Taiwan	20.3	38.9	40.8	0.329	1.084
Philippines	11.9	34.1	54.0	0.494	1.020
Thailand	16.8	38.0	45.2	0.385	1.014
South Vietnam	19.2	39.5	41.3	0.340	1.010
Average	(16.9)	(35.8)	(47.2)	(0.407)	
Africa					
Madagascar	13.0	26.9	60.1	0.562	1.520
Ivory Coast	16.5	31.7	51.8	0.456	1.453
Dahomey	15.8	32.5	51.7	0.467	1.428
Malawi	15.0	32.1	52.9	0.470	1.277
Chad	19.3	35.9	44.8	0.369	1.253
Tanzania	13.5	30.8	55.7	0.503	1.25
Senegal	9.4	28.1	62.5	0.587	1.139
Uganda	16.6	36.8	46.6	0.401	1.071
Sierre Leone	7.2	30.0	62.8	0.612	1.031
Sudan	13.9	36.0	50.1	0.446	1.016
Average	(14.02)	(32.08)	(53.9)	(0.487)	
Latin America					
Argentina	16.6	32.5	50.9	0.437	1.321
Chile	13.0	31.2	55.8	0.506	1.203
Venezuela	8.2	26.4	65.4	0.622	1.146
Costa Rica	13.6	33.2	53.2	0.416	1.122
Colombia	10.1	29.8	60.1	0.557	1.088
Brazil	9.2	29.3	61.5	0.574	1.074
Mexico	11.2	31.9	56.9	0.524	1.081
Dominican Rep.	12.4	33.3	54.3	0.493	1.071
Panama	9.8	30.8	59.4	0.557	1.066
El Salvador	10.1	31.8	58.1	0.539	1.031
Ecuador	10.5	32.3	57.1	0.526	1.021
Barbados	14.7	38.4	46.9	0.426	0.960
Average	(11.6)	(31.7)	(56.6)	(0.515)	

Table 17.2 (*Continued*)

Country	Income share of bottom 40 percent	Income share of middle 40 percent	Income share of top 20 percent	Gini index	α/β
Developed Countries					
United States	19.5	41.4	39.1		
Sweden	16.0	39.5	43.3	0.406	0.918
Canada	19.0	41.0	40.0	0.333	0.924
Denmark	16.3	39.7	44.0	0.386	0.932
Germany, Fed. Rep. of	18.9	40.8	40.3	0.334	0.930
Australia	20.0	41.1	38.9	0.318	0.933
Norway	17.1	41.9	41.0	0.362	0.838
France	10.0	35.3	54.7	0.518	0.939
Netherlands	13.7	37.0	49.3	0.449	0.987
Finland	11.7	37.9	50.4	0.473	0.899
New Zealand	16.7	41.3	42.0	0.371	0.867
United Kingdom	18.5	41.2	40.3	0.362	0.838
Japan	16.0	39.9	44.1	0.393	0.921
Greece	17.4	37.9	44.7	0.381	1.045
Hungary	23.7	42.7	33.6	0.251	0.839
Yugoslavia	18.4	40.2	41.4	0.347	0.955
Spain	16.5	38.0	45.5	0.393	1.019
Average	(17.0)	(39.8)	(43.1)	(0.380)	

tries, with an average of 56.6 percent. In the African countries, the average is 53.9 percent, whereas in Asian countries it is 47.2 percent. In the developed countries the same group has the lowest average share of 43.1 percent. These results are clearly in agreement with Kuznets' hypothesis about the shares of upper income groups.

With respect to the share of the bottom income group (bottom 40 percent), the differences between the Asian and the developed countries do not appear significant. The share is considerably lower in African and Latin American countries. From these observations, it is difficult to determine whether the lower income group receives higher, lower, or even equal shares in the developing countries in comparison with the developed countries.

The income share of the intermediate group, that is, from the 40th to the 80th percentile, is appreciably larger in the developed than in the developing countries. This fact corresponds to the earlier observation that the Lorenz curves for developed countries are skewed toward (1, 1).

An International Comparison of Poverty

In order to make an international comparison of poverty, it is necessary to specify the poverty line for each country. Ideally, this should be determined by the socially accepted minimal standard of living of a society. Because the scope of this study is necessarily limited, a single, somewhat arbitrarily determined, subsistence income will represent the poverty line for all countries. This subsistence income is set at $150. a head (1970 U.S. dollars).

The specification of the poverty line in U.S. dollars involves the conversion of the per capita GDP of different countries to U.S. dollars, a conversion that, at existing exchange rates, is misleading because official exchange rates do not necessarily reflect the purchasing powers of different currencies. Although this problem has attracted the attention of several economists,[3] the most thorough and extensive study was made by Kravis, Heston, Summers, and Kenessey (1975), and financed jointly by the World Bank and the United Nations. In this study the authors developed estimates of the purchasing power parity (PPP) of the currencies of ten countries, the U.S. dollar being the PPP base. It is evident from their results that the PPP differs considerably from the existing official exchange rate. For example, in the case of India the official exchange rate was Rs 7.5 to the U.S. dollar in 1970, whereas the PPP gave only Rs 2.04 to the dollar. These figures demonstrate that the use of the official exchange rate would substantially bias the estimates of poverty. (In order to avoid this bias, the PPP rates provided by Summers and Ahmad (1974) are used here to convert the GDP of different countries.) The authors derived these estimates for one hundred one countries by fitting a nonlinear debiasing equation to thirteen observations provided by earlier studies.[4] These estimates may not have adequate precision, but they will still be superior to the GDP estimates calculated on the basis of official exchange rates.

The detailed numerical results on poverty are presented in tables

3. See Balassa (1964, 1973), Beckerman (1966), and David (1972).

4. Kravis, Heston, Summers, and Kenessey (1975) obtained PPP estimates for three additional countries. The term "debiasing" has been used by Summers and Ahmad (1974) to signify the adjustment to be made between the PPP and the official exchange rate estimates of the per capita GDP.

17.3 to 17.6. The formats of these tables are identical. The second column gives the population of each country in 1970, obtained from the World Bank's data files. The third column presents the 1970 per capita GDP in U.S. dollars. These figures are based on the official exchange rates during the same period. The fourth column reports the adjusted per capita GDP in U.S. dollars, which has been calculated by means of the PPP of each country as given by Summers and Ahmad. These adjusted values of the GDP have been utilized to estimate the proportion of population below the poverty line, the values of which are reported in the fifth column. The sixth column gives the actual population living in poverty, whereas the seventh column presents the adjusted mean income of the poor. Column 8 presents the per capita poverty gap, which is obtained by subtracting each figure in column 7 from the common poverty level $150. Column 8 reports the value of the poverty index P introduced in (15.1), whereas column 9 gives the percentage contribution of each country to the total poverty in the region.

Table 17.3, relating to poverty in Asia, shows that 35.6 percent of the population in the countries reported for this area lives below the poverty line. The maximum poverty is observed in India, where 41.33 percent of the population is considered poor. Indonesia comes next, the proportion of the poor at 41.06 percent.

Note that Hong Kong has the lowest percentage of population living in poverty, although it has the highest per capita poverty gap. The poverty index P for Asia is computed at 5.95, which implies that 5.95 percent of the total income must be transferred from the nonpoor to the poor to eliminate poverty. India accounts for 66.9 percent of the total population in Asia, although it contributes as much as 81.4 percent to total poverty. In contrast, 13.68 percent of the contribution to total poverty comes from Indonesia, and the remaining countries contribute less than 5 percent. It may be concluded, therefore, that among the Asian countries considered, poverty is concentrated mainly in two countries, India and Indonesia.

Table 17.4, relating to Africa, shows that 35.93 percent of the population of the countries listed is poor, which is slightly higher than that for the Asian countries of table 17.3. The Ivory Coast has the lowest percentage of population living in poverty; the percentages for the remaining African countries are more even than among the Asian countries.

(*text continues on page 398*)

Table 17.3. *Poverty in Asia, 1970* [a]

Country	Population (in thousands)[b]	GDP per capita, 1970 (U.S. dollars)	Adjusted GDP per capita, 1970 (U.S. dollars)	Percentage of population living in poverty	Population living in poverty (in thousands)	Adjusted mean income of poor	Per capita poverty gap	Poverty index	Percentage of contribution by country to total poverty
Hong Kong	3,960 (0.49)	745	1,210	1.21	48	69	81	0.08	0.03
India	583,129 (66.90)	98	250	41.33	222,397	98	52	8.60	81.40
Indonesia	115,567 (14.37)	101	250	41.06	47,453	109	41	6.73	13.68
Korea	31,793 (3.95)	260	530	3.84	1,222	109	41	0.30	0.35
Malaysia	10,945 (1.36)	353	680	9.90	1,083	95	55	0.80	0.42
Philippines	36,850 (4.58)	259	530	18.08	6,663	97	53	1.81	2.49
Sri Lanka	12,514 (1.55)	174	390	11.69	1,463	132	18	0.54	0.18
South Vietnam	18,332 (2.28)	235	490	5.39	989	100	50	0.55	0.35
Thailand	36,218 (4.50)	183	410	13.83	5,007	117	33	1.11	1.16
Total	804,308 (100)	127	299	35.60	286,325	100	50	5.95	100.00

a. Poverty level: per capita GDP of $150 at U.S. prices, 1970.
b. Figures in parentheses are the percentage population shares of each country.

Table 17.4. *Poverty in Africa, 1970*[a]

Country	Population (in thousands)[b]	GDP per capita, 1970 (U.S. dollars)	Adjusted GDP per capita, 1970 (U.S. dollars)	Percentage of population living in poverty	Population living in poverty (in thousands)	Adjusted mean income of poor	Per capita poverty gap	Poverty index	Percentage of contribution by country to total poverty
Ivory Coast	4,941 (9.05)	347	670	1.87	92	111	39	0.11	0.33
Malawi	4,440 (8.13)	74	200	58.23	2,585	92	58	16.89	13.77
Senegal	3,870 (7.09)	217	460	32.01	1,239	93	57	3.97	6.49
Sierra Leone	2,555 (4.68)	177	390	37.27	952	64	86	8.22	7.52
Sudan	15,695 (28.75)	117	290	36.63	5,750	96	54	6.82	28.51
Tanzania	13,270 (24.31)	100	250	49.53	6,573	94	56	11.09	33.79
Uganda	9,814 (17.98)	135	320	24.71	2,425	107	43	3.32	9.58

a. Poverty level: per capita GDP of $150 at U.S. prices, 1970.
b. Figures in parentheses are the percentage population shares of each country.

Table 17.5. *Poverty in Latin America, 1970* [a]

Country	Population (in thousands)[b]	GDP per capita, 1970 (U.S. dollars)	Adjusted GDP per capita, 1970 (U.S. dollars)	Percentage of population living in poverty	Population living in poverty (in thousands)	Adjusted mean income of poor	Per capita poverty gap	Poverty index	Percentage of contribution by country to total poverty
Brazil	92,764 (41.46)	391	730	17.31	16,055	104	46	1.09	50.68
Chile	9,780 (4.37)	684	1,140	0.93	91	112	38	0.03	0.23
Colombia	21,632 (9.67)	409	760	13.11	2,837	115	35	0.60	6.77
Costa Rica	1,727 (0.77)	544	950	1.54	27	118	32	0.05	0.06
Dominican Rep.	4,068 (1.82)	363	690	9.30	378	107	43	0.58	1.12
Ecuador	6,093 (2.72)	269	550	21.46	1,307	99	51	1.99	4.57
El Salvador	3,534 (1.58)	291	580	20.82	736	96	54	1.94	2.73

Guyana	745 (.33)	358	680	8.47	63	53	97	1.21	0.42
Honduras	2,520 (1.13)	276	560	27.46	692	88	62	3.04	2.95
Jamaica	1,888 (0.84)	721	1,180	11.15	211	81	69	0.65	0.99
Mexico	50,670 (22.64)	682	1,130	4.24	2,150	97	53	0.20	7.86
Panama	1,464 (0.65)	731	1,200	6.79	99	82	68	0.38	0.45
Peru	13,586 (6.07)	332	650	25.34	3,443	74	76	2.96	17.94
Uruguay	2,886 (1.29)	815	1,300	6.12	177	67	83	0.39	1.00
Venezuela	10,399 (4.65)	999	1,530	4.60	479	116	34	0.10	1.09
Total	223,756 (100)	501	879	12.85	28,763	99.78	50.22	0.73	100.00

a. Poverty level: per capita GDP of $150 at U.S. prices, 1970.
b. Figures in parentheses are the percentage population shares of each country.

Table 17.6. World Poverty: Asia, Africa, and Latin America, 1970[a]

Region	Population (in thousands)[b]	GDP per capita, 1970 (U.S. dollars)	Adjusted GDP per capita, 1970 (U.S. dollars)	Percentage of population living in poverty	Population living in poverty (in thousands)	Adjusted mean income of poor	Per capita poverty gap	Poverty index	Percentage of contribution by country to total poverty
Asia	804,308 (74.29)	127	299	35.60	286,325	100.00	50.00	5.95	84.96
Africa	54,585 (5.04)	193	299	35.93	19,616	94.00	56.00	6.72	6.51
Latin America	223,756 (20.67)	501	879	12.85	28,763	99.78	50.22	0.73	8.53
Total	1,082,649 (100)	208	419	30.91	334,704	99.63	50.37	3.71	100.00

a. Poverty level: per capita GDP of $150 at U.S. prices, 1970.
b. Figures in parentheses are the percentage population shares of each country.

Table 17.7. *Quintile Shares of Income in Fifty Countries*

	0–20	21–40	41–60	61–80	81–100
Asia					
Hong Kong	5.6	10.0	14.3	21.1	49.0
India	5.5	10.0	13.7	18.9	51.9
Indonesia	6.8	10.5	13.4	17.3	52.0
Korea	7.2	11.5	15.8	22.1	43.4
Malaysia	4.1	8.3	12.7	19.9	55.0
Philippines	3.9	8.0	12.9	21.2	54.0
Sri Lanka	7.4	10.5	14.8	21.7	45.6
South Vietnam	7.1	12.1	16.6	22.9	41.3
Thailand	6.4	10.4	15.2	22.8	45.2
Pakistan	8.4	12.2	16.0	21.9	41.5
Taiwan	7.8	12.5	16.6	22.3	40.8
Average	6.4	10.5	14.7	21.1	47.2
Africa					
Chad	7.7	11.6	15.2	20.7	44.8
Dahomey	5.5	10.3	13.9	18.6	51.7
Ivory Coast	6.6	9.9	13.3	18.4	51.8
Madagascar	5.2	7.8	11.0	15.9	60.1
Malawi	5.7	9.3	13.1	19.0	52.9
Senegal	3.2	6.2	10.4	17.7	62.5
Sierra Leone	1.1	6.1	11.1	18.9	62.8
Sudan	5.0	8.9	13.9	22.1	50.1
Tanzania	5.1	8.4	12.2	18.6	55.7
Uganda	6.2	10.4	14.9	21.9	46.6
Average	5.1	7.6	12.9	19.2	53.9
Latin America					
Argentina	6.9	9.7	13.3	19.2	50.9
Barbados	4.0	10.7	15.8	22.6	46.9
Brazil	3.0	6.2	10.6	18.7	61.5
Chile	4.8	8.2	12.2	19.0	55.8
Colombia	3.5	6.6	10.9	18.9	60.1
Costa Rica	5.0	8.6	12.9	20.3	53.2
Dominican Rep.	4.3	8.1	12.8	20.5	54.3
Ecuador	3.5	7.0	11.9	20.5	57.1
El Salvador	3.2	6.9	11.7	20.1	58.1
Mexico	3.7	7.5	12.1	19.8	56.9
Panama	3.0	6.8	11.4	19.4	59.4
Venezuela	2.7	5.5	9.6	16.8	65.4
Average	4.0	7.6	12.1	19.6	56.6

(*table continues on the following page*)

Table 17.7   (*Continued*)

	0–20	21–40	41–60	61–80	81–100
Developed Countries					
Australia	7.1	12.9	17.6	23.5	38.9
Canada	6.7	12.3	17.2	23.8	40.0
Denmark	5.2	11.1	16.3	23.4	44.0
Finland	2.7	9.0	14.7	23.2	50.4
France	2.3	7.7	13.3	22.0	54.7
West Germany	6.9	12.0	16.9	23.9	40.3
Greece	6.3	11.1	15.6	22.3	44.7
Hungary	8.5	15.2	19.1	23.6	33.6
Japan	4.6	11.4	16.5	23.4	44.1
Netherlands	4.0	9.7	14.7	22.3	49.3
New Zealand	4.9	11.8	17.1	24.2	42.0
Norway	4.7	12.4	17.6	24.3	41.0
Spain	6.0	10.5	15.4	22.6	45.5
Sweden	4.6	11.4	16.4	23.1	43.3
United Kingdom	6.6	11.9	17.0	24.2	40.3
United States	6.8	12.7	17.5	23.9	39.1
Yugoslavia	6.6	11.8	16.7	23.5	41.4
Average	5.5	11.5	16.4	23.4	41.7

Note that, according to table 17.5, the incidence of poverty is considerably lower in the Latin American countries than in the Asian and African countries considered. In Latin America, only 12.85 percent of the population lives in poverty, compared to about 35 percent in Asia and Africa.

Table 17.6 gives the disaggregation of world poverty according to three regions. It can be seen that, of a population of about one billion, approximately 334 million people live below the poverty line of $150., with maximum concentration (186 million) in Asia.

Bibliography

Adelman, I., and C. Morris. 1971. "An Anatomy of Patterns of Income Distribution in Developing Nations." Part III of the final report (Grant AID/Csd-2236). Evanston, Ill.: Northwestern University.

Ahluwalia, M. S. 1974. "Income Inequality: Some Dimensions of the Problem." In H. Chenery and others, *Redistribution with Growth*. London: Oxford University Press.

————. 1976. "Income Distribution and Development: Some Stylized Facts." *Papers and Proceedings of the American Economic Association*. Paper presented at the 88th meeting of the American Economic Association, December 28–30, 1975, Dallas, Texas.

Ahsan, S. M. 1974. "Progression and Risk Taking." *Oxford Economic Papers*, vol. 26, pp. 318–28.

Aigner, D. J., and A. S. Goldberger. 1970. "Estimation of Pareto's Law from Grouped Observations." *Journal of the American Statistical Association*, vol. 65, pp. 712–23.

Aigner, D. J., and A. J. Heins. 1967. "A Social Welfare View of the Measurement of Income Equality." *Review of Income and Wealth*, vol. 13, pp. 12–25.

Aitchison, J., and J. A. C. Brown. 1954. "On Criteria for Description of Income Distribution." *Metroeconomica*, vol. 6, pp. 88–107.

————. 1957. *The Lognormal Distribution*. Cambridge: Cambridge University Press.

Aitken, A. C. 1934. "On Least-Squares and Linear Combination of Observations." *Proceedings of the Royal Society of Edinburgh*, vol. 55, pp. 42–48.

Allen, R. G. D., and A. L. Bowley. 1935. *Family Expenditure*. London: Staples.

Allingham, M. G. 1972. "The Measurement of Inequality." *Journal of Economic Theory*, vol. 5, pp. 163–69.

Allingham, M. G., and A. Sandmo. 1972. "Income Tax Evasion: A Theoretical Analysis." *Journal of Public Economics*, vol. 1, pp. 323–38.

Amoroso, L. 1925. "Ricerche intorno alla curva dei redditi." *Annali di mathematica pura ed applicata*, Series 4–21, pp. 123–59.

Anand, S. 1973. "The Size Distribution of Income in Malaysia." Part I. Washington, D.C.: Development Research Center, World Bank. Processed.

Apostol, T. M. 1958. *Mathematical Analysis.* Reading, Mass.: Addison-Wesley.

Arrow, K. J. 1951. *Social Choice and Individual Values.* New York: John Wiley.

———. 1965. *Aspects of the Theory of Risk-Bearing.* Helsinki: Yrjö Jahnssonin Säätiö.

Arrow, K. J. and others. 1961. "Capital-Labour Substitution and Economic Efficiency." *Review of Economics and Statistics,* vol. 43, pp. 225–50.

Atkinson, A. B. 1970. "On the Measurement of Inequality." *Journal of Economic Theory,* vol. 2, pp. 244–63.

———. 1973. "How Progressive Should Income Tax Be?" In *Essays on Modern Economics.* Edited by M. Parkin. London: Longman Group Ltd.

Balassa, B. 1964. "The Purchasing-Power Parity Doctrine: A Reappraisal." *Journal of Political Economy,* vol. 72, pp. 584–96.

———. 1973. "Just How Misleading Are Official Exchange Rate Conversions? A Comment." *Economic Journal,* vol. 83, pp. 1258–67.

Bardhan, P. 1970. "On a Minimum Level of Living and the Rural Poverty." *Indian Economic Review,* vol. 5, pp. 54–67.

Barten, A. P. 1964. "Family Composition, Prices and Expenditure Patterns." In *Econometric analysis for national economic planning.* Edited by P. Hart, G. Mill, and J. Whittaker. 16th Symposium of the Colston Society. London: Butterworth and Company.

Batty, I. Z. 1974. "Inequality and Poverty in Rural India." *Sankhyā: The Indian Journal of Statistics,* vol. 36, pp. 291–336 and 430.

Becker, G. S. 1962. "Investment in Human Capital: A Theoretical Analysis." *Journal of Political Economy,* vol. 70, pp. 9–49.

———. 1967. *Human Capital and the Personal Distribution of Income.* Ann Arbor: University of Michigan Press.

Beckerman, W. 1966. *International Comparisons of Real Incomes.* Paris: Organization for Economic Cooperation and Development. Processed.

Bentley, P., D. J. Collins, and N. T. Drane. 1974. "Incidence of Australian Taxation." *Economic Record,* vol. 50, pp. 489–510.

Bentzel, R. 1970. "The Social Significance of Income Distribution Statistics." *Review of Income and Wealth,* series 16, no. 3 (September), pp. 253–64.

Bergson, A. 1938. "A Reformulation of Certain Aspects of Welfare Economics." *Quarterly Journal of Economics,* vol. 52, pp. 310–34.

Bjerke, K. 1961. "Some Income and Wage Distribution Theories: Summary and Comments." *Weltwirtschaftliches Archiv,* vol. 86, pp. 46–66.

Blinder, A. S. 1974. *Toward an Economic Theory of Income Distribution.* Cambridge, Mass.: MIT Press.

Bowles, S. 1969. *Planning Educational Systems for Economic Growth.* Harvard Economic Studies, vol. 133. Cambridge, Mass.: Harvard University Press.

Bowley, A. L. 1937. *Elements of Statistics.* New York: P. S. King and Company.

Bowman, M. J. 1945. "A Graphical Analysis of Personal Income Distribution in the United States." *American Economic Review*, vol. 35, pp. 607–28.

Bracewell-Milnes, B. 1971. *The Measurement of Fiscal Policy*. London: Confederation of British Industry.

Bresciani-Turroni, C. 1910. "Di un indice misuratone della disugaglianza dei redditi." *Studi in onone di B. Brugi*, pp. 54–61. Palermo.

Bronfenbrenner, M. 1971. *Income Distribution Theory*. Chicago: Aldine-Atherton.

Budd, E. C. 1970. "Post-War Changes in the Size Distribution of Income in the U.S." *American Economic Review*, vol. 60, pp. 247–60.

Burr, I. W. 1942. "Cumulative Frequency Functions." *Annals of Mathematical Statistics*, vol. 13, pp. 215–35.

Champernowne, D. G. 1952. "The Graduation of Income Distributions." *Econometrica*, vol. 20, pp. 591–615.

———. 1953. "A Model of Income Distribution." *Economic Journal*, vol. 63, pp. 318–51.

———. 1956. "Discussion on Paper by Hart and Prais." *Journal of the Royal Statistical Society*, part II, vol. 119, pp. 181–83.

———. 1973. *Distribution of Income between Persons*. Cambridge, England: Cambridge University Press.

———. 1974. "A Comparison of Measures of Inequality of Income Distribution." *Economic Journal*, vol. 84, pp. 787–816.

Chenery, H. B., and others. 1974. *Redistribution with Growth*. London: Oxford University Press.

Chenery, H. B., and M. Syrquin. 1975. *Patterns of Development, 1950–1970*. London: Oxford University Press.

Chipman, J. S. 1974. "The Welfare Ranking of Pareto Distribution." *Journal of Economic Theory*, vol. 9, pp. 275–82.

Chiswick, B. R. 1968. "The Average Level of Schooling and the Intraregional Inequality of Income: A Clarification." *American Economic Review*, vol. 58, pp. 495–501.

———. 1971. "Earning Inequality and Economic Development." *Quarterly Journal of Economics*, vol. 85, pp. 21–32.

———. 1974. *Income Inequality: Regional Analysis with a Human-Capital Framework*. New York: National Bureau of Economic Research.

Clement, M. O. 1960. "The Quantitative Impact of Economic Stabilizers." *Review of Economics and Statistics*, vol. 42: pp. 56–61.

Cohen, L. 1959. "An Empirical Measurement of the Built-in Flexibility of the Individual Income Tax." *American Economic Review*, vol. 49, pp. 532–41.

Cramer, H. 1946. *Mathematical Methods of Statistics*. Princeton, N.J.: Princeton University Press.

Cramer, J. S. 1964. "Efficient Grouping, Regression and Correlation in Engel

Curve Analysis." *Journal of the American Statistical Association*, vol. 59, pp. 233–50.

———. 1969. *Empirical Econometrics*. Amsterdam: North-Holland.

Current Population Reports. 1965. "Income in 1964 of families and persons in the United States." U.S. Bureau of the Census, Department of Commerce. Series P-60, No. 47.

Dalton, H. 1920. "The Measurement of the Inequality of Incomes." *Economic Journal*, vol. 30, pp. 348–61.

———. 1955. *Principles of Public Finance*. New York: Frederick A. Praeger.

Dandekar, V. M., and N. Rath. 1971. *Poverty in India*. Poona: Indian School of Political Economy.

Das Gupta, P., A. K. Sen, and D. Starrett. 1973. "Notes on the Measurement of Inequality." *Journal of Economic Theory*, vol. 6, pp. 180–87.

David, P. A. 1972. "Just How Misleading Are Official Exchange Rate Conversions?" *Economic Journal*, vol. 82, pp. 979–90.

De Wolff, P., and A. R. D. Van Slijpe. 1972. *The Relation between Income, Intelligence, Education and Social Background*. Institute of Actuarial Science and Econometrics, University of Amsterdam.

Dhrymes, P. J. 1970. *Econometrics: Statistical Foundations and Applications*. New York: Harper and Row.

Dodge, D. A. 1975. "Impact of Tax, Transfer, and Expenditure Policies of Government on the Distribution of Personal Income in Canada." *Review of Income and Wealth*, series 21, no. 1 (March), pp. 1–52.

Dorrington, J. C. 1974. "A Structural Approach to Estimating the Built-in Flexibility of United Kingdom Taxes on Personal Income." *Economic Journal*, vol. 84, pp. 576–94.

Dougherty, C. R. S. 1971. "Estimates of Labour Aggregate Functions." Harvard Center for International Affairs, Economic Development Report, no. 190. Cambridge: Development Research Group.

———. 1972. "Substitution and the Structure of the Labour Force." *Economic Journal*, vol. 82.

Drane, N. T., H. R. Edwards, and R. C. Gates. 1966–68. *The Australian survey of consumer expenditures and finances*. Macquarie University Data Archive Ltd.

Elteto, O., and E. Frigyes. 1968. "New Inequality Measures as Efficient Tools for Casual Analysis and Planning." *Econometrica*, vol. 36, pp. 383–96.

Engel, E. 1957. "Die Produktions—und Consumptionsverhältnisse des Königreichs Sachsen." *Zeitschrift des Statistischen Büreaus des Königlich Sächsischen Ministerium des Innern*, vol. 22 (November).

Fair, R. C. 1971. "The Optimal Distribution of Income." *Quarterly Journal of Economics*, vol. 85, pp. 551–79.

Feller, W. 1966. *Introduction to Probability Theory and Its Applications*, vol. II. New York: John Wiley.

Fields, G. S., and John C. H. Fei. 1974. "On Inequality Comparisons." Economic Growth Center, Yale University, discussion paper No. 202.

Fishlow, A. 1972. "Brazilian Size Distribution of Income." *American Economic Review*, vol. 62, pp. 391–402.

Fisk, P. R. 1961a. "Estimation of Location and Scale Parameters in a Truncated Group Sech Square Distribution." *Journal of the American Statistical Association*, vol. 56, pp. 692–702.

———. 1961b. "The Graduation of Income Distributions." *Econometrica*, vol. 29, pp. 171–85.

Forsyth, F. G. 1960. "The Relationship between Family Size and Family Expenditure." *Journal of the Royal Statistical Society*, vol. 123, pp. 367–97.

Friedman, M. 1953. "Choice, Chance and Personal Distribution of Income." *Journal of Political Economy*, vol. 61, pp. 277–90.

———. 1962. *Capitalism and Freedom*. Chicago: University of Chicago Press.

Gastwirth, J. L. 1971. "A General Definition of the Lorenz Curve." *Econometrica*, vol. 39, pp. 1037–39.

———. 1972. "The Estimation of the Lorenz Curve and Gini Index." *Review of Economics and Statistics*, vol. 54, pp. 306–16.

———, and J. T. Smith. 1972. "A new goodness of fit test." *Proceedings of the American Statistical Association*, pp. 320–22.

Geary, R. C. 1949–50. "A Note on a Constant Utility Index of the Cost of Living." *Review of Economic Studies*, vol. 18, pp. 65–66.

Gibrat, R. 1931. *Les inégalités économiques*. Paris: Sirely.

Gini, C. 1912. *Variabilità e mutabilità*. Bologna.

———. 1913–14. "Sulla misura della concentrazione e della variabilita dei caratteri." *Transactions of the Real Instituto Veneto di Scienze, Lettere ed Arti*, vol. 53, pp. 1203–12.

———. 1921. "Measurement of Inequality of Incomes." *Economic Journal*, vol. 31, pp. 124–26.

Goldberger, A. S. 1964. *Econometric Theory*. New York: John Wiley.

———. 1967. "Functional Form and Utility: A Review of Consumer Demand Theory." University of Wisconsin, Social Systems Research Institute, Systems Formulation, Methodology and Policy Workshop paper 6703. Processed.

Gradsheteyn, I. S., and I. M. Ryshik. 1965. *Tables of Integrals Series and Products*. New York: Academic Press.

Green, C. 1966. "Negative Taxes and the Poverty Problem." Conference monograph prepared for the Brookings Institute Studies in Government Finance (June 9–10).

Gupta, S. 1977. *A Model for Income Distribution, Employment and Growth: A Case Study of Indonesia*. World Bank Staff Occasional Papers, no. 24. Baltimore: Johns Hopkins University Press.

Hadar, J., and W. R. Russell. 1969. "Rules for Ordering Uncertain Prospects." *American Economic Review*, vol. 59, pp. 25–34.

Hanoch, G., and H. Levy. 1969. "The Efficiency Analysis of Choices Involving Risk." *Review of Economic Studies*, vol. 36, pp. 334–46.

Hardy, G. H., J. E. Littlewood, and G. Polya. 1929. "Some Simple Inequalities Satisfied by Convex Functions." *Messenger of Math*, vol. 26, pp. 145–53.

———. 1934. *Inequalities*. Cambridge: Cambridge University Press.

Hart, P. E., and S. J. Prais. 1956. "The Analysis of Business Concentration: A Statistical Approach." *Journal of the Royal Statistical Society*, vol. 119, pp. 150–80.

Hayakawa, M. 1951. "The Application of Pareto's Law of Income to Japanese Data." *Econometrica*, vol. 19, pp. 174–83.

Henderson, R. F., A. Harcourt, and R. V. A. Harper. 1970. *People in Poverty: A Melbourne Survey*. Melbourne: Cheshire.

Henrici, P. 1967. *Elements of numerical analysis*. New York: John Wiley.

Husen, T. 1968. "Ability, Opportunity and Career: A 26 Year Follow-up." *Education research*, vol. 10, pp. 170–79.

Itsumi, Y. 1974. "Distributional Effects of Linear Income Tax Schedules." *Review of Economic Studies*, vol. 41, pp. 371–81.

Iyenger, N. S. 1960. "On a Method of Computing Engel Elasticities from Concentration Curves." *Econometrica*, vol. 28, pp. 882–91.

Jain, S. 1975. *Size Distribution of Income: A Compilation of Data*. Baltimore: Johns Hopkins University Press.

Jain, L. R., and S. D. Tendulkar. 1973. "Analysis of Occupational Differences in Consumer Expenditure Patterns in India." *Sankhyā: The Indian Journal of Statistics*, vol. 35, pp. 140–56.

Johnston, J. 1963. *Econometric Methods*. New York: McGraw-Hill.

Kakwani, N. C. 1974. "A Note on the Efficient Estimation of the New Measures of Income Inequality." *Econometrica*, vol. 42, pp. 597–600.

———. 1976. "On the Estimation of Income Inequality Measures from Grouped Observations." *Review of Economic Studies*, vol. 43, pp. 483–92.

———. 1977a. "Measurement of Poverty and Negative Income Tax." *Australian Economic Papers*, vol. 17, pp. 237–48.

———. 1977b. "On the Estimation of Engel Elasticities from Grouped Observations with Application to Indonesian Data." *Journal of Econometrics*, vol. 6, pp. 1–17.

———. 1977c. "Applications of Lorenz Curves in Economic Analysis." *Econometrica*, vol. 45, pp. 719–27.

———. 1977d. "Measurement of Tax Progressivity: An International Comparison." *Economic Journal*, vol. 87, pp. 71–80.

———. 1977e. "Redistributive Effects of Alternative Negative Income Tax Plans." *Public Finance*, vol. 32, pp. 77–91.

———. 1977f. "On the Estimation of Consumer Unit Scale." *Review of Economics and Statistics*, vol. 59, pp. 507–10.

———. 1978a. "Taxation in an Inflationary Economy: A Note." *Economic Record*, vol. 54, pp. 140–42.

————. 1978b. "A New Method of Estimating Engel Elasticities." *Journal of Econometrics*, vol. 8, pp. 103–10.

————. 1978c. "Tax Evasion and Income Distribution." In *Taxation and development*. Edited by J. F. J. Toye. London: Frank Cass.

————, and N. Podder. 1973. "On the Estimation of Lorenz Curves from Grouped Observations." *International Economic Review*, vol. 14, pp. 278–91.

————. 1976. "Efficient Estimation of the Lorenz Curve and Associated Inequality Measures from Grouped Observations." *Econometrica*, vol. 44, pp. 137–48.

Kalecki, M. 1945. "On the Gibrat Distribution." *Econometrica*, vol. 13, pp. 1961–70.

Kats, A. 1972. "On the Social Welfare Function and the Parameters of Income Distribution." *Journal of Economic Theory*, vol. 5, pp. 90–91.

Kendall, M. G. 1956. "Discussion on Paper by Hart and Prais." *Journal of the Royal Statistical Society*, vol. 119, pp. 183–84.

————, and A. Stuart. 1969. *The Advanced Theory of Statistics*. London: Charles Griffin.

Klein, L. R., and H. Rubin. 1947. "A Constant Utility Index of the Cost of Living." *Review of Economic Studies*, vol. 15, pp. 84–87.

Kloek, T. 1966. *Indexcijfers: enige methodologische aspecten*. Doctoral dissertation. Netherlands School of Economics, Rotterdam.

Kolm, S. C. 1973. "A Note on Optimum Tax Evasion." *Journal of Public Economics*, vol. 2, pp. 265–70.

Kondor, Y. 1971. "An Old-New Measure of Inequality." *Econometrica*, vol. 39, pp. 1041–42.

Kravis, I. B. 1959. "Relative Income Shares in Fact and Theory." *American Economic Review*, vol. 49, pp. 917–49.

————. 1960. "International Differences in the Distribution of Income." *Review of Economics and Statistics*, vol. 42, pp. 408–16.

————. 1962. *The Structure of Income: Some Quantitative Essays*. Philadelphia: University of Pennsylvania Press.

————, and others. 1975. *A System of International Comparisons of Gross Product and Purchasing Power*. Baltimore: Johns Hopkins University Press.

Kuznets, S. 1953. *Share of upper income groups in income and savings*. New York: National Bureau of Economic Research.

————. 1955. "Economic Growth and Income Inequality." *American Economic Review*, vol. 45, pp. 1–28.

————. 1957. "Quantitative Aspects of the Economic Growth of Nations, II: Industrial Distribution of National Product and Labour Force." *Economic Development and Cultural Change*, supplement to vol. 5, pp. 1–80.

————. 1963. "Quantitative Aspects of the Economic Growth of Nations, III: Distribution of Income by Size." *Economic Development and Cultural Change*, vol. 11, pp. 1–80.

Lampman, R. J. 1964. "Prognosis for Poverty." *National Tax Association Proceedings of the 57th Annual Conference*, pp. 71–81. Pittsburgh.

———. 1971. *Ends and Means of Reducing Income Poverty*. Chicago: Markham.

Levine, D. B., and N. M. Singer. 1970. "The Mathematical Function between the Income Density Function and the Measurement of Income Inequality." *Econometrica*, vol. 38, pp. 324–30.

Levy, P. 1925. *Calcul des probabilités*. Paris: Gauthier-Villars.

Lluch, C. 1973. "The Extended Linear Expenditure System." *European Economic Review*, vol. 4, pp. 21–32.

Lluch, C., A. Powell, and R. Williams. 1977. *Patterns in Household Demand and Saving*. New York: Oxford University Press.

Lorenz, M. O. 1905. "Methods of Measuring the Concentration of Wealth." *Journal of the American Statistical Association*, vol. 9, pp. 209–19.

Lydall, H. F. 1968. *The Structure of Earnings*. Oxford: Oxford University Press.

Mahalnobis, P. C. 1960. "A Method of Fractile Graphical Analysis." *Econometrica*, vol. 28, pp. 325–51.

Mandelbrot, B. 1960. "The Pareto-Levy Law and the Distribution of Income." *International Economic Review*, vol. 1, pp. 79–105.

Mann, H. B., and A. Wald. 1943. "On Stochastic Limit and Order Relationship." *The Annals of Mathematical Statistics*, vol. 14, pp. 217–26.

Martic, L. 1970. "A Geometric Note on Income Inequality Measures." *Econometrica*, vol. 38, pp. 936–37.

Mexico Household Survey. Bank of Mexico, 1968.

Mincer, J. 1958. "Investment in Human Capital and Personal Income Distribution." *Journal of Political Economy*, vol. 66, pp. 281–302.

Minhas, B. S. 1970. "Rural Poverty, Land Redistribution and Development." *Indian Economic Review*, vol. 5, pp. 97–128.

———. 1971. "Rural Poverty and Minimum Level of Living." *Indian Economic Review*, vol. 6, pp. 110–13.

Mirrlees, J. A. 1971. "An Exploration in the Theory of Optimum Taxation." *Review of Economic Studies*, vol. 38, pp. 175–208.

Monthly Labor Review. April 1975. Washington, D.C.: U.S. Department of Labor.

Morgan, J. 1962. "The Anatomy of Income Distribution." *Review of Economics and Statistics*, vol. 44, pp. 270–83.

Mossin, J. 1968. "Taxation and Risk Taking: An Expected Utility Approach." *Econometrica*, vol. 35, pp. 74–82.

Muellbauer, J. 1974a. "Prices and Inequality: The United Kingdom Experience." *Economic Journal*, vol. 84, pp. 32–55.

———. 1974b. "Household Composition, Engel Curves and Welfare Comparisons between Households." *European Economic Review*, vol. 5, pp. 103–22.

————. 1975a. "The Cost of Living and Taste and Quality Change." *Journal of Economic Theory*, vol. 10, pp. 269–83.

————. 1975b. "Inequality Measures, Prices and Household Composition." *Review of Economic Studies*, vol. 41, pp. 493–504.

————. 1975c. "Identification and Consumer Unit Scale." *Econometrica*, vol. 43, pp. 807–9.

Mukharji, M. N., N. Battacharya, and G. S. Chatterjee. 1972. "Poverty in India: Measurement and Amelioration." *Commerce*, vol. 125, pp. 275–99.

Musgrave, R. A., and M. H. Miller. 1948. "Built-in Flexibility." *American Economic Review*, vol. 38, pp. 122–28.

————, and T. Thin. 1948. "Income Tax Progression, 1929–48." *Journal of Political Economy*, vol. 56, pp. 498–514.

National Sample Survey of India. All India Rural, Central Statistical Organization, Government of India. 7th round, October 1954–March 1955; 9th round, May–November 1955; 10th round, 1955–56; 16th round, 1960–61.

National Social and Economic Survey. Indonesian Government Publication, 1969.

Newbery, D. 1970. "A Theorem on the Measurement of Inequality." *Journal of Economic Theory*, vol. 2, pp. 264–66.

Nicholson, J. L. 1957. "The General Form of the Adding-up Criterion." *Journal of the Royal Statistical Society*, vol. 120, pp. 84–85.

Ojha, P. D., and V. V. Bhatt. 1964. "Patterns of Income Distribution in an Underdeveloped Economy: A Case Study of India." *American Economic Review*, vol. 54, pp. 711–20.

Oshima, H. T. 1962. "The International Comparison of Size Distribution of Family Incomes with Special Reference to Asia." *Review of Economics and Statistics*, vol. 44, pp. 439–45.

————. 1970. "Income Inequality and Economic Growth: The Postwar Experience of Asian Countries." *Malaysian Economic Review*, vol. 15, pp. 7–41.

Pareto, V. 1897. *Cours d'économique politique*. Vol. 2, part I, chapter 1. Lausanne.

————. 1919. *Traité de sociologie générale*. Vol. 2. Lausanne and Paris.

Paukert, F. 1973. "Income Distribution: A Survey of the Evidence." *International Labour Review*, vol. 108, pp. 97–125.

Pearse, P. H. 1962. "Automatic Stabilization and the British Taxes on Income." *Review of Economic Studies*, vol. 29, pp. 124–39.

Pechman, J. A. 1956. "Yield of the Individual Income Tax during a Recession." In *Policies to Combat Depression*. Princeton, N.J.: Princeton University Press.

Pietra, G. 1948. *Studi di statistica metodologica*. Milan: Giuffre.

Pigou, A. C. 1932. *Economics of Welfare*. London: Macmillan.

————. 1947. *A Study in Public Finance*. New York: Macmillan.

Podder, N. 1972. "Distribution of Household Income in Australia." *Economic Record,* vol. 48, pp. 187–98.

Podder, N., and N. C. Kakwani. 1975a. "Distribution and redistribution of household income in Australia." *Australian Taxation Committee Commissioned Studies.* Canberra: Australian Government Publishing Service, pp. 111–52.

———. 1975b. "Incidence of indirect taxes and company income tax." *Australian Taxation Review Committee Commissioned Studies.* Canberra: Australian Government Publishing Service, pp. 201–10.

———. 1976. "Distribution of Wealth in Australia." *Review of Income and Wealth,* series 22, pp. 75–91.

Post Enumeration Survey of the 1970 Census. Data from tape data base, Department of Statistics, Government of Malaysia. N. p.

Prais, S. J., and J. Aitchison. 1954. "The Grouping of Observations in Regression Analysis." *Review of the International Statistical Institute,* vol. 22, pp. 1–22.

Prais, S. J., and H. S. Houthakker. 1955. *The Analysis of Family Budgets.* Cambridge, England: Cambridge University Press.

Pratt, J. W. 1964. "Risk Aversion in the Small and the Large." *Econometrica,* vol. 32, pp. 122–36.

Psacharopoulos, G., and K. Hinchliffe. 1972. "Further Evidence on the Elasticity of Substitution among Different Types of Educated Labor." *Journal of Political Economy,* vol. 80, pp. 786–96.

Pyatt, G. 1975. "On the Interpretation and Disaggregation of Gini Coefficients." Washington, D.C.: Development Research Center, World Bank. Processed.

———. 1976. "On the Interpretation and Disaggregation of Gini Coefficients." *Economic Journal,* vol. 86, pp. 243–55.

Quandt, R. 1966. "Old and New Methods of Estimation and the Pareto Distribution." *Metrica,* vol. 10, pp. 55–82.

Ranadive, K. R. 1965. "The Equality of Incomes in India." *Bulletin of the Oxford Institute of Statistics,* vol. 27, pp. 119–34.

———. 1968. "Pattern of Income Distribution in India, 1953–54 to 1959–60." *Bulletin of the Oxford Institute of Statistics,* vol. 30, pp. 110–22.

Rao, V. M. 1969. "Two Decompositions of Concentration Ratio." *Journal of the Royal Statistical Society,* series A, vol. 132, pp. 418–25.

Report of the Commissioners of Her Majesty's Inland Revenue 1958–59 to 1966–67. Great Britain's Board of Inland Revenue.

Reynolds, M., and E. Smolensky. 1974. "The Post-Fiscal Distribution: 1961 and 1970 Compared." Institute for Research on Poverty, discussion paper no. 191–74. Madison: University of Wisconsin.

Rolph, E. R. 1967. "The Case for a Negative Income Tax Device." *Industrial Relations,* vol. 2, pp. 155–65.

Romer, T. 1975. "Individual Welfare, Majority Voting and the Properties of a Linear Tax." *Journal of Public Economics,* vol. 4, pp. 163–85.

Rosenbluth, G. 1951. "Note on Mr. Schutz's Measure of Income Inequality." *American Economic Review*, vol. 41, pp. 935–37.

Rothschild, M., and J. E. Stiglitz. 1970. "Increasing Risk: A Definition." *Journal of Economic Theory*, vol. 2, pp. 225–43.

————. 1973. "Some Further Results on the Measurement of Inequality." *Journal of Economic Theory*, vol. 6, pp. 188–204.

Roy, A. D. 1950. "The Distribution of Earnings and of Individual Out-put." *Economic Journal*, vol. 60, pp. 489–505.

Roy, J., I. M. Chakravarty, and R. G. Laha. 1959. "A Study of Concentration Curves as a Description of Consumption Patterns." *Studies in Consumer Behaviour*. Calcutta: Indian Statistical Institute.

Rutherford, R. S. G. 1955. "Income Distributions: A New Model. *Econometrica*, vol. 23, pp. 277–94.

Salem, A. B. Z., and T. D. Mount. 1974. "A Convenient Descriptive Model of Income Distribution: The Gamma Density." *Econometrica*, vol. 42, pp. 1115–27.

Samuelson, P. A. 1947. *Foundation of Economic Analysis*. Cambridge, Mass.: Harvard University Press.

————. 1947–48. "Some Implications of Linearity." *Review of Economic Studies*, vol. 15, pp. 88–90.

Sargan, J. D. 1958. "Linear Models for the Frequency Distributions of Economic Variables." Paper presented at the Chicago meeting of the Econometric Society, December 27–29. See *Econometrica*, vol. 27, p. 315.

Schutz, R. R. 1951. "On the Measurement of Income Inequality." *American Economic Review*, vol. 41, pp. 107–22.

Sen, A. K. 1969. *Collective Choice and Social Welfare*. San Franscisco: Holden-Day.

————. 1972. "Utilitarianism and inequality." *Economic and Political Weekly*, vol. 7, pp. 54–57.

————. 1973. *On Economic Inequality*. Oxford: Clarendon Press.

————. 1974a. "Informational Bases of Alternative Welfare Approaches: Aggregation and Income Distribution." *Journal of Public Economics*, vol. 4, pp. 387–403.

————. 1974b. "Poverty, Inequality and Unemployment: Some Conceptual Issues in Measurement." *Sankhya: The Indian Journal of Statistics*, vol. 36, pp. 67–82.

————. 1976. "Poverty: An Ordinal Approach to Measurement." *Econometrica*, vol. 44, pp. 219–31.

Sheshinski, E. 1972a. "The Optimal Linear Income Tax." *Review of Economic Studies*, vol. 39, pp. 297–302.

————. 1972b. "Relation between a Social Welfare Function and the Gini Index of Inequality." *Journal of Economic Theory*, vol. 4, pp. 98–100.

Shirras, G. F. 1935. "The Pareto Law and the Distribution of Income." *Economic Journal*, vol. 45, pp. 663–81.

Singh, B. 1973. "Making Honesty the Best Policy." *Journal of Public Economics*, vol. 2, pp. 257–63.

Singh, B., and A. L. Nagar. 1973. "Determination of Consumer Unit Scales." *Econometrica*, vol. 41, pp. 347–56.

Singh, S. K., and G. S. Maddala. 1976. "A Function for Size Distribution of Income." *Econometrica*, vol. 44, pp. 963–73.

Slitor, R. E. 1948. "The Measurement of Progressivity and Built-in Flexibility." *Quarterly Journal of Economics*, vol. 62, pp. 309–13.

Smith, D. B. 1965. "A Simplified Approach to Social Welfare." *Canadian Tax Journal*, vol. 13, pp. 260–65.

Stark, T. 1972. *The Distribution of Personal Income in the United Kingdom, 1949–1963.* Cambridge, England: Cambridge University Press.

Stiglitz, J. E. 1969a. "Distribution of Income and Wealth among Individuals." *Econometrica*, vol. 37, pp. 382–97.

————. 1969b. "The Effects of Income, Wealth and Capital Gains Taxation on Risk-Taking." *Quarterly Journal of Economics*, vol. 83, pp. 263–83.

Stone, R. 1954. "Linear Expenditure Systems and Demand Analysis: An Application to the Pattern of British Demand." *Economic Journal*, vol. 64, pp. 511–27.

Srinivasan, T. N. 1973. "Tax Evasion: A Model." *Journal of Public Economics*, vol. 2, pp. 339–46.

————, P. N. Radha Krisnan, and A. Vaidyanathan. 1974. "Data on Distribution of Consumption Expenditure in India: An Evaluation." *Sankhya: Indian Journal of Statistics*, vol. 36, pp. 148–62.

Summers, R., and S. Ahmad. 1974. "Better Estimates of Dollar Gross Domestic Product for 101 Countries: Exchange Rate Bias Eliminated." Paper presented at the Meeting of the Econometric Society, December, San Francisco.

Tax Foundation. 1966. *Tax Burdens and Benefits of Government Expenditures by Income Classes,* 1961 and 1965. New York: Tax Foundation.

Taxation Statistics (Australia). 1961–62, 1971–72, and 1972–73. Canberra: Government Printer of Australia.

Taxation Statistics (Canada). 1966–72. Ottawa: Department of National Revenue, Taxation Division.

Theil, H. 1963. "On the Use of Incomplete Prior Information in Regression Analysis." *Journal of the American Statistical Association*, vol. 58, pp. 401–14.

————. 1967. *Economics and Information Theory.* Amsterdam: North-Holland.

————. 1971. *Principles of Econometrics.* New York: John Wiley.

————. 1975. *Theory and Measurement of Consumer Demand.* Vol. 1. Amsterdam: North-Holland.

Thurow, L. C. 1970. "Analyzing the American Income Distributions." *American Economic Review*, vol. 60, pp. 261–69.

Tinbergen, J. 1975. *Income Distribution: Analysis and Policy.* Amsterdam: North-Holland.

Titmuss, R. M. 1962. *Income Distribution and Social Change.* London: Allen and Unwin.

Tobin, J. 1965. "Improving the Economic Status of the Negro." *Daedalus,* vol. 94, pp. 878–98.

Trends in the Income of Families and Persons in the United States, 1958–70. Washington, D.C.: U.S. Government Printing Office.

Tsuji, M. 1972. "A Note on Professor Stiglitz's Distribution of Income and Wealth." *Econometrica,* vol. 40, pp. 947–49.

Vaidyanathan, A. 1974. "Some Aspects of Inequalities in Living Standards in Rural India. *Sankhya: Indian Journal of Statistics,* vol. 36, pp. 215–41.

Vickrey, W. 1949. "Some Limits to the Income Elasticity of Tax Yield." *Review of Economics and Statistics,* vol. 31, pp. 140–45.

Von Bortkiewicz, L. 1930. "Die Disparitats Masse de Einkommensstatistik." *Bulletin de l'Institut International de Statistique,* vol. 25, pp. 189–298.

Von Neumann, J. and O. Morgenstern. 1947. *Theory of Games and Economic Behavior.* 2nd edition. New York: John Wiley.

Weisskoff, R. 1970. "Income Distribution and Economic Growth in Puerto Rico, Argentina, and Mexico." *Review of Income and Wealth,* vol. 16, pp. 303–32.

Wesson, J. 1972. "On the Distribution of Personal Incomes." *Review of Economic Studies,* vol. 39, pp. 77–86.

Wilks, S. S. 1944. *Mathematical Statistics.* Princeton, N. J.: Princeton University Press.

Yntema, D. W. 1933. "Measures of the Inequality in the Personal Distribution of Wealth or Income." *Journal of the American Statistical Association,* vol. 28, pp. 423–33.

Zellner, A. 1962. "An Inefficient Method of Estimating Seemingly Unrelated Regressions and Tests for Aggregation Bias." *Journal of the American Statistical Association,* vol. 57, pp. 348–68.

————, and T. H. Lee. 1965. "Joint Estimation of Relationships Involving Discrete Random Variables." *Econometrica,* vol. 33, pp. 382–94.

Indexes

Subject Index

Utility function, 54, 55–56, 59, 91–94, 186, 188; Cobb-Douglas, 302; consumer-unit scales and, 352–54

Wage rates, 312–13
Work, leisure and, 302–09

Author Index

Adelman, I., 381
Ahluwalia, M. S., 381
Ahmad, S., 390
Ahsan, S. M., 241
Aigner, D. J., 64, 91
Aitchison, J., 2, 26
Allen, R. G. D., 198
Allingham, M. G., 64, 234, 240, 242
Amoroso, L., 29
Anand, S., 342
Arrow, K. J., 56, 94, 133
Atkinson, A. B., 48, 51, 53–59, 63, 64, 68n., 73, 74, 93–95, 114, 119, 198, 206, 207, 212, 302

Barten, A. P., 352
Becker, G. S., 2
Bentley, P., 262
Bentzel, R., 64
Bergson, A., 56
Bowles, S., 2
Bowley, A. L., 113, 198
Bresciani-Turroni, C., 79
Brown, J. A. C., 2, 26
Budd, E. C., 96, 113
Burr, I. W., 24

Chakravarty, I. M., 159n., 161
Champernowne, D. G., 2, 17–20, 25–26, 28, 42n, 64
Chenery, H. B., 133
Chipman, J. S., 73, 74
Clement, M. O., 272
Cohen, L., 272
Collins, D. J., 262
Cramer, H., 212

Dalton, H., 54, 64, 65, 67, 72, 80, 88, 90, 91–92
Dandekar, V. M., 348
Das Gupta, P., 48, 59, 64, 73, 74
De Moivre, A., 13
De Wolff, P., 2

Dodge, D. A., 262
Dorrington, J. C., 272
Dougherty, C. R. S., 2
Drane, N. T., 114, 130, 262, 357

Edwards, H. R., 114
Engel, Ernst, 185

Fisk, P. R., 24–25, 26, 28, 35
Forsyth, F. G., 352
Friedman, M., 284, 287
Gastwirth, J. L., 30, 37–38, 97–98, 101, 115, 153
Gates, R. C., 114
Gibrat, R., 2, 17, 27, 28
Gradsheteyn, I. S., 138
Green, C., 284, 287

Hadar, J., 53n
Hanoch, G., 53n
Harcourt, A., 366n
Hardy, G. H., 51, 97
Harper, R. V. A., 366n
Heins, A. J., 64, 91
Henderson, R. F., 366n
Heston, A., 390
Hinchliffe, K., 2
Houthakker, H. S., 198, 205, 210, 215, 224, 351, 352
Husen, T., 2

Itsumi, Y., 302
Iyenger, N. S., 216

Jain, L. R., 130, 384

Kakwani, N., 30, 36, 103, 129, 130, 153, 156, 180, 199, 219, 245, 327, 328, 352
Kalecki, M., 27
Kats, A., 73
Kenessey, Z., 390
Klein, L. R., 186
Kondor, Y., 82n